WHERE LAND AND WATER INTERTWINE

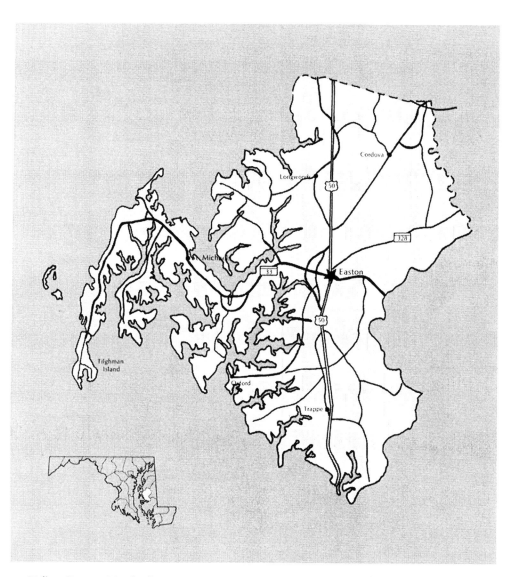

Talbot County, Maryland

WHERE LAND AND

An Architectural History of Talbot County, Maryland

WATER INTERTWINE

CHRISTOPHER WEEKS

With Contributions by

MICHAEL O. BOURNE

JOHN FRAZER, JR.

MARSHA L. FRITZ

GEOFFREY HENRY

THE JOHNS HOPKINS UNIVERSITY PRESS

AND

THE MARYLAND HISTORICAL TRUST

This inventory was originally financed in part with federal funds from the National Park Service, Department of the Interior. However, the contents and opinions do not necessarily reflect the views or policies of the Department of the Interior.

The Johns Hopkins University Press
2715 North Charles Street
Baltimore, MD 21218-4319
The Johns Hopkins Press Ltd., London

All illustrations are from the files of the Maryland Historical Trust except for material borrowed from the following: The Enoch Pratt Free Library, Baltimore, the painting on p. 4; Mr. John Frazer, Jr., the copies of his family portraits on pp. 64, 79 (both), and 81; The Historical Society of Talbot County, Easton, the material on pp. ii–iii, 18, 19 (upper), 21, 22 (lower), 23 (upper), 26, 28, 30 (both), 31 (all), 37 (lower), 45, 46, 47, 48 (both), 49, 50, 51, 52, 55 (lower), 57 (lower), 59, 60, 75, 76, 78, 80, 82 (upper), 85 (upper), 86, 87, 90, 96, 102, 107 (lower), 110 (left), 111 (lower), 114, 116, 118 (lower), 122, 124, 126, 128, 129, 130 (upper), 132, 134, 135, 136, 137 (lower), 138, and 158 (T-54); The Library of Congress Prints and Photographs Department, Historic American Buildings Survey, the material on pp. 10, 12, 13, 15 (lower), 17 (both), 19 (lower), 20, 22 (upper), 23 (lower), 24, 37 (upper), 40, 55 (upper), 82 (lower), 83, 87 (lower), 89, 94, 97, and 99; The Maryland Historical Society, Baltimore, the material on pp. 5, 7, 8, 9, 24, 67, 72, 98, 117 (both), 118 (upper), 119, 120, 121 (both), 133; The Peale Museum, Baltimore, the photograph on p. 66 and the drawings on p. 137 (top and middle).

Library of Congress Cataloging in Publication Data

Main entry under title:

Where land and water intertwine.

  Includes bibliographical references and index.
  1. Architecture—Maryland—Talbot County.   I. Weeks, Christopher,
1950-   .   II. Bourne, Michael O.   III. Maryland Historical Trust.
NA730.M32T358   1984   720'.9752'32   84–7186
ISBN 0–8018–3165–2

A catalog record for this book is available from the British Library.

Contents

Preface and Acknowledgments

The Maryland Historical Trust is charged by the Maryland General Assembly with preserving the best of Maryland's architectural, archaeological, and historical resources. Government agencies have occasionally been known to follow their mandates in a logical manner; this may be the case with the Trust, whose policy acknowledges that it is easier to preserve "the best" of Maryland's historical treasures if the state's citizens help. The Trust's policy also recognizes that before either the state bureaucracy or citizenry can intelligently begin preserving X building or Y archaeological site, it is necessary for as many people to know as much about the state's built environment as possible.

The Trust is working toward these ends in two ways. First, since the early 1960s, its Survey and Planning Division has been conducting architectural and archaeological surveys across the state. Second, the Trust's Community Education Division has been working to educate the public, in part through the volumes in this series of historic-site inventories.

Where Land and Water Intertwine represents the culmination of sixteen years of architectural research in Talbot County. This book has two sections: a narrative and an inventory. The narrative presents an analysis of Talbot County's architectural history from the Indian settlements through the mid-twentieth century in the context of the county's social and economic history; it considers how changes affected, and were reflected in, the county's architecture. This book is in no way intended to be a comprehensive history of Talbot County; politics, for example, has largely been ignored. But it is hoped that this approach will interest people who are not professionally involved in architectural history.

Part 2 is a catalog of Talbot's architecture. The sites included were chosen either because they are significant as examples of a formal style of architecture or its adaptation or because they are typical of the vernacular kinds of buildings found in the county. The entry number (e.g., T–245) denotes the chronological order in which the property was surveyed. Because surveyors often did not number sites in strict sequential order, and because the Maryland Hall of Records lists these sites according to the surveyors' numbering, some gaps occur between site numbers in Part 2. Each entry in this section includes the popular name of the property or its street address, the date or approximate date of its construction and alteration, its general location, a mention if the structure is listed in the National Register of Historic Places (or if, as at Wye, a structure is a National Historic Landmark), a photograph, and a brief description. In the case of many rural properties, in order to respect the privacy of the occupants, exact locations are not given. In addition, sites have been listed numerically, not geographically, to further guard against uninvited visitors. Hence, too, no detailed maps—and, at the owners' requests, few floor plans—are included. Every attempt was made to record and photograph each structure as closely as the property's owner would allow. The contents reflect the condition and appearance of the structures as of June 1983. The Trust freely acknowledges the likelihood of errors or of conflicting judgments regarding these historic sites. Evaluation was based upon current professional knowledge of architectural history.

The inventory does not contain every building—probably not even every "historic" building—in the county. It does include, however, every building that the Trust's various historic-site surveyors felt was important. Of course, these surveyors are no more perfect than other human beings, and the Trust encourages readers to point out sins of omission. The surveyors' reports are on file in the Trust's library in Annapolis and on microfiche at the Maryland Hall of Records, also in Annapolis; they are also available in the archives of the Historical Society of Talbot County and in the Talbot County Public Library, both in Easton. Interested readers are encouraged to borrow the fiche from the Hall of Records through interlibrary loan—at no cost—or to peruse the files during normal business hours at any of the other three places mentioned.

Careful readers may think they detect a discrepancy regarding the use of photographs in the inventory and the use of the word *site*. Some structures listed as "sites" are accompanied by a photograph; some are not. This seeming paradox is easily explained. The Trust has been sending surveyors to Talbot County since 1967. The first surveyors recorded sites—plots of ground with no buildings—they felt were important, but because there were no standing structures, they did not take photographs. (One soybean field looks like another.) Later, other surveyors discovered that some buildings included in the first list were no longer standing. In this case, a photograph of the vanished building is included, but the entry is referred to as "site."

The surveyors who worked with the Trust deserve mention, and we gratefully acknowledge them and their work: Michael O. Bourne, Paul A. Brinkman, James W. Clark, Marsha L. Fritz, Geoffrey Henry, Ann Hill, Cynthia B. Ludlow, and Peter L. Teeling. The surveyors' job was made easier by the uniform cooperation and welcome extended them by the various property owners throughout the county.

We are also indebted to those who contributed to the production of this book, particularly Norman Harrington and the staff of the Talbot County Historical Society, Pamela J. Caldwell, Orlando Ridout V, Dr. Albert T. Dawkins, Jr., Mrs. Morgan B. Schiller, John Frazer, Jr., Miss Mary H. Cadwalader, Mrs. Brodnax Cameron, Sr., Michael Trostel, John Dorsey, Mary Ison of the Library of Congress, Mary Ellen Hayward, Eric Kvalsvik, and Stiles Colwill of the Maryland Historical Society in Baltimore, Rita Brunner, Will Culen, John Devine, Glorian Dorsey, and Coscealia Saunders. Very special thanks are due Nancy C. Essig of the Johns Hopkins University Press, who has patiently nurtured this project for years.

PART I

AN ARCHITECTURAL HISTORY OF TALBOT COUNTY

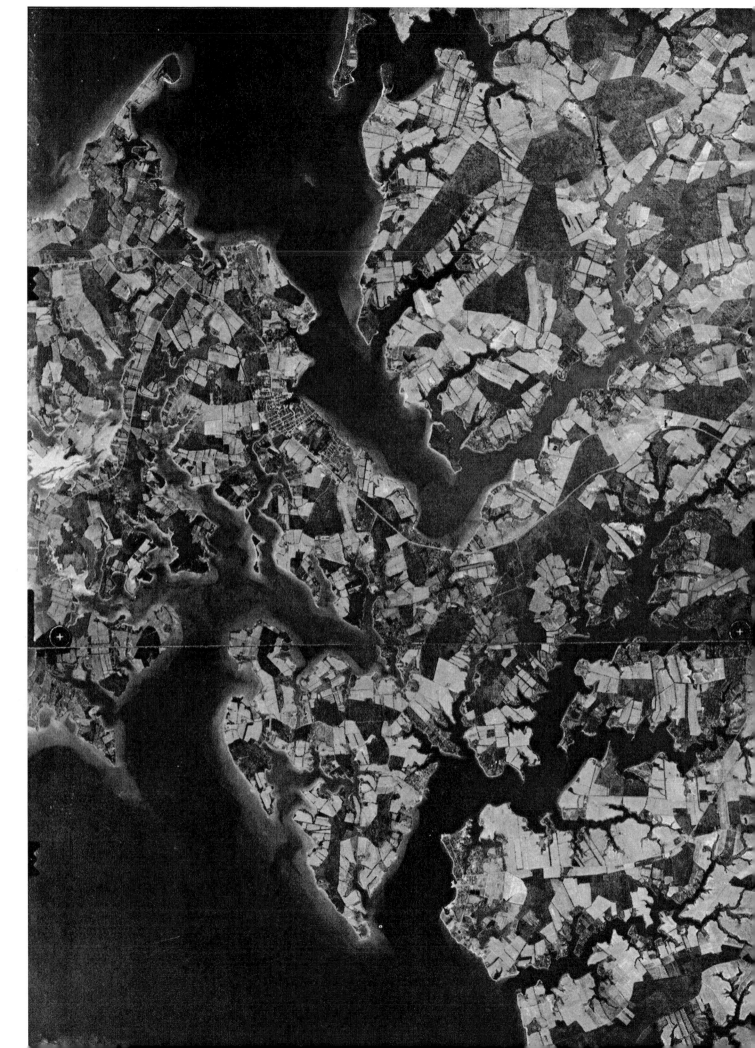

CHAPTER 1

Child of the "Mother of Waters"

Since earliest times, the waters of Talbot County have lured settlers to its shores. Today, those magnificent waters remain the county's most prized and priceless possession. The Chesapeake Bay, with its attendant rivers and creeks, dominates every county it touches, but it expresses itself most generously in Talbot. The county is small in land area (279 square miles), but its "heritage is steeped in the benefits of 600 miles of tidal shoreline . . . the longest in the United States."[1] Tidal inlets in this flat land twist, divide, and turn upon themselves in such convolutions that necks and peninsulas reach out to the Bay like welcoming but gnarled fingers. "It is an intimate place," writes William W. Warner, "where land and water intertwine in infinite varieties of mood and pattern."[2]

The word *Chesapeake* is of Indian origin. Its exact meaning, however, is uncertain. Some feel that it was originally *Tschischiwapeki,* meaning both "a highly salted body of standing water" and "Great Waters"; others favor *Kchesepiock,* meaning "a country on a great river"; Captain John Smith's "Chesapeack" has been interpreted simply as "Mother of Waters."[3]

Names may be the Indians' most enduring legacy to Talbot County, which served as a buffer between the Eastern Shore's two great tribes, the Nanticokes and the Susquehannocks. Most Eastern Shore Indians lived south of the Choptank and were Nanticokes, a powerful tribe formed of Wicomicoes, Choptanks, and Assateagues. The northern part of the Eastern Shore was dominated by the warlike Susquehannocks, a branch of the fierce Iroquois nation. This split is reflected in modern names: the Susquehanna River is north of Talbot County; Nanticoke, Wicomico, Choptank, and Assateague refer to rivers, counties, and islands to the south. The exact border between the two tribes constantly shifted, as the Nanticokes moved north only to be pushed back when the Susquehannocks moved south. That they passed back and forth through modern Talbot County is evidenced by the many arrowheads, spear points, ax blades, and other artifacts that have been plowed up in Talbot's fields or uncovered along the shore. But the waterways were the Indians' main travel routes. For them, they made canoes of giant tree trunks, burning and scraping them into shape, forming vessels 10 to 30 feet long.

The Nanticokes were peaceful people, living in villages surrounded by stockades. These towns were situated along rivers, where the Indians could fish with spears, arrows, bone hooks, and nets and weirs made from stakefences. Shad, sturgeon, crabs, eels, oysters, and clams were taken from the waters. Then, as now, the climate was moderate, with a long growing season conducive to lush crops, and the Nanticokes raised maize, beans, peas, squash, pumpkins, tobacco, and sunflowers, tilling the soil with a crooked tree limb.

The Indians' shelters provided only the most basic protection from the elements. The huts themselves, the first buildings in Talbot County, sometimes resembled a modern Quonset hut in basic construction. They were made of long poles, often curved or bent for

OPPOSITE:
Talbot County's shoreline from the Wye River on the north to the Choptank: "Land and water intertwine in infinite varieties of mood and pattern."

1. Norman Harrington, "Talbot County and the Good Life," in *Heartland,* vol. 8, no. 3 (Fireside 1983): 136.
2. William W. Warner, *Beautiful Swimmers* (Boston: Little, Brown & Co., 1976), p. 11.
3. Swepson Earle, *The Chesapeake Bay Country* (Baltimore: Thomsen-Ellis Co., 1923), p. 251.

Cecil Calvert, Second Lord Baltimore, by Gerard Soest. Courtesy, Enoch Pratt Free Library.

strength and laid in rows. Other popular building methods included the construction of a lean-to against a large tree trunk and the use of forked tree limbs as corner posts on which heavy branches could be rested. Lighter branches and twigs were then woven into the basic framework of the chosen form. If a degree of waterproofing was desired, clay or mud was packed between the branches.

One April day in 1607, Captain Christopher Newport's fleet of three vessels was involuntarily thrown into the mouth of the Chesapeake. "Scudding before a gale, these storm-tossed boats found a haven of rest and a safe anchorage in the waters of this great inland sea."[4] The year after Newport's "scudding," Captain John Smith left Jamestown and sailed up the Bay, mapping what he saw north to the Susquehanna River. In his role as "America's first press agent,"[5] he penned the following oft-quoted lines:

> A faire Bay compassed but for the mouth with fruitful and delightsome land. Within is a country that may have the prerogative over the most pleasant places of Europe, Asia, Africa or America, for large and pleasant navigable rivers. Heaven and earth never agreed better to frame a place for man's habitation.

If Newport was the first Englishman to see the Bay and if Smith was the first to explore it, the first white man actually to set foot in Talbot County was William Claiborne, a gentleman by birth and a man of education. King Charles I had appointed Claiborne secretary of state for Virginia, and, in 1625, Claiborne was commissioned to discover the source of the Chesapeake. He also obtained a license to trade with the Indians. Acting under the license, Claiborne established a trading post at the southern end of what he called the "Kentish Isle" (Kent Island) in 1631. Claiborne surrounded his settlement with a protective stockade, possibly following the Nanticokes' example.

Charles I may have had too many friends; he certainly had a genius for granting overlapping claims. For, while Claiborne was firming up his trading post on Kent Island, the king, in London, was in the process of granting George Calvert rights over the entire newly created colony of Maryland.[6] Calvert, Baron Baltimore (taking his title from the manor of Baltimore in County Longford, Ireland), was a close friend of the young king and named his colony "Mary's land" after Charles's wife, Henrietta Maria.

It is said that George Calvert, called the Projector, drew up Maryland's charter with his own hand. In it, he projected a scheme for the happiness of his fellow men, a scheme that was carried out by his son and heir, Cecil, after the Projector died on April 15, 1632.[7] George Calvert was probably the best-informed man in the world on Anglo-American colonization. He sought to lay down a practical program that would avoid all mistakes made in earlier colonies. Using the plantation system the English had used in Ireland, Maryland's charter invested the Lords Proprietary (the Calverts) with various rights: the right to make all laws public and private with the assent of the freemen; the right to establish courts of justice and appoint all judges, magistrates, and civil officers; the right to erect and found churches and chapels; the right to call out and arm the whole fighting population, wage war, and exercise martial law; and the right to levy duties and tolls on ships and merchandise. To the colonists, the charter gave the right to remain English subjects and as such to inherit, purchase, and possess land or other property in England; the right to have freedom of trade with English ports; the right to participate in making the laws; and the right to be exempt from taxation by the Crown. They also had the right to trade with Holland and elsewhere, which Virginia lacked—this would, in the future, enable Marylanders to undersell Virginia in the staple of tobacco.[8] The charter passed the royal seal and was issued to Cecil Calvert, Second Lord Baltimore, in June 1631. Thus, at twenty-six years of age, Cecil became the sole Lord Proprietary and vice-regal governor of an English county palatine.[9]

Cecil immediately set about finding desirable people to settle in his colony. Enemies beset him on every side, motivated by religious bigotry or distrust, political animosities, court intrigues, and personal enmities left over from his father's official duties under James

4. Ibid.
5. Warner, *Beautiful Swimmers*, p. 11.
6. Matthew Page Andrews, *Tercentenary History of Maryland* (Chicago: S. J. Clarke Publishing Co., 1925), p. 7.
7. Ibid., pp. 8–9.
8. Ibid., pp. 7–8.
9. For a discussion of the term *palatinate*, see ibid., pp. 44–48.

I. He also had to raise money through subscription because of his father's large losses in the earlier colony of Avalon in Newfoundland.

Finally, however, on November 22, 1633, the *Ark* and the pinnace *Dove* set out. Cecil, who had to stay home to keep his foes from destroying the enterprise, appointed his brother Leonard to be commander and first governor. Leonard sailed on the *Ark,* with Master Thomas Lowe as captain. Another younger brother, George, went along. Four months later, the expedition reached the Chesapeake with some 320 men, including Father Andrew White, S.J., the first eyewitness historian of the colony. They made a tentative landing at St. Clements Island in the Potomac on March 25, 1634, later establishing a permanent settlement on the nearby mainland at St. Mary's. Cecil Calvert, however, was to die without ever seeing the colony he fought so hard to advance.

Thanks to Lord Baltimore's (the Projector's) careful study and preparation, the Maryland colonists in 1634 had come properly equipped for many of the hazards of their settlement. Unlike the earliest Virginians, who had been forced to use canoes because they lacked other watercraft, the Marylanders had been instructed about the exact equipment each was to bring from England, including "necessaries for a boate of 3 or 4 Tunne; as Spikes, Kayles, Pitch, Tarre, Ocome, Canvis or a Sayle, ropes, anchor, iron for each other."[10]

According to Lord Baltimore's "Conditions of Plantation," the amount of land granted to a freeman was to vary in proportion to the number of persons he brought with him. "First settlers" who brought other people were entitled to a grant of 2,000 acres. If an immigrant brought fewer than five people, he received 100 acres for each person over

Talbot County is clearly marked on John Ogilby's 1671 map *Nova Terra-Maria.*

10. Ibid., pp. 58–66.

sixteen years of age, including his wife and himself, with 50 additional acres for every person under that age. The grants were subject to annual quit-rents varying from twelve pence for every 50 acres in small holdings to twenty shillings for a manorial estate. These rents were to be paid to the Lord Proprietary "in commodities of the country." An independent woman had the same privileges as a man.[11]

Meanwhile, back on Kent Island, William Claiborne was making considerable profit trading with the Indians, and he had persuaded many of his fellow Virginians, including a clergyman, the Reverend Richard James, to sail up the Bay to the Kentish Isle. "Burgesses were elected and represented the Island in the Virginia Assembly, and until King Charles granted the Charter of Maryland . . . the Isle of Kent was considered, and rightfully, a part of the Virginia Colony."[12]

Conflict between Claiborne and the Calverts was inevitable. Leonard Calvert, upon arriving in Maryland in 1634, erected the county of St. Mary's, which then included the entire province. He divided this large county into "hundreds," one being the "Hundred of the Isle of Kent." Claiborne fought his case in London, but the Commissioner of the Colonies decided in the Calverts' favor.

Maryland's earliest settlers conducted what legal business they had either in St. Mary's or on Kent Island. As settlement increased—greatly abetted by the 1649 Toleration Act—pressures to create more convenient sites for courts became stronger, and several other counties were erected, including Talbot County, which was carved out of Kent in 1662. At that time Talbot included all the land between the Choptank and Chester rivers. Border disputes followed, but after Queen Anne's County (1706) and Caroline County (1773) were taken entirely or partially out of Talbot, the borders were fixed; except for erosion, the county has remained geographically intact ever since.[13]

All these legal-political squabbles and changes suggest settlement—intelligent men are not going to worry about marking boundaries of land where no one lives. In fact, the Calverts had been granting land in what is now Talbot County since 1649. One early grant, or patent, in the county seems to have been for a 100-acre tract called Salter's Marsh, which was surveyed on October 13, 1658, for John Salter;[14] several other patents date to the autumn of 1658, but they are of only limited interest until November 5, 1658, when Linton, a tract of 600 acres, was granted to Edward Lloyd. From this point, several names with a true Talbot ring begin to appear: Martingham, a tract of 200 acres, was surveyed on July 28, 1659, for William Hambleton; Hier-Dier-Lloyd, 3,050 acres, was surveyed on August 11, 1659, again for Edward Lloyd; Plimhimmon, 600 acres, was surveyed on August 15, 1659, for Henry Morgan; Otwell, 500 acres, was surveyed on August 15, 1659, for William Taylor; Ratcliffe Manor, 800 acres, was surveyed on August 25, 1659, for Captain Robert Morris; and two separate 1,000-acre Tilghman tracts were surveyed—Canterbury Manor on August 23, 1659, for Richard Tilghman and Tilghman's Fortune on August 24, 1659, for Samuel Tilghman.[15] It is of some interest to reflect on the phenomenon that there were Lloyds and Tilghmans and Hambletons speaking of Otwell, Plimhimmon, Ratcliffe Manor, and Martingham before there was a Talbot County.

The county's first lawmakers were called justices of the peace and were, like their counterparts in Tudor and Stuart England, "to execute all the ordinary functions of local government. . . . The judicial, political, and economic powers of the Justice of the Peace were so various, and taken together so important, that the Justices of the Peace became the most influential men in England." In England, as in colonial Talbot County, according to Sir George Trevelyan, these justices "were country gentlemen, living on their own estates and all their own rents. In the last resort what they valued most was the good opinion of their neighbors, the gentry and the common folk of the shire."[16] His discussion continues:

> Moreover, there were habits of self-government in old English society that were easily
> transplanted overseas. This the squirarchial tradition at home, the local government of
> the English shire by Justices of the Peace who were the local landowners, gave rise ere
> long in Virginia to the rule of an outdoor equestrian aristocracy of planters, whose life

11. Ibid., p. 82.
12. Earle, *Bay Country*, p. 276.
13. Oswald Tilghman, *History of Talbot County*, vol. 2, reprint of original 1915 edition (Baltimore: Regional Publishing Co., 1967), pp. 1–3. Curiously, authorities disagree as to just when Talbot was erected, 1661 or 1662.
14. Ibid., p. 11
15. Ibid., pp. 11–13.
16. G. M. Trevelyan, *English Social History* (New York: David McKay Co., 1965), p. 171.

differed from that of English country gentlemen chiefly in the possession of Negro slaves. This aristocratic system grew up naturally with tobacco plantations that soon became the staple of that Colony's wealth.[17]

Early Maryland's economy was based on nearly endless fields of tobacco.

Like the English justices of the peace, Talbot County's j.p.'s took turns hearing cases in their houses: "The first court of Talbot after its separation from Kent . . . was held at the house of Mr. William Coursey on the 25th of April 1662, at which no business seems to have been transacted. It met, perhaps, merely for organization."[18] Legal activity continued to be less than bustling. Some "trifling business" was transacted at the second court held June 25, 1662, at the house of Richard Woolman.[19] The third court was again hosted by William Coursey. This met on October 25, 1662, and "among other business transacted was the 'laying' of the 'county and publique leavy' for the year, amounting to 7473 pounds of tobacco." Nothing else much happened in the world of jurisprudence until the seventh court, held June 3, 1663, at the house of Edward Lloyd, when "William Hambleton took the oath of High Sheriff and gave his bond."[20]

The tenth court was held back at the ever-welcoming William Coursey's; here "Edward Lloyd first [took] his seat as one of the Justices, in virtue of his being one of the Governor's Council and Judge of the provincial courts." That court heard an interesting case. It appears that John Shorte, an indentured servant of Thomas South, was about to receive a whipping and, rather than suffer that punishment, "John Shorte ran into the

17. Ibid., p. 217.
18. Tilghman, *History*, vol. 2, p. 203.
19. Ibid., p. 204.
20. Ibid., p. 205.

A nineteenth-century engraving showing the history of tobacco transport.

creek, and there in a considerable depth of water remained, while his master stood threatening him upon the bank. Then it came to pass that John Shorte was drowned—some say by his own act, rather than be chastised, and others say by the act of his master." The court nonetheless passed post-mortem judgment on Shorte, ruling that the "late servant unto Mr. Thomas South is Fielo Desi: and this is our verdict that he ought not to have a Christiall Buriall [sic] by Law."[21]

The twelfth court, held at Richard Woolman's on March 15, 1663, was also lively. Thomas South reappears, now possibly as Talbot County's first lawyer, and was sued by Anthony Griffin "for use of his 'cannew' which Mr. South had borrowed for a fortnight for the Indians to hunt for him. Griffin claimed ten pounds of tobacco per day." At the same court, Thomas Hynson, Jr., one of the justices of the court, and Ann Gaine were presented "for committing fornication, contrary to the Act of Assembly." Hynson confessed he was guilty but "prayed indulgence from the court" because he had later married Ann. The court spared him both the prescribed fine of 600 pounds of tobacco and "the corporal punishment by whipping upon his bare body, till the blood do appear." Instead, it merely relieved him of his judicial robes for a year and a day. Ann escaped punishment entirely.[22]

Even the county's first official courthouse had a rollicking atmosphere to it. In 1679, the county commissioners entered into agreement with one Elizabeth Winkles "to have the Court House which is now used to Keepe Court in, with the room adjoining" and that one Richard Swetnam was to "come to the aforesaid house to keep ordinary." From this it seems that Talbot County's first Hall of Justice was also a pub, partly occupied by its caretaker. Oswald Tilghman suggests that "apparently Elizabeth Winkles kept the house as a kind of ordinary or tavern," that Captain Philemon Lloyd had selected "the Widow Winkles's" house, and that the commissioners allowed her 3,100 pounds of tobacco. Later that year, on August 19, appears the following record:

> The Court hath agreed with Richard Swetnam (the same who was invited in June of the same year, to come to the place where the court was held, to keep an ordinary, and to confer with reference to the erection of a county building), to build a Court House upon the County land in Wye River; the said house to be fivety foote by twenty-three, with a Court Hall, eighteen foote by eighteen, according to a plot delivered to the court by the said Swetnam. In consideration whereof the commissioners have condescended to payd unto him the s'd Swetnam, One Hundred & Fifty Thousand Pounds of Tobacco; the one moyety or half part to be payd this year, the remainder at the cleare finishing the Premises, and the said Swetnam to live in the said house when finished, seven years Rent free: the said Swetnam is to repair forthwith to the house where the court is now keep, and lay in provision ag't the next Court.[23]

Notice the phrase "condescended to pay" in the agreement with Swetnam. One justice of the peace was found to be welshing on his canoe rental; in 1664 another was publicly accused of hog stealing.[24]

Several conclusions and implications may be drawn from these early records. One was made by Oswald Tilghman in his *History of Talbot County*:

> It may be mentioned incidentally that the white servants in the early times of our State, were treated with a cruelty that would be incredible if it were not a matter of public record. The death of John Shorte evinces this—but there are hundreds of cases mentioned of great barbarity in which this court was called upon to interpose. One cannot but remember that a similar case of alleged drowning to escape a whipping occurred upon Wye river nearly two hundred years after the death of John Shorte, which case Frederick Douglass has embalmed in his memoirs.[25]

Another implication is that, clearly, Trevelyan may have painted a too-romantic picture of the justices and lawyers in that crude era; Talbot County was very much a rough-and-ready society in its early years. This suggestion is further supported by the peripatetic nature of the courts; the county was unable—or felt no need—to have a settled, courthouse-based system of justice.

Further, Talbot County's economy was clearly based on tobacco. The widely grown weed served as the colony's medium of exchange, and apparently had an agreed-upon

21. Ibid.
22. Ibid., pp. 206, 207.
23. Ibid., p. 212.
24. Ibid.
25. Ibid., p. 206.

A nineteenth-century engraving showing the history of tobacco storage and curing.

value: 7,473 pounds of it was the needed revenue to run the county, 10 pounds would allow one to rent a canoe for two weeks, and it would cost 600 pounds in fines to commit fornication "contrary to the Act of Assembly."

It is also clear that there were still a few Indians around—but they must have been fairly tame if Thomas South was able to hire them to hunt for him. This also suggests that South, an attorney, had too many other things to do than hunt for his own food, and we may be seeing Talbot County's first class distinctions being formed. Hunting reminds us of the county's riches in game, and the "cannew" recalls the county's hundreds of miles of rivers and creeks that provided protected shelters and easy egress for her early pioneers and for their cargo-laden ships.

Finally, it is remarkable that in all the above only two women have been mentioned: the "licentious" Ann Gaine and the tavern keeper-barmaid, the "Widow Winkles." Maryland and Virginia suffered, at that time, "a severe shortage of women. Men outnumbered women by six to one among immigrants who left London for the Chesapeake in the middle 1630s." Women came over in greater number as the century wore on, "but men still outnumbered women about two and a half to one among new arrivals at the end of the century."[26]

26. Thad W. Tate and David L. Ammerman, eds., *The Chesapeake in the Seventeenth Century: Essays of Anglo-American Society* (Chapel Hill: University of North Carolina Press, 1979), p. 209.

CHAPTER 2

Earliest Architecture in Talbot County

Within a few years after the first patents in the area had been granted, enough settlers were living along the Wye, the Miles, and the Choptank to warrant the founding of a new county. But how did those first citizens live? What sort of buildings did they erect in the century before there was enough cash to build a Wye House, a Hope, or a Myrtle Grove?

Recently, scholars have done much work in seventeenth-century Tidewater architecture and have come up with some conclusions and several hypotheses. [1] Any discussion of the architecture of this period in this place must begin with the curious observation that, unlike New England, where there are 200 to 300 seventeenth-century buildings, the Chesapeake area, the richest and most populous of England's American colonies, has only five structures with a secure seventeenth-century date. There are two places of worship (St. Luke's Church near Smithfield, Virginia, and Easton's wonderful Third Haven Friends Meetinghouse) and three houses (the original section of Holly Hill in Anne Arundel County; Bacon's Castle in Surry County, Virginia; and the Adam Thoroughgood House in Virginia Beach—although there is some debate over the Thoroughgood House). As a result of this dearth, researchers have had to rely on documentary evidence and archaeology and have had to take what little solid information is available and make generalizations about the basically homogeneous region.

Many of the very first houses were hardly that at all but were primitive shelters, temporary structures that colonists from Massachusetts to Georgia created upon arrival, whose only purpose was to protect the settlers from the weather. It is to be expected that men such as the first colonists would have abandoned these "improvised expedients"[2] as quickly as they could financially afford to, and they did.

> For many newcomers a hut was followed, as soon as they could be, by a weatherproof but cheaply built house, which was not expected to last longer than it took its owner to accumulate enough capital to build yet another more substantial dwelling. Over and over again homesteaders on each new frontier moved in the same three steps from primitive shelters to temporary impermanent buildings, to the "fayre houses" that many yeomen and even husbandmen were used to from England. [3]

There is some argument among scholars as to just what form these replacement houses took, but there is no debate that, whatever form, whatever size, they can all be classed as *vernacular*, "a term invented by archaeologists to describe buildings that are built according to local custom to meet the personal requirements of the individuals for whom they are intended."[4] Englishmen settled in the Chesapeake area, and it is reasonable to suspect that these settlers' first response to the need to build was to behave as they had done in England, to try to duplicate what they had left behind simply because it was all they knew. But a more severe climate, new and diverse building materials, and a different economy all resulted in new building requirements.

OPPOSITE:
Troth's Fortune.

1. Note, in addition to sources cited herein, proceedings of organizations such as the St. Mary's City Commission, the Colonial Williamsburg Foundation, and the Vernacular Architecture Forum.
2. Cary Carson, Norman F. Barka, William M. Kelso, Garry Wheeler Stone, and Dell Upton, "Impermanent Architecture in the Southern American Colonies," in *Winterthur Portfolio* 16 (1981):139.
3. Ibid., p. 140.
4. Cary Carson, "The Virginia House in Maryland," in *Maryland Historical Magazine*, vol. 69, no. 2 (1974):185.

Sarum, in Charles County—a "Virginia House" in Maryland.

A considerable amount of adjusting took place wherever colonists from different backgrounds were thrown together in frontier communities. At first, everyone dealt with his new surroundings in ways he had been accustomed to at home. But sooner or later some fewer customs usually predominated, because they were better suited or more adaptable than the rest. In housing, the variety of competing building traditions imported by settlers from all over England gave way in every colony to standardized types of dwellings, which answered local needs more exactly. What is so surprising about the home-grown vernacular building traditions in Maryland and Virginia is the speed and thoroughness with which they departed from all English precedent.[5]

In 1974, Cary Carson, then working for the St. Mary's City Commission, published a piece called "The 'Virginia House' in Maryland" in the *Maryland Historical Magazine*. There and in subsequent articles, he argued that the "Virginia House" was, in the seventeenth century, "universally acceptable to tobacco planters on both sides of the Potomac"[6] and that "it proved unusually adaptable to planters' requirements for a simplified, economical system of framing that minimized joinery and took full advantage of the structural quality of riven clapboards."[7] The Virginia house was one of several replacement house forms popular in the Chesapeake region.

There are few, if any, Virginia houses left in Talbot County, but, because they were so popular throughout the region, one can assume that Talbot contained its share and that, therefore, it will be worthwhile to determine just what these houses were like. Carson chose the extant Sarum in Charles County, Maryland, as conforming "in about every detail to what seventeenth-century carpenters seem to have meant by a 'Virginia House'." Sarum is

a one story, frame dwelling with two rooms on the ground floor, the whole being covered with unpainted riven clapboards. It needs only exterior gable end chimneys to complete the picture, and, in fact, there definitely was one such stack built against the east gable, with a fireplace opening into the downstairs room and maybe another into the chamber above. Presumably it had a twin on the opposite gable, which was obliterated when the house was later enlarged westwards. What little we know about the interior conforms to a type no less than its exterior appearance and its manner of construction. Exposed, but unchamfered, the beams framed high ceilings downstairs. The wall posts were also visible in both rooms. Whitewash covered the ceiling and the lath and plaster walls in the west room. In the other the exposed timberwork was painted, the tie beams a dark rust red and the posts a pale blue-green.[8]

The Virginia house was a relatively large replacement house. Dell Upton, now teaching at the University of California at Berkeley, has written that "building in the early Chesapeake was of remarkably low quality"; he continued:

Numerically, the most significant plan form was the one-room house. Usually flimsily built and frequently extremely small—as little as eight or ten feet square—these houses form the background against which everything else must be set. As late as the eighteenth century, one-room houses characterized the accommodations of 80 to 90 percent of the white population of much of the Chesapeake, and, of course, all of the black population. It is important to keep this context in mind as we consider the larger houses that follow.[9]

While speculation as to just what the oldest house in Talbot County is may be an amusing after-dinner game, it ultimately leads nowhere simply because no one knows the answer. Nor does it really matter. Instead, it can safely be said that there are about a dozen very early houses in the county, nearly any of which could be the oldest. More important, together they form a priceless group that gives great insights into the way of life successful Chesapeake Bay planters enjoyed in the years around 1700. This group includes Crooked Intention, Troth's Fortune, White Marshes, Martingham, Orem's Delight, Bloomfield, Combsberry, Boston Cliff, Hampden, Ferry Farm House, Lloyd's Landing, Long Point (Elston's Point), and the Captain's House at Wye.

Troth's Fortune (T–50), possibly built between 1686 and 1710, shines as one of the best-preserved examples of early colonial Maryland vernacular architecture. In 1686, William Troth I bought a tract of 300 acres called Acton, on which he built the house

5. Ibid., p. 186.
6. Ibid.
7. Carson et al., "Impermanent Architecture," p. 158.
8. Carson, "Virginia House," pp. 192–93.
9. Dell Upton, "The Origins of Chesapeake Architecture," in *Three Centuries of Maryland Architecture* (Annapolis: Maryland Historical Trust, 1982), p. 45.

today known as Troth's Fortune.[10] Although Troth's Fortune may seem small to us, by today's standards, its two good-sized rooms on the first floor and two original rooms upstairs made it twice the size of nearly any of Troth's contemporaries' dwellings. William Troth's 1711 inventory, completed after his death in 1710, lists fire "doggs" in the hall and in the parlor, which may correspond to the fireplaces in the gable-end chimneys present today. (The chamber and an unnamed room did not have andirons listed in 1711.)[11] The unusual medieval-style stair tower on the rear facade, the detailed circa-1720s interior woodwork, and the glazed headers in the first story's Flemish-bond brick walls, give Troth's Fortune an individuality that adds to the charm of the house.

In addition to its architectural importance, Troth's Fortune provides insights into the economic and religious life of colonial Talbot County, and the house and the Troths need to be discussed at some length. William Troth I was a member of that small class of colonial planters, now referred to as merchant planters, who augmented agriculture with business and trade to make a living considerably above that of the average farmer.

In 1676 Troth patented two parcels of land, 400 acres of Troth's Fortune and 100 acres known as Troth's Addition. Seven years later he purchased 300 acres of a tract called Acton from John Acton, son of the original patentee. At his death in 1710, William Troth possessed 1,216 acres in Talbot county, 500 in Dorchester County, and an undetermined amount (but exceeding 240 acres) in Queen Anne's County—about 2,000 acres in all.[12]

But Troth's wealth did not come from farming alone. His estate inventories illustrate Troth's economic success, and show the reason for it. The total value of the goods

Troth's Fortune, as photographed in 1936 for the Historic American Buildings Survey.

10. Troth patented 400 acres as Troth's Fortune in 1676. He may have built a house on this tract, but it is not known today as Troth's Fortune, as that house now stands on the tract called Acton. This confusion may be attributed to Dr. H. Chandlee Forman's record of the house in his book *Early Manor and Plantation Houses of Maryland* (1934). He calls the house Troth's Fortune although it is called Acton or the Troth farm in the property deeds for both 1932 and 1936. This error was picked up and repeated by many people who later wrote about the house, and Troth's Fortune has become its common name.

11. Troth Inventory, Talbot County Inventory No. 33C, pp. 69 et seq. in Maryland Hall of Records, Annapolis; Troth's Last Will and Testament is in Talbot County Will Book E.M. no. 1, p. 264; it is dated January 11, 1709, and was probated November 6, 1710.

12. Troth's Fortune nomination to the National Register of Historic Places; on file at the Maryland Historical Trust, Annapolis.

evaluated in the 1711 inventory is £929.18.3½. The larger part of this inventory, which included his household goods, consisted of goods listed "in the store." An additional inventory, made in 1712, is for £276.6.2¾, of which £216 was "cash in . . . ye hands of Jonath. Searth & Thomas Bond—merchants in London as per Account current." These two amounts combined give Troth a net worth in goods of approximately £1,206, a large amount for the early eighteenth century, when only 0.7 percent of Maryland's planters were worth over £1,000 in 1710.[13]

Troth achieved his wealth through mercantile rather than agricultural activities. Although most larger tobacco growers traded directly with England, the smaller ones usually sold their crops to men such as Troth. The advantages enjoyed by the middlemen in this system are explained by Arthur Pierce Middleton in his book *Tobacco Coast*:

> [They] competed with the factors [employed by the London merchants] in buying tobacco from the smaller planters, and shipped it along with their own to England on consignment. In order to enter the purchasing market they were obliged to import large quantities of European and West Indian goods and to keep a store. . . . In return for tobacco sent to Great Britain on consignment, they imported goods for their stores as well as for their own use, and marked them up in price and extended credit, much as factors did, in order to obtain control of the smaller planters. Thus emerged a group of powerful merchant-planters, peculiar to the tobacco colonies, who engaged in all the mercantile pursuits yet considered themselves primarily planters.[14]

Middleton also mentions that this system was more prevalent in the eighteenth century than in the seventeenth, which makes William Troth one of the first to participate in and profit from it.

Stores such as Troth's, according to P. A. Bruce in his *Economic History of Virginia*, were "found in great numbers in every navigable stream" in colonial Virginia, "the store [being] one of the principal institutions . . . whether the property of a foreign or a native merchant."[15] Margaret Shore Morris suggests that this was also true in Maryland in her book, *Colonial Trade in Maryland, 1689–1715.*[16]

The housing for these stores is also considered by Bruce, who says that they were sometimes kept in a room of the dwelling house, but were more often housed in a separate building. This, he suggests, would have been a "boarded house with a loft and with a shed."[17] That Troth's store was probably in a separate building can be determined by comparing the rooms listed in the 1711 inventory with those in the house today. The two downstairs rooms, the chamber, and the unnamed room upstairs would leave no space in the house itself for a store; thus, it was probably kept in another building, which, of necessity, would have been located at the waterfront. The dwelling house was and is located about a quarter of a mile back from the river bank.

Stores such as Troth's were almost the only source of manufactured goods available to the colonists, so they were stocked with a wide variety of wares, from tin pans and needles to powder and shot. Many lines in Troth's inventory were taken up by bolts of cloth, including calico, damask, crepe, serge, linsey, and "lining" (linen). Nor was there a shoe shortage: fifty-two pairs for men and twenty-two for women were listed. Leather, window glass, iron, paper, nails, carpenters' tools, hoes, two old guns, and two old chafing dishes are a further sampling of the goods Troth offered for sale.[18] Troth's mercantile ventures placed him economically far above the overwhelming majority of his customers, who lived in one-room houses, enjoyed net incomes of about £8 to £15 sterling a year from two or three hogsheads of tobacco raised with their own hands, and counted their entire visible estates at something less than £200.[19]

The Troths were also important to Talbot's religious history. Quakerism had arrived in Talbot County in the 1650s, spreading there from Kent Island, where it first appeared in Maryland. Although subject to widespread and violent persecution in the 1660s, by the following decade the sect had become more widely accepted in the entire colony. Three well-known traveling Friends visited Talbot County at this time, encouraging men with education to become leaders in the meetings, and, by the time William Troth first appears

13. Ibid.
14. Arthur Pierce Middleton, *Tobacco Coast: A Maritime History of Chesapeake Bay in the Colonial Era* (Newport News, Va.: Mariner's Museum, 1953), p. 108.
15. Philip Alexander Bruce, *Economic History of Virginia in the Seventeenth Century,* vol. 2 (New York: Macmillan & Co., 1896), p. 380.
16. Margaret Shaw Morris, *Colonial Trade of Maryland, 1689–1715* (Baltimore: Johns Hopkins Press, 1914), p. 103.
17. Bruce, *Economic History,* p. 381.
18. Troth Inventory. Much of this material has also appeared in Norman Harrington, "Talbot's Hidden Heritage" (Easton: Talbot County Historical Society, 1980), pp. 47, 48.
19. Aubrey C. Land, "The Planters of Colonial Maryland," in *Maryland Historical Magazine,* vol. 67, no. 1 (1972):114.

The venerable Third Haven Meeting House, Maryland's oldest documented building.

Interior of the Third Haven Meeting House.

in the records of the county in 1676, Talbot had become a strong center of Quakerism on the Eastern Shore, and our William Troth was a prominent member.[20] It is important to note that while it may jar the sensibilities of today's Friends, three hundred years ago slavery was not regarded as inconsistent with the tenets of Quakerism: William Troth, for instance, owned thirteen slaves when he died in 1710.[21]

As noted, Troth's Fortune has a medieval-style stair tower; it is not the only house in the area with such a feature. If one were to sail easterly from Troth's Fortune down the Choptank to a small branch of Island Creek, one would come to Combsberry, (T-156) on Oxford Neck, a three-part brick dwelling whose central (oldest) section is five bays long and two-and-one-half stories tall with a two-story stair tower in the center of the north facade. Its south facade is laid in all-header bond above the stepped water table, with English bond below. This use of all-header bond sets Combsberry apart from its contemporaries. In fact, it sets it so far apart that one might question its popularly given date of circa 1700; that type of brickwork is far more common to the 1740–80 period. English bond is used on the rest of the building. The first-story windows have deep segmental arches, and a semicircular arch rises above the door. On the north, the tower contains the stair and entrance thereto. East of the tower, the main facade is punctuated by one window on each story; the tower itself has a semicircular headed window between floors, apparently a modern introduction.

Inside, the plan consists of two rooms separated by a passage leading from the south entrance to the stair tower. The partition creating the passage was added later. With the exception of the fireplaces, the first story is devoid of any period work. The stair does, however, have raised-panel spandrel and closet and a good, late-eighteenth-century close-string balustrade. An early brick kitchen, separate from the house, is still standing.

Flemish bond and English bond were more common than all-header bond—and they were more economical, too. Lloyd's Landing (T–124), a superior example of the "replacement house" constructed by prosperous farmers in the early eighteenth century, is unique in Talbot County in that all four facades are laid in English bond. Its hall-and-parlor floor plan is somewhat unusual in so early a house, but is repeated in several later houses in Dorchester County, just across the Choptank. The old house was doubled in size around 1950, but its interior is noteworthy for the fine paneling that still graces the living room. According to the 1798 federal direct tax, the building was owned and occupied by James Lloyd and the property was called "Part of Jamaica." The farm's buildings included, besides the main house, a framed kitchen, 16 by 22 feet; a log meat house, 12 feet square; a framed milk house, 10 by 12 feet; and a fowl house of unknown dimensions.

Another example of a replacement house can be seen at the Ferry Farm House (T–187), also known as Aker's Ferry, near Trappe. Here a horse and rider could be ferried across the Choptank to what is now Cambridge. Although the original house (which was used as a tavern) has had additions, the oldest section can still be discerned. It is an early eighteenth-century frame dwelling with a gambrel roof, and it is three bays long and two bays deep. The house is built on a brick cellar whose bricks are large and laid in English bond that resembles early-eighteenth-century work on the Eastern Shore. The first floor joists are huge flitched logs still retaining their bark. The walls of the house are covered with plain weatherboard. While the interior has been remodeled, it still has a good, early-eighteenth-century stair, and the east rooms retain some period woodwork. For example, the major posts protrude from the walls and are encased in fluted pilasters with a design similar to the fluting that can be seen at White Marshes (T–105), several miles up the Choptank.

That house, located near the headwater of Kings Creek, which flows into the Choptank, has a new kitchen wing, but the original two-and-one-half-story structure is essentially unchanged from the early eighteenth century. It is a three-bay-long structure laid in English bond, except for the west facade, which is laid in Flemish bond with glazed headers. There is a central door on the first story and two windows with jack arches of

20. For a good general discussion of Maryland's early Quaker history, see Norman Harrington, *Shaping of Religion in America* (Easton: Historical Society of Talbot County, 1980), pp. 67–73.
21. An interesting event in the life of William Troth occurred on December 18, 1682, an event that is a further indication of the rough-and-ready lives Talbot's seventeenth-century planters led. Troth was attacked at his home on the Choptank by an Indian named Poh Poh Caquis, first with a gun and then with a tomahawk. Troth escaped uninjured. Poh Poh Caquis was captured and pleaded intoxication as his defense. The Talbot County judges did not accept this defense, however, and sentenced the Indian to twenty lashes on the bare back and banishment.

Combsberry's north facade has a two-story stair tower; photo by Frances Benjamin Johnston.

Combsberry's south facade is laid in all-header bond, rare in Talbot County; photograph by Frances Benjamin Johnston.

rubbed and gauged brick. A two-brick beltcourse wraps around all sides of the building, with a narrow string course at attic level on both gable ends. Glazed brick chevrons just below the rake decorate both gable ends. The east facade has a central door flanked by two windows, with the same arrangement on the second story. The first-floor door is sheltered by a small, finely detailed porch; the second-floor door leads to a balcony with a Chinese Chippendale railing. The early porch trim is repeated on the addition. Lines in the whitewash and the second-story door suggest there once was a two-story wing on the east facade.

The interior of the old house has a hall-and-parlor plan. The hall's gable-end paneling is similar to that of nearby Troth's Fortune, except that White Marshes's contains an enclosed stair on the east side of the fireplace. The closet retains original shelving, and the window jambs are fluted.

Hampden, one of the best survivors from early Talbot County.

This house is laid in Flemish bond; that house is laid in English bond. But not all of these early houses have uniform bonding patterns. In fact, many houses have bonding like that of White Marshes, where the pattern varies from facade to facade. There are also houses like Hampden (T–68), on Island Neck overlooking Dividing Creek, which has foundations built of stone to grade, English-bond brick to the water table, Flemish bond to the second-floor level, and common bond in the gable ends. Hampden also has lintels of rubbed and gauged brick on the east facade and segmental arches on the west. The central entrance has its original molded frame and wide-paneled door. Architecturally, Hampden is like Compton and Boston Cliff in plan and like White Marshes and Troth's Fortune in date and detail. It is one of the best survivors from early Talbot County, retaining most of its original exterior and interior detail. Hampden represents the dwelling of a well-to-do planter of the period and is an interesting combination of vernacular form and early Georgian interior design. It is said that Thomas Martin, one of the first vestrymen for old Whitemarsh Church (see chapter 4), built this house in the seventeenth century on part of the Hier-Dier-Lloyd grant, 200 acres of which he purchased from Edward Lloyd I. Some historians deem it the oldest existing brick house in Talbot County. Other authorities, however, date the house to circa 1720.

Another bi-bonded house is Bloomfield (T–175), a Bartlett–Dixon family dwelling that has been the product of continual growth. The oldest section, one of the earliest extant dwellings in Talbot County, is a brick, one-room, story-and-loft house. (Care should be taken not to confuse Bloomfield's one-room core with the one-room houses Dell Upton discussed above. Bloomfield's original section is larger and better built than the houses Upton was describing.) The brick bonding is visible only on the southeast end: the first floor is Flemish bond, while the gable end above that level is English bond. Additions include a one-and-one-half-story section with brick gable ends and brick nogged-frame facades, and a late-nineteenth-century, two-story, frame kitchen that joins the middle part of the house at its south corner. All frame parts of the house are covered in rectangular lapped weatherboards.

Two of the best of Talbot's early replacement houses are Orem's Delight (T–193) and Boston Cliff (T–122); both are laid in Flemish bond. Orem's Delight is, in fact, one of the

Bloomfield: the oldest section is the brick wing to the right.

Boston Cliff, romantically photographed by Frances Benjamin Johnston in the 1930s.

The best-executed early Georgian interior in Talbot County: the stair with flowered step-ends at Boston Cliff, as photographed in the 1930s.

few small eighteenth-century dwellings that has survived without being incorporated into a larger dwelling. It is a one-and-one-half-story brick structure that measures 20 by 25 feet. The east and north facades are laid in Flemish bond with glazed headers. The north gable end is given some refinement by a two-brick-wide beltcourse with two glazed interlocking diamonds below the wide chimney. Both the south and west sides are laid in Flemish bond, without glazing, but portions have been relaid. Both also have a stepped water table. The south wing's gable end is covered with shiplap siding and is pierced by two small windows. This wing is a modern replacement of a very early wing, which was demolished in the 1960s. The entrance door rests below a rubbed segmental arch and is flanked by matching windows; the openings have been slightly altered, but it is possible to see where the original work exists. The roof has been replaced, as has the dormer.

Inside, the structure is divided into two rooms by a beaded board partition. There is some late-eighteenth-century fielded paneling above the fireplace; the entire composition is flanked by a cupboard and by an enclosed stair which leads to the one-room, unfinished second story. Originally, the building had a huge fireplace with a mitre-arch recess in the cheeks and a large wood lintel, and the floor was about ten inches lower than it is at present. The 1798 tax assessment, however, shows that by the end of that century the house was essentially the same size and configuration it is now and that there were a spinning house, a kitchen, and a meat house close by. Architecturally, Orem's Delight is important for several reasons. It possesses many unusual original features, including the glazed diamonds on the gable and the early fireplace. It also possesses good late-eighteenth-century detail in the paneling and woodwork. But its real significance is that it is a rare survival of a wonderful early house essentially undisturbed by later additions. As such, its importance is hard to overestimate.

While comparisons are invidious, it may safely be said that Boston Cliff (T–122) has the best-executed early Georgian interior in Talbot County. It is certainly the earliest example that can be positively dated: it was built in 1729. The house is a five-bay, one-and-one-half-story, brick building with a three-bay, one-and-one-half-story twentieth-century extension on the east end. The walls are laid in Flemish bond with random glazing. Its stepped water table jogs above the basement window (similar to Cloverfields in Queen Anne's County and several houses in Chestertown), and there is a beltcourse at second-floor level on the gable end. The splendid interior is divided into stair hall, living room, and dining room, with a modern den in an addition behind the dining room. Original woodwork remains in most of the rooms, but the most significant detail is the open-string stair with carved flowers on the stair spandrels; the stair's bold handrail extends over the newels, and is similar to handrails found at Fernwood (T–114), Hampden (T–68), and Otwell (T–164).

Crooked Intention (T–48) got its interesting name in 1681 when Hugh Sherwood took out a patent for 130 acres in Talbot County. According to one widely circulated legend, Sherwood had planned to return to England, but this intention was never fulfilled, and he decided to settle in Maryland instead, naming the land he bought here Crooked Intention to signify his revised plans for the future.

In 1690, Sherwood sold fifty acres of the tract to Robert Harrison, who, in 1717, left the land, apparently still unimproved, to his son Robert.[22] This second Harrison *probably* built the brick one-and-one-half-story house we see today soon after he acquired the property; we know that some sort of Harrison house was in existence by 1753 when Robert II died, leaving his "now Dwelling plantation with all the Dwelling houses, outhouses," etc., to his wife, Elizabeth, to be transferred to his son Joseph in the event of her death or remarriage.[23] The (presumed) oldest part of the present house has a simple hall-and-parlor plan with a kitchen wing. (While this is the sort of house that could have been built in the mid-eighteenth-century, it is not unique to that era.) Later in the century—and we are on firmer ground now—Thomas Harrison (Joseph's son) made additions to the rear of the building that is now standing, creating the present quaint roof line; simultaneously, he

22. Material in the Maryland Hall of Records, Annapolis.
23. Ibid.

installed paneling, a built-in cupboard, and the other interior woodwork that still survives intact in Crooked Intention. This important, if puzzling, structure was restored in 1948 by Mr. and Mrs. G. A. Van Lennep, Jr.

Then there is Otwell. As has been discussed, the 500-acre tract called Otwell was surveyed in 1659 for William Taylor. In 1662 a court for Talbot County convened "at the house of William Taylor,"[24] which must have stood on the property before the present dwelling. From this point, the plantation was conveyed to Taylor's son Samuel who sold it to Colonel Vincent Lowe, a province deputy, in 1687. From Lowe, the property passed to a distant relative, Foster Turbutt, who was a justice or commissioner for Talbot County. Foster Turbutt's will, probated in 1721, leaves "my now dwelling plantation" to his daughter Sarah, who had married Nicholas Goldsborough III around 1720. And Nicholas and Sarah Goldsborough, socially prominent and wealthy, were the probable builders of the house's oldest section, although there are those who maintain that the present Otwell is a product of the seventeenth century.

After the Goldsboroughs' deaths Otwell immediately fell into a decline and for years

Crooked Intention, an old house with an interesting name.

24. See Tilghman, *History,* vol. 1, pp. 201–9.

Otwell: the oldest portions form the T-shaped front sections.

Otwell: the stair before the 1958 fire. Note the floral step-ends that are somewhat similar to those at Boston Cliff.

the house was probably uninhabited—or at least uncared for—accounting for the following description in the 1783 tax assessment: 850 acres and one brick dwelling house "in bad repair," as well as a frame kitchen, three tobacco houses, a fowl house, a milk house, and three logged dwelling houses, "all mostly in bad repair."[25]

The Goldsboroughs' story-and-one-half house was unusual in that it had a **T** plan. Beginning with the top of the **T** (west elevation), the building is three bays long with two windows on the first story and dormers above. Both the north and south ends are two bays deep with two windows on each story, flanking a flush chimney; on the south end the pairs of windows are aligned exactly while the north windows on the second story are placed slightly closer together than their first-story counterparts. In addition, each end features jack-arch lintels over the windows and two symmetrically placed ventilators on either side of the corbel-capped chimney just under the eaves line. On the east side of the head of the **T**, flanking the stem, are two dormer windows, the northernmost of which tops a window in the first story. The interior still retains the original floor plan: the early, **T**-plan section has two parlors in the cross of the **T** with a squarish stair hall and dining room in the stem. This was extremely complex for its date, making Otwell notably more sophisticated than most of its contemporaries. Unfortunately, much of the decorative interior detailing was destroyed in a disastrous fire in 1958, although Mr. and Mrs. John E. Jackson restored or replaced it with great accuracy after the blaze.

Dating the houses discussed above was hard, but it is nothing short of maddening for the next two dwellings, Martingham (T–210) and the "Captain's House" at Wye (T–54).

In the mid-seventeenth century, Robert Martyn was granted 500 acres of land for transporting his wife and five children to the province. Of this, Martyn assigned 200 acres

Martingham, once the seat of the venerable Hambleton family.

Frances Benjamin Johnston photographed Martingham's outbuildings in the 1930s; the dairy and meat house are still standing.

25. See Otwell's Nomination to the National Register of Historic Places, on file at the Maryland Historical Trust, Annapolis.

The Captain's House at Wye; although it
has been much altered, it may have been
the original home of the Lloyds.

to William Champe, who in turn assigned that parcel called Martingham to the Scotsman William Hambleton. By 1663 Hambleton had been appointed high sheriff of the county and a justice of the peace. The following year he was elected a delegate to the General Assembly by the freemen of Talbot County, people who had a freehold of fifty acres within the county or who were residents and had a visible estate of £40 sterling. Hambleton died in 1675, leaving his dwelling plantation to his sons, John and William. The estate passed from father to son through successive generations.

Martingham is a frame dwelling composed of three portions, an early, one-and-one-half-story, center part with two, flanking one-story wings. The main part of the house and the east wing are of great historic interest; the west wing was built in 1945 to balance the original kitchen wing. Martingham began as a two-room (per floor) dwelling with central chimney. Rear rooms were added later and the roof was altered to cover both rooms; at that time the center chimney was also replaced by the gable end fireplaces.

Inside the original (central) section, there is a small entrance hall with an enclosed stairway on the back wall; two rooms flank the hall, and both rooms have fireplaces. Boxed posts on the lateral walls of the south half of the original building divide the main facade into three bays. The south posts have large quarter-round molding like the summer beam on the second-story ceiling of Carvill Hall in Kent County. All other trim is very plain. The old yellow-pine floor is an early replacement. The corner posts of the house are exposed in both the living room and dining room, which provides an interesting decorative touch.

There are two early outbuildings north of the kitchen: a dairy and a meat house. The dairy is a small square building with a brick foundation, a pyramidal roof, and a lean-to porch. The original floor is below grade and has been covered by a makeshift wood floor. The frame meat house rests on brick piers and is sheathed with white pine weatherboard.

All the above structures seem ripe for further investigation, possibly using dendrochronology, a modern method whereby scientists can determine the year the timber in the house was cut. This is also true for the "Captain's House" at Wye.

The history of Wye and the Lloyds will be explored elsewhere (see chapter 5). Still, it should be noted here in this chapter on circa 1700 houses that the "Captain's House" (so called because during the nineteenth century it was the dwelling of the captain of the Wye House vessels) *may* date to the seventeenth century. The late J. Donnell Tilghman has written that "the records of Talbot County show that court was held in June of 1663 at the house of Edward Lloyd. It is quite possible that court was held in this building, since there is neither evidence nor tradition suggesting that Edward Lloyd ever lived on any of his other Talbot County lands."[26] Lloyd was then based in Anne Arundel County and was rich enough to have had his house built in its entirety after he began patenting land in Talbot County in the 1650s. It is clear that a house was definitely in place by 1685 when an inventory was made of the estate of Colonel Philemon Lloyd (Edward's son and heir). This inventory listed the following rooms: hall, new room, upper chamber, blue chamber, study chamber, black chamber, stair case, Madam Lloyd's room, nursery, kitchen, kitchen loft, closet, and store. Tilghman continues:

> Until evidence to the contrary is found, one may safely accept the family tradition that the Captain's House is the earliest structure. This is well borne out by the architectural design. Though the interior trim and mantels are obviously of later date than the walls, the steep roof and the massive north chimney suggest a building that may well be among the oldest still standing in the state. This chimney, with its ornamental bands and its brick pilaster, has few counterparts in Maryland and strongly suggests the influence of Jacobean models in England.[27]

This may be the exception that proves the rule. For if Wye makes it clear that not every Chesapeake planter lived in a shanty or in a small "replacement" house, it is equally clear that the assessors in 1685 felt that the Lloyds were enough apart that it was appropriate to use the respectful appellation "Madam."

26. J. Donnell Tilghman, "Wye House," in *Maryland Historical Magazine*, vol. 47, no. 2 (1953):91.
27. Ibid.

CHAPTER 3

A Grain-based Georgian Splendor

U ntil the middle of the eighteenth century, tobacco was by far the most commonly grown crop in Maryland. Tobacco, however, exhausts the soil when not rotated with other crops. While some Talbot County planters failed to rotate their crops and by 1750 were suffering the consequences—depleted soil, poor production, and lower income—many of the county's farmers had diversified and were enjoying an economic boom. Architectural historian Orlando Ridout V has described the impact of changing agricultural and economic conditions on the Eastern Shore:

> By the mid eighteenth century, a gradual shift was underway on the Eastern Shore. While Southern Maryland remained firmly committed to tobacco production, many Eastern Shore farmers found grain increasingly attractive as a cash crop. Although grain prices were not always as high as tobacco prices, they remained relatively stable and were not subject to the fluctuations of the tobacco market. These farmers were further encouraged by merchants, particularly in Philadelphia, who sought new sources of grain for the booming export trade to the West Indies and Southern Europe. By the close of the colonial period, grain had replaced tobacco as the principal market crop on the Eastern Shore, and by the end of the eighteenth century, tobacco production had all but ceased.[1]

Others have noticed the same phenomenon: "The fertile plain along the Choptank River . . . became the bread basket of the Chesapeake in this period. . . . Wheat superseded tobacco as the major market crop in Kent County by 1750 and was becoming a significant source of income for planters as far south as Talbot County."[2]

Several studies have shown that all along the Chesapeake, whenever farmers began to diversify, to augment their tobacco income with grains (or to replace the "noxious weed" altogether), their profits increased enough to allow them to build houses, barns, churches, and mills substantial enough to have endured to this day.

The Chesapeake area, and Talbot County in particular, enjoyed a steady eighteenth-century prosperity based on a bountiful rural economy, steady growth, and a fixed social order. The populations of Talbot, Queen Anne's, and Kent counties, which then, as now, resemble each other enough to form a unit, more than trebled, from 10,800 in 1713 to 37,000 by the Revolution. "As long as the economy allowed a father to establish his children on their own farms, sons and daughters remained on the Eastern Shore, and with each new generation, ties of kinship and land among families multiplied." Further,

> since the seventeenth century, Eastern Shore society had changed in three respects. The number of middling family farmers, the importance of slave labor, and the power of the merchant-planter all had grown. In the continuing predominance of small farmers who mixed production for home and the market, the Eastern Shore shared much with the Middle Colonies and still resembled rural England. In their growing reliance on slaves, Eastern Shore planters followed a path previously taken in Virginia. And in the coming of age of third-generation merchant-planter families, the Eastern Shore acquired an elite that rivaled the landlords of New York's Hudson Valley, the great sugar planters of the West Indies, and the gentry of England.[3]

OPPOSITE:
Gross Coate, a Tilghman house from 1760 until 1983.

1. Orlando Ridout V, "Agricultural Change and the Architectural Landscape," in *Three Centuries of Maryland Architecture* (Annapolis: Maryland Historical Trust, 1982), p. 7. See also Paul G. E. Clemens, *The Atlantic Economy and Colonial Maryland's Eastern Shore* (Ithaca: Cornell University Press, 1980).
2. Carson et al., "Impermanent Architecture," pp. 168–71.
3. "The Planters of Talbot County," Chapter 5 in uncertain book; stray photocopy in archives of the Talbot County Historical Society, Easton, and the Maryland Historical Trust, Annapolis, pp. 120–21.

Conjectural sketch of George Robins's Peachblossom.

In Talbot this third generation elite had solidified by about 1730 when the county had sixteen men and one woman who each owned more than 1000 acres of land and 10 slaves.

All of this can, of course, be seen in Talbot's architecture. Unfortunately while there is virtually nothing left to give an indication of how Talbot's yeomen lived, the middling and upper classes shared in the cereal-based prosperity and the county is filled with their mid-Georgian structures. Some, of course, shared more equally than others—the "merchant planters" met in Chapter 2 did particularly well and secured their hold on the county's wealth, but nearly all classes enjoyed a better life than they had before. The names of Talbot's Georgian masterpieces are still beautifully evocative: Myrtle Grove, Ratcliffe Manor, Richland, Rolles Range, Wickersham, Plimhimmon, Gross' Coate, Pleasant Valley. These were and are great houses built by great men who had great fortunes and represent what has been called "the triumph of the merchant-planter class."[4]

The term "Georgian" is as tricky to use as the term "Victorian." Both, by strict definition, refer to English monarchs, not to architecture, yet over the years both have acquired connotations that *suggest* definite styles of building. And, for better or worse, "Georgian" is too much a part of the American architectural vocabulary to be ignored. It is used to describe structures that are symmetrical in facade and plan, well-ordered, typically three or five bays long, have double-hung sash windows, and have gable or hipped roofs. Many of these features had by the late eighteenth century become so widely accepted that in modified form they were virtually vernacular. Higher-style Georgian buildings are usually further enriched by quoins, pediments, pilasters, elaborate cornices, and belt-courses. The most formal buildings of all can be subcategorized *Palladian*, a term that in Talbot County should probably be reserved for Wye House and Hope.

Not surprisingly, almost all these "Georgian masterpieces" are bound together by ties of friendship, shared inheritances, business partnerships, and blood. From the early days in the county there has been much intermarriage among "merchant-planter" families, and these families developed similar tastes in cultural areas, one of which was architecture. The overlapping, interlocking mazes that make up the Lloyd, Goldsborough, Hollyday,

4. Ibid., p. 121.

Tilghman, et al. families will bewilder all but the most persistent of geneologists; non-Talbot residents, after only a brief study of the county's family trees, may never want to hear the words "Henrietta Maria" again. But it is important to attempt to make some sense of some of the bloodlines, if only to see which Henry and Sarah built X house and how they and X are related to Robert and Anna Maria and Z house down the creek.

The marital and economic history of the Robins family—whose early family tree was leafy with artisans, adventurers, and merchant planters—illustrates these points.[5] George Robins (1646–1677) arrived in Talbot County around 1670 from London. He originally came to oversee an elaborate trading enterprise, but he found life at Job's Content (later renamed Peachblossom) so pleasantly profitable that he settled down to the life of a planter. His son Thomas (1672–1721) was sufficiently successful in shoemaking, tobacco, and grain to be styled "esquire." At Thomas's death, he left his son George II (1697–1742) seventeen slaves, a herd of livestock, a large inventory of leather goods, and four farms that produced crops of corn, tobacco, and wheat. George Robins II took his diversified wealth and increased it even further through commerce with the West Indies and England, having accumulated 4,624 acres by 1731, when he married Henrietta Maria Tilghman, a niece of Edward Lloyd II.[6]

Two daughters of George Robins II married two sons of Samuel Chamberlaine (1697–1773), who had himself, in 1729, married Henrietta Maria Lloyd (1710–1748), another of Edward Lloyd II's nieces. Samuel Chamberlaine, the first of his name in Talbot County, had immigrated as a seventeen-year-old apprentice seaman in 1714. He settled near Oxford and married twice: Henrietta Maria Lloyd was his second wife and the mother of his children; his first wife, Mary Ungle, had died in 1726. Mary Ungle's father, Robert, was a rich Oxford merchant, important in politics and "notorious for his crude humor and excessive drinking."[7] Chamberlaine prospered, buying and building in booming Oxford, and was appointed justice of the peace. In 1733, thanks in part to his wives' dowries, he owned 2,686 acres and seventeen slaves; when Chamberlaine died in 1773, he owned 4,169 acres.[8]

Finally, the Robinses were matrimonially linked to the Goldsboroughs, the first of whom, Nicholas, appeared in Kent Island (by way of Dorset, London, Barbados, and New England) in 1670 and died shortly thereafter. Nicholas Goldsborough's widow, Margaret (Margaretta) Howes Goldsborough, married George Robins I. The Goldsborough children had moved to Talbot County by the 1690s; one of them, Robert, made a career in law, serving as chief justice of Maryland's highest court. Robert saved his money to invest in land, and in 1733 owned 1,941 acres, twenty-six adult slaves, and a fine home at Ashby.

The Goldsboroughs probably owed more of their wealth to agriculture and office and less to commerce than any of their equally prominent contemporaries, but marriage of two of Robert Goldsborough's children to children of George Robins (the eighteenth century merchant) and the marriage of his brother Charles into the Ennalls family, then the wealthiest merchants in Dorchester County, united the profits of agriculture, office and commerce.[9]

Robert Goldsborough (1704–1777) was a distinguished barrister and a scion of many of the county's leading families. Still, he will probably be most fondly remembered as the builder of the original section of Myrtle Grove (T–53); the house is still owned by his descendants. It is said that Robert's father gave him Myrtle Grove as a wedding present in 1739; others date it to 1724–34.[10] Myrtle Grove is on land carved out of the senior Goldsborough's Ashby estate, a tract that meandered two-and-one-half miles along the Miles River. Myrtle Grove's oldest section, the central section of today's house, is five bays wide and one-and-one-half-stories tall. Built on an English bond foundation, the walls are covered with beaded weatherboard, while wood shingles cover the steep gable roof. The entrance, with its wide, ten-panel door, forms the central bay. Each of the other bays contains a nine-over-nine sash window with thick muntins and three-panel shutters.

5. The Robins family has remained prominent: the twentieth-century photographs of H. Robins Hollyday form an invaluable tool for Eastern Shore historians.
6. "Planters of Talbot County," p. 129; see also Samuel Chamberlaine, Chamberlaine (Cottonport, La.: Polyanthus, 1973), pp. 59–67.
7. "Planters of Talbot County," pp. 126, 127.
8. Ibid., p. 128.
9. Ibid., p. 131; see also Eleanor Goldsborough, The House of Goldsborough, 6 vols. (unpublished manuscript, 1932); a typed copy is in the library of the Maryland Historical Society, Baltimore.
10. Dr. H. Chandlee Forman, Old Buildings, Gardens and Furniture in Tidewater Maryland (Cambridge, Md.: Tidewater Publishers, 1967), p. 95.

Myrtle Grove, one of the most beloved houses in Talbot County. Robert Goldsborough's original house is the taller frame section. The 1790 brick addition rises above, and the 1927 kitchen is in the foreground.

Myrtle Grove: paneling in the sitting room of the circa 1735 structure.

Archaeological investigations have revealed that Myrtle Grove's kitchen originally extended to the northwest, where a 1927 addition now stands (see also chapter 9).

The original house has an L-shaped central hall with one room on each side. The hall retains its original floor, and there is a closed-string stairway in the ell. The dining room is northwest of the hall and boasts much of its original elaborate paneling. This room was originally divided into two rooms, as is indicated by remnants of the corner fireplaces' brick supporting arches which are visible in the dining room's cellar. Across the hall from the dining room is the sitting room, whose northeast and fireplace walls are entirely paneled. The ell of the hall connects with the hall in the superb two-story, hall-and-double-parlor, brick addition, completed in 1790.

The legal activities of the early Goldsboroughs are given architectural expression in the circa-1770 frame, story-and-a-half law office, still at Myrtle Grove, one of the oldest law offices in the country. Robert Henry Goldsborough, grandson of the Robert who built the original section of Myrtle Grove, served as burgess in the general assembly, justice of the peace, deputy commissary for Talbot County, and register of wills.

Ratcliffe Manor (T–42) is another one of Talbot's great mid-eighteenth-century houses. Henry Hollyday (1725–1789) and his wife Anna Maria Robins (married in 1749) built the house shortly before 1760. Mrs. Hollyday was a daughter of the aforementioned George Robins II, while Hollyday's grandfather had settled on the western shore in the 1670s as a factor for an English tobacco merchant. As will be seen, the Hollyday family continued to maintain close personal and business ties with England until the Revolution.

Henry Hollyday's father James (1695–1747) became a vital figure in the development of Talbot County after his marriage in 1721 to Sarah Covington Lloyd, the widow of Edward Lloyd II. James and Sarah Hollyday lived at an early Wye House, where their three children were born, and James was guardian of the vast Lloyd estates until Edward Lloyd III came of age in 1729. James served as commissioner of peace for Talbot County in 1723, 1729, 1732, and 1736; he was a member of the provincial court in Annapolis in 1732, a member of the lower house of the Maryland Assembly from 1724 through 1732, and he held many important posts including treasurer of the Eastern Shore (1727–1747) and naval

Myrtle Grove's 1790 addition.

Myrtle Grove: reception room in the 1790 section. Note the particularly fine cornice.

Myrtle Grove: stair and hall in the 1790 section.

31

Ratcliffe Manor, a delight to "connoisseurs of the colonial."

11. Chamberlaine, *Chamberlaine*, pp. 63–67; also Tilghman, *History*, vol. 1, p. 47.
12. John Martin Hammond, *Colonial Mansions of Maryland and Delaware* (Philadelphia: J. B. Lippincott Co., 1914), p. 148.

officer of the port of Oxford. When Edward Lloyd III came of age and the Hollydays left Wye, they moved north into Queen Anne's County and built Readbourne, the great house on the Chester River.[11]

It is clear that Henry Hollyday, one of James and Sarah's Wye-born children, and his wife were used to the life of the provincial *gratin*. And Ratcliffe Manor is the beautiful outward and visible sign of the Hollydays' refined taste. "The site of Ratcliffe Manor is such that it has a charming outlook. One sees the windings of the Tred Avon and the fine farms of this rolling, fertile country."[12] Swepson Earle neatly sums up Ratcliffe Manor by noting that the house is "more distinguished in appearance than the majority of houses built at the same period. The rooms are capacious, the ceilings are high, and the quaintly carved woodwork delights the connoisseurs of the colonial."[13] This "distinguished" building is a large, impressive, well-maintained, and superb example of colonial Georgian architecture. The jerkinhead-roofed house is a very large five bays wide and four deep. It sits on a high cellar above a beveled water table. There is a central door on the front with a segmental arch. All of the windows have flat brick arches. The windows have the hierarchy that builders at that time deemed proper: twelve-over-twelve panes on the ground floor and twelve-over-eight on the second. There are huge twin chimneys at each end of the house. To the west of the main house is a one-and-one-half-story, three-bay brick wing.

The interior has a floor plan with two large rooms overlooking a terraced garden and two rooms and a central stair hall on the approach side. Raised-paneled dado is in place around the hall except adjacent to the door. The stair ascends in three flights and is superb: walnut is used on the balustrade; square newels have carved recessed panels on each exposed surface; there are two bold-turned balusters per step. Beneath the second-story landing is an elliptical arch with reeded pilasters.

The east room or office has a diagonal fireplace flanked by fluted pilasters upon paneled bases. Above the fireplace is a large plaster panel. All paint has been removed from the woodwork to reveal the color and grain of the native yellow pine. The drawing room is the largest and best-appointed room in this thoroughly impressive house. It is fully paneled to the ceiling on all sides and the fireplace is flanked by fluted pilasters and arched closets. Above the fireplace are two large horizontal panels, the lower being smaller than the upper panel. The fluted pilasters, like those in the office, rest on paneled bases, but, unlike those in the office, there is stop fluting at the base of each pilaster, which stops abruptly at the base molding. One closet was originally a cabinet, but the doors have been removed and the shell dome and scalloped shelves are now visible. With the exception of the pilasters, the overall feeling of the room resembles the woodwork originally installed at Readbourne, the boyhood home of the builder of Ratcliffe Manor. John Martin Hammond has written that "Ratcliffe Manor has no ghosts and no stories of violent death or suicide. It speaks simply of gentility and good living."[14]

When the Hollydays built Ratcliffe Manor, they apparently laid out the garden at the same time. The perfect relation of house and garden is one of Ratcliffe Manor's greatest charms. It is probable that Hollyday had studied Miller's great *Gardner's Dictionary* and had obtained from it a good deal of helpful information for his design of Ratcliffe's grounds. It is known that his mother-in-law, in writing to Peter Collinson, an English naturalist and a friend of her husband George Robins, quotes Miller in some detail. One of her letters to Collinson, dated June 5, 1768, suggests her botanical expertise, her knowledge of Miller, and her friendliness with Collinson:

> Kind Sir—Yesterday morning I received your very obliging letter, with seeds, (a part of which I will put in the ground, and keep the rest for next Spring,) and Zananculus which you so kindly favor me with, and which I have long desired to see. I will follow your directions in planting them. . . . Finding in Miller that the ——— is poisonous, I think best to forbear sowing the seed just now, as I have several grandchildren, at times running in the garden, who might handle the plant and suffer by it. Being so much in your debt sir, I had an inclination to send half a dozen tulip roots of my own raising, but I am several miles from the ship. If I thought they might be cruising about I should be discouraged by thinking yours so far superior, that mine would not be acceptable. I shall be always glad to hear of your welfare, but writing may be troublesome in your advanced age, and I cannot expect you to continue your correspondence as you have doubtless many to write to.
>
> I am with the greatest respect, your much obliged friend and servant.[15]

Miller's publication is known to have been on sale in Oxford by the factor for Foster Cunliffe and Sons as well as by the *Virginia Gazette* in Williamsburg. It is of interest to note

13. Earle, *Bay Country*, p. 366.
14. Hammond, *Colonial Mansions*, p. 151.
15. Chamberlaine, *Chamberlaine*, pp. 41–42.

that the broad avenue approach to Ratcliffe Manor is equal in width to the dimensions Miller advocated.

Richland (T–77), dating to the 1740s, is located on a peninsula that juts out into the Tuckahoe Creek. The house is important to this study of Talbot County architecture because it illustrates how, as the county's more remote areas got settled, people carried the building traditions of the circa-1725 period upstream from the Bay. One can see how a house form, popular in the 1720s at the mouth of the Miles or the Choptank, would, by the next generation, appear in the county's more inland reaches. Richland has echoes of Otwell, Hampden, Compton, and other early Talbot residences. The long, one-and-a-half-story frame structure stretches its five regularly placed bays between two large chimneys. (There is a later, two-bay kitchen to the west.) Richland's main facade faces south and is punctuated by nine-over-six sash windows that flank a central paneled door. The north facade has a small lean-to addition on one side; on the other side there are a door and two windows with a small casement window adjacent to the door to light the stair within; this arrangement of casement and door can also be seen at Otwell. The house's interior contains two rooms with a center stair hall and a third room to the rear; in this general plan, Richland continues a room arrangement that was found at Hampden and Compton, as well as at Richland's contemporary, Anderton, near Oxford. The parlor, on the west end of the house, has one paneled wall across the face of the fireplace and two closets. In composition, the paneling resembles Troth's Fortune's (T-50), but lacks the pilasters, that is, there are two horizontal panels above the fireplace with vertical panels flanking the fireplace. The stair hall is of the same period as the living room. It is a close-string structure with turned balusters and bold handrail having molding on the outside and only a bead on the base of the inside. It ascends in three flights to the second story.

Fernwood (T–114), near Easton, is a more ambitious circa-1740 house. This large, two-and-one-half-story, five-bay structure is one room deep. Its north facade is laid in Flemish-bond brick above a plain water table and in English bond below; English bond is also used on the south facade. Fernwood has been added to over the years (one ell dates to circa 1870; another dates to 1960), but some woodwork has survived in the original section, a section that has the "customary" Georgian center-stair-hall plan. The stair itself is original to the second quarter of the eighteenth century. Its open string has three turned balusters per step and a bold handrail that curves over the intermediate newels, like the handrail at Boston Cliff (T–122). There is a paneled spandrel that matches the raised-panel dado. The doors and trim appear to date from around 1870. West of the hall, the living room contains eighteenth-century raised paneling on the chimney breast; the paneling was taken from the old Dover ferry house and installed here in 1960. There are, however, original paneled wainscot, window sections, and jambs.

Talbot County has many well-known houses, houses whose fame has spread well beyond the Chesapeake area. Firmly among these, by anyone's reckoning, is Gross' Coate (T–87). A Tilghman house from when it was built in 1760 until it was sold in 1983, Gross' Coate grew and changed in a leisurely fashion with the family fortunes.

The history of the place goes back, however, to Roger Gross, who patented the 300-acre tract in 1658. The land, a peninsula between Gross Creek and Lloyd Creek, passed back and forth among various Grosses until Henrietta Maria Lloyd, widow of Philemon Lloyd, bought it in the 1680s for 50,000 pounds of tobacco. She renamed it "Henrietta Maria's Purchase." Mrs. Lloyd's daughter Anna Maria married Richard Tilghman II of the Hermitage, bringing her mother's purchase to the union as part of her dowry; in 1748 Anna Maria Tilghman deeded the property to her son William for five shillings. [16]

This William Tilghman changed the name of his plantation back to Gross' Coate. More important, he built the two-story nucleus of the present house about 1760. The earliest parts of the existing house consist of the present north parlor and back parlor, with that part of the hall that adjoins them, and three bedrooms, with a passage on the second

16. J. Donnell Tilghman, "Gross' Coate," unpublished typescript in the library of the Maryland Historical Society, Baltimore.

floor. In the 1798 tax assessment that portion of the building is described as a two-story brick dwelling house, 38 by 34 feet. The building appears to have faced north and south since the original chimney bases exist in the basement on the east and west walls. There was probably a hip roof, but that was replaced in the early nineteenth century by a gable roof with pedimented facade. (Some suggest that was to honor Wye House: a pencil sketch of circa 1850 shows that this facade does resemble other Lloyd houses of the period, e.g., Wye Heights, Presqu'isle, and The Anchorage.) Tilghman died in 1782 and left the house to his wife for the rest of her lifetime, and to their son, Richard, after her death. It is not known when Richard took over at Gross' Coate, but his account books for the 1794–97 period contain expenses for 80,000 bricks and refer to a "new kitchen."[17] This kitchen is extant, and, with the milk house, overseer's house, meat house, and quarter, it marks the post-Revolutionary era as a period of great building on the plantation. There is a service wing beyond the kitchen about which are arranged extensive outbuildings, including a dairy, wash house, schoolhouse, carriage house, and barn; the barn incorporates an eighteenth-century brick stable and forms the terminus of the work yard.

According to Richard's descendant the late Donnell Tilghman, the house was referred to as "Grocer's" in the 1790s.[18] More importantly, Richard is remembered today as a patron of the arts, at least as an employer of Charles Willson Peale; in 1790 Peale visited Gross' Coate and painted three portraits that rank among his best works. The group picture of Richard's wife and their two sons went to England in 1976 to represent Peale's mastery of group portraiture. Peale also painted two Tilghman children, Richard and his young and beautiful sister, Mary. The forty-nine-year-old artist caused a family crisis by inconveniently falling in love with Mary. Peale, a widower, was in search of a new mother for his six small children. Richard Tilghman, who expected his sister to marry someone of her own social position, was enraged and is said to have locked his sister in her bedroom until Peale had finished the assignment and was safely gone. Peale fulfilled his commission and left, but not until he had painted a scowl on Richard's face.[19]

The house continued to grow: around 1850, a dining room was added east of the parlor and north of the entry; other additions date to 1863 and 1882. The last major rebuilding occurred in 1914—it was still a Tilghman project, but was done under the guidance of Wilson L. Smith, architect of the Maryland National Bank Building in Baltimore. Smith designed a Georgian revival house. He raised the roof by adding a third story to the oldest part of the house and made this the central part of his composition. He had the south wing lowered about half a story and had a new north wing constructed to balance the south. Hip roofs cover the three sections, all of which are joined by a modillion cornice. Across one bay of the north wing and extending around the south wing is a one-story verandah that, with the cornice, helps turn a potentially ramshackle farmhouse into a unified, cogent structure.

Built by a member of the Trippe family, Avonville (T–168) is another large, two-and-one-half-story, brick dwelling that has, like Gross' Coate, grown for 200 years. The oldest portion (1760) is three bays wide and two deep and is located in the center of the long composition; it has a center stair hall flanked by two small rooms. From evidence in the cellar, however, the original floor plan consisted of a central stair hall on the north half of the building flanked by two small rooms, with two larger rooms on the south side of the house. Thus, in plan it would have resembled a small-scale Ratcliffe Manor and suggests that Talbot County's gentry shared a well-ordered aesthetic sensibility. Its north facade is laid in Flemish bond with both water table and beltcourse. The first-story, nine-over-nine sash windows have three centered arches and flanking shutters; the second-story sash windows also have louvered shutters, but have twelve-over-twelve panes. Two dormers light the third-floor room. The entrance is located in the easternmost bay of the house and is shaded by a small portico. Originally, the door was located in the center bay of the house. Adjacent to that former door, the date 1760 is inscribed in one of the bricks. The one original window on this facade has been lengthened.

17. Ibid.
18. Ibid.
19. Edward C. Papenfuse, Gregory A. Stiverson, Susan A. Collins, Lois Green Carr, eds. *Maryland: A New Guide to the Old Line State* (Baltimore: Johns Hopkins University Press, 1976), p. 158.

It appears that the first alteration to the house, the change of floor plan, occurred around 1840. About two generations later, the owner added on the east a large, frame, four-bay wing including a kitchen and dining room. When a large drawing room was added on the west side of the house in 1937, the east wing had its surface covered with brick and its roof raised. In more recent years, a porch was added to the south side of the dining room and to the old main section.

A description of two large houses, Pleasant Valley (T–84) and Galloway (T–104), both in the Easton area, will serve to end this discussion of Talbot County's grand Georgian domestic architecture, bringing it up to the Revolution.

Architecturally, Pleasant Valley is clearly among the very greatest of Talbot County's late Georgian houses. Not only was the building constructed of superior materials by able craftsmen, but most of those materials are still intact. In 1773 Howes Goldsborough and his wife Rebecca built Pleasant Valley on part of the tract called St. Michael's Fresh Run. The house is mentioned in the 1783 tax assessment as "a large brick dwelling house and kitchen" along with several quarters, barns, and shops. It is described in detail in the 1798 federal direct tax, which notes the presence of a schoolhouse, quarters, and smokehouse. The main house is a five-bay-long, two-and-one-half-story brick building, two bays deep, with a one-and-one-half-story brick wing, three bays long and one bay deep. It is located near the headwaters of the Miles River between the towns of Longwoods and Easton. The brick is a uniform color laid in Flemish bond above the cyma-reversa water table and English-bond foundation. The two long facades are identical, with central entrances having a semicircular fanlight above the door and twentieth-century porches. Pleasant Valley's interior has appropriately elegant paneling and woodwork. The main stair is particularly well-known: it rises three stories in graceful walnut magnificence with three turned balusters to each step. A semicircular fanlight tops the door leading from the stair hall to the northwest parlor; it matches and is on axis with the fanlight on the two exterior doors, a further refinement.

Galloway, also near Easton, is a suitable companion for Pleasant Valley, even though nineteenth-century alterations have caused it to lose some of its Georgian impact. The brick building is 37 feet square and two-and-one-half stories tall with a two-story shingled frame kitchen wing. The two long walls are laid in Flemish bond above the chamfered water table and in English bond below. The foundation below grade is stone masonry; the gables each are laid in common bond. There is a three-brick beltcourse.

Inside, the floor plan was originally similar to Pleasant Valley's. The northwest half of the house was originally divided into stair hall and parlor, but the partition has been removed to create one large room. This room contains the open-string stair, which has square, fluted newels and turned balusters like those once found at Cranberry in Harford County (now on exhibit in the American wing of the Baltimore Museum of Art). Its soffit is paneled and there are turned pendants from the newels. The remainder of the room has raised-panel dado and a heavy cornice. There is a diagonal fireplace at the south corner of the room; it is embellished with a paneled chimney breast complete with fluted pilasters. The other two ground-floor rooms have similarly elegant woodwork. The second story has the same floor plan as the ground floor, but with plainer paneling above the fireplaces and simpler trim throughout. There are two rooms in the attic.

Those houses discussed above were the great houses of mid-eighteenth-century Talbot County, the mansions the Hollydays, the Tilghmans, the Lloyds, the Goldsboroughs built to house themselves. But, as noted above, the wealth of the period was not enjoyed solely by the county's upper class, and enough small, vernacular, relatively unambitious period houses have remained to give a picture of life among Talbot County's flourishing middle class in the years a generation or so on each side of the American Revolution.

The fascinating, two-section house called Saulsbury (T–128) well deserves the sobriquet doubly unique. Located east of Trappe and south of the Miles Creek, Saulsbury (properly called Nomini), in its main facade and floor plan, is like no other house in Talbot

Rolles Range, near St. Michaels, as photographed by Frances Benjamin Johnston for the Historic American Buildings Survey in the 1930s.

Rolles Range as it appears today, with the date and builders' initials exposed.

County. The entrance facade is exceptional because it is placed in the gable end of the gambrel-roofed structure; the plan is unique in having a central vestibule with a stair against the centrally placed chimney and with a room to each side. The same plan is found on the second story. The house's current name, Saulsbury, is of recent vintage. Its tract was patented as Nomini in 1663 by William Robinson, John Smith, and George Watts. The house is often dated to the 1660s, but this probably refers to the patent.[20] It is known that some house stood on this site by 1705, but whether the existing structure is that old is unclear.

As noted, Saulsbury (Nomini) is difficult to pinpoint in time. Among methods of dating buildings, the dated brick—a brick in the masonry with a date glazed or carved into it—is one of the most reliable. Although not absolutely dependable, the dated brick is a help. Obviously the less disturbed the mortar around the brick is, the happier for all concerned. Talbot County has at least three brick-dated houses: Rolles Range (T–209) and Wickersham (T–56) date to around 1750; Avonville (T–168) is from a decade later.

The date at Rolles Range is found on the north gable where glazed headers boldly proclaim 1751 and the initials of the builders, F. L. (Feddeman and Lydia Rolle). The house stands on the upper reaches of Broad Creek northwest of St. Michaels. It is a two-part dwelling with the original brick, gambrel-roof, five-bay section and a two-story, twentieth-century wing at right angles to the south. The facade of the early part is laid in Flemish-bond brick above a simple stepped water table and English bond foundation. The cellar windows and those on the main floors have centered arches. There is a flat rowlock arch above the entrance. The entrance itself is interesting, with nineteenth century side-lights and transom around an eighteenth century door. Apparently the brickwork has not been changed on each side of the door, so there were probably double doors and a wide frame originally. Three dormers provide light for the second story of both sides of the building.

Inside, the floor plan consists of a hall, a stair passage, and a parlor. Some early paneling in the hall may be original to the house; its design is certainly unusual: the small flanking panels have square panels above long panels, the reverse of any other paneling in the county. The stair structure is original, but the balustrade, paneled spandrel, and soffit were all replaced in the early nineteenth century; there is some original paneling in the second-story hall. All of the roofing appears original: there is a common rafter system with pegged mortise-and-tenon joints at the apex; two braces nailed onto the underside of the rafters are still in place. Rolles Range is important architecturally as a dated building of the 1750s: few Talbot County buildings of this period can be dated so securely and this is the only dated gambrel-roof structure. The period paneling is equally significant.

One-and-one-half-story Wickersham, closer to Easton, boasts three dated bricks. All are located on the house's east gable end; one is inscribed with 1750, one with June 26, 1750, and one with RR 1750. That entire east wall is a triumph of colonial brick work, arguably the most impressive and ambitious in Talbot County. Between the four windows is a complicated diamond design in glazed headers consisting of a large diamond composed of sixteen smaller diamonds with other small diamonds at top and bottom. Its design is similar to, though more elaborate than, that found in Orem's Delight on Ferry Neck. There is a bricked-in door on the west gable end; it once led to the original kitchen. Traces of the colonnade walls can still be seen where it was bonded to the gable wall. Similar broken bonding can be seen on the north side of the original cellar entrance.

Edward Lloyd III of Wye House built the Wye Mills Miller's House (T–70) as his miller's residence. The two-and-one-half-story, three-bay, Flemish bond building has a hall-and-parlor plan within and a three-brick beltcourse without. This fine mid-eighteenth-century vernacular dwelling exemplifies the position millers enjoyed in the Georgian era. The Society for the Preservation of Maryland Antiquities now owns the entire Wye Mills complex and plans to restore it to its circa 1770 condition, back, in other words, to the days when corn and wheat ruled Talbot's economy, back to the days when the Tilghmans were living in a newly-completed Gross' Coat and when Anna Maria Robins Hollyday was planting the garden at Ratcliffe Manor.

20. Maryland Hall of Records, Annapolis.

The Wye Mill, a property of the Society for the Preservation of Maryland Antiquities.

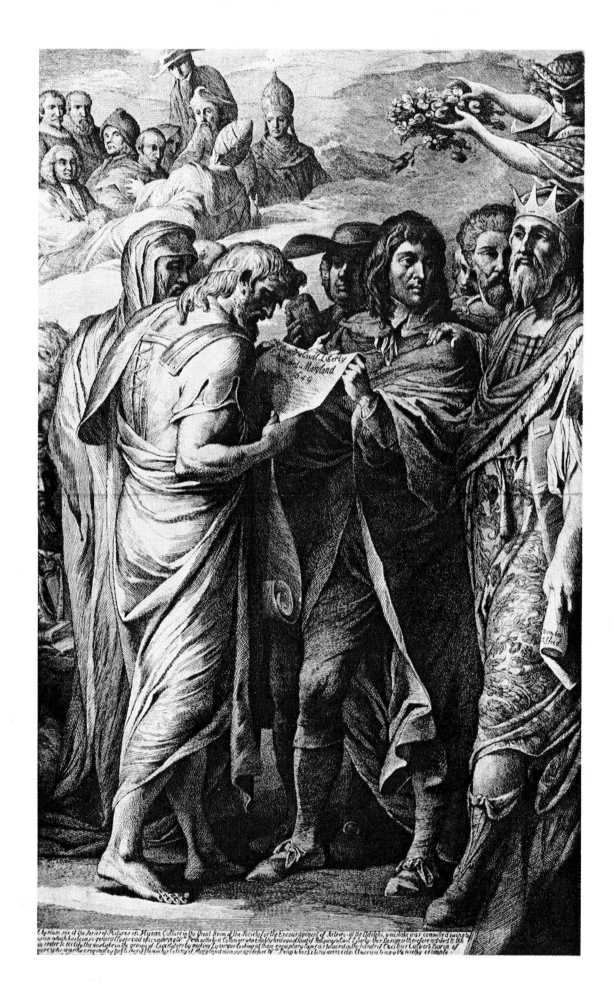

Civil Liberty
and Maryland
1649

CHAPTER 4

Not Everyone in Talbot Was a Farmer

As has been discussed, Talbot County's early history was dominated by farmers; they, in turn, were dominated by merchant-planters, a term used by Aubrey C. Land and others to describe the generation or so of late-seventeenth- and early-eighteenth-century entrepreneurs who accumulated enough capital to make the golden Georgian age possible:

> No one in those years, planter or bondsman, actually pronounced that phrase [merchant-planter] as the process itself dragged along in sweat and tears and—occasionally—blood. This was the price paid for every acre won by clearing the primeval woodland, for every dwelling house and every curing barn erected, for fences put around planted fields (Maryland horses developed astonishing appetites for tender young tobacco), for roads, crude as they were, drainage ditches, for orchards planted, in short for all those things our colonial forebears lumped together under the heading of "improvements". They created the wealth of the province, gave value to the wild country that had previously had none, provided the conditions for a viable economy.[1]

Not everyone in Talbot, however, was a farmer and many of the county's early settlers brought with them other touches of civilization, including churches and schools, trades and towns.

Cecilius Calvert's determination that his new colony would grant religious freedom to all was expressed in his written orders of instructions, which outlined the orderly development of his venture known as "Mary's Land." Leonard Calvert, as of 1636, made all officeholders take an oath swearing them to permit religious freedom. But the Catholic Calverts' struggles with the Puritan William Claiborne coincided with the English Civil War, and Charles I's supporters included the English Catholics: "When the Puritans succeeded in the king's arrest, trial, and execution it was a bleak day for adherents of the Church of Rome in England and the colonies."[2]

In an effort to save Maryland from the ravages of a civil war over religion, the Calverts appointed William Stone, a Protestant, governor for their colony. Stone prepared an official "Act Concerning Religion," which passed the colonial assembly on April 21, 1649. At that time Maryland's assembly was composed of Protestants and Catholics in nearly equal numbers and "not only did the act guarantee a policy of toleration in matters of religion, but the joint action of Protestants and Catholics on so sensitive or volatile an issue was unprecedented":

> And whereas the inforceing of the conscience in matters of Religion hath frequently fallen out to be of dangerous Consequence in those commonwealthes where it hath been practised. . . . Be it Therefore . . . enacted . . . that noe person or persons whatsoever within this Province . . . professing to believe in Jesus Christ, shall from henceforth bee any waies troubled, Molested or discountenanced for or in respect of his or her religion nor in the free exercise thereof.[3]

The act was almost immediately violated and Maryland entered a period of religious bigotry. The Church of England became the Established church in the colony in 1692; in 1704 it became a crime to say mass or to have a child baptized by a Catholic priest.

OPPOSITE:
Allegory depicting Lord Baltimore and Religious Freedom; engraving by James Barry, 1793.

1. "Planters of Colonial Maryland," pp. 112, 113.
2. Harrington, *Religion*, p. 29.
3. Ibid., p. 29.

As a gesture of conciliation, in 1705 Queen Anne ordered that Catholics could hold private worship, and this set the pattern for the colonies: private services held in private chapels at private houses—the best-known example is the chapel at Doughoregan Manor in Howard County. The most public Catholic colonial institution in Maryland was the St. Francis Xavier Mission at Old Bohemia in Cecil County. There Father Thomas Mansell acquired 458 acres in 1706 (it eventually grew to 1,700 acres), on which the Jesuits built living quarters, grist and saw mills, brick kilns, and other buildings to house income-producing ventures. Their profits supported the mission and gave the Jesuits the opportunity to practice their religion and to conduct a boys' school.[4]

That mission's prosperity led to similar ventures. In 1765 another Jesuit, Father Joseph Mosley, established St. Joseph's Mission (T–73) in the Tuckahoe district of Talbot County. Father Mosley, a native of Lincolnshire, had come to Maryland in 1758. He worked in St. Mary's and Charles counties before going up to the head of the Bay to work at Old Bohemia in 1764. Father Mosley wrote a letter to his sister in 1776 in which he discusses the whys and wherefores of St. Joseph's founding:

> It's a Mission that ought to have been settled above these sixty years past by means of the immense trouble and excessive rides it had given our gentlemen that lived next to it; till these days no one would undertake it, either for want of resolution or fear of the trouble, notwithstanding it had contributed to the deaths of several of ours and had broken the constitution of everyone who went down to it; although it was but twice a year, except calls to the sick.
>
> I was deputed in August 1764 to settle a new place in the midst of this Mission; accordingly, I set off for those parts of the country; I examined the situation of every congregation within sixty miles of it; and, before the end of the year, I came across the very spot, as providence would have it, with land to be sold, nigh the center of the whole that was to be tended. I purchased the land, and took possession in March following.[5]

Missions like St. Joseph's were intended to be self-supporting, but Father Mosley's 200 acres may not have been large enough to turn a profit, and he had to depend on subsidies from Old Bohemia.[6] He certainly did not indulge in grand buildings: he wrote his sister that the mission was housed in a shack built of some boards "riven from oak trees, not sawed plank, and these nailed together to keep it out the coldest air. Not one brick or stone about it, no plastering and no chimney, but a little hole in the roof to let out the smoke. In this I lived till the winter when I got it plastered to keep off the cold, and built a brick chimney."[7]

It is interesting to see how "replacement churches" parallel replacement houses. In 1782, after eighteen years of farm income and subsidies, Father Mosley was able to build something more substantial. Again a letter to his sister: "I've built on my farm a brick chapel and dwelling house. It was a difficult and bold undertaking at that time I began it, trusting on Providence, and I've happily finished without any assistance from our gentlemen or my congregation." This chapel and house are still standing. The original structure had an addition in 1848, and the cloverleaf apse where the present altar is now located was added in 1903. The remains of Father Mosley and at least three other early priests are interred under the church floor.

Quakers arrived in Talbot County in 1658 or 1659, only six or seven years after Quakerism had started in England (as has been discussed in chapter 2). They were soon joined on the shore by refugees from New England and Virginia, where Quakers suffered whipping, hanging, and imprisonment. Bayside Meeting near Wittman may have been their earliest meeting. The Kemps, Balls, Lowes, Fairbanks, Fishbournes, and many other families attended.[8] Another early meeting was the Choptank Meeting near Trappe, where Dickinsons, Sharpes, Powells, Stevenses, Webbs and other families met. Wilsons, Parrotts, Neals, Jadwins, Berrys, Pitts, Clarks, Turners, and others worshiped at Tuckahoe near Mathewstown. The fourth meeting was at Betty's Cove just outside Easton, at North Bend, where the Bartlett, Dixon, Harwood and Edmondson families were the backbone; George Fox, the founder of Quakerism, visited Betty's Cove in 1672–73. The Quaker belief of "God in every man" brought about reconsideration of slave-holding. In 1705 John

4. Ibid., p. 30.
5. Archives of the Maryland Province of the Society of Jesus.
6. Harrington, *Religion*, p. 32.
7. Ibid., p. 34.
8. Tilghman, *History*, vol. 2, pp. 38, 39.

St. Joseph's Roman Catholic Church; building began under Father Joseph Mosley.

Jadwin freed his one slave. When William Dixon freed his two slaves in 1712, he gave them fifty acres, built them a house and barn and gave them a cow and other things with which to support themselves. By the end of the American Revolution, hundreds of Quaker-owned slaves had been freed and the Society of Friends became the first denomination in the county—and in the United States—to become free of slave-holding.[9]

Talbot County Quakers, like their Quaker brethren elsewhere, emphasized the importance of education. Probably all four meetings had schools by 1680. One such school—though built much later—was the little brick building on Bay Street, Easton, constructed in 1874 as a Friends school. Quakers subscribed to buy books in 1676. George Fox (1625–1691), the English founder of the Society of Friends, sent books to Quakers here; after his death, another bundle arrived. The books Fox gave augmented the existing volumes, which represent the earliest public library in Talbot County, and what must have been one of the earliest in America.[10]

Talbot County's—indeed, Maryland's—Anglican church history began with the first settlers, and the church's colonial period is neatly divided in two eras based on the official Establishment—the 1692 act for "the Service of Almighty God and the Establishment of the Protestant Religion Within This Province."[11]

The first years of Maryland's history suggest that the pioneers were not, to be charitable, overly concerned with the betterment of their souls; the fires of hell seem to have held little fear for them. As early as 1638, for example, some colonists complained about "this heathen country where no Godly minister is to teach and instruct ignorant people in the grounds of religion."[12] But little action was taken: a generation later, in 1676, there were only four ministers in the entire colony: a 1677 letter to Lord Baltimore contained the news that "many inhabitants of Maryland live very dissolute lives"; the writer was probably right—recall those early law cases. The writer went on to ask Lord Baltimore to correct "this wicked kind of living." But Lord Baltimore did not, and his colony continued its "dissolute" existence.[13]

9. See Harrington, *Religion*, pp. 67–73; see also ibid., pp. 521–30.
10. Tilghman, *History*, vol. 2, pp. 521–30.
11. Harrington, *Religion*, p. 93.
12. Ibid.
13. Ibid., p. 94.

In 1691, however, King William and Queen Mary apparently decided that his had gone on long enough and decreed that "we have thought fitt to take our Province of Maryland under our immediate care and protection." They appointed Sir Lionel Copely the colony's first royal governor and instructed him to "take especial care" that the colonists became more religious. On June 2, 1692, Sir Lionel signed the act establishing the Protestant religion "on behalf of their Majesties."[14]

Thirty parishes were erected under this act of establishment; thirteen of these were on the Eastern Shore. The justices of each county were instructed to hold meetings, establish parish boundaries, choose vestrymen, build churches as needed, and collect a tax of forty pounds of tobacco from each taxable person in each parish to pay for all this.

Talbot County probably (the pre-1692 records are sketchy) had four churches in existence before the establishment: St. Peter's (at Whitemarsh), Wye Church, St. Michael's, and St. Paul's. Because St. Paul's is now, of course, in Queen Anne's County, it is beyond the scope of this book.

The 1692 Establishment Act divided what is now Talbot County into three parishes: St. Peter's, which extended from Oxford to Tuckahoe Branch and was centered at Old Whitemarsh; St. Paul's, which covered the northern part of what was then Talbot County and included both the church at Wye and some land that is now in Queen Anne's County, and the new St. Michael's parish, consisting of Mill and Bay hundreds, the area that now stretches from Easton north to the Wye River.[15]

Old Whitemarsh Cemetery and the ruins of Old Whitemarsh Church (T–137) are significant as tangible remains of the early history of the Protestant Episcopal Church in Maryland. The first church on this site is believed to have been built between 1662 and 1665, but the first date mentioned in the parish records is 1690, when Joseph Leech was acting minister. There is, however, a courthouse record in Talbot County for June 21, 1687, authorizing repairs to the road "from Cooleys' gate to the Church at Whitemarsh." And, as noted, when the Maryland assembly made the Church of England the established church of the colony in 1692, it included the parish where Whitemarsh Church was located as one of the thirty original parishes.[16]

The location of Old Whitemarsh Church was chosen in the seventeenth century because of its accessibility to the trade and commerce of that day. It was a focal point on the main public road, lying midway between the town of Oxford and the now extinct town of Dover (Maryland). The church fell into disrepair but in 1751 was nearly doubled in size, largely because of the popularity of the rector, the Reverend Thomas Bacon. Bacon deserves immortality as the compiler of *Bacon's Laws*, a compendium of Maryland's colonial statutes that was for many decades an authoritative guide for the state courts.[17] Membership began to decline when Bacon left, and after 1795 services were alternated between Whitemarsh and Easton, which had by then become the county seat and the center of mercantile activity in the area. By 1847 fewer services were held in Old Whitemarsh and the rector lived in Easton while Christ Church (T–15) was being built. Whitemarsh's old Bible, communion service, and wooden alms box were moved to St. Paul's Church (T–282), Trappe, where they remain today. Old Whitemarsh was abandoned during the Civil War; in 1896 a fire completely destroyed it except for the portions of brick wall that stand today.[18]

There are several famous Maryland names connected with Whitemarsh. Robert Morris, Sr., father of George Washington's financier, died in July 1750 and was buried in Whitemarsh Churchyard in a grave adjacent to the walls of the old church. General Tench Tilghman (1810–1874, a grandson of Washington's aide-de-camp) was a lay reader at Whitemarsh Church. There are also several local traditions of foggy morning duels fought near the church.[19]

But Whitemarsh has an even more intriguing story, however, one that is probably best told on a stormy Halloween night. It concerns the wife of Reverend Daniel Maynadier, a Huguenot and Whitemarsh's first rector (1714–1746) after the Establishment. According

14. Ibid.
15. For a general history of the Episcopal Church in Maryland, see ibid., pp. 75–130.
16. Tilghman, *History*, vol. 2, pp. 271–73.
17. Papenfuse, et al., *New Guide*, p. 135.
18. Ibid.
19. "History of Talbot County," unpublished manuscript, Oxford, Maryland.

Old Whitemarsh Cemetery, an ideal spot for Halloween tales.

to the tale Mrs. Maynadier died, and a few hours after she was buried, two grave robbers dug her up and tried to take a valuable heirloom ring off her finger. It wouldn't budge, so, according to legend, they got a knife and severed her finger at the joint. The flow of blood and the fresh air then revived the lady: she uttered a cry, sat up, and nothing more was heard of the grave robbers. "Mrs. Maynadier, wrapped in her grave clothes, made her way on foot to the rectory, an old brick mansion on the Glebe farm about a mile from the church, and there astonished her husband."[20]

Whitemarsh's records date to 1690, but evidence suggests to some historians that Whitemarsh may actually go back as far as the 1660s.[21] Early rectors associated with the parish include Reverend John Lilliston (Lillingstone?), Reverend John Leech, and Reverend John Clayland, the last of whom apparently escaped the "especial care" of Governor Sir Lionel Copely: a 1698 letter to the then Governor Nicholson complained that "Mr. Jno. Clayland in Talbot is scandalous."[22]

In 1672 the Reverend Mr. Clayland received fifty acres on the Miles River to be used as a glebe. Clayland became rector of Christ Church (T–260), St. Michaels, when the parish was erected twenty years later. It is uncertain when or where the first churches was/were located, but someone wrote in the 1736 vestry records that one old church had decayed so badly it had been replaced "and none but very aged persons had any knowledge of the time when it was built."[23] The present Christ Church dates to 1878 and replaces an 1812 structure.

Old Wye also predates the 1692 establishment as a parish, if not as a structure, and the present Old Wye Church (T–55), is the only eighteenth-century Anglican church remaining in Talbot County. On October 28, 1717, the vestry contracted with Talbot carpenter William Elbert to construct a church at the headwaters of the Wye River "either where the old church stands or hard by the same." The church opened in October 1721.[24] Located at the southern extremity of Wye Mills on the west side of state route 662, the small, one-story brick structure measures approximately 25 by 50 feet with a sanctuary 16 by 18 feet; both are covered by a gable roof. The church walls are laid in Flemish bond above and English bond below a chamfered water table. Alternating glazed headers are used in the semicircular arched heads of the church's windows, which are separated on the building sides by brick buttresses. Glazed-header Flemish bond is employed in the west gable end. The entrance, with its double doors and Doric architrave, is built upon a

20. Harrington, *Religion*, p. 122.
21. Ibid., p. 103.
22. Ibid., p. 104.
23. Ibid., p. 124; see also Tilghman, *History*, vol. 2, pp. 311, 312.
24. Tilghman, *History*, vol. 2, p. 276.

Wye Church, in its idyllic setting, is the only remaining eighteenth-century Anglican church in Talbot County; it was restored in 1949.

projecting plane of the west gable; the gable itself contains three windows, two small and round, one large and round. The large window dates to 1949, when the entire church was restored through a grant from Arthur A. Houghton, Jr., and under the guidance of the Boston architect William Perry of the firm Perry, Shaw and Hepburn. All of the interior dates from the restoration, as does the large Palladian window over the altar, but many of the details are based upon evidence that was found in the original structure.

The first schools in this county were what may be designated as plantation, or home, schools. These were small in size, and the instruction was elementary in character. As soon as a sufficient number of pioneers had settled in any vicinity, schools of another order, but scarcely of a different grade, were instituted. Neighbors would unite to employ a teacher, and students were permitted to avail themselves of the services of the master for a fee. The teacher's salary was exceedingly small, but there was the additional compensation of "boarding around" with the families of the chief patrons. These neighborhood subscription schools continued down to the time when the state and county gave support to the public schools, but even then it was customary for the neighborhoods to contribute a sum for an increase in the teachers' salaries.[25]

In 1750 the Reverend Thomas Bacon founded the Charity Working School for Talbot County, the only training school in the province for poor and black children. The school was established in part of a brick building, near Bacon's Whitemarsh church. One of its articles of incorporation stated "that such Negro children as shall be sent by order of the Trustees . . . shall be taught to read and write and introduced to the knowledge and fear of the Lord, gratis; but maintained at the expense of their respective owners." This school was maintained entirely by private subscription, and it flourished for a generation. By the 1780s, however, Bacon and many of the original trustees had died and the property was turned over to the county; it was used as a poorhouse or almshouse, hence the origin of the name Alms House Road.[26] The almshouse was discontinued in the 1930s; it was demolished and the bricks were stored until 1976 when some were used to help stabilize the Whitemarsh ruins.

25. Ibid., pp. 13–15 and 457–95.
26. Ibid., pp. 457–95.

In 1696 an act of the General Assembly made a provision for the founding of two public schools, one for the Western Shore at Annapolis and one for the Eastern Shore at Oxford. Lack of funds prevented the school at Oxford from being built, but twenty-seven years later enough money had accumulated to make the establishment and maintenance of a Talbot County school feasible. The state legislature passed an act in 1723 that funded schools throughout Maryland, including the Free School of Talbot County, and that nominated The Reverend Henry Nichols, Mr. Robert Goldsborough, Colonel Matthew Tilghman Ward, Mr. William Clayton, Robert Ungle, Esq., Mr. Thomas Bozman, and Mr. John Oldham as visitors. These men were to select a place for the school near the center of the county; they chose a parcel on a large tract called Tilghman's Fortune near the head waters of the Tred Avon River, bought it, and erected such buildings as were necessary. The school's teachers had an annual salary of twenty pounds; they did not board around, but, as a benefit, enjoyed the use of the school farm.[27]

Tilghman's Fortune, the site of that early school, was a 1,000-acre tract patented by Samuel Tilghman, a man who reinforces the idea that if not all of Talbot's citizens farmed neither did they all pray or teach. In July 1658, Cecil, Lord Baltimore, named Samuel Tilghman, mariner, as first admiral of the province of Maryland, "not only because of his navigational skill but because he seemed to have been a principal champion of the proprietary. . . . [A] contemporary letter to Lord Baltimore stated 'Captain Tilghman and his mate Master Cook are very honest men and do stand up much for your honor.' "[28] Tilghman was based in Oxford, then the leading port on the Eastern Shore. Oxford not only was a port of entry but also served as one of Maryland's leading shipbuilding centers. A 1707 map of Oxford shows one shipyard; by 1730 another establishment produced schooners. Oswald Tilghman comments that:

It is difficult at this day [1915] to discover the causes of the concentration of trade at the pretty town of Oxford. . . . The most rational of these are the excellence of its harbor, its proximity to and ready approach from the great bay, its accessibility to water by means of boats from all the regions bordering upon the Chesapeake, at a time when roads were

Bacon's school; later the county almshouse; still later demolished.

27. Ibid., pp. 13–15.
28. L. G. Shreeve, *Tench Tilghman: The Life and Times of Washington's Aide-de-camp* (Cambridge: Tidewater Publishers, 1982), pp. 13–14.

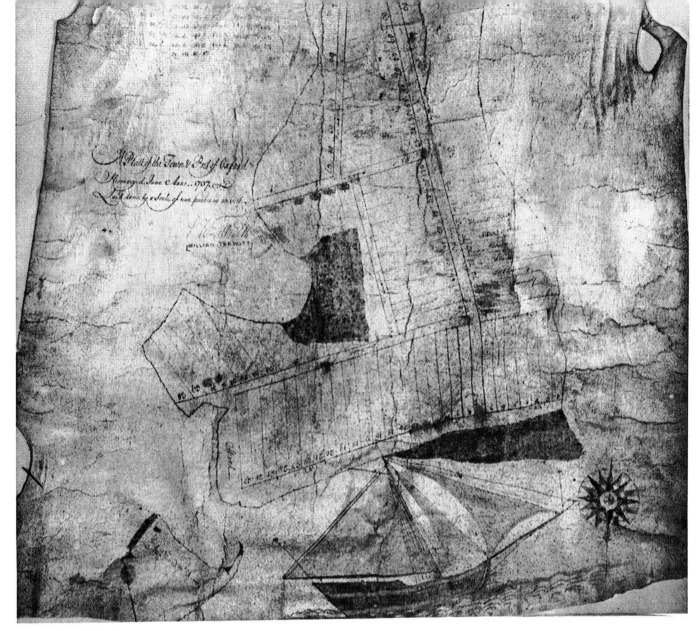

Oxford as mapped in 1707.

Oxford harbor circa 1750, with ships that plied the waters between the Mersey and the Chesapeake "with detours to Madeira, the coast of Africa and the West Indies." Fanciful drawing by John Moll.

What is now the Robert Morris Inn in Oxford as seen in 1910.

either wanting or were mere bridle paths, and lastly the remarkable salubrity of its atmosphere, then as now unpoisoned by malaria. And the causes of decline after the middle of the century are almost as obscure; for if those of its prosperity, which have been assigned, were the true causes, inasmuch as they were permanent in their influence, they should have secured permanence of commercial prominence. But there was really another cause for the decadence of Oxford as a center of trade, and this was the absence of a back country dependent upon this place for an outlet of its products and an inlet for its supplies. The growth of the vast west demanded a port of entry and departure upon the opposite shore, and this port was furnished by the town of Baltimore which grew proportionately with the growth of the country north and west, and finally absorbed the foreign and the greater part of the domestic trade of the Province.[29]

Tilghman also credited Oxford's mid-eighteenth-century prosperity to her enterprising businessmen, singling out Robert Morris, Sr. (1711–1750). There were seventeen large warehouses in Oxford in the early eighteenth century, several of which were operated by Morris, factor for Foster Cunliffe & Sons of Liverpool, England. Foster Cunliffe had ships that plied the water between the Mersey and the Chesapeake "with detours to Madeira, the coast of Africa and the West Indies."[30] Morris became their man in Oxford in 1738. His importance in Oxford's economic growth is made clear by certain contemporary comments: Jeremiah Banning wrote that

29. Tilghman, *History*, vol. 1, pp. 66, 67.
30. Ibid., p. 67.

The Tred Avon Ferry and its slip. This ferry is believed to be the oldest free-running ferry in the United States.

Oxford was at the time of his death and during his agency, for he was its principal supporter, one of the most commercial ports of Maryland. The storekeepers and other retailers both on the Western and Eastern sides of the Chesapeake repaired there to lay in their supplies. . . . Oxford's streets and Strand were once covered by busy crowds ushering in commerce from almost every quarter of the globe. . . . After the death of Mr. Morris commerce, splendor and all that animating and agreeable hurry of business at Oxford declined to the commencement of the civil war, which broke out in April 1775, when it became totally deserted as to trade.[31]

Perhaps Morris's greatest contribution was introducing a system of accounting to replace the use of tobacco as currency.

As tobacco was the staple commodity of the country at the time it was the principal object of trade; and as it was the medium by which values were estimated, and debts paid it was the common currency. Of course scarcely anything could have been worse for this latter purpose, for it varied in quantity and quality year by year. . . . The evils enumerated had been long felt in the community, but the legislation necessary for their amelioration had not been secured. The difficulty of securing the reform of any mischievous system which has grown up in any society, and penetrated the whole body by its roots, is one of [the] familiar facts of practical politics.[32]

But Morris tried, and he is generally acknowledged to have been the first to do so in Maryland. His premature death prohibited total success, but the county records show that by 1750 (the year Morris died), it was common for merchants to keep accounts in currency, not tobacco. He and his son of the same name are memorialized in Oxford by Morris Street and the Robert Morris Inn (T–249), an institution whose fame for comfort and hospitality has spread far beyond the Tred Avon.

One of the most interesting features in Oxford is the Tred Avon Ferry. Its ferry slip is near the Robert Morris Inn, and it is believed to be the oldest ferry that runs "free"—that is, not attached to a cable—in the United States. Connecting Oxford and Bellevue, the line was started in 1683 by Richard Royston, who collected his fare in tobacco, the currency of the pre-Morris era.[33]

Oxford thrives today on a recreation-based economy, but not all of the county's early towns have been so fortunate. Recently a good deal of research has been focused on Talbot County's "ghost towns," Dover, Doncaster, Kingston, and York.

Dover existed as a port partially because of the prevalence of fresh water from the Choptank, which killed the troublesome teredo worms that may have been in the ships' planking. The port thrived until the late eighteenth century but has now completely disappeared.

Doncaster may be the best known of these now-extinct hamlets. It was founded as a result of Lord Baltimore's 1683 order to establish shipping points within the province: "ports and places where all ships . . . shall unload and put on shore and sell, barter, and traffic." Doncaster was located on the banks of the Wye River hard by Bruff 's Island, and hard by the lands of the Lloyds. One of the Lloyds' kinsmen was Richard Bennett, shipper, planter, and one of the richest men in the province. "He owned many vessels, gave employment to the best shipbuilding of Miles and Chester Rivers,"[34] and he would have benefited enormously from a town on this site. Similarly, it would be reasonable to believe that the Lloyds, who lived nearby at Wye House and who were then the county's largest landholders, would have been interested in the creation and development of Doncaster as a port for the shipment of tobacco from their large plantations in the area. In fact, the Lloyds may indeed have been responsible for the General Assembly's decision in 1683 to establish a town and port at the Doncaster site. Colonel Philemon Lloyd's wife is credited with building a Roman Catholic chapel at Doncaster, thus giving the town the distinction of having the first edifice of the Catholic faith on the Eastern Shore.[35] On Doncaster's original plat, still preserved at Wye House, lot number five, the corner of High and Landing Streets, is marked "E. Lloyd's Lott" and, opposite, "#6 R. Bennett's Lott."

31. Quoted in ibid., p. 70.
32. Ibid., vol. 2, p. 11.
33. Papenfuse et al., *New Guide*, p. 172.
34. Andrews, *Tercentenary History*, p. 404.
35. Mrs. Morgan B. Schiller in conversation with Christopher Weeks, May 23, 1981.

Oxford thrives today.

York, on the south bank of Skipton Creek, enjoyed an existence from about 1681 to around 1710. But it was an important place in its time, for it has the distinction of being an early county seat of Talbot and thus the site of a courthouse and jail. As a port of entry, little York probably had at least one tobacco warehouse, but it also had something that no other town in the province possessed in those early days—a measured race track. This was a half-mile track located, according to tradition, directly in front of the courthouse. It was in place as early as 1689 and was probably the first race track in Maryland.[36]

York's decline began in 1706 when the General Assembly created Queen Anne's County out of that portion of Talbot County lying between the Chester and Wye rivers. With the new county formally established, York was no longer the center of Talbot County, now much reduced, and there immediately arose a public demand to move the courthouse to a location more convenient to the majority of the county's population. Hence the start of Easton, the most successful town in Talbot County, in terms of size, power, and influence. Easton's early history is discussed in chapter 6, but the town serves as a good place to end this chapter and as a reminder that no, not everyone in Talbot was a farmer.

36. Tilghman, *History*, vol. 2, pp. 217, 218.

CHAPTER 5

Wye and the Lloyds: A Summation and a Preamble

Lloyd. The name reverberates through Talbot County's history like the boom of an exceptionally resonant gong. For over 300 years the Lloyds have been the county's fulcrum; for over 300 years Wye House (T–54) has been the Lloyds' home.

The family is at the center of the entire region through an intricate system of marriage and intermarriage. The Lloyds' marital complex not only has bound them to some of Maryland's most influential families, but has also served to put them at the center of a system of alliances which forms an aristocratic encirclement of the entire Chesapeake Bay, from the Cadwaladers in Philadelphia to the Tayloes in Virginia. This need not be gone into at any depth here, except to quote the late J. Donnell Tilghman on Henrietta Maria Lloyd (1647–1697):

> Henrietta Maria Lloyd is perhaps better known to Marylanders of today than any of the men of the Lloyd family, no matter how important their services to the country may have been. She probably vies with Mistress Margaret Brent for the distinction of being the most famous woman of early Maryland. According to tradition she was named for Queen Henrietta Maria who was, it is claimed, her godmother. The descendants of Henrietta Maria Lloyd appear to be exceptionally numerous, a thing explained by the fact that any one descended from her knows it, no matter how ignorant he or she may be of the rest of their ancestors, and claims that descent with intense pride. This pride cannot be explained by the usual reasons for there is no record that this woman accomplished anything unusual for one of her time and position. Nor is there any tradition that she did among her descendants (of whom this writer is, as proudly as the rest, one). In all probability, Henrietta Maria Lloyd was a woman of such outstanding virtues, of such graciousness and generosity, such charm, intelligence and warmth, that she was greatly beloved during her life. Her memory must have persisted vividly. Grandchildren who had known her told of her to great grandchildren born after her death and in a generation or two she became the beautiful and romantic legend she remains today.[1]

Perhaps more important to this architectural history of the county is the phenomenon that one modern architect called "Wye's Pups."[2] When generations of Lloyds married and left Wye, these daughters and sons were set up in houses of their own, which created an architectural cat's cradle that includes Presqu'isle, Wye Heights, Wye Plantation, Wye Town Farm, The Anchorage, The Rest, Lloyd's Landing, Hope, Knightly, and Gross' Coate. The system spread into other counties and, arguably, includes Readbourne and Kennersley in Queen Anne's County, as well as, of course, the Chase-Lloyd House in Annapolis.

Further, the Lloyds and Wye combine all the seemingly disparate threads that made up—and make up—life on the Eastern Shore; the Lloyds' threads may be silken, not homespun hopsack, but they can still serve as syntheses of the seventeenth- and eighteenth-century Talbot that has been discussed above, and will serve to act as a prelude to what will be described in the chapters that follow. This examination of the Lloyds has intentionally been placed at the center of this book on Talbot County; moreover, it might be wise to view the chapter itself as being divided into thirds: symbolically at its

OPPOSITE:
Wye House today. It is conjectured that the original dwelling stood ninety degrees from the mansion, between the present house and the Orangery, and that the gardens, still somewhat evident, were on axis with it. The farm road and, beyond it, Lloyd's Creek, which leads to the Wye River, can be seen. The cove at Lloyd's Creek was the scene of much commercial activity from circa 1660 through the Civil War.

1. Tilghman, "Wye House," p. 93.
2. Warren Cox, FAIA, in conversation with Christopher Weeks, June 12, 1982.

center—thus forming the nucleus of the entire narrative—is Edward Lloyd IV (1744–1796), builder of the present Wye House. He and his house are preceded by Edward Lloyd I (?–1695), Philemon Lloyd (1646–1685), Edward Lloyd II (1670–1718), and Edward Lloyd III (1711–1770) and their house (or houses); his line has been directly continued through Edward Lloyd V (1779–1834), Edward Lloyd VI (1798–1861), Edward Lloyd VII (1825–1907), Charles Howard Lloyd (1859–1929), and, to bring the story up to our own time, Mrs. Morgan B. Schiller (née Elizabeth Key Lloyd), who died in 1993.

In the 1630s, the progenitor of this family, Edward Lloyd I, came to Virginia, probably from the Wye Valley, which weaves its way through western England and eastern Wales. Edward Lloyd I was a man of some ambition. He undoubtedly wanted high position, and by 1645 he sat in the Virginia House of Burgesses.

Trevelyan observed that "English Puritanism of the Cromwellian type did not attract the Welsh, who remained Cavalier so far as they took any side at all."[3] Lloyd was an exception and, being a religious nonconformist, in 1649–50 he led a group of Puritan settlers from Virginia to Maryland, where "he immediately became embroiled in the politics of Lord Baltimore's strife-torn province."[4]

Material and political ambition were probably as important to him as religion, and, shortly after settling in Anne Arundel County, he was prominent enough to become a member of the General Assembly (1654), commander of Anne Arundel County, commissioner to the Susquehanna Indians, burgess for Anne Arundel County, and member of council.[5] He was also buying and patenting lands in Anne Arundel County and, across the Bay, in Talbot. With the bulk of his holdings in Talbot, Lloyd moved there, where he continued to dominate; as has been observed, the precourthouse court often met in "the house of Edward Lloyd" (see chapter 2).

He also met Richard Bennett, and the meeting proved memorable. Bennett had been "a leader of the small but influential Puritan community in Virginia. When Oliver Cromwell took power in England, he commissioned Bennett to obtain the submission of the recalcitrant governments of Maryland and Virginia and later appointed him governor of Virginia."[6] Bennett's son, also named Richard, had married Henrietta Maria Neale. This younger Richard died and his widow soon married Philemon Lloyd, Edward's son: "The marriage united two of the greatest fortunes in the Chesapeake, for Lloyd was probably the richest man in Maryland."[7] Edward Lloyd had returned to England in 1668, leaving his concerns in the hands of his son Philemon then aged twenty-two.[8] Philemon and his wife lived on the Wye tract and either built or inherited what must have been early Maryland's largest house, the original Wye, of which the "Captain's House," mentioned at the close of chapter 2, may have been a part. In 1685 Philemon predeceased his father (but still leaving 7,430 acres of land);[9] his father Edward died in 1695 and willed Wye to Philemon's eldest son, Edward II. Henrietta Maria died in 1697 and the inventory of her estate, dated November 2, 1697, and of Philemon's in 1685 are among the most important documents of their age in that they give us a very clear glimpse at the life at the top in seventeenth-century Maryland.[10]

So what did the early Wye House look like? Philemon's inventory suggests several separate rooms as recited in chapter 2. Henrietta Maria's is more complex—and more confusing. Several rooms reappear, including the hall, the "New Room," the black chamber, the blue chamber, the staircase, Madam Lloyd's room, the nursery, the closet, the kitchen, and the kitchen loft. New (?) rooms, however, are included: a "High Chamber," a study, an "Old Study," an "Entry," a "Lodging Room," and a "Passage." There are also a wash house and a pantry. Andirons, indicating fireplaces, were cited in the hall (in 1685 and 1697), in the new room (1697), in the upper chamber (1685), in Madam Lloyd's room (1685), in the lodging room (1697), and in the kitchen (1685 and 1697). The exact configuration of this house (when more than 90 percent of Marylanders huddled in one-room hovels) has long been of interest to writers. In 1953 the late J. Donnell

3. Trevelyan, *English Social History*, p. 233.
4. "Planters," p. 125.
5. Tilghman, "Wye House," p. 92.
6. "Planters," p. 122.
7. Ibid.
8. Tilghman, *History*, vol. 1, pp. 132–44.
9. Material in Maryland Hall of Records, Annapolis.
10. Hall of Records; note especially Inventory, Book 9, p. 398 *et seq.*, and Book 15, p. 198 *et seq.*

Wye House: photograph by Jack Boucher for the Historic American Buildings Survey.

Wye House: north facade.

From Vicenza to Talbot County: Wye House's south porch.

Detail of the Villa Rotonda: plate XIII, book 2 of Palladio's *Four Books of Architecture*.

11. Tilghman, "Wye House," p. 91.
12. Paul G. E. Clemens, "Economy and Society on Maryland's Eastern Shore, 1689–1733," in *Law, Society, and Politics in Early Maryland* (Baltimore: Johns Hopkins University Press, 1974), p. 157.

Tilghman speculated that Philemon's 1685 inventory suggests "that the main house may have been of two full stories or that there was, at the time, a south dependency balancing the present Captain's House."[11] Fourteen years later, Dr. Chandlee Forman also suggested that the Captain's House was "an integral part" of a three-part balanced composition. This seems unlikely and it is difficult to imagine that even the Lloyds would have had the time or the money to live on such an elaborately grand scale in the 1680s. A century later, emphatically yes, but not then in what was still a fairly primitive part of the world. They were, after all, shrewd businessmen who probably would have put any extra capital to work in ways that would produce further income—in land, in slaves, in ships, or in tangible goods of fairly firm value, such as furniture and jewels.

Thus it is interesting to note how the seventeenth-century Wye was furnished. It is important to bear in mind, when considering the personal property from the Lloyds' inventories, that a typical inventory of that time would read something like William Holter's: "he owned a blanket, two iron posts, some old lumber or furniture, a file, two cows with calves, and two small hogs, or £4 in property. Shortly before his death in 1709, he planted enough tobacco to yield a crop of 1750 pounds, which his administers sold for £5."[12]

In 1697 the hall at Wye House contained, among other things, 45 pounds of brown sugar, two small tables, twelve turkey-leather chairs, ten guns, one looking glass, and one pair of fire irons. The new room contained eighteen chairs, one table, one drawing table and carpet, one olive table, one stand and looking glass, one chest of drawers of olive wood, one chest of drawers of walnut, two dozen damask napkins, two damask tablecloths, one dozen diaper napkins, twenty-one old napkins, two diaper tablecloths, one Holland tablecloth, five pairs of Holland sheets, a "stock" of pillow slips, three table baskets, one hourglass, etc. The high chamber was furnished with one bed with curtain and hangings and blankets and sheets, "all furnished fit to lyve in," seven cane chairs and a couch, seven "cushings" and a pallet for a couch, brass tongs, and brass candlesticks. The black chamber had two feather beds with curtain and valance, rug and blanket, "bolster and pillows, etc"; the blue chamber had a feather bed and its furniture, six turkey work chairs, five leather chairs, one chest, and one glass. The staircase was no boxed stair; it contained "8 old rugs, 1 old clock, and 2 chests."

In Henrietta Maria's lodging room, which must have also served as a sort of storeroom, were eleven pairs of wooden shoes, one bed and its furniture and valances and a large quilt, 7,000 pins, ten ounces of silk, a dozen threads of lace, a parcel of thread and lace, a gross and nine dozen buttons, "twenty five yards of stuff and crape," four Mantua gowns, Scotch cloth, eight ells of Hollands, six yards of striped silk, eighteen pairs of gloves and a looking glass, twenty ells of dowlass, sheets, bolster, and pillow cases, towels, plate valued at £88.17.6, four trunks, one chest of drawers, two looking glasses, four old chairs and a little table, etc., etc., etc.

There were twenty-eight slaves at Wye House and ten at another plantation, an astonishingly large number for that time. "Madam Lloyd's cloaths" were inventoried as: one satin gown and petticoat, one silk gown and petticoat, one old silk gown and coat, one mourning gown and quilted petticoat, one silk mantel, two silk petticoats and scarf, a "good warm gown," two smock coats and two waistcoats, a parcel of laces, a pair of bodices, a gauze coat, one flowered satin party coat, four party coats, four pairs of shoes and one pair of galoshes, silk and worsted stockings, two head dresses, a box of handkerchiefs, a parcel of neck laces, a flowered "satting" morning gown, a "long scarfe lyned with velvet," a parcel of silver lace and footings, two pairs of stays, one black scarf, one parcel of beads and silver cross and snuffbox, one gown and party coat, one silk petticoat with silver fringe, one silk mourning gown, one riding gown, one sable tippet and strings, two short aprons, "girdle and mask, etc." Her other personalty included one diamond ring, one mourning ring, four stone rings, three rings and a pair of earrings, five pictures, a little box of cash, one parcel of

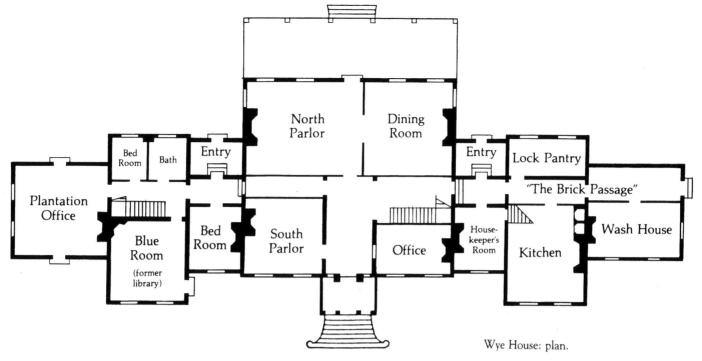

Wye House: plan.

beads, a silver snuffbox, and a silver cross. Among other items of interest is the especially mentioned "great wrought silver dish" that she left to her three daughters jointly.

Thus, in the thirty years after their arrival in Maryland, the Lloyds had, through their skillful business dealings, buttressed by a good marriage or two, managed to create a life far superior to nearly any of their contemporaries. They were even better off than their near-peers—"the nucleus of a landed planter class [that] had emerged" by 1689.[13] Ignoring, for a moment, their mercantile enterprises, the Lloyds' wealth had been increased by rising land values:

> Land prices rose because Talbot planters had cleared land and erected homes on most of the bayside. The fertile necks of land between the Chesapeake and the county's rivers provided the resident access to the market. The population was denser here, most tobacco was produced here, and most buying and selling of land occurred here. Consequently . . . land prices for this region of the bayside soared. Edward Lloyd's patent, Hier Dier Lloyd, for example, increased in value from 30 pounds of tobacco per acre in 1663 to 80 pounds by 1700.[14]

This increase in wealth is obviously reflected in the Lloyd inventory, with its abundance of the finest material goods of the period. But it is important to reemphasize that these goods should be viewed as investments: the bolts of cloth and the 7,000 pins certainly were, and diamonds are usually safe things to buy.

It is no doubt the Lloyds' extraordinary wealth that has encouraged speculation as to their early house and gardens. Forman, for example, has written not only that their seventeenth-century house was the "integral part" of a symmetrical composition, but that there was an elaborate, "symmetrical and balanced" 435-foot boxwood garden laid out on axis with the house. He has further suggested that there were, "on either flank of the axial promenade . . . conjecturally, nine elongated rectangles of box—panels, as it were—filled with grass, vegetables, flowers, and fruit trees. The right-hand, or northern, box rectangles were each approximately 150 feet long and varied from 38' to 60' in width."[15]

Donnell Tilghman discusses the old house:

> Consider the present cross axis of the garden as the main axis and the whole scheme immediately reveals itself. The old house faced east towards the now silted up cove and west across a rectangular lawn. . . . In the left corner of the lawn [was] . . . [a] brick wall forming the south boundary. Both walls ended at the deep ditch, still in existence, which formed the west boundary and an invisible barrier, like a ha-ha, against stock grazing in the fields beyond. The space between the walls appears to have been divided into long rectangles enclosed by box hedges. Four of these still exist and there may well have been two more to the east of them. The path dividing them through the center is the cross axis

Wye House: stair. The cannon in the lower right is from the Lloyds' eighteenth-century yacht.

13. Ibid., p. 153.
14. Ibid., p. 158.
15. Forman, *Old Buildings*, p. 55.

of the present garden but was the main axis of the old and centers on the site of the original main house.

If the box hedges of the west end of the garden were kept trimmed and low, as probably they were, from the old house one could have looked across them to the wide sweep of Shaws Bay, Bruffs Island and the mouth of Wye River.[16]

These speculations need further archaeological work; Edward Lloyd II's 1718 last will and testament makes references to "my dwelling plantation with all houses, orchards, and gardens thereupon," but everyone then had gardens and the word alone does not mean a formal, designed layout. Edward Lloyd III's will (dated 1750 and probated in 1770) left his wife Wye House and its furniture, "the kitchen both old and new and the hen houses and all that spot of ground that encompassed with pailing and is called a garden;" this "garden" again probably refers to a vegetable garden and pailed gardens are a standard inventory reference. So, while it is relatively safe to assume that some sort of pre-Revolutionary gardens existed, their elaborateness is uncertain. If the house and garden are so sophisticated as Forman suggests, then the original Wye house and garden become of international importance as a very early expression of the Palladian ideals of balance and integration generally thought to have first appeared in America two generations later at Drayton Hall, near Charleston, and at Rosewell in Gloucester County, Virginia.

Still, it is possible. Garden books were not unknown in seventeenth-century England; John Parkinson's well-known *Paradisi in Sole Paradisus Terrestris* appeared as early as 1629. English architectural historian John Harris has written that

> the question of axiality was to dominate fashionable garden planning after the Restoration [1660]. Influences were French rather than Italian, and the textbook of modern design was André Mollet's *Le Jardin de Plaisir* of 1651. The house was now seen as the fulcrum of a planned garden that extended from its four fronts and was in firm visual control of the whole. Principles of perspective played a decision role and coordinated water, *allees* (avenues), *parterres de broderies* or embroidered parterres (level spaces ornamented with flower beds of elaborate shape) and *bosquets* (groves of trees). In the house, of course, was the owner, who lived at the center of this plan. It reflected the French autocratic position, and the triumph of the style was enacted at Versailles and the satellite palaces around Paris.[17]

But even so, for such an *au courant* scheme to have appeared in England's colonies—not even in her provinces—would be extraordinary.[18]

In any event, 1695, with Philemon's son Edward II controlling the estate, marks the beginning of over two hundred years of Edward Lloyds succeeding each other as master of Wye. All, concurrent with managing their estates, took an active role in the affairs of their county, their state, their nation. This second Edward (1670–1718) was justice of Talbot County and a member of the assembly; appointed a member of council in 1701, he became council president and was, in effect, governor of Maryland from 1709 until 1714.

His 1719 inventory suggests that much had changed since his parents' deaths in 1685 and 1697. The compilers of the inventory noted twelve rooms, including several holdovers and some additions. To determine whether these are actual additions or merely changes in name and/or use, and to attempt a floor plan would be, at best, speculative.

Intriguing is a reference to "the new room in the shed" and its furniture—"a legacy left to Madam Sarah Lloyd by her husband Col. Edward Lloyd, Esq., d'c'd." This room had a fireplace; it also had two decanters and three pieces of "Japanned" furniture: a "fine chest of drawers," a "table and glass with a nest of drawers," and a "tea table": items decidedly rare in America in 1719.

There was also a "Store Seller" fully equipped with "120 gal. Brandy, 65 gal. Molasses, 285 gal. rum, 30 gal. brandy, 4000 oz. sugar, and an additional 184 gal. rum."

In all, Edward II's estate, which fills forty folio pages, was valued at £8,946 and included 108,283 pounds of tobacco; for comparative purposes, the next inventories listed—obviously a random sampling—are valued at £196, £5, £6, £15, and £12.

The third Edward (1711–1770) was a minor when his father died and his affairs were

16. Tilghman, "Wye House," pp. 95, 96.
17. John Harris, "The Formal Garden 1660 to 1710," in *The Garden* (London: New Perspectives Publishing, 1979), pp. 25, 26.
18. Charles Willson Peale supplies one curious bit of supportive evidence that some sort of Palladian building may have been at Wye before the present house, In 1771 Peale went to Wye to paint a group portrait of Edward Lloyd (IV), his wife, Elizabeth Tayloe Lloyd, and their daughter, Anne. This date is a decade or so before the generally agreed upon date for the present house Wye, but in the background of the picture, beyond Lloyd's hip, is a Palladian villa that is very elegant indeed. In portraiture, it is not unknown to put a subject's house in the background of a portrait. Peale himself did it often—most famously in his portrait of William Paca, in which he put Paca's Annapolis garden pavilion in the distance. But, of course, it was not unknown to use merely symbolic structures, and Peale could have decided that this lively yet dignified edifice would suitably suggest the sitters' distinguished family backgrounds. Moreover, Orlando Ridout IV and Michael Trostel have proven that Peale and the Annapolitans of the 1770s were fond of the "structure" in the Lloyd portrait: it is plate 39 from Isaac Ware's *A Complete Body of Architecture* (London: T. Osborne and J. Shipley, 1756). On the other hand, John Harris, during a 1983 visit to Wye, became convinced that the Lloyds did live on the grand scale Forman suggested. It is, at present, impossible to know.

run by his mother and stepfather, Sarah and James M. Hollyday, as was discussed in chapter 3. At age 22, when he came into possession of over 3,000 acres of land in Talbot County, he became the greatest landowner, the most prominent creditor, and the largest shipper in the region. He married Anne Rousby, daughter of a wealthy Calvert County planter and a relative of Richard Bennett's wife. In developing Eastern Shore trade with Philadelphia and Southern Europe, Lloyd used his contacts with Robert Morris, a Philadelphia speculator and merchant (whose father, a Liverpool factor, had been a business partner of both Lloyd and Richard Bennett; see chapter 4). Politics were a part of his life and in 1743 he followed his father on the Maryland council, a position he held until 1767. When Lloyd died in 1770, his estate, including 160 slaves and "ca. 43,000 acres in Dorchester, Talbot, Anne Arundel, Kent, and Queen Anne's counties," came to almost £100,000, "making him perhaps the richest man who ever lived in colonial Maryland."[19]

Unfortunately, there is no orphan's court inventory for Edward III, as there had been for his father and grandparents. After his death, however, his children had an informal inventory ("Inventory of Sundry Household Furniture") made of their father's possessions to make the estate's division easier. They listed nine rooms in a two-story Wye House, and the rooms compare nicely with those listed in 1719: a parlor, a dining room, a passage, Mrs. Lloyd's chamber, and a nursery on the ground floor; the second story contained a "Room over the Passage," a "Room over the Dining Room," a "Room over the Parlor," and "the great Passage."[20] Items such as chimney glasses, andirons, fire screens, shovels, and tongs suggest that there were fireplaces in all five ground-story rooms and in the three upstairs bedrooms. The three nonpassage second-floor rooms all have bedsteads and other items that suggest a sleeping use. But even so, it is difficult to establish the exact configuration of the house. Was there a center hall on both floors? If so, did the ground floor have the parlor in half the space with the dining room and Mrs. Lloyd's chamber across the passage from it? There is no room listed as being above the nursery; was it a one-story appendage off (presumably) Mrs. Lloyd's room? And where was the stair?

Wye House: the north parlor. Furniture was built especially for this room and has always remained in place.

19. "Planters," p. 126; see also *A Biographical Dictionary of the Maryland Legislature 1635–1789*, vol. 2; manuscript being prepared for publication by the Maryland Hall of Records Commission.
20. Lloyd papers on file at the Maryland Historical Society, Baltimore; Ms 2001; Roll 39; microfilm reel 1243.

Wye House: dining room. A portrait of Governor Edward Lloyd V is over mantel; his uncle Richard Bennett Lloyd, whose portrait—by Benjamin West—is over the sideboard, was a Loyalist in the Revolution.

The parlor had "2 window curtains," which might suggest two windows; but the dining room had "2 silk Damask Window Curtains and Brass Rods" and the Chamber had "2 Window Curtains." No curtains were listed in the passage, which does suggest that it occupied a place in the center of the house, although it is impossible to know if it ran through the house. It must, however, have served as something of a picture gallery, because it held "2 maps and 13 pieces of Painting": could they have been viewed in so dark a space? It also had a "Breakfast Table," but it is difficult to imagine people breakfasting in a sunless room. The inventory suggests a definite refinement in the Lloyds' style of living. Daily existence was much more comfortable than it was in 1719, as a large number of pier glasses and flower pots indicates. Those wonderful "Japanned" pieces also remained at Wye. There were also included three shops, presumably outbuildings: a cooper's shop, a smith's shop, and a carpenter's shop.

Table 1 might help clarify what rooms existed in the house at various times, although their arrangement remains unclear. Is the old hall the parlor (which seems possible)? But why are they both, then, in the 1719 list? Maybe the dining room is the old hall? Is the 1719 "Mr. James's Room" the old "Madam Lloyd's Room"? What of the three upstairs bedrooms in 1770—could one be the 1685 upper chamber, and could that, in turn, be the high chamber mentioned in 1697 and 1719? All four lists indicate a house of a similar scale, but as to the configuration, no one can be sure.

The fourth Edward (1744–1796) for a time confined himself to the management of the Lloyd fortune. But, as with his ancestors, a (presumed) sense of noblesse oblige led him into politics. From 1771 to 1776 he served in the lower house of the General Assembly; drawn into "national" issues, he was a member of the committees of correspondence formed in reaction to the tea tax and the Boston port bill; he signed the articles of association of the freemen of Maryland; he was elected to Maryland's council of safety in 1775; he held a seat on the council of the State of Maryland from 1777 to 1779; he was chosen as a state senator for the Eastern Shore in 1781, 1786, and 1791; he was one of Talbot County's representatives at the state constitutional convention of 1788; and he served as a delegate to the Congress of the United States in 1783 and 1784.[21]

This Edward (nicknamed "the magnificent" by his descendants) is generally credited with building the present Wye House. He had one of the largest fortunes in America; his

21. Tilghman, *History*, vol. 1, pp. 176–83.

TABLE 1

1685	1697	1719	1770
Hall (fireplace)	Hall (fireplace)	Hall (fireplace)	
New Room	New Room (fireplace)		
Upper Chamber (fireplace)	High Chamber	High Chamber	
Blue Chamber	Blue Chamber		
Study Chamber			
Black Chamber	Black Chamber	Old Black Room	
Staircase	Staircase		
Madam Lloyd's Room (fireplace)	Madam Lloyd's Room	Mr. James's Chamber	Mrs. Lloyd's Chamber (fireplace)
Nursery	Nursery		Nursery (fireplace)
Kitchen (fireplace)	Kitchen (fireplace)	Kitchen	
Kitchen Loft	Kitchen Chamber	Kitchen Garret	
Closet	Closet	Closet	
Store	Store		
	Lodging Room (fireplace)		
	Study		
	Old Study		
	The Entry		
	Passage	Passage	Passage (fireplace)
	Lodging Room		
	Pantry		
	Wash House		
		New Closet	
		Parlor	Parlor (fireplace)
		Hall Chamber	Room over the Passage (fireplace)
		New Room in the Shed (fireplace)	
			Dining Room (fireplace)
			Room over the Dining Room (fireplace)
			Room over the Parlor (fireplace)
			Great Passage

wife (née Elizabeth Tayloe) had been reared at the great Palladian house Mt. Airy, overlooking the Rappahannock River in Virginia. To both of them Wye, grand as it probably was, must have seemed incommensurate with their position in life and with the way they wished to live. And they probably felt it was old fashioned. The Lloyds, in ordering furnishings for their "new" house in 1780s and '90s, constantly used phrases like "the most up to date," "the most stylish," and we can assume that they would have wished a suitable container for their "up-to-date" Chippendale furniture.[22]

Moreover, the Lloyds must have been growing weary of the site and orientation of the old house. If earlier speculations are correct,

the old house had faced what was once known as the 'long green,' which led to the waterfront. Along this moved all the bustle and confusion of a vast agricultural under-taking. At one end, vessels were being loaded and unloaded. Through the green moved carts, drays and wagons. Many buildings stood along its perimeter, overseers' houses, slave quarters, storage houses, corn cribs, barns. Some of the buildings still stand, in use, and

22. Lloyd papers at Maryland Historical Society.

many of the barns existed well into this century. Here were also . . . blacksmith and cooper's shops and loom houses. It must have been not only a busy but a noisy place and the family would have been glad to move their dwelling a hundred yards back behind a barrier of trees and shrubbery.[23]

The Tayloes' Mt. Airy sits calm and elegant, lordly and serene, miles from the Rappahannock and its attendant activity. This seclusion, this separation from commercial chaos, must have appealed to the Lloyds, and the appeal was probably as much political and psychological as aesthetic. These "changes in ceremony and hierarchy" had begun in England in the medieval era at the highest—i.e., royal—level.[24] American architectural historian Dell Upton has cited several late-seventeenth-century colonial examples, on a much smaller scale than Wye, and notes that "to a certain extent . . . the Chesapeake change is part of the larger Anglo-American transformation and . . . social reorganization."[25] The ninety-degree shift of Wye House thus reflects changes that had been underway for generations, from Yorkshire to the Chesapeake Bay. Once again, Wye is exemplary.

The architect of Edward and Elizabeth's Wye, the Wye that is (nearly) that of today, is unknown. So is the date the house was built. These lacunae are extraordinary considering the vastness and thoroughness of the Lloyd family papers, yet generations of historians have been through them without finding any definite answer.

> It is impossible to give an accurate, documented date for the building of the present house. For the present it can only be stated that the family was still living in the old house in 1770. . . . On April 18, 1792, Edward and Elizabeth Lloyd scratched their names and the date on a window pane of the existing house. For the rest, Wye House papers are filled, throughout these years and well into the next century, by references to extensive building. For example, there are references in 1773 to "the new house on Wye." A letter from Richard Grason, the agent or overseer at Wye House, addressed to Edward Lloyd at Annapolis, November 22, 1774, states, "the new house I expect, will be covered tomorrow." This could be Wye House but also it could be any of numerous other houses on the vast Lloyd holdings.[26]

Donnell Tilghman, speculating that the architect was Robert Key, argued that Key's *ouevre* contained work in Annapolis with which the Lloyds would have been familiar and noted that the Lloyd account books are filled with transactions with Key beginning in 1775 and ending in 1798.[27] But research since Tilghman wrote his article has shown that Key's reputation as an architect may have been exaggerated and that he might better be called a "gifted artisan."[28] Rosamond Randall Beirne has grappled with the Key issue:

> If ever Key was in need of a meal or a little pocket money, he could count on the patronage and generosity of Edward Lloyd IV of "Wye" and Annapolis. For a period of twenty-eight years, 1774 to 1802, he served the Lloyds at both town house and plantation. Often the entries in the Lloyd business ledgers are for small repairs such as: "Repairing Stable with one new Slate, making a coach jack, etc." More pretentious was his "Building a Temple," presumably a garden house at "Wye." Once he is credited with 51½ days' work at Wye House and again for "106 days' work about Green House, Mansion House and Sundry Repairs."

These lengths of time—in all, more than five months—are intriguing, but, as Mrs. Beirne notes,

> The sum of £279, roughly the total of his collections from Edward Lloyd, does not seem sufficiently great to accept him as the designer and builder of "Wye House." He received at that time ten shillings a day, larger than the five and a half Lloyd paid to both William Buckland and William Noke for work on his town house. This would seem to indicate that the ten shillings were for Key and his workman and that they were serving as independent journeymen.[29]

To compound the manifold mysteries that surround Wye, no one seems to know just which part of the present house was built when. Forman speculates that the house underwent five separate phases of construction; he suggests that the phases (and dates) are as follows:

23. Tilghman, "Wye House," p. 100.
24. Mark Girouard, *Life in the English Country House* (New Haven: Yale University Press, 1978), pp. 45, 46.
25. Dell Upton, "The Origins of Chesapeake Architecture," in *Three Centuries of Maryland Architecture* (Annapolis: Maryland Historical Trust, 1982), p. 50.
26. Tilghman, "Wye House," p. 97.
27. Ibid., p. 99.
28. Rosamond Randall Beirne, "Two Anomalous Architects: John Horatio Anderson and Robert Key," in *Maryland Historical Magazine*, vol. 55, no. 3 (1960):200.
29. Ibid., pp. 197, 198.

I. Main block and pavilions (1782–84)

II. "Hyphen" to connect the above and the front porch (c. 1790)

III. End additions (office to the west, wash house to the east), and rear vernanda (c. 1800).

IV. Rear entries to hyphens (c. 1830–60s)

V. Raising the roofs of the two pavilions (1914).[30]

The editors of *A New Guide to the Old Line State* note that "the house was probably finished by 1784, when some of the present furnishings were ordered from England." They add, however, that many of the other furnishings came from an earlier Wye House, including the grandfather clock in the hall, made by a clockmaker who died in 1725.[31]

Tilghman suggests that the house, pavilions, and hyphens were all built at the same time, and he lumps the rest together: "The porches, wing 'entries,' the plantation office at the end of the west wing and, probably, the wash house at the end of the east wing, are all additions."[32]

It seems most likely that Tilghman is correct insofar as the main sections' dates go: by the 1770s and '80s the various parts of houses in Maryland and Virginia were connected, not freestanding; separate buildings, such as Forman postulates, would have been the practice one or two generations earlier. Examples abound: in Maryland, some of Wye's connected contemporaries would include Mt. Clare in Baltimore (hyphens added in 1768), Annapolis's Hammond-Harwood House, and Whitehall (in its second phase) in Anne Arundel County.

At this time, architecture in the colonies—and to a large degree in England, too—depended on pattern books. There were few architects as such, so, generally speaking, a traveling carpenter, or joiner, or plasterer, or mason would sell a design from a builder's manual to a prospective client and would then attempt to reproduce the pattern. Much more rarely, a sophisticated client would have these books in his own library and would tell the artisan what he wanted. The most influential pattern books were various editions in translation of Palladio's *Four Books of Architecture*, James Gibbs's *A Book of Architecture* and *Rules for Drawing the Several Parts of Architecture*, William Adam's *Vitruvius Scoticus*, Colen Campbell's *Vitruvius Britannicus*, Robert Morris's *Select Architecture*, and William Salmon's *Palladio Londinensis*.

These—and many others—were copiously illustrated with clearly engraved plates that made copying (or interpreting) as easy for a colonial builder as using a dress pattern is for a seamstress today. They were of especial value, as Gibbs wrote in the preface for his *Book of Architecture* "in the remote parts of the Country, where little or no assistance for Designers can be procured."[33] Architects like Gibbs had, of course, themselves read Palladio and saw an impressive and practical invention in his many part plans, which, Palladio wrote, sensibly allowed the master "to go every place under cover. . . . neither the rains nor the scorching sun of the summer [would] be a nuisance to him."

The multinational—someone has called it "the true International Style"— phenomenon of Palladianism is too broad to explore here. James Ackerman posed the question, "What is it about Palladio's villas that made them so popular throughout the ensuing centuries?" He partially answered himself by stating that the Protestant northern Europeans "liked the cerebral, abstract quality in Palladio" and by commenting that the success of the *Four Books* was due to Palladio's abstractness: "a designer who thinks in terms of proportions in the plane can communicate the essence of his concepts in line." Moreover,

Palladio's clients were country gentry in much the same way that British squires and American plantation owners were. The country landowner in eighteenth-century Anglo-Saxon culture, like his predecessor in the Veneto of the sixteenth century, was economically tied to the land as overseer of the crops and the herds, but a classical education and the ambitions of a Humanist gave him city tastes. . . . Northern weather and an agrarian economy did not encourage vast ornamental landscaping schemes in which the utility

30. Forman, *Old Buildings*, pp. 63–65.

31. Papenfuse et al., *New Guide*, p. 159.

32. Tilghman, "Wye House," p. 100.

33. Quoted in William Rasmussen, *Building by the Book* (Charlottesville: University Press of Virginia, 1984), p. 78.

Deborah Lloyd (1741–1811). Portrait by John Hesselius circa 1755; some people feel that the orange she is holding is from Wye's Orangery.

structures were pushed into the background by pools and fountains. He preferred the Palladian Villa, designed for an economic and social situation nearly identical to his own.[34]

One possible model for Wye may be seen in the "Roman Country House" as depicted in Robert Morris's *Select Architecture* (1757):

> At the time the English nobility began to look to Robert Adam for a new style, which he gave to them in a late Roman adaptation of his own, the Virginians turned to Palladio's smaller houses for novelty. Thomas Jefferson, with Monticello in 1770, initiated the purely Palladian phase of this period, but there were several houses, probably complete this time, that were in the same manner but were based on plates of Palladian adaptations from Robert Morris' *Select Architecture*, published in London in 1757. These marked the breaking away from the large-scale rectangular block. . . . In the new style a small scale central block with a series of connected, decreasing units was evolved, sometimes with terminal buildings. This plan had manifest practical advantages, as rooms more often had cross ventilation and great central stair halls were no longer required. . . . Also, the kitchen wing was removed from the family's living quarters, the old semi-enclosed court scheme being abandoned and the units arranged in one long line. This plan was not entirely new . . . but for the first time the whole was formalized and the central block brought down in scale by subdivision.[35]

When Edward IV died in 1796, his estate inventory listed "the largest eighteenth-century Maryland book collection . . . 2,500 volumes."[36] (Happily, many are still at Wye.) While Morris's *Select Architecture* is not included in the inventory, several architectural books are. Most notable are an unidentified *View of County Seats in Ireland*, the two-volume *A Collection of Designs in Architecture* by Abraham Swan (1757), James Gibbs's *A Book of Architecture* (2nd ed., 1739), Gibbs's *Rule for Drawing the Several Parts of Architecture* (2nd ed., 1738), and, significantly, two editions of Palladio's *Four Books of Architecture*: Isaac Ware's 1738 translation and the 3rd edition (1742) of Giacomo Leoni's translation. While it is speculation, at best, to attempt to cite a source, an inspiration, for Wye House, it is easy to see the basis for Wye's monumental front porch: it is a reduced version, lifted with great care, of Palladio's Villa Rotonda, as even a cursory comparison of the porch and plate 13, (book 2) of Leoni's translation, the translation Lloyd had, illustrates.

Wye's plan is, however, totally different from these Roman Country Houses. For one thing, the main block is two rooms deep, thus creating a more livable, if darker, house in that the reception rooms are more compactly arranged. It should also be pointed out that a main tenet of Palladianism is symmetry; all of the Roman Country Houses are balanced on the exterior and are symmetrical around an axis (usually a through center hall) that runs the width of the house: Wye is balanced on its exterior, and has an interior axis of sorts, but this axis runs the *length* of the house and the rooms are only vaguely balanced around it. Variations of this sort of plan, dubbed by some "the Annapolis plan," can be seen in Annapolis at the Hammond-Harwood House and the Brice House, and in Baltimore, at Mt. Clare. It also exists in Virginia—for example, at Kenmore and Menokin.[37]

The moment one enters the front door [of Wye], one is struck with the quality of spaciousness: high ceilings, openness, light. It is a house designed, like so many of the old houses of the Tidewater, to be cool in summer. The six panel doors are, characteristically of the late eighteenth century, wide and low, a fact that accentuates the height of the ceilings. Their trim is crowned by frieze and horizontal cornices. All the first floor rooms of the main house have fireplaces with panelled overmantels.

Standing in the entrance hall, one may look north through the house via a jib door for a vista of the bowling green and orangerie, or south for the length of the avenue to the top road gate. . . . To the left of the hall, the south parlor has the intimate furnishings of a family living room. The fireplace is considerably off center and it is probable that the passage to the west wing was taken off this room.[38]

At the end of the hall, opposite the entrance, a door opens into the north parlor, the most beautiful room in the house and one of the most distinguished of its era in the state. Its furnishings, like those of most of the rooms, consist largely of pieces that have

34. James S. Ackerman, *Palladio* (Baltimore: Penguin Books, 1974), pp. 77, 78.
35. Thomas T. Waterman, *The Mansions of Virginia* (Chapel Hill: University of North Carolina Press, 1945), p. 341.
36. Edwin Wolf II, "The Library of Edward Lloyd IV of Wye House," in *Winterthur Portfolio*, no. 5, (1969):87.
37. Waterman, *Mansions*, pp. 308 et seq.
38. Michael Trostel has suggested that structural evidence indicates that this is not true, that the south parlor has always been where it is, as it is (conversation with Christopher Weeks, May 25, 1983).

always been in the house. The four tall windows are hung with blue damask and between two of them are gilt mirrors, made to order for these spaces in London. The bill for these mirrors as well as those for the crystal girandoles on the console tables beneath them are still in existence.

The Orangery.

From the north parlor a wide arch leads into the dining room. A line on the floor gives evidence that this room was once enlarged at the expense of the parlor. In the panelled overmantel beyond the dining table hangs a portrait of Governor Lloyd. Over the sideboard is the colorful painting, by Benjamin West, of Captain Richard Bennett Lloyd in the scarlet uniform of the Coldstream Guards.[39]

The library was in the west pavilion; besides the books on architecture, Lloyd also owned a group of books whose titles bespeak another of the Lloyds' interests, gardening. Among the books in the library at Wye are Thomas Collins Overton's *Original Design of Temples, And other Ornamental Buildings for Parks and Gardens* (1776), Seeley's *A Description of the Gardens of Lord Viscount Cobham at Stowe* (4th ed., 1747), Gilbert Brookes's *The Complete British Gardener* (1779), William Marshall's *Planting and Ornamental Gardening* (1785), and John Randall's *The Semi-Virgilian Husbandry* (1764). There is also John Abercrombie's *The Hot-House Gardener or the General Culture of the Pine-apple* (1789).

This interest in hothouse gardening brings up a building at Wye that is at least as interesting as the house itself, the Orangery (called "the greenhouse" by earlier generations of Lloyds). It faces the north (rear) of Wye House across a bowling green. The stuccoed brick building, decidedly French Renaissance in style, was almost certainly erected by Mr. and Mrs. Edward Lloyd IV. Its two-story, hip-roofed central portion features piers of rusticated stonework dividing the floor-length windows at the first story; the stone quoins running up to the cornice at the corners help give the structure a monumental effect. The second-story room in the Orangery contained an elaborate John Shaw billiard table, removed to Winterthur in this century. The one-story flanking hip-roofed wings, raised just one step above grade, have large arched windows that give the appearance of glass-enclosed arcades. A central heating system once augmented the sun's heat, and the orange and lemon trees that were grown here were planted in square tubs that the editors of the *New Guide* say were identical to tubs used at Versailles.[40]

Wye's citrus trees were moved out into the open-air garden in summer and were put

39. Tilghman, "Wye House," p. 103.
40. Papenfuse et al., *New Guide*, p. 129.

The brick-walled Lloyd graveyard contains the graves of ten generations of Lloyds, their descendants, and their in-laws. Photograph by A. Aubrey Bodine.

41. Chamberlaine, *Chamberlaine*, note to illustration 12.
42. Lloyd papers at the Maryland Historical Society.
43. McHenry Howard, "Wye House, Talbot County, Maryland," in *Maryland Historical Magazine*, vol. 18, no. 4 (1923):298.
44. Mrs. Morgan B. Schiller in conversation with Christopher Weeks, May 20, 1983.
45. Rasmussen, *Building by the Book*, p. 85.
46. Ibid.
47. Forman, *Old Buildings*, p. 59.
48. Girouard, *Life*, pp. 210, 211.
49. Wye also had a deer park, as did many similar estates in England and America. The deer park generally proved a mixed blessing; Mr. Baker, George Washington's gardener at Mt. Vernon, complained that he was often bitten by his deer, which also ate shrubs. "I am at a loss," wrote the general, "in determining whether to give up the shrubs or the deer." Quoted in Rasmussen, p. 85.
50. Forman, *Old Buildings*, p. 60.

back into the south-facing Orangery in winter. The Orangery's date is as troublesome as that of the house (or, rather, houses). A circa-1755 John Hesselius portrait of Deborah Lloyd (1741–1811) shows the sitter holding an orange "very possibly from the orangery of 'Wye' ";[41] Edward and Elizabeth Tayloe Lloyd's 1783 tax assessment includes "one greenhouse." It also includes, at Lloyd's Addition to Woolman (the tract containing the greenhouse) "one brick dwelling, one kitchen, four quarters." The "brick dwelling" means that if the Orangery was standing in 1783 it predates the present *frame* dwelling. (The tract Linton is generally considered to have contained the various Wye Houses; the 1783 assessment, however, shows that that tract was unimproved.)

The Orangery, a truly remarkable structure, remained in use for several generations. The Lloyd papers at the Maryland Historical Society contain a letter from Robert Goldsborough of Myrtle Grove to Edward Lloyd V, dated October 27, 1810, in which Goldsborough speaks of a request by Dr. Tristram Thomas for "a Lemon" prescribed for Mrs. Goldsborough, who was ill. He conveys thanks for the lemon and reports on Mrs. Goldsborough's condition.[42] McHenry Howard, reminiscing about Wye in the *Maryland Historical Magazine* in December 1923, commented that "the oranges were hardly edible but the lemons were of fine quality."[43] The present (1984) owner of Wye, Elizabeth Key Lloyd Schiller, has said that her "earliest and fondest memories are of the Orangery. My grandparents kept tubs and tubs of oleanders and gardenias there in the winter and brought them out in the spring and summer. The place was filled with blossom. Then when we took over—oh my!—we used it for everything. We raised baby quail in it and we gave dinner parties in it—sometimes with Viennese string quartets."[44] The Orangery was restored in 1981 under the watchful eye of Baltimore architect Michael Trostel and in cooperation with the Society for the Preservation of Maryland Antiquities.

When growing up at Mt. Airy, Elizabeth Tayloe Lloyd was much exposed to fashionable tastes in gardening; her father, John Tayloe II, probably designed the extensive gardens there "with the aid of his copy of Phillip Miller's popular *Gardener's Dictionary*, which he purchased in 1760."[45] The Tayloes' garden had large marble statues, a spacious bowling green in the center flanked by the formal parterre to the east and boxwood to the west. Beyond the box was the Tayloes' Orangery (now in ruins), which had, according to early nineteenth-century insurance policies, a central greenhouse covered with a wooden roof, flanked on each end by a "Hothouse" with "sides of glass" and "cov[ere]d with glass." William Rasmussen has written that "in 1827 note was made of orange and lemon trees put out on the grass before this structure, where raspberries were produced at about the same time and sent to Yorktown for an October dinner there in honor of the visiting Lafayette."[46]

Beyond Wye's Orangery is the brick-walled Lloyd graveyard, a shaded, sequestered two-acre plot containing the graves of ten generations of Lloyds, their descendants, and their in-laws.

Writers discussing Wye always make reference to the Orangery's being off-center from the main house: "definitely off the center of the axis of the mansion," one historian fusses.[47] But that should be no surprise. During the third quarter of the eighteenth century, garden fashion changed in England and "axial planning, and straight avenues, canals or walks all converging on the ceremonial spine of the house disappeared in favour of circular planning." This "circular planning" encouraged perambulations, and "walking round a garden or driving round a park, whether one's own or somebody else's, loomed large in the ample leisure time of people in polite society."[48] The Wye garden contained several features that would make such a walk amusing: a rose arbor, parterres, box-lined walkways, a variety of structures placed at strategic points.[49] Forman has noted "the 'Terrace' running beside a ditch, where members of the family used to walk on summer evenings to take the air."[50] Moreover, "the replacement of axial by circular planning, inside houses and out, affected the way people looked at buildings. They no longer thought in terms of rigidly intersecting axial vistas, each neatly ending in a terminal feature. They liked to see buildings in a series and from a variety of constantly changing angles. Their compactly planned houses were visually circumscribable and were made more so by having their extremities hived off instead of being subsidiaries to the main block, as in many formal houses. Stable blocks became separate incidents in the landscape."⁵¹

All of this, of course, affected the way people approached the house—and the configuration of Wye's driveway to the house from the road becomes suddenly explainable. The drive, lined with the oaks and beeches beloved of the English, is certainly contemporaneous with the present house. The visitor enters through modern (1929) gates and, for a few hundred yards, proceeds straight as an arrow's shaft, with the goal, the house's Palladian-porticoed door, directly in front. Then, suddenly, the road divides; for a while the house disappears from view, then it reappears at an angle—it disappears, reappears, disappears, reappears. Finally, the visitor crosses the ha-ha, goes through an inner pair of gates, and enters the elliptical forecourt.

Wye's system of ha-has is, by the way, as interesting as any other feature of the estate. A ha-ha, simply, is a ditch used to make an invisible boundary that is impassable by animals. The *Oxford English Dictionary* (OED) says it is "a boundary to a garden, pleasure-ground, or park, of such a kind as not to interrupt the view from within and not to be seen till closely approached, a sunken fence." Graham Stuart Thomas, in his book *Gardens of the National Trust*, says it was first "described by Dezalliers d'Argenuille in his book *La Théorie et la Pratique du Jardinage*"⁵² in 1709, and the OED dates its first written appearance in England to 1712. Thomas notes that "this one feature made possible the whole idea of expansive eighteenth-century gardening." Washington's ha-ha at Mt. Vernon is probably a contemporary of the Lloyds' at Wye (it certainly is not much earlier), and these may have been the first in America. The ha-ha is yet another example of how aware the Lloyds were of the latest trends in design, whether architectural or horticultural.

How did these late-eighteenth-century Lloyds live? The Maryland Historical Society in Baltimore possesses many archival treasures; certainly among the most interesting is the collection called the Lloyd Papers, over 30,000 items spanning 250 years. The material was given to the Society in installments in 1948, 1967, and 1969 by Mrs. Morgan Schiller (née Elizabeth Key Lloyd), was processed between 1969 and 1970, and was microfilmed in 1972. The papers provide invaluable insights into the history of the Eastern Shore.

Although the papers are most complete for the nineteenth century, there is enough material from the mid- and late eighteenth century to form a picture of day-to-day life on a large-scale plantation during that period; although they focus on the Lloyds—specifically on Edward Lloyd IV and Elizabeth Tayloe Lloyd—the papers can be used to illustrate some generalizations about Chesapeake society and economy. Unless otherwise noted, the following discussion is entirely based on material from the society's Lloyd Papers.

In 1783 tax men assessed 167,883 acres of land in Talbot County, of which Edward Lloyd IV owned 11,884 acres, or 7.1 percent. Within district number two, the northwestern third of Talbot (which seems to have been the county's most valuable area), Lloyd owned 18.2 percent of the land, including a substantial part of the shoreline of the peninsula formed by the Wye and St. Michaels (Miles) rivers.

Lloyd had, as has been noted, inherited all this from his father in 1770: his inheritance included not only the land at Wye House and elsewhere in the colony, but also slaves (themselves worth more than £7,000), stock, household furnishings, crops, 500 ounces of plate (£200), bills of exchange held by London merchants, colonial bonds, a mill, full or partial ownership of several schooners, and an interest in a number of stores on the Eastern Shore, in all a material estate amounting to 45,867 pounds of tobacco, £14,547 current money and £8,539 sterling; the entire estate had a total value of £40,155. For comparative purposes, the same assessment gives Henry Hollyday, a man who was hardly destitute, "one large brick dwelling house" (Ratcliffe Manor, T–42; see above page 32) and a total estate of £3,097. Lloyd was worth almost as much as everyone else in the district combined: his closest monetary competitors were his brother, Richard Bennett Lloyd (£11,236), and his maiden sister, Henrietta Maria Lloyd (£4,564). The richest non-Lloyd was Peregrine

This nineteenth-century photograph, taken in the gardens at Wye, suggests that life at Wye resembled the lives described by Jane Austen in *Mansfield Park:* "Fanny made the first interruption by saying: 'I wonder that I should be tired with only walking in this sweet wood; but the next time we come to a seat, if it is not disagreeable to you, I should be glad to sit down for a while . . . ' [A]nd standing back, well shaded and sheltered, and overlooking a ha-ha into the park, was a comfortable-sized bench on which they all sat down."

Note: On pages 67 through 71 of this book certain passages are taken verbatim and others are paraphrased from an unpublished paper by Jean B. Russo entitled "The Plantations of Edward Lloyd IV, Talbot County, Maryland, 1770–1796: A Case Study in Estate Management." The paper was presented to the American Seminar of the Department of History, The Johns Hopkins University, on 7 February 1979.

51. Girouard, *Life*, pp. 210, 211.
52. Graham Stuart Thomas, *Gardens of the National Trust* (London: Weidenfeld and Nicolson, 1979), pp. 61, 62.

Wye from across the ha-ha.

Tilghman (£3,412), but his wife was Deborah Lloyd, the young woman with the Orangery (?) orange.[53]

Beginning the first year of his inheritance, Edward Lloyd IV began to divest himself of his commercial assets and to expand his initial inheritance of slaves and farms so that by the end of the 1780s he was totally agrarian, deriving almost all his income from the sale of agricultural products, interest paid by bondholders, and rents paid by tenants.[54]

Thus it is interesting to note that, although the Lloyd fortune had been built up over several generations by men whose wide range of mercantile interests stretched from Maryland to England, Edward Lloyd IV contracted these interests, restricting his commercial pursuits to the marketing of his own crops.

His actions resemble those his sister Elizabeth, and her husband, John Cadwalader, were taking in Philadelphia. She had married Cadwalader on September 25, 1768, bringing with her "plantations totaling 2,478 acres on the Sassafras River in Kent County, and plantations on the Wye River of 1,213 acres more. Her personal wealth at the time of her marriage, not counting a present from Colonel Lloyd of £1,000, was estimated at £10,000, for, in addition to her land, she owned seventy-eight slaves, one hundred and twenty-five horses, a large stock of cattle, hogs, and sheep, and £427 worth of Lloyd family plate."[55]

Cadwalader was wealthy in his own right, but Nicholas B. Wainwright, the eminent Pennsylvania historian, has surmised that Elizabeth Lloyd's dowry enabled her husband to retire "from business soon after his marriage. Early in 1769, he and his brother gave up their store." It also allowed him to complete a house that was grander than anything else in Philadelphia at that time. Moreover, right after the wedding the Cadwaladers commissioned some superb locally made furniture, by Thomas Affleck and others. This furniture has recently been in the news: one chair brought a record price at auction in 1983.[56] No wonder, then "Edward the Magnificent"; no wonder then, that the Lloyds have cast such a long, and long-lasting, shadow throughout the Chesapeake region.

Lloyd had inherited four schooners from his father in 1770: he sold three immediately and kept only one. And there is only one record of that vessel's ever making a voyage to London: he used it instead locally—to transport his products to market in Baltimore, Annapolis, and on the Eastern Shore and to carry goods from one plantation to another. (During the Revolution the schooner was lost "while being used by the State—probably captured by the British in the Yorktown campaign—for which he received 37,500 pounds

53. Material in the Maryland Hall of Records. See also Jean Russo, "The Plantations of Edward Lloyd IV," unpublished manuscript, Maryland Historical Trust, Annapolis.
54. To oversee the operation of the farms and the work force, Lloyd, absent in Annapolis for much of the year (and perhaps generally disinclined to pursue an active managerial role), employed several categories of assistants.
55. Nicholas B. Wainwright, *Colonial Grandeur in Philadelphia* (Philadelphia: Historical Society of Pennsylvania, 1964), p. 3.
56. Mary Helen Cadwalader in conversation with Christopher Weeks, October 10, 1982.

of tobacco in compensation.")[57] Lloyd also inherited Wye Mill from his father. The Lloyds' miller operated the mill during the 1770s, but Lloyd sold it in 1778 for £1,000; similarly, Edward Lloyd III had also owned several stores, and accounts in the early 1770s refer to his son's interest in stores in Queenstown and at Wye Mill and Wye Town—by the end of the decade such references cease.

Within three years after his father's death, Lloyd significantly increased his slave labor force and the number of farms he operated and greatly diversified the production of those farms. According to one employee of Lloyd's, "there was nothing but a continual Expense in Settling the farms and no profit arising therefrom the first 2 or 3 years after the present Colonel Lloyd took possession of his Estate." The inheritance from his father and the income from rents and bonds would have been sufficient to see Lloyd through this period; once the initial period of expansion was over, his agricultural operations were very prosperous. Production figures cover most of the years from 1770 to 1784, and show that all of Lloyd's farms grew wheat, tobacco, and corn, with additional crops of barley, oats, beans, peas, and potatoes in some years. The three major crops showed great fluctuation in output, rising to high levels before the Revolution, moving erratically during the war years, and reaching new peaks for some crops at the end of the war. Cultivation of oats and barley apparently began during the war and showed a much more stable pattern of harvest size.

Chase-Lloyd House: interior; this was "the grand one." Photograph by Marion E. Warren.

No evidence from the harvest records suggests that total acreage was shifted among the major crops, although there are indications that the crop planted on a given area of ground did rotate from year to year. Given that Lloyd cultivated the same nine farms for twenty-seven years, with increased production over that period, there must have been some effective form of crop rotation and fertilization to maintain soil fertility. The agricultural reformer John Beale Bordley was a neighbor of Lloyd's on the Wye River, and it is possible that Lloyd, who sold oats, barley, and corn to Bordley in the 1780s, was aware of Bordley's recommendations and followed them. Lloyd's cultivation of potatoes, turnips, peas, barley, oats, and clover—all part of Bordley's proposed plan of eight-field crop rotation—suggests such a conclusion; this will be gone into further in chapter 7.

As discussed in chapter 3, diversification had begun in Talbot County by mid-century, so this shift in emphasis from tobacco alone to tobacco, wheat, and corn was not an innovation of Lloyd's, but his extensive production of wheat was unusual. Records from the early 1770s indicate total sales ranging from 2,000 to 5,000 bushels each year; by the 1790s, Lloyd was selling 10,000 bushels a year. At the same time, there is no evidence that tobacco harvests had decreased in size from the fifty to seventy hogsheads produced yearly in the 1770s and 1780s; rather, correspondence with London refers to shipments of one hundred or more hogsheads by the 1790s. No sales figures for corn exist for the years after 1777, but the planting of 431,000 corn hills on the home plantation alone in 1796 seems to show that production of that crop was not insignificant. A comparison of two records for livestock, the 1783 tax assessment and the 1796 inventory, indicates that the number of all stock raised had increased as well.

As efficient a farmer as Lloyd seems to have been, his interests were not solely agricultural. He was the heir to the family's tradition of political leadership and was elected to the house of delegates in 1771. This required an Annapolis residence, so, the year he was elected, Lloyd bought the shell of a house on Maryland Avenue from Samuel Chase. Chase had bought the lot in 1769 from Denton Hammond and had begun to build a large three-story structure, unlike any other private house in Annapolis. Chase's ambitions exceeded his funds and construction progressed slowly: by 1771, only the cellar, brick walls, and structural carpentry appear to have been completed. This was Lloyd's "shell." Chase's sale of the house and land for £504.8.2 sterling and £249.17.7 Maryland currency was believed by his acquaintances to have been a wise move. Charles Carroll of Carrollton commented on the transaction in a letter to his kinsman Charles Carroll, Barrister:

Colonel Lloyd has purchased Chase's house . . . ; it is agreed on all hands that Chase has acted very wisely in selling it; he has got rid of an encumbrance which must have ruined

57. McHenry Howard, "Wye," p. 295.

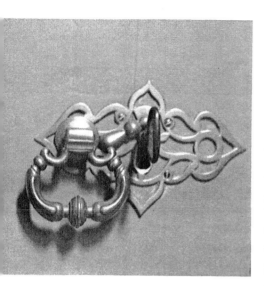

Hardware at Wye. That in the Annapolis house has the same design but was executed in silver.

him at ye long run; the money received of Lloyd will extricate him from all difficulties; he is now independent and may if he pleases continue so and become more serviceable to the Public. [58]

Eventually, Lloyd acquired another neighboring lot.

The present owner of Wye House deprecates (almost seriously) her rural inheritance by referring to it as "just an old farmhouse." She says that "the Annapolis house was the grand one. The details at Wye are scaled-down and simplified versions of the town house's."[59] This follows the contemporary English practice of stressing the town house over the country house. The similarities between the two Lloyd structures are interesting. The main door scheme is the same at both Wye and the Annapolis house: the doors are flanked by two, quarter-engaged columns with a semicircular fanlight above which extends through a broken cornice to the pediment. There are two small side windows (making reference, therefore, to the three-part "Palladian window" scheme); the whole ends in pilasters. Reflecting the difference between city formality and country informality, the Annapolis house entrance uses the more elaborate Ionic order and modillions; Wye's order is Doric and lacks modillions.

Inside, both houses have similar hardware, but the city-country split can again be seen: silver drop handles and lock escutcheons in Annapolis, brass at Wye. Tilghman wrote that "the unusual treatment of the frieze in the entablature over the doors of the first floor at Wye House occurs in several places" in the Annapolis house and he speculates that "it is quite possible that the construction of the two houses was being carried on at the same time and that the same designer or architect is responsible for both."[60]

The documentation for the Annapolis house is clear. Lloyd used the finest designer he could find—no less than William Buckland. (Buckland was known to the Lloyds because he had done the interior work on Mt. Airy.) Few people dare speculate that Buckland did any work at Wye. What is possible, however, is that once the elaborate work was done in Annapolis, some of the same workmen might have been sent across the Bay to attempt less formal, more "country" versions of their work.

Letters written to London merchants and Edward Lloyd's estate inventory of 1796 illustrate the luxurious and elegant style in which the Lloyds lived in their two houses. (Again, bear in mind that a total estate of £100 would have been respectable.) The inventory lists over £1350 in furnishings: mahogany furniture, carpets, draperies, custom-made chandeliers, mirrors, and ornaments. In August 1791, Lloyd wrote to Thomas Eden and Company in London and ordered fourteen "handsome strong fashionable mahogany chairs for a dining room" and in January 1792 he ordered a "handsome mahogany sideboard table" as well as "fashionable or ornamental decorations to set off a dining or supper table that will accommodate twenty people." The Annapolis residence was supplied with four complete sets of Wedgewood china, 253 pieces in all, decorated with Lloyd's coat of arms, testimony to the style of entertainment which the Lloyds provided when they resided in town.

Also in January 1792, Lloyd placed orders with five different firms for a wide variety of other goods. Among the items of clothing requested from England were caps, shawls, stockings, over five dozen pairs of gloves, two silk dresses and two pair of stays for his wife, a winter suit for himself, and sixteen pairs of shoes for his wife and eldest daughter. Medicines and cosmetics were ordered from three merchants, while all five were asked to supply food items, including tea, cheese, raisins, nuts, chocolate, capers, anchovies, and India mangoes, as well as six dozen "finest champaign," burgundy, and claret. The inventoried items included over £1000 worth of wines and liquors. William Anderson was also asked to send a saddle and bridle for Lloyd's son, and Thomas Eden and Company to provide magazines and books. In August of the preceding year, Lloyd ordered a phaeton built by the "best maker in London," with his coat of arms or "what is most fashionable" to be put on the carriage, and an assortment of fruit trees for his Orangery, asking for "only the

58. Quoted several places. Note, for example, Rosamond Randall Beirne, "The Chase House in Annapolis," in *Maryland Historical Magazine*, vol. 49, no. 3 (1954):181.
59. Mrs. Morgan B. Schiller in conversation with Christopher Weeks, May 20, 1982.
60. Tilghman, "Wye House," p. 101.

choicest fruits of each kind and not less than four trees of each sort which I beg may be handsome healthy well grown Trees."

Lloyd kept a "Pleasure-Boat" for fishing and hunting parties on the Bay. He wrote to his merchants in London for two cannons for his yacht, "such as will make a thunderous report." They are still at Wye, in the hall, now quietly mounted on wooden blocks. "Probably a vessel was maintained at Wye continuously until after the Civil War, when it was discontinued, the last two being successively the 'Petrel' and the 'Wave of Wye.' When not in use they were kept moored to a cluster of piles in the Quarter Cove; they were of about 80 tons of burden."[61]

A keen horseman, Lloyd was a member of the Maryland Jockey Club, bred and raced pedigreed horses, and his stable, one of the finest of the time, provided stud services to his Talbot County neighbors. His hunting dogs came from England.

The Lloyds' interests also extended to the sciences and the fine arts, as the estate inventory indicates: Lloyd possessed two pianofortes, one a "grande" valued at £75, and several other instruments; numerous prints and paintings, including several by Charles Willson Peale, one a family triple portrait painted in 1771; a microscope, telescopes, and globes; and the library.

Edward Lloyd IV died in 1796 and his estates—and houses—passed to his only son, Edward V, nicknamed "the Governor" because of his extreme interest in politics. From 1800 to 1805 he served as a Democratic-Republican delegate to the General Assembly, directing his efforts toward reducing suffrage restrictions and toward reforming the judicial system. On September 27, 1806, he was chosen to complete Joseph H. Nicholson's unexpired term in the U.S. House of Representatives. During his stay in Congress, he was called upon to consider the pros and cons of dispensing with surplus revenue; he voiced opposition to conspiracy charges involving Aaron Burr, voted against the 1807 proposal to outlaw the African slave trade, and supported the government's attempt to resist British encroachments on the high seas. In 1808 he campaigned for James Madison when the Virginian ran for president. On June 5, 1809, he was elected to complete the unexpired term of Maryland's Governor Robert Wright; he was reelected to that office on October 2, 1809, and again in 1810. The following, taken from the *Republican Star* of November 27th, 1810, may illustrate the political and agricultural sentiment of the time:

> Yesterday Governor Lloyd took the oaths of office in the Senate Chamber both Houses attending. It was with sincere gratification we observed his Excellency, cloathed in the manufactures of the State. It was a beautiful suit of green, in fineness, softness and texture equal to imported cloths. The wool was grown upon his own farm and was produced from merino blood, with which he has lately enriched the State. It is by these means alone that domestic manufacturers can be encouraged. The heads of departments by wearing those manufactures tend more than anything else to encourage them. Many persons with a foolish pride will not wear them because they are not exactly equal to foreign manufactures; but in this instance a specimen is exhibited in Maryland, equal to any from the other side of the Atlantic, which at once meets the objection originating from pride and vanity. With pleasure we state that this truly patriotic Governor to be a Republican, and before he obtained the wool of this superior quality, he had cloathed himself (during the last session) in inferior manufacture, which evinced his patriotism and desire to encourage America to shake off entirely her dependence upon foreign countries.[62]

While still governor, he was chosen as a state senator for the Eastern Shore. It was in the latter capacity that he advocated a military solution to the Anglo-American problem, and he got his wish with the War of 1812. In January 1815 he left the Maryland Senate but in October of the same year was chosen as a delegate to the lower house of the assembly. Defeated in 1816, Lloyd retired from politics until December 18, 1819, when he was elected to the U.S. Senate. There he opposed adoption of Henry Clay's American System and was also against the attempt to exclude slavery from the territories lying north of 36 degrees 30 minutes, but he abstained on the Missouri Compromise (which proposed

61. Howard, "Wye," p. 294.
62. Quoted in Tilghman, *History*, vol. 1, p. 191.

The dairy near Wye House.

admitting Maine and Missouri to the Union at the same time, one free, the other slave). In 1826 he resigned because of illness.

Despite political preoccupations, Edward Lloyd V was the largest wheat grower in the state. He also assisted in the formation of the Farmers' Bank of Maryland (serving on the board of directors of its Easton branch) and was in regular attendance at the Annapolis Jockey Club, "and won and lost his money with as much equanimity as comported with a proper interest in the contests of the turf."[63] He also invested in coal-rich land in western Maryland. At the time of his death, he was probably the richest of the Lloyds of Wye.[64]

Renowned, respected, and resplendent as "the Governor" must have been, he is (ironically) best known today not because of his own actions, but because he employed a man who owned a slave. Not just any slave: Frederick Douglass, a man described by Theo. Lippman, Jr., *Sunpapers* editorial writer, as "the most influential man of any color in the English-speaking world, insofar as the slavery issue was concerned." Douglass was born into slavery on one of the Lloyd farms on the Tuckahoe Neck. His name was originally Frederick Augustus Washington Bailey, but he changed his surname to Douglass once he became a free man in Massachusetts. Lippman comments that "many great heroes are thrown up by mass movements. But Douglass was not merely a spokesman for a cause. He defined the cause."[65]

Douglass was sent to Wye as a child when the estate may well have been at its peak—under "the Governor," Edward V. This Lloyd, the son of the builders, did not create his environment, he was born into it and, one assumes, took it, a well-oiled luxurious machine, for granted. Lloyd must have viewed it all as natural, as the only way things could be. This was a point of view that Douglass, whom Lippman called the "personification of the hero in history," spent all his life trying to change.

Douglass's autobiography, *My Bondage and Freedom* (published in 1855), agrees with the picture of life suggested in the Lloyd Papers; his description of Wye and its setting closely resembles the Wye that has physically endured. Donnell Tilghman suggests that "the grandeur of the house and grounds and luxury of life there are greatly exaggerated by

63. Ibid., pp. 205, 206.
64. Ibid., p. 206.
65. Theo. Lippman, Jr., "Notes & Comments," in the *Sun*, February 14, 1980.

Douglass, for excellent political reasons," but he concedes that "the rest of the account is probably factual."

Douglass's thoughts on hearing that he would go to Wye are revealing:

It was, evidently, a great thing to go to Colonel Lloyd's; and I was not without a little curiosity to see the place; but no amount of coaxing could induce in me the wish to remain there. The fact is, such was my dread of leaving the little cabin, that I wished to remain little forever, for I knew the taller I grew the shorter my stay. The old cabin, with its rail floor and rail bedsteads upstairs, and its clay floor downstairs, and its dirt chimney, and windowless sides, and that most curious piece of workmanship of all the rest, the ladder stairway, and the hole curiously dug in front of the fireplace, beneath which grandmammy placed the sweetpotatoes to keep them from the frost, was my home.[66]

He comments on the self-sufficiency of Wye, a self-sufficiency that he argues was necessary if slavery was to be maintained:

Just such a secluded, dark, and out-of-the-way place, is the "home plantation" of Colonel Edward Lloyd, on the Eastern Shore, Maryland. It is far away from all the great thoroughfares, and is proximate to no town or village. There is neither schoolhouse, nor townhouse in its neighborhood. The schoolhouse is unnecessary, for there are no children to go to school. The children and grandchildren of Colonel Lloyd were taught in the house, by a private tutor—a Mr. Page—a tall, gaunt sapling of a man, who did not speak a dozen words to a slave in a whole year. The overseers' children go off somewhere to school; and they, therefore, bring no foreign or dangerous influence from abroad, to embarrass the natural operation of the slave sytem of the place. . . . Its blacksmiths, wheelwrights, shoemakers, weavers, and coopers, are slaves. Not even commerce, selfish and iron-hearted as it is, and ready, as it ever is, to side with the strong against the weak—the rich against the poor—is trusted or permitted within its secluded pre-cincts. . . . [I]t is a fact, that every leaf and grain of the produce of this plantation, and those of the neighboring farms belonging to Colonel Lloyd, are transported to Baltimore in Colonel Lloyd's own vessels; every man and boy on board of which—except the captain—are owned by him. In return, everything brought to the plantation, comes through the same channel. Nearly all the plantation or farms in the vicinity of the "home plantation" of Colonel Lloyd, belong to him; and those which do not, are owned by personal friends of his, as deeply interested in maintaining the slave system, in all its rigor, as Colonel Lloyd himself. Some of his neighbors are said to be even more stringent than he. The Skinners, the Peakers [Pacas?] the Tilghmans, the Lockermans, and the Gipsons, [Gibsons?] are in the same boat; being slaveholding neighbors, they may have strengthened each other in their iron rule. They are on intimate terms, and their interests and tastes are identical.[67]

Douglass is a fair enough reporter to note that, despite the iniquities of the system, Wye "is, nevertheless, altogether . . . a most strikingly interesting place, full of life, activity, and spirit." His recollection of the house seems, as noted, accurate:

[T]here stood the grandest building my eyes had then ever beheld, called, by every one on the plantation, the "Great House." This was occupied by Colonel Lloyd and his family. They occupied it; I enjoyed it. The great house was surrounded by numerous and variously shaped outbuildings. There were kitchens, wash-houses, dairies, summer-house, green-houses, hen-houses, turkey-houses, pigeon-houses, and arbors, of many sizes and devices, all neatly painted, and altogether interspersed with grand old trees, ornamental and primitive, which afforded delightful shade in summer, and imparted to the scene a high degree of stately beauty. The great house itself was a large, white, wooden building, with wings on three sides of it. [He must be calling the Palladian porch a wing.] In front [the Orangery and water side], a large portico, extending the entire length of the building, and supported by a long range of columns, gave to the whole establishment an air of solemn grandeur. . . . The carriage entrance [life then was water-based, so Douglass would have thought of the river side as the main facade] to the house was a large gate, more than a quarter of a mile distant from it; the intermediate space was a beautiful lawn, very neatly trimmed, and watched with the greatest care. It was dotted thickly with delightful trees, shrubbery, and flowers. The road, or lane, from the gate to the great house, was richly paved with white pebbles from the beach, and, in its course, formed a complete circle around the beautiful lawn. Carriages going in and retiring from the great house, made the

66. Frederick Douglass, *My Bondage and Freedom* (New York: Arno Press, 1968), p. 43.
67. Ibid., pp. 62, 63.

circuit of the lawn, and their passengers were permitted to behold a scene of almost Eden-like beauty. Outside this select inclosure, were parks, where—as about the residences of the English nobility—rabbits, deer, and other wild game, might be seen, peering and playing about, with none to molest them or make them afraid. The tops of the stately poplars were often covered with the red-winged blackbirds, making all nature vocal with the joyous life and beauty of their wild, warbling notes. These all belonged to me, as well as to Colonel Edward Lloyd, and for a time I greatly enjoyed them.[68]

Despite the cruelties of the slaves' day-to-day life, the overwork, the whippings, the constant threat of being "sold south," despite all that, there is never a word against the Lloyds. If anything, Douglass's writings praise them or, at least, place them so much above the sordid details of life as to absolve them. "Col. Lloyd was not in the way of knowing much of the real opinions and feelings of his slaves respecting him. The distance between him and them was far too great to admit of such knowledge." Douglass seems to realize—and this is where the saga of Douglass and the Lloyds acquires the makings of a true classic tragedy—the force of fate. It was Douglass's fate to be born where he was, as he was, just as it was the Lloyds' to be born as they were. Men—brilliant, and eloquent—were born to be adversaries because of circumstance. Had each not had his role cast before his birth. . . . This is made even more poignant by an 1881 *Baltimore American* account that reveals much about all concerned:

> A notable incident in the history of Wye House, one illustrative of the great social revolution that had been effected in the county, through the changed relations of the races, was the visit of Frederick Douglass in the year 1881, to the scenes of his youth. He was politely received by the sons [including the present owner's father] of Colonel Lloyd, he being absent, and invited to partake of the hospitalities of the house. He who left a slave of a poor man, came back a great nation's officer, to receive from the scions of a proud family the courtesies due an honored guest. He was deeply affected by all he saw, but more by the consideration and kindness that was shown him by the young men who were doing the honors in the absence of their father. He plucked flowers from the graves of the Lloyds that he had known but had passed away, as mementoes, and he drank with an effusion that marked its sincerity, the health of "the Master of the Old House" and of his children, with the wish that the horn of plenty might be poured out abundantly upon them, and that they and their descendants to remote generations might "worthily maintain the fame and the character of their ancestors."[69]

In 1834 Edward V was succeeded by Edward Lloyd VI, his eldest son, who, unlike his ancestors, had not received a scholarly education. His father, "the Governor," was convinced that agricultural training would yield greater benefits. By way of an apprenticeship, Edward Lloyd VI learned the intricacies of plantation management at Wye Heights (T–81). During the years that followed, he used this knowledge to handle problems resulting from industrialization, soil exhaustion, cyclical depressions, and population fluctuations. While many of his neighbors went bankrupt, Edward Lloyd VI prospered, becoming, according to Oswald Tilghman, "the greatest farmer in the state of Maryland."[70] This was true at least as far as his Talbot holdings went; his land acquisitions in Arkansas, Louisiana, and Mississippi would prove to be bad investments. Lloyd was too preoccupied with running his estates for much political activity, but in 1836 and 1840 he found time to serve as a presidential elector for Martin Van Buren, and he was elected to the Maryland Senate in 1850.

The last Edward Lloyd to own Wye, Edward VII, succeeded on his father's death in the ominous year of 1861. Edward VII suffered the effects of the Civil War and Emancipation—120 years ago his lost slaves were valued at $350,000[71]—effects felt not only at Wye, but also on the farms his father had purchased in the slave states of Mississippi, Arkansas, and Louisiana. While coping with this devastation, he nonetheless did his political duty and was a member of the Maryland Senate from 1874 to 1882 and from 1890 to 1894. He died in 1907.

Donnell Tilghman summarizes the dramatic twentieth-century history of Wye, a drama highly satisfactory in that, after no little suffering, there is a happy ending:

68. Ibid., pp. 64–68.
69. Quoted in Tilghman, *History*, vol. 1, p. 227; confirmed in conversation: Mrs. Morgan B. Schiller with Charity V. Davidson and Christopher Weeks, May 20, 1983.
70. Tilghman, *History*, vol. 1, p. 212.
71. Ibid., p. 225.

The once great fortune that had created and maintained Wye House through so many generations had, by the end of the last century, vanished. To the after effects of the Civil War and the abolition of slavery, factors which had ruined almost every southern fortune based on land, were added the very unwise stipulations of a will. The maker of the will had never imagined, much less foreseen, a day in which the owners of the great southern plantations would be called land poor, and had placed upon his sons and their heirs financial burdens that eventually ruined them. Edward Lloyd [VII] was faced with the necessity of selling Wye House. Fortunately, his second son, Charles Howard Lloyd together with his wife, Mary Donnell Lloyd, were able to buy in and save the family home.

Upon the deaths of both Charles Howard Lloyd and his wife, the place descended to their two daughters. Mrs. Morgan B. Schiller acquired the half interest of her sister, Mrs. Thomas Hughes, and . . . after having been closed for many years, the house is again open and modernized, a center, as it was through previous generations, of the life and activity of the county.[72]

Wye House: "a center . . . of the life and activity of the county."

72. Tilghman, "Wye House," pp. 108, 109.

CHAPTER 6

Talbot County and the New Republic

I t is always difficult to attempt to pin down any area's "golden era." Nevertheless, one could argue that Talbot County certainly glistened in the two-generation period encompassing the American Revolution and the War of 1812. One would, in fact, be hard-pressed to name any place of similar size and population that produced, in those politically hot fifty years, more notable and exciting people and events, or that contributed as much to the martial activities that dominated the age, the Federal period. Nor, as will be seen, does Talbot County's Federal-period architecture disappoint.

Revolutionary sentiment in Talbot County first climaxed on November 25, 1765, when a public meeting produced the following:

> The Freemen of Talbot County assembled at the Court House of said County do declare to the world:
>
> That they bear faith and true allegiance to His Majesty King George III.
>
> That they are most affectionately and zealously attached to his person and family; and are fully determined, to the utmost of their power, to maintain and support his crown and dignity . . . and do unanimously resolve:
>
> That under the Royal Charter granted to this Province, they and their ancestors have long enjoyed, and they think themselves entitled to enjoy, all the rights of British subjects.
>
> That they consider the trial by jury, and the privilege of being taxed only with their consent, given by their legal representatives in Assembly, as the principal foundation, and main source, of all their liberties.
>
> That by the Act of Parliament lately passed, for raising stamp duties in America, should it take place, both of these invaluable privileges enjoyed in their full extent, by their fellow subjects in Great Britain, would be torn from them; and that therefore the same is, in their opinion, unconstitutional, invasive of their just rights, and tending to excite disaffection in the breast of every American subject.
>
> That they will at the risk of their lives and fortunes endeavor, by all lawful ways and means, to preserve and transmit to their posterity their rights and liberties in as full and ample a manner as they received them from their ancestors; and will not by any act of theirs countenance or encourage the execution or effect of the same Stamp Act.
>
> That they will detest, abhor, and hold in utmost contempt, all and every person or persons who shall meanly accept of any employment or office relating to the Stamp Act; or shall take any shelter or advantage under the same; and all and every Stamp-pimp, informer or favorer of the said Act; and that they will have no communication with any such persons, except it be to upbraid them with their baseness.
> And in testimony of this their fixed and unalterable resolution they have this day erected a gibbet, twenty feet high, before the Court House door, and hung in chains thereon the effigy of a stamp informer, there to remain *in terrorem*, till the Stamp Act shall be replaced.[1]

In 1774, another group of men gathered in Talbot County and introduced another notable, and perhaps more revolutionary, document, the Talbot Resolves. This meeting

OPPOSITE:
What may be the first public school in Talbot County lies sheltered by the massive limbs of the Wye Oak.

1. Tilghman, *History*, vol. 2, pp. 53, 54.

Washington and his Generals: Tench Tilghman (right), Washington (left), and Lafayette (center).

was a reaction to the Boston Port Bill, England's response to the Boston Tea Party, and was the first such to be held in Maryland. The resolves put forth concern not for local interests, or even national interests, but for the "interests of mankind." The proceedings, taken from the *Maryland Gazette,* read as follows:

> Alarmed at the present situation of America and impressed with the most tender feelings for the distresses of their brethren and fellow subjects in Boston, a number of gentlemen having met at this place, took into their serious consideration the part they ought to act as friends of liberty and the general interests of mankind.
>
> To preserve the rights and to secure the property of the subject, they apprehend is the end of government. But when those rights are invaded—when the mode prescribed by the laws for the punishment of offences and obtaining justice is disregarded and spurned—when without being heard in their defence, force is employed in the severest penalties inflicted; the people, they clearly perceive, have a right not only to complain, but likewise to exert their utmost endeavors to prevent the effect of such measures as may be adopted by a weak and corrupt ministry to destroy their liberties, to deprive them of their property and rob them of the dearest birthright as Britons.
>
> Impressed with the warmest zeal for and loyalty to their most gracious sovereign, and with the most sincere affection for their fellow subjects in Great Britain, they have determined calmly and steadily to unite with their fellow subjects in pursuing every legal and constitutional measure to avert the evils threatened by the late act of Parliament for shutting up the port of Boston; to support the common rights of America, and to promote that union and harmony between the mother country and the colonies on which the preservation of both must finally depend.[2]

"Unfortunately," as Tilghman's *History of Talbot County* notes, "no record is preserved of the officers and active members of this meeting, which marks the beginning of the Revolution in a stricter sense,"[3] but it is believed that Matthew Tilghman may have been in the chair here as he was at many other such meetings (see pages 79–81). On June 22, 1774, Matthew Tilghman, Edward Lloyd IV, Nicholas Thomas, and Robert Goldsborough IV went to Annapolis to represent Talbot County in the standing committee of correspondence.

Once the Revolution actually began, Talbot had more than its share of heroes. Certainly the first among these equals must be Tench Tilghman, son of Matthew Tilghman's brother, James. Tench Tilghman was born on December 25, 1744, at Fausley (T–338), his maternal grandfather's plantation two miles from Easton. (The house no longer stands.) After receiving his education—probably in Easton—he joined his uncle, Tench Francis, Jr., in business pursuits in Philadelphia. When the Revolution came, he wrote, "Upon the breaking out of the troubles, I came to a determination to share the fate of my country, and that I might not be merely a spectator, I made as hasty a close as I possibly could, of my commercial affairs."[4]

Tench Tilghman was an aide-de-camp to General Washington and served beside him in every engagement from Rhode Island to Yorktown: he saw the disastrous battles of Long Island and White Plains; he took part in the retreat through New Jersey to Pennsylvania; he crossed the ice-clogged Delaware on Christmas Eve, 1776; he shared the glories at Trenton and Princeton as well as defeat at the Brandywine; and he suffered the horrible hardships of the winter at Valley Forge.[5] When Cornwallis surrendered at Yorktown on October 19, 1781, General Washington selected Colonel Tilghman to carry the official news to the Continental Congress in Philadelphia. "Sir," wrote General Washington to Thomas McKean, president of the Continental Congress, "Col. Tilghman, one of my aides-de-camp, will have the honor to deliver these dispatches to your excellency. He will be able to inform you of every minute circumstance which is not particularly mentioned in my letter. His merits, which are too well known to need my observations at this time, have gained my particular attention, and I could wish that they be honored by the notice of your excellency and congress."[6] In an exciting and hazardous passage in an open boat from Yorktown to Rock Hall in Kent County (via Annapolis) and finally a hundred-mile posthaste horseback ride from Rock Hall to Philadelphia, he carried the official document: Cornwallis's "Articles of Capitulation."

2. Ibid., pp. 60, 61.
3. Ibid., p. 61.
4. Ibid., vol. 1, p. 9.
5. Ibid., pp. 19, 20.
6. Ibid., pp. 23, 24.

On October 29, 1781, Congress gave Colonel Tilghman a vote of thanks for his service and awarded him a horse and an elegant sword. Two years later, on December 23, 1783, Colonel Tilghman was at General Washington's side when the latter surrendered his commission as commander in chief of the American armies of the United States.

After the war, Tilghman reentered the commercial world he had left in 1776. He was Washington's agent in Baltimore "for the transaction of almost every kind of business . . . even down to the china that adorned Mrs. Washington's tea-table."[7] He also formed a business partnership with Robert Morris II of Philadelphia, whose father lies buried at Whitemarsh cemetery. This was ended by Tilghman's death in 1786.

On hearing of Tilghman's death, Washington wrote Thomas Jefferson, "Col. Tilghman, who was formerly of my family, died lately, and left as fair a reputation as ever belonged to a human character. Thus some of the pillars of the revolution fall. May our country never want props to support the glorious fabric."[8]

Washington's letter of condolence to James Tilghman, Tench's father, deserves to be quoted at length:

> Of all the numerous acquaintances of your lately deceased son, and amidst all the sorrowings that are mingled on that melancholy occasion, I may venture to assert (that excepting those of his nearest relatives) none could have felt his death with more regret than I did, because no one entertained a higher opinion of his worth or had imbibed sentiments of greater friendship for him than I had done. That you, sir, should have felt the keenest anguish for this loss, I can readily conceive—the ties of parental affection, united with those of friendship could not fail to have produced this effect. It is however a dispensation, the wisdom of which is inscrutable; and amidst all your grief, there is this consolation to be drawn; that while living no man could be more esteemed, and since dead, none more lamented than Col. Tilghman.[9]

In 1783 Tench had married a first cousin, Anna Maria Tilghman, a daughter of Matthew Tilghman (1718–1790); in 1787 Matthew Tilghman bought Plimhimmon (T–162) and "after the death of her husband Mrs. [Tench] Tilghman returned to her father's house . . . but subsequently removed to her beautiful estate of Plimhimmon . . . Here she lived in great comfort and simple elegance."[10]

This is easy to imagine: inside and out the house has stylish details that bespeak a world beyond the Chesapeake. As, indeed, does the name: among the curiosities preserved in the Bodleian Library at Oxford is the 1360 Gough map of Britain. It shows the nation of Wales grossly out of shape and quite dominated by a central mountain called Plimelemon, from which most of the country's rivers radiate. This totally false idea of Welsh geography seems to have persisted for centuries afterwards and later writers often spoke of Plimelemon, Plinlimmon, Plynlimon (or in Welsh, Pumlumon) as the great mountain of Wales. What the British today call Plynlimon today ranks far down the list of Welsh mountains in order of height, but it must, however, always have had a romantic appeal to Welshmen and to Marylanders: note the names of two of the peak's rivers, the Wye and the Severn.

Miraculously, the original section of Talbot's Plimhimmon is in almost untouched condition. The old house is composed of a two-bay, two-story brick structure; there are also a five-bay, two-story frame wing and a three-bay, two-story kitchen. The frame wing was constructed in the 1870s by William Myers, grandfather of the present owner, to replace an earlier one-and-one-half-story wing.

The brick section is sited upon a man-made terrace. Inside, the old portion of the house has a hall-and-parlor plan. Its open-string stair is located in the north end of the hall and has a walnut balustrade with two balusters per step and turned newels with a continuous handrail. On the wall adjoining the wing is a large arched recess with fluted pilasters, paneled soffit, and keystone trim. Around the room is a chair rail, which is a half profile of the handrail and the same as the shadow-rail. A mantel around the fireplace is the focal point of the parlor. It has fluted pilasters supporting the shelf with a course of triglyphs, a course of fluting, and Wall-of-Troy molding. The windows are recessed from

Matthew Tilghman (1718–1790), the "Patriarch of Maryland," by John Hesselius.

Mrs. Matthew Tilghman, née Ann Lloyd (1723–1794), by John Hesselius. Mrs. Tilghman was a daughter of the "beautiful Ann Grundy" and the Honorable James Lloyd.

7. Ibid., p. 32.
8. Ibid., p. 38.
9. Ibid., p. 39. For a thorough and modern account of Tench Tilghman, see also Shreeve, *Tench Tilghman.*
10. Ibid., p. 41.

Samuel Hambleton, fourth-generation Talbot countian and veteran of the War of 1812.

the interior wall and their trim rests upon pilasters. There are recessed paneled jambs and a panel beneath the window with applied molding. A chair rail interrupts the pilasters. It is composed of a cap with a course of triglyphs beneath. Most of the woodwork in the room retains its original paint, including the grained door, black baseboards, and gray trim.

Matthew Tilghman, Tench's father-in-law, was a man of no little interest himself. He was the youngest son of Richard Tilghman of Queen Anne's County. At age 15 he went to live at Ward's Point (the house is now known as Rich Neck, T–211), the home of his much older first cousin Matthew Tilghman Ward. Tilghman was adopted by Mr. Ward and eventually secured a fortune from him. In 1741 he married Ann Lloyd, a granddaughter of Colonel Philemon Lloyd. He served as a justice of the peace for Talbot County, represented the county in the General Assembly from 1751 to 1757, and was speaker of the house in the 1770s. An ardent patriot who was widely regarded as the "Patriarch of Maryland," Tilghman missed signing the Declaration of Independence only because his dutes in Annapolis kept him from going to Philadelphia. He did, however, serve as president of the provincial convention in 1776, where he was chairman of the committee that drafted the constitution of Maryland, "and to him, therefore, in some good measure Maryland was indebted for that admirable code of fundamental laws which gave . . . healthful vigor to its functional operations."[11] It would be hard to overstate Matthew Tilghman's importance to Maryland's history. Yet, as Oswald Tilghman has written, the Patriarch of Maryland's "name is hardly known beyond the limits of the county of his home."[12]

Talbot County and its citizens also figured prominently in what is often referred to as the second war for independence. Following the declaration of war in 1812, Congress, on June 26, 1812, formally authorized the issuance of letters of marque and reprisal. When this second war with England threatened, many men who had taken an active naval role in the Revolution were still young enough to man privateers again. In the 1812 period Baltimore built half of all the Chesapeake privateers, but St. Michaels built one quarter of them. Prior to 1812, an even larger percentage had come from the Eastern Shore.[13]

The Chesapeake-built privateers formed a force that, according to William M. Marine in his book, *The British Invasion of Maryland, 1812–1815,*

> was the most powerful agent for peace [as] is shown by dispatches in the English press of which the following is a specimen: "At a meeting of shipowners, merchants, manufacturers, and underwriters of the city of Glasgow—held September 8, 1814, it was unanimously resolved: 'that the number of American privateers with which our channels have been infested, the audacity with which they approached our coasts, and the success with which their enterprise has been attended, have proved injurious to our commerce humbling our pride and discreditable to the direction of the naval power of the British nation, whose flag till of late waved over every sea and triumphed over every rival.'"[14]

Not surprisingly, the British found it necessary to strike at the Chesapeake base of these privateers. They ordered Admiral Sir George Cockburn "to destroy and lay waste such towns and districts on the coasts as might be assailable." He carried out his orders well, and many Maryland farmers and merchants were reduced to poverty: he devastated Calvert County; he burned Havre de Grace; in the summer of 1813, he held Kent Island with a force of 2,000 men and looked towards St. Michaels. He attacked that Talbot village twice, first on August 9, then again on August 26.[15]

One of Talbot's many citizens to gain immortality during the War of 1812, Samuel Hambleton, was born March 29, 1777, the fourth generation of the family to whom Cecil, Lord Baltimore, had granted Martingham in 1659 (see chapter 1). Hambleton was appointed a purser in the Navy at the age of twenty-nine. In 1812, he was ordered to Newport under Oliver Hazard Perry; he accompanied Perry to Lake Erie in 1813 to complete the building and equipping of the American fleet intended to protect our northern frontier from a Canada-based invasion. After the battle of Lake Erie, which popularized the slogan "Don't give up the ship," medals were struck with the likeness of Commodore Perry on one side, and, on the reverse, a squadron of vessels closely spaced.

11. Ibid., p. 428.
12. Ibid., p. 430.
13. "History of Talbot County."
14. William M. Marine, *The British Invasion of Maryland, 1812–1815* (Baltimore: Society of the War of 1812, 1913), pp. 100–27.
15. Tilghman, *History*, vol. 2, pp. 148, 149.

Each commissioned officer received one and Purser Hambleton's silver medal is one of the most valued treasures of the Talbot County Historical Society. Samuel Hambleton eventually retired to Perry Cabin (T–206), named for his beloved friend and commander. He died there in 1851, and was buried at Martingham.

During this era Talbot County also experienced significant developments in architecture. While American buildings of the 1780–1810 period are generally referred to by the patriotic adjective *Federal*, they nevertheless display certain European influences. In England, late eighteenth-century building was dominated by works of the brothers Adam, who lent their surname to a style. Based on archaeological findings from such places as Pompeii, the Adams' style is characterized by attenuated proportions and delicacy of form, terms that are also used to describe American Federal structures. Not every Talbot countian possessed a fortune large enough to build a great Federal structure, but many, many were financially able to be up-to-date in inexpensive ways, and, generally speaking, it is in interior trim—such as thin delicate mantels—that we see most of Talbot County's experience with Federal-period design.

Talbot's Federal architecture began with complex and great seats like Hope; it was then used by prosperous farmers and merchants who used Federal dicta in details of their houses. Finally, Federal precepts, like those of the Georgian period (see chapter 3), became thoroughly absorbed into Talbot's architectural psyche and appeared in the vernacular urban and rural dwellings that housed most of the county's population.

One of the finest—certainly one of the most interesting—Federal-period houses in Talbot County is Hope (T–90), a sprawling, highly rhythmic, seven-part mansion located on Woodland Creek south of Wye House. A 100-acre tract called Hope was granted in 1665 to Henry Hawkins, a relative of the first Edward Lloyd. It was purchased in 1720 by James Lloyd, younger brother of Edward Lloyd II and a man in a position to put together a considerable estate. Lloyd bought a number of adjacent tracts, including Hope, Pickbourne, Talley Farm, Elliott's Discovery, The Adjunction, Scotland, and Lloyd's Discovery.

Robert, the eldest son of James Lloyd and his wife, a lady known for over two hundred years as "the beautiful Ann Grundy," inherited the farm on the death of his father in 1723. This Robert Lloyd married Anna Maria Tilghman Hemsley, widow of the great tobacco merchant William Hemsley, and lived at the Hemsley home—Cloverfields—on the Wye River in Queen Anne's County. Robert Lloyd devised Hope to his elder daughter, Deborah. When she inherited Hope, she was married to Peregrine Tilghman (d.1808), a

Portrait by Johns Hesselius of "the beautiful Ann Grundy" (1690–1732). She was the daughter of the Honorable Robert Grundy (d. 1720) of Talbot County, the wife of the Honorable James Lloyd (1680–1723), and the first mistress of Hope, where she is buried. Her daughters were Margaret Tilghman (b. 1714), the first mistress of Gross' Coate; Deborah, who married Jeremiah Nichols, rector of St. Michael's Parish; Henrietta Maria Chamberlaine, the first mistress of Plaindealing; and Ann, who married the Honorable Matthew Tilghman of Rich Neck.

Plimhimmon.

Hope underwent considerable alteration in the late nineteenth century before it was saved in 1907 by William J. Starr.

Hope: hall and stair, photographed in 1935 by Robert W. Tebbs for the Historic American Buildings Survey.

son of Richard Tilghman of The Hermitage in Queen Anne's County.[16] It is thought that
Peregrine and Deborah Tilghman were already living on the Hope property at the time of
Robert Lloyd's death, and some sources suggest that the Peregrine Tilghmans built the
large central section of the present-day mansion. (They could certainly have afforded it;
see page 67.) The local tradition that gives a 1740 date to the house can be dismissed, for
there is nothing in the tax assessments of 1783 or 1798 to substantiate such a date. In 1804
the Tilghmans had Hope, Pickbourne, Scotland, and other tracts resurveyed and unified
into one large farm they called Hope. It is likely that the house was erected either shortly
after the 1804 resurvey, or in 1810 when Deborah Lloyd Tilghman died and devised Hope
to her son Robert Lloyd Tilghman (1778–1823). Robert Lloyd Tilghman devised Hope to
his wife, the former Henrietta Maria Forman. The property was finally sold out of the
family in 1863.

Hope's original configuration consisted of the present central section (but with a roof
not quite so high) with two one-and-one-half-story frame wings connected by ogee-roofed
hyphens, a truly dramatic composition. The house is similar in design to Mt. Clare in
Baltimore, home of Margaretta Tilghman Carroll, widow of Charles Carroll, Barrister, and
a cousin of Robert and Henrietta Maria Tilghman.

The north facade of the main block of the house is three bays long and almost as deep.
It is two-and-one-half stories high with a replacement classical Doric porch. The entrance
has a wide single door that gives the appearance of being double and is flanked by fluted
pilasters and sidelights, with a wide, elliptical fanlight over all. Both sidelights and
fanlights have designs typical of great Federal buildings. Above the entrance is a three-part
window, the large central window of which has a semi-elliptical arch. In the apex of the
pavilion is an elliptical window. All of the above mentioned openings have rubbed-and-
gauged-brick arches and Flemish-bond brickwork with exceptionally narrow convex
mortar joints. The windows, which have nine-over-six sashes on both stories, have stone

Another view of nineteenth-century
Hope.

16. Chamberlaine, *Chamberlaine*, pp. 25–27.
Thanks are heartily given to John Frazer, Jr.,
for his inestimible help in explaining Talbot's
genealogical complexities.

The Wilderness.

sills and louvered shutters. As in most houses of the period, the walls lack water table and beltcourse: these horizontal features would detract from the desired sense of height.

In the main block the stair ascends in the east end of the entrance hall, which is somewhat unusual in that it runs across the front of the main block, not through the center; in this, Hope resembles Kennersley, a slightly earlier house in Queen Anne's County. The bottom of the balustrade begins in a volute and has a mahogany handrail and two balusters per step. There are fretwork step spandrels. Along the stair wall is a recessed, paneled dado that is a continuation of the dado around the entire room. The two doors opposite the entrance open into the parlors; with the exception of the mantels, both parlors are identical. They have recessed paneled dado, doors and jambs, a jib door to the porch and overdoors like the ones in the hall.

The house was subsequently mutilated by the construction of a large, rectangular, flat-roofed brick addition at the west end, and by the end of the nineteenth century had deteriorated, but it was restored and remodeled by William T. Starr in 1907, using old photographs for inspiration. The best craftsmen of the area were employed to execute the restoration of the brickwork and interior and to erect brick wings and two-story hyphens that retain the ogee roofline. A new porch was added to each front and extensive landscaping—walls, allees, and formal gardens—was carried out in true Edwardian exuberance.

The Federal move toward delicacy noted in Hope's details can also be seen at The Wilderness (T–149), a house perched on a bluff with views "unrivaled for beauty in this country."[17] Daniel Martin, son of Nicholas Martin, began the building of the larger portion of the house in 1815. The wing of the house dates to circa 1785.[18] Daniel Martin was a man of some thoroughness: "In the construction of this house care was taken that haste should not affect the solidity nor mar the finish. . . . It is said that the floors were allowed to season a year before the house was occupied."[19] The house seems somehow taller and slenderer than earlier two-and-one-half-story structures. This effect was doubtless intended and is furthered by the tall chimneys that lead the viewer's eye skyward. The builders of the addition were as sophisticated and urbane as their pocketbooks would allow: they etched fine reeding in the windows' jack arches; they gave the building a side-

17. Earle, *Bay Country*, p. 372.
18. Papenfuse et al., *New Guide*, p. 136.
19. Earle, *Bay Country*, p. 372.

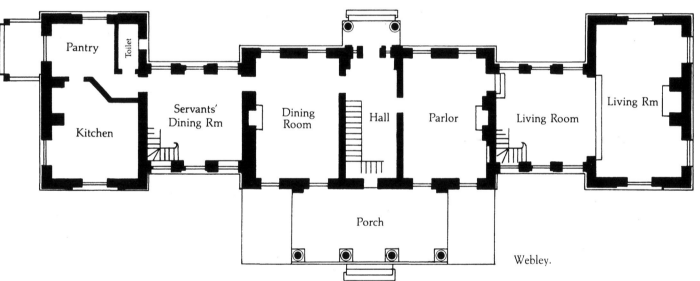

Webley.

hall–double-parlor plan (a plan probably more common to town than to country houses); and they separated the parlors with a graceful arched opening complete with pilasters and keystone. Other interior refinements include a finely reeded chair rail and a weavelike design on the step ends. The Wilderness marks Martin as a man of the world. This is borne out in his life: he was twice elected governor, first in 1828, then again in 1830. He died in office July 11, 1831.

Love's Folly (T–185), circa 1800, on Oak Creek near the hamlet of Royal Oak, is another important Federal house. The original part of the dwelling has a side entrance with a transom over the door. First- and second-floor windows and doors have rusticated stone lintels with keystones and may anticipate Hope in this refinement. The south facade's exterior walls are laid in Flemish bond with glazed headers—a further decorative touch. The interior of the old section is composed of a stair hall and living room. The open-string stair retains all original work including delicate turned newels, two fine balusters per step, and a good, shaped handrail typical of the early Federal dwellings. It also retains original recessed panel doors, window jambs, and three-part trim.

Easton grew up around its courthouse, seen here circa 1895 with William Elston Shannahan's horse and carriage. Photo by William Barnwell Shannahan.

Webley (T–214), also known as Mary's Delight, is located at the end of a long lane on a rise of ground overlooking the Bay. The house is a five-part structure built in two periods. Its central block is a substantial circa-1805 Federal mansion, built by the noted scholar and jurist John Kersey. Webley's central entrance has a transom flanked by two small narrow windows, similar in composition to Bloomingdale in Queen Anne's County. Most of the interior woodwork in the center-hall house is original and well-preserved. The stair has a delicate walnut balustrade, turned newels, two balusters per step, and a shadow rail above paneled wainscoting. Its spandrel is plain, but the ends of the steps have fine fretwork scrolls. Before the facades were painted, Webley enjoyed a contrast between stone window arches and brick walls, a lively refinement that few other country houses in Talbot County could claim, but that would have been appreciated by Federal-period builders with their love of decoration. Webley's history is not uneventful. It was purchased by one of the Kersey's sons-in-law, Dr. Absalom Thompson, in 1826, and four years later he converted the dwelling into the first hospital on the Eastern shore.[20] Thompson was a famous surgeon, and contemporaries describe him "riding bareback and barefoot on a mule on his way to visit patients, carrying a jar of calomel, a lancet, and a syringe with a nozzle as big as a gun barrel."[21] One must allow for some poetic license regarding the syringe, but Dr. Thompson's "reputation was more than state-wide. Almost as famous as a surgeon was his profanity."[22] Thompson had a flair with Christian names, too; his son was christened Absalom Christopher Columbus Americus Vespucius Thompson. In 1924 Mrs. Harold Walker of Washington, D.C., bought Webley; she built the hyphens and wings according to designs by Arthur Blakeslee, AIA.

Good workmanship is by no means exclusive to large houses and wealthy owners. Jena (T–163), for example, is among the most charming of Talbot County's buildings. Situated on an inlet of Goldsborough Creek near Oxford, the house is a three-part building composed of a tall, one-and-one-half-story brick section with later wings on the northeast. The old part of the house is similar in form to Bullen's Chance (T–150) only a few miles south. It has the same three-bay facade consisting of a side door and two windows. These windows have a nine-over-six sash on the first story and a six-over-nine sash on the second. Its main facade is laid in Flemish bond; the gable end is laid in common bond.

The principal facade's windows retain most of their original surrounds: a thinnish outside fascia bounded by a quarter-round bead, a fillet, a wider fascia and a small bead outlining the opening itself. Their sills consist of a projecting torus molding atop two small fillets and a fascia. The replacement door is surmounted by a four-light transom with a thick bead characterizing the entire wooden surround. A boxed cornice with complex crown moldings extends across the length of the facade, as does a brick water table.

The main block has a side-hall–double-parlor plan. The stairhall is entered through the east, main doorway, which is a six-panel door with a brass box lock. The door surround is of interest because of its involved series of moldings: fascia, cyma, recessed fascia, raised fascia, recessed fascia, cyma, fascia, and finally an inner bead abutting the door jamb. On the north side of the hallway, immediately preceding the stair, is the doorway to a nineteenth-century addition; here the surround is the same as described in the hall and the reveal is about eighteen inches deep. The baseboard of the north wall of the hallway continues up the stairway and is beaded. The handsome stair appears to be a replacement.

Typically, just as one of Jena's original facades is obscured by an addition, so, too, has a complicated history of ownership obscured the exact date of the house. The 1798 federal direct tax lists a house of almost the same dimensions on this site; the editors of *Maryland: A New Guide to the Old Line State* simply say that Jena is "a small one-and-one-half-story yellow brick house built after 1700." The *Guide* adds, however, that the property was named Jena by Jacob Gibson, "a well-known Talbot County eccentric, who named his various estates in the county after victories won by Bonaparte; others were Marengo, Austerlitz, and Friedland."[23] Another source says, however, that Gibson never owned

20. Early legal documents refer to houses on the tract; a 1735 estate report refers to "one large dwelling with several rooms," and a 1734 appraisal mentions "one dwelling house with two large rooms 40 feet long and 15 feet wide." The dimensions do not coincide with the present building. Kersey had his land re-surveyed in 1805 and probably built Webley at that time.
21. Papenfuse et al., *New Guide*, p. 167.
22. Sara Seth Clark and Raymond B. Clark, Jr. "Webley, or Mary's Delight, Bay Hundred, Talbot County," in *Maryland Historical Magazine*, vol. 49, no. 1 (1954):51.
23. Papenfuse et al., *New Guide*, p. 169.

Jena, that instead, Gibson's friend, Perry Spencer, owned it and merely followed his friends' Napoleonic naming system.[24]

Jamaica Point (T–63) is one of the finest representatives of the late Federal style in Talbot County. William R. Hughlett (1816–1885) built the house in 1838, one year prior to his marriage to Lydia Ann Carter. (A brick beside one door has "WRH 1838" scratched into it.) Hughlett was a prosperous shipyard owner and was a director of the Easton National Bank from 1847 to 1875. He was also in the lumber business and farmed a portion of the lands that his father had amassed. His wealth is clearly evident at his house. It is a two-part brick structure composed of a three-bay, two-and-one-half-story part with a four-bay, two-story wing. The principal portion of the house is raised above a cellar. Two sides of the building are laid in Flemish bond (northwest and northeast) and the jack arches above the windows splay widely. The two chimneys within the gable are joined above the roof with a curtain wall, giving the impression of great mass. Jamaica Point's two-story wing is composed in an arrangement often seen in vernacular structures; there is a door (flanked by two windows) opening to the middle room, and another door (and window) opening into the kitchen.

The word "urbane" is sometimes used to describe Talbot's Federal-period houses, just as it has been suggested that the side-hall double-parlor or "townhouse" plan seems somewhat unusual in the countryside. All this is by way of introducing the theme that during the Federal period, for the first time, Talbot County's architecture in town matched the level of its architecture in the country.

Inns and hotels were important in Easton's early days; the Brick Hotel, seen here circa 1895, was completed in 1812.

24. Forman, *Manor Houses*, p. 117.

In this period Easton came into its own. At the time Easton was founded, the town was not on navigable water; and it is particularly curious that the county seat of this water-oriented county was inland. (Today the extended town boundaries include access to the water at Easton Point.) The Talbot County court records and the transcripts of debates of the provincial assembly in the early 1700s discuss the location of the courthouse at Pitts Bridge, the site of present-day Easton, so the town's cause for being was law, not trade. Easton grew up around its courthouse. These early records and debates show that when the colonists of the 1700s established the courthouse, they were interested primarily in locating it at a point central to all sections of the county. The possibility that a large town might grow up around the courthouse seems not to have entered their minds. This would have been fully in keeping with the prevailing custom in the colonial south; even today in these areas, many courthouses are located, without a town, alone in the countryside.

Easton's early history was also closely associated with its taverns. When the village came into existence, first as Talbot Courthouse, there may have been a few scattered houses in the vicinity, but there was no town, no accommodations for the judges, court officials, jurists, and others on court business. That there were at least two or more taverns by 1722 is evident by a judicial ruling of June 5; "Order: that the Publick Houses at the Courthouse in this County are hindered from keeping their nine pins in the streets during the sitting of this court." The early Talbot taverns—the Golden Plough, the Indian Queen, the Sign of the Seven Stars, Willie Weaver's Tavern, and others—doubtless were counterparts of the English inns where male guests slept in dormitorylike quarters, often two or three to a bed.[25]

This worked for a while, but by around 1810 Easton had become the largest town on the Eastern Shore. Moreover, the state legislature had made the city the semi-official capital of the Shore in 1788[26] and the federal judiciary act, which designated communities in which the district court should sit, divided Maryland so that the courts should be held alternately between Baltimore and Easton. "The first was held in Baltimore on April 17, 1790, with William Paca presiding. The second session was held in Easton, and so delighted the community that it set about building a new and larger court. Completed in 1794, portions of the structure survive in the present building."[27] Clearly this growing town needed a real hotel with individual rooms and the amenities one would associate with a place of such distinction. Samuel Groome, with funds and vision, chose the important corner of Washington and Federal streets and built an imposing three-story brick building. Completed in 1812, the Brick Hotel (T–26) instantly became the Eastern Shore's leading hostelry and helped promote Easton's progress through much of the nineteenth century. It still stands today, no longer as a hotel, but as housing for professional offices.

With towns come tradesmen. For example, when Philemon Hemsley of Queen Anne's County was awarded the contract to build the courthouse in 1710, he promptly set up a forge and anvil east of the construction site, and by early 1711 rods and nails were being produced for the courthouse. Hemsley found much other work in repairing wagons, and his blacksmith shop continued for many years: manufactured tools were not available and the ironworker's shop made everything. During periods when work was slow, tools for farming and shipbuilding, tongs for oystering, and wood cutting tools were hammered out and set aside for the trade that grew in front of the courthouse.[28] As Philemon Hemsley added other items to those he made, shopkeeping eventually became his main endeavor, and so what is believed to have been the oldest hardware store—later known as Shannahan-Wrightson Hardware Company—in the United States came into being.

The Bruff family's history is another example of the growth of Easton's commerce. Thomas Bruff came to Talbot in 1668. The son of a London silversmith, he practiced his father's trade, as did two of his grandsons, Thomas and James Earle, and one of his great grandsons, Richard. Joseph Bruff (1730–1784) bought a lot in town in 1775, and, during the Revolution, worked as an armorer. The Maryland archives show that on June 12, 1777, the council of safety of Maryland directed him to deliver all the public arms that were

25. George O. Garey, *History of Easton*, reprint of original 1881 edition (Easton: Historic Easton, 1974); see also Tilghman, *History*, vol. 2, pp. 221–45.
26. Harrington, "Good Life," p. 146.
27. Ibid.
28. Tilghman, *History*, vol. 2, pp. 222–24.

repaired and in his possession to the proper officials. The following year he was made collector of clothing for the army in Talbot County.

Silversmiths were apparently in great demand, for in 1807 William Needles (Needels) used the *Republican Star* to "beg leave to inform his fellow citizens, that he has opened a Silversmith's Shop in Easton near the Market House." This must be the same Needles who, as Bowdle and Needles, had occupied the shop cited in the 1798 federal direct tax. Needles was a member of a prominent Talbot Quaker family; his punch, "W. Needles," appears on many pieces of silver still in the county.

There were other Talbot silversmiths: James Bowdle, Jonathan Benny, James Berry, Edward Corner, William Skinner, Benjamin Willmott, and James Troth. Most of these craftsmen have left no identifiable silver. Few of them had distinct marks, and the use of initials as marks leads to frustration among collectors because three of them had the same initials, J. B.[29]

These early artisans wore many hats and wore them well. For example, Bruff, Benny, Willmott, and Troth augmented their silversmithing by clock-making. John Needles surveyed and laid out the town of Easton in 1785. Colonel Jeremiah Banning named the streets. The issue of early Easton (laying the town out, naming the streets, etc.) has been often dealt with, but the 1947 article "How Easton's Streets Were Named" in the *Star Democrat* remains a classic:

> With such a patriotic man as Banning having to do with the layout of Easton, it is little wonder that the main street was named after the Father of His Country. Goldsborough Street was named in honor of the family of that name so prominent in the history and development of Talbot. Dover Street was so named because it was the highway which led to the then important town of that name on the Choptank near the ferry across that river. Hanson Street was named after John Hanson, the Revolutionary patriot, at that time president of the Continental Congress. South Street was named because, at that time, it was the southern boundary of the town; the inspirations for the names of West and North Streets can probably be deduced. Harrison Street was named in honor of the prominent family of that name. August Street, it is believed, originally ran to Washington Street in front of the Courthouse, but the origin of the name or the reason for so naming this street is in doubt, though in the early days it was a street of great importance. The only remains of this street from Harrison to Washington is the alley between the old market house and Shannahan & Wrightson's building, . . . known as Magazine Alley.[30]

These were the only streets the new town had; the additions came after Banning's death.

With towns come tradesmen: Washington Street, as photographed in the 1930s for the Historic American Buildings Survey; the Shannahan and Wrightson building is at the extreme left.

29. J. Hall Pleasants and Howard Sill, *Maryland Silversmiths, 1715–1830* (Baltimore: Lord Baltimore Press, 1930), pp. 106–13.
30. "How Easton's Streets were Named," in *Easton Star-Democrat*, October 17, 1947.

Some of Easton's superb Federal row-houses on Washington Street.

For a hundred years Easton would be the richest, largest, most important, and most progessive town on the Eastern Shore. It was the home of the Shore's first newspaper (1790), first bank (1805), and first steamboat line (1817). All this sophistication is reflected in the town's Federal-period architectural boom: the area around the courthouse was quickly developed, and the buildings hastily erected after 1794 still make up the core of Easton's business section.

The Dyer Antiques Gallery building (T–35) is an example of a rowhouse form commonly constructed in Easton: it is two-and-one-half stories high with a gable roof and broad end chimneys and has dormers to light the upper floor. Three bays wide, the structure has a side-hall plan and Flemish-bond facade. One of a group of numerous surviving Federal buildings, it has had many alterations, but the delicate woodwork of the third floor and the gouge work of the cornice attest to its former elegance.

The probable builder, Lambert Hopkins, purchased this property in 1785. In the federal tax assessment of 1798 he is listed as owning and living in a house that may be this one. It remained a dwelling at least until 1818, when his daughter, Elizabeth Vickers, lived there. Little else is known, either of Hopkins or of the use of the building, until the late nineteenth century. At that time it became a drug store, which it remained until 1969 when it was remodeled into offices and the present front was added.

The barrel-vaulted walkway, now enclosed, running between the gallery and 8 North Washington Street (T–36) indicates that the two structures are contemporaries. A typical Federal building, 8 North Washington Street is three bays wide and has a Flemish-bond brick facade. It was probably constructed between 1791 and 1798 by a William Mebuy, who held a lease on the property during that period. When he sold the lease to Bennett Wheeler in 1798, a brick building was standing at this location; Wheeler occupied it and may have kept a store in the first floor. Its use for many years after has not been discovered, but by the turn of this century it housed a drug store, as did its neighbor, 6 North Washington Street; it is now connected to 10 North Washington Street, a similar structure.

Up the street, at 24 North Washington Street (T–38), is a tall and well-proportioned structure that adds to the interest of the Washington Street commercial district. Built before 1805, it is one of Easton's earliest structures and survives as an example of a Federal-period building erected to serve a large mercantile business. Three-and-one-half stories in height, it has Flemish-bond brick on the front facade and keystone window arches of tan sandstone that suggest those at Webley in the country and at the Neall House in town (see below). The builder was probably Owen Kennard, a prominent figure in early Easton and the owner of several lots along Washington Street and a house that stood at the site of the present Maryland National Bank building.[31] Alterations, including the mansard roof that now covers the building, are interesting and well scaled.

Several other buildings in town date to the Federal period. Their elegant details suggest the prosperity of their owners and the skill of their craftsmen. Number 107 North Washington Street (T–21) is notable for the Federal detailing—fluted pilasters and Adamesque sunbursts—on its single dormer; 111 North Washington Street (T–22) has elegant double keystone arches above its window openings.

Number 115 North Washington Street (T–23) is particularly fine: it is a four-bay brick building, two-and-one-half stories high and covered with a gable roof with two dormers in each slope; two double chimneys at the south gable end have corbelled caps and are connected by a brick curtain; the curtains rise above the gable-end bearing walls and visually separate the building from its neighbors. The Flemish-bond brick of the front facade was laid with great care: the narrow mortar joints are toled into a bead. The bricks themselves are deep red in color and perfectly formed. The ground floor has been altered, but the second and third floors are still intact and are graced by two Federal mantels in the formal second-floor rooms: each has a rectangular opening flanked by reeded pilasters and a frieze decorated with shallow carving in a star-and-chain motif. Door frames are trimmed with narrow composite moldings. Three-part chair rails are used in major rooms. No mantels on the third floor remain, but other detailing—chair rails, doors, and trim—does. The deep barrel vaults of the dormers fronting on Washington Street are copied in several other Federal buildings of the town.

Federal buildings abound south of the courthouse square. One of the finest is 109 South Washington Street (T–10). Its Flemish-bond facade is enriched with double-keystone lintels at window openings that resemble those seen at 111 North Washington Street. The main entrance is outstanding: fluted pilasters carry an entablature decorated with Adamesque pineapples and sunbursts. The transom light has diamond panes, a detail also used on the building's exquisite interior woodwork. The well-proportioned two-and-one-half-story structure shows influence of both the Federal and Georgian periods, and may be considered a transitional building.

The nearby Askins House (T–9) is one of the many early brick row buildings constructed along Washington Street in Easton's first boom period. Like its contemporaries, it has a fine Flemish-bond brick facade and tall end chimneys. The structure is two-and-one-half-stories tall and four bays wide. Some of its interior woodwork is intact—particularly on the ground floor—and is representative of the period.

Superb brick work can also be seen at the Hughlett-Henry House (T–17), 10 South Street. Although damaged by time and inadequate repairs, the main facade is exceptional. The perfectly formed bricks laid in Flemish bond, the fine mortar joints, the molded-brick cornice all attest to the skill of the brick makers and masons.

Foxley Hall (T–30) at 24 North Aurora Street, is an impressive free-standing Federal house. Once called Burnside, Foxley Hall is, at least, Federal on the outside; Dr. Samuel Harrison and his son-in-law, local historian Oswald Tilghman, created the gloriously extravagant late Victorian interior circa 1889 with the help of architect Thomas Buckler Ghequir.

The Talbot County Historical Society is developing a complex of Federal structures as headquarters, museum, residence of the curator, and garden. The grandest of these, 29

29 South Washington Street, built by the Neall family and now a house museum of the Talbot County Historical Society.

31. Talbot County Land Records, Hall of Records, Annapolis.

South Washington Street, is an extraordinary period house built by James and Rachel Cox Neall between 1804 and 1810. The Neall brothers, Joseph and James, were Quakers and cabinetmakers, and James's elaborate house is carefully constructed. By 1798 Joseph Neall had built Joseph's Cottage (T–33) at 20 West Street, to be used as his shop and residence. That one-and-one-half-story frame building has two rooms per floor and a central entrance. Walls and ceiling are covered with boards inside; there is an enclosed corner stair. The steeply pitched roof is complemented by the large brick exterior chimney.

The three-story, brick Neall House is a superb interpretation of Federal design principles. Just as correct, the Bullitt House (T–12) at 108 Dover Street was built in 1801. To the west of the house is a steeply roofed frame wing reputedly built by Bullitt for use as a law office. Designed as a free-standing building, the old office—three bays long and one-and-one-half stories high—is now connected to the main house by a one-story brick hyphen and displays the same touches of elegance, such as the beaded and decorated window frames, as the main house sports. Further, the office's box cornice has crown-and-bed moldings, and its wide random-width siding is beveled, a detail also seen on the central portion on 108 South Harrison Street (T–472). Inside and outside, the Bullitt House is carefully detailed. Ornamental motifs are sophisticated and restrained; the workmanship of brick mason and wood-carver make it one of Maryland's outstanding period pieces. The house stayed in the Bullitt-Hayward-Chamberlaine family continuously from 1801 until the Great Depression of the 1930s.

North of the courthouse square at 119 North Washington Street is the Perrin Smith House (T–24). Its significance can hardly be overemphasized: along with the Bullitt and Neall houses, it is the most elaborate of Easton's Federal period dwellings and is also among the best preserved. In every aspect, it displays supreme attention to fine craftsmanship and delicacy of detailing, and it is generous in its use of ornamental mantels and of cornice, door, and window trim. If the Neall and Bullitt houses are examples of fine freestanding townhouses, the Perrin Smith House is their companion row house. The building has played an equally illustrious part in the social and political life of the town. Although he did not build the structure, Perrin Smith, founder of the *Republican Star*, Easton's oldest newspaper (now the *Star-Democrat)*, purchased the property in 1801 and used it as his office and residence for many years. The structure was purchased by The Chesapeake Bay Yacht Club in 1911.

Smith's *Republican Star*, or the *Eastern Shore Political Luminary*, was established in 1799 to compete with the *Maryland Herald*, one of the few newspapers on the Shore at that time. The *Star-Democrat* is the third oldest paper in Maryland and one of the oldest in the United States: when Thomas Perrin Smith founded the *Star*, his idol, Thomas Jefferson, was running for the presidency.

The *Star* became widely known all over the state. As events were leading up to the War of 1812, the *Star*, in defiance of the British-claimed right to seize and search American ships on the high seas, issued a call: "To the citizens: Your independence, the legacy of the heroes of '76, has been attacked by a band of sea robbers and pirates. You are now called upon to assemble around the standards of your country and adopt measures that will convince the cowardly assassins that we are descendants of those heroes who once drove them from our country, that we are willing and ready to do it again or perish with our constitution."[32] Both the Republicans and the Federalists of the Shore were united against Great Britain, and it cannot be doubted that when the War of 1812 finally broke out, part of the intensely patriotic sentiment of the Shore toward the government can be attributed to the *Star*. When the enemy threatened St. Michaels in 1813, it is said that editor Smith shouldered his musket, left his presses, and served as a private; the *Star* appeared on Tuesdays as usual.

The mention of St. Michaels is a reminder that not all of Talbot's Federal townhouses are in Easton, however, rich as that city is in period architecture. Down the Miles River, St. Michaels was enjoying its own boom. Probably the best-known house in St. Michaels is

32. Clippings in Talbot County Historical Society, Easton.

The elegant Cannonball House in St. Michaels.

the so-called "Cannonball House" (T–61). Similar in appearance to the Bullitt House, the Cannonball House ranks as one of Talbot's, indeed, one of Maryland's, most elegant Federal townhouses, comparable to the few structures of that period in Baltimore or Georgetown. The house, constructed in the first decade of the nineteenth century by William Merchant, is an imposing brick town residence that dominates its corner location and the surrounding neighborhood. Its fully articulated Federal style reflects St. Michaels's status as a thriving port and shipbuilding center in the early nineteenth century.

Much attention was given to the house's architectural detail; both the north entrance facade and the west gable end, which face the street, have been executed in Flemish bond characterized by extremely thin and delicate mortar joints and finely laid splayed arches over each window. The arched sash of the dormers on the north facade is particularly noteworthy, distinguished as it is by carefully scaled pilasters supporting complex molded architraves. On the interior of the side-hall double-parlor house, the woodwork is almost entirely intact and includes herringbone chair rails, mantels with reeded corners blocks and central panels, six-panel doors, and architrave surrounds. But the most extraordinary interior features of the Merchants' house are the archways in the first and second floor hallways.

St. Michaels's building boom is reflected in the Cannonball House's history, and the structure's name is one of the longest-lasting results of the sieges of St. Michaels. (See above.) According to local legend, during the sieges, the citizens of St. Michaels kept their houses lightless and hung lanterns in treetops to confuse the British gunners. This ruse was a success and the British overshot their mark. But a single cannonball, it is said, grazed the chimney stack on this house, ricocheted, entered the building through a dormer window, and bounced down the steps to the surprise of Mrs. Merchant. Burn marks on the stair survive to support this account of the origin of the nickname "Cannonball House."

The Old Inn (T–257) in St. Michaels is also of note. It is a four-bay, two-and-one-half-story brick building with a two-bay, two-story kitchen wing. (In form, the wing resembles the Cannonball House's kitchen.) The street facade has two windows and two doors; both main facades are shaded by two-story porches that appear to be original.

Compton: the original house and Governor Stevens's additions.

Not all of Talbot County's citizens followed the Federal fashion in the 1780–1830 period. Vernacular structures, structures based on tradition rather than on academic style, continued to be built.

Clay's Hope (T–189), one of the county's finest late-eighteenth-century houses to have survived, is of excellent, although simple, workmanship and is a vernacular structure that reflects the influence of grander houses of the period, like Galloway (T–104). It is a large, two-story, brick building measuring 36 by 26 feet with a long, two-story frame wing. The principal facade of the main part of the house is three bays wide and is laid in Flemish bond; and other walls are laid in common bond. There is a chamfered water table and three-brick beltcourse around the three exposed sides of the building, betraying some lingering Georgian ideals. Within the old, brick portion, the floor plan consists of a stair hall in the southeast corner, a living room in the northeast corner and what is now a den in the west half, where originally there were two rooms with diagonal fireplaces. The stair's chair rail and trim are all typical of the late eighteenth century. The house is described in the 1798 federal direct tax with an adjoining 20-by-20-foot brick kitchen, and James Colston is listed as the owner of the property. He owned the same land in 1783, but he then lived in a frame house, so we may assume that the brick Clay's Hope was built between the two dates.

More obviously vernacular is the Eberhard House (T–130), near Trappe. Significantly, most of these vernacular structures are located in the remote areas of the county, not near the towns that drew the more sophisticated citizens who were, through communication with the outside world, able to be kept abreast of changes in architectural fashion. The Eberhard House could have been built any time from the seventeenth to the twentieth century, but it probably dates to around 1800. It is a small farmhouse composed of two, three-bay sections, one two stories tall, and the other one-and-one-half stories. Both sections are built on brick piers (useful in a moist climate and in a low-lying area) and are covered with brown wood shingles. A one-story porch shades the facade of the two-story part, while a small chimney rises between the two sections.

A contemporary of the Eberhard House, Grace Creek Farm (T–219) is located south of Bozman overlooking the confluence of Grace and Leadenham creeks into Broad Creek. The house faces southeast and is typical of the early-nineteenth-century frame dwellings found in the outer reaches of Talbot, Dorchester, and Caroline counties. It is composed of a three-bay, one-and-one-half-story section with single-bay addition. The central entrance of the northwest facade has a porch protecting the 1840s six-panel door. On each side is a single window with six-over-six sash framed by louvered shutters. Two dormers light the rooms above. Since the original two sections were built, ambitious owners have continuously kept vernacular traditions alive by making, as they felt like it, several additions to create a long, low dwelling with a new "glass room" overlooking the water.

Beauvoir (T–147), also near Trappe, was greatly enlarged over the years, but it began as a simple one-story vernacular cottage. Perhaps just as interesting as the main house is the large, square, board-and-batten meat house to the north of the dwelling.

At Compton (T–146) there is another notable outbuilding, a brick, two-story milk house; its first story rests below a moat-like retaining wall. The main house itself is of note in that it shows what often happens when people leave home, prosper, and return. Samuel Stevens (1778–1860) inherited a simple one-and-one-half-story brick house from his father, John Stevens, in 1794. Samuel grew interested in politics, and intermittently represented Talbot County in the house of delegates in Annapolis from 1807 through 1820. Then on December 9, 1822, he was elected to what would be the first of three terms as governor. His progressive administrations are remembered for the enfranchisement of Jews, the abolition of religion as a test for Maryland officeholders, the extension of the civil liberties guaranteed in the Bill of Rights to state law, and the creation of the Chesapeake and Ohio Canal. During Lafayette's visit to the United States (1824), Governor Stevens is said to have ridden from Compton to meet him wearing swallow-tailed blue jeans.[33] Despite such homespun liberalism, Stevens must have acquired some sense of self-importance while in Annapolis because, when he returned, he raised the roof of his old house to give it two full stories and added a one-and-one-half-story wing to the east. H. Chandlee Forman waxes poetic on Compton: "Like the rose colour seen in the depths of the Grand Canyon of Arizona are the bricks of this old Stevens home."[34]

Tilghman's Fortune (T–247) is another fine circa-1800 vernacular house built with great care. The Talbot County chamber of commerce moved the small brick house from Easton Point to its present location in 1969, put it on a new brick basement, and now uses it as an office. Its east facade is expertly laid in Flemish bond and has a center door and two windows. The other sides are laid in common bond, and their openings vary: there is a window on the south gable and a door and window on the west facade. One chimney is located within the north gable, to which gable has been added a two-bay, one-story frame office on brick piers. The interior of the older part has only one room with late-eighteenth/early-nineteenth-century mantel and trim. There is a door to the new office end and an enclosed stair to the loft beside the fireplace. The chamber of commerce is to be congratulated in its decision to move the house and to adapt it to this new use.

Building took place throughout Talbot County in the years around 1800, and not all of it was domestic. Beneath the long limbs of the Wye Oak stands a one-and-one-half-story, brick, one-room building (T–57) said to be the first public school on the Eastern Shore. Interestingly, it is almost identical in form to Tilghman's Fortune. Both structures—and the great, shady oak—form a tranquil end to this otherwise explosive chapter.

33. Papenfuse et al., *New Guide*, p. 137.
34. Forman, *Manor Houses*, p. 197.

CHAPTER 7

Victorian Talbot: Calm

Talbot's nineteenth-century architectural history may be divided conveniently—if stormily—by the Civil War. At the risk of oversimplifying, antebellum Talbot resembled a Currier and Ives print: all was peaceful and rural and serene; after the war the county's builders engaged in the same eclectic battles that took place elsewhere in America.

But in Talbot County these battles were fought on a somewhat limited scale. They might even better be termed skirmishes. Actually, few buildings of *any* style were constructed in Talbot during the 1830s, '40s, and '50s. This is easily explained: after the flourishing Federal era, the county suffered an economic decline:

> An Assessment of the property in Easton was made in 1823, and the amount as placed on the tax books exhibited a total of $328,576.25. From this time till the close of the late war [Civil War], but little progress was made: indeed the assessment of 1830 exhibited but $235,059—an actual reduction of more than one third in seven years. True there was the establishment of several industries that the progress of the times demanded, but there was the utter abandoning of others that hitherto were conducted on an extensive scale. . . .
>
> The tanning business, once carried on extensively in Easton, there being no less than four establishments in operation at one time, became completely extinct. Between 1850 and 1860, there was an actual loss in population, the census of 1850 reporting the total population as 1413, and that of 1860 as 1358—a loss of 55. From 1830 to 1840, the entire county was going backwards in population, and after that made but slow progress until the close of the war. Many persons left here to find homes in the then developing South and West, which accounts in a great measure for this retrograde movement.[1]

If the county was spared the blighted landscapes so often associated with nineteenth-century industry, it also missed most of the money. It maintained a solid agricultural base, but missed the rich-rich of the late nineteenth century. And without large infusions of new money to spur people to build, the most expansive years architecturally were indeed over—at least until the colonial revival era in the twentieth century. This is not to say that nothing was built—quite a bit was and much of it first rate—but the county stopped being at the national foreground, where it had been in the seventeenth and eighteenth centuries, when the best of Talbot's architecture was equal to the best anywhere in America. Of course, to say that early Victorian Talbot wasn't equal to colonial Talbot is to speak relatively and to apply the very highest standards.

There were exceptions. The county did achieve greatness in architecture in the nineteenth century: Christ Church in Easton, for example, was at the vanguard of a new intellectual, religious philosophy that began in England and came to Talbot via New Jersey, thus showing that the county retained some of its earlier architectural sophistication. Similarly, any town in America would be proud to have some of Easton's Victorian splendors, such as the Chaffinch House and the Miller Lodge of the International Order of Odd Fellows (see chapter 8).

So, while Talbot County has not been stagnant or idle, it is important to remember that the countians' inventions and changes and experiments have been of an evolutionary

VENERATE THE PLOUGH

"Venerate the Plough" could well have been the motto of Talbot County's agricultural society.

OPPOSITE:
Presqu'isle in its serene setting.

1. Garey, *History of Easton*.

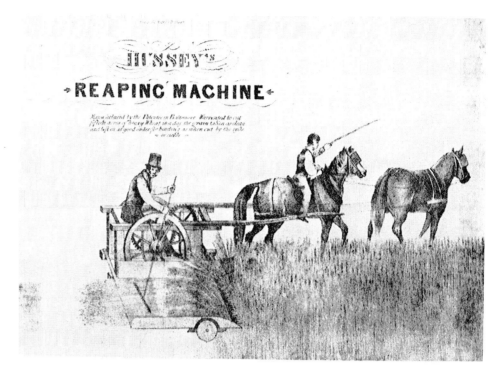

HUSSEY'S
REAPING MACHINE

The development of Hussey's reaping machine was financed by Tilghman money, and the machine was first tested at Plimhimmon. Unfortunately, the Tilghmans had only a verbal, gentleman's agreement with the maker, and the machine was taken over by Cyrus McCormick.

nature. Doubtless most countians would think this is as it should be: "If it works, don't fix it." In 1959 the *Star-Democrat* ran a piece on this subject:

> Talbot County is sometimes referred to as 'the hereditary county,' because until modern times the manner of living had continued unchanged since the coming of the English colonists. Even nowadays, in this twentieth century era of automobiles, airplanes, radios, televisions and atom bombs many . . . Talbot countians . . . live . . . a mode of life which had its beginnings with pre-Revolutionary days.[2]

This "mode of life" is, of course, based on land for farming and water for transport.

And farming was very much on the minds of Talbot's citizens in the early nineteenth century, when the county's "agriculture received its first and greatest impulse," and when countians formed "the first Agricultural Society . . . in the county, probably the first in the state, and certainly among the first in the United States."[3] The earliest discussion of a Talbot County farmers' association was in a *Republican Star* article of May 28, 1805. Bylined "Agricola," the article noted:

> The manner in which such a society would be productive of good effects, would be, that by farmers forming themselves into an association, their minds would be more particularly and ardently devoted to husbandry and rural economy; premiums would be given for the suggestion of the best systems, and the greatest practical productions; an emulation would be excited, which is always the parent of excellence in anything, and agriculture, instead of being deemed an inferior, low bred and degraded pursuit, would rise in the public estimation, and become a science that would command the attention, the genious [sic] and talents of the age . . . Intimate alliance between philosophy and agriculture, would afford an ample field for mental exertion.[4]

Agricola went on to discuss some of the "new developments" he would like to see used more widely: "Rotation of crops, the extended use of clover, and the employment of Plaster of Paris as a fertilizer." And he blamed tobacco for soil exhaustion and hoped his innovations would cure the ill effects of tobacco-planting.

On July 19 of that year a group of men met at the courthouse in Easton, chose William Hayward as president and Robert H. Goldsborough as secretary of their agricultural society, and adopted some resolutions. One of these resolves read "that it is the opinion of this meeting, that a *Society*, formed on liberal principles, for the promotion and improvement of agriculture in this and neighboring counties, will be highly useful, and tend to increase the value of lands, and the general interest of the inhabitants."[5]

2. The *Easton Star-Democrat*, August 7, 1959, Section C, p. 1.
3. Tilghman, *History*, vol. 2, p. 23.
4. Ibid.
5. Ibid., p. 24.

Then, after (the usual) many organizational meetings and formations of committees, the constitution for the "Society for the Promotion of Agriculture and Rural Economy for the Eastern Shore of Maryland" was adopted on September 9, 1805. Article 2 reads:

> The great end of the present institution being the improvement of Agriculture in this and the neighboring counties, in all its branches, every communication that shall relate to systems of husbandry—rotations of crops in grass and grain—the nature, qualities and kinds of soil—the improvement of every kind of soil by manures, and the fit application of these to different soils—the cultivation of all sorts of grain and grasses and their suitableness to different soils and systems—the construction of ploughs and other implements of husbandry—improved methods of raising and ameliorating the breed of horses, cattle, sheep, swine, and relieving them from disorders to which they are subject—the improvement of soils by particular cultivation, and the employment of peas, beans and other pulses—the practicability of raising to advantage cabbages, potatoes, carrots, parsnips, beets and other roots, as winter food for cattle, sheep and swine—the substitution of hedges for wooden fences, and the methods of raising sets and planting them for use—the general advantages of drains and ditches as a means of improving lands and crops, of benefiting the public highways and of advancing the health of the inhabitants—the cultivation of flax, hemp, hops and cotton, and the proper care of wool, bark, timber and hides, as connected with some of the arts and manufacture—the rearing and management of fruit trees to supply the absence for those which are daily diminishing—the methods of preventing and destroying insects which are found to be injurious to the farmer—and in general, every communication which shall relate in any way to these subjects, or others connected with the department of Agriculture and rural economy in any degree, shall be considered as a proper object of the Institution and shall always receive a merited attention from members.[6]

Interest in agriculture led to many charming farm buildings, such as this one at Perry Hall, photographed in the 1930s by Frances Benjamin Johnston for the Historic American Buildings Survey.

6. Quoted in ibid., pp. 25, 26.

Fairview, one of Talbot County's great
Greek revival mansions.

The members held a few meetings, but their society seems to have died on the vine.
There were a few other unsuccessful attempts to establish similar organizations, until the
Board of Agriculture for the Eastern Shore was formed and held its first meeting December
1, 1825, at Wheatlands (T–100), the residence of General Perry Benson.

Throughout the nineteenth century that twelve-member board met monthly at
various members' houses "to discuss agricultural topics and to enjoy a good Maryland
dinner," and the list of the organization's presidents reads like a familial and architectural
Who's Who: Nicholas Hammond of Saint Aubins, Robert H. Goldsborough of Myrtle
Grove, Samuel Hambleton of Perry Cabin, Samuel Stevens of Compton, Nicholas
Goldsborough of Otwell, Kennedy R. Owen of Marengo, Matthew Tilghman Goldsborough of Ellenborough and Otwell, and Edward Lloyd VII of Wye House. Among the causes
advocated were the use of machinery, improved grain and grass seeds, and the use of lime
and commercial fertilizer. Nor did they merely talk about agricultural change; they acted.
For example, General Tench Tilghman (1810–74), grandson of Washington's aide-de-
camp, experimented with Peruvian guano as a fertilizer, was the first Marylander to use a
newly invented mechanical reaper, and built the first steam-powered sawmill on the
Eastern Shore.[7]

It might not be too far-fetched to suggest that these improvements in agriculture were
paralleled by the introduction of eclecticism, of choice, in architecture, that if, after the
1830s and '40s, farmers were free to choose from among different crops, so, too, were they
free to choose from different building styles. And there were many styles to choose from:
Greek, Gothic, Italianate, Egyptian, Moorish, each had its proponents, each had its own

7. Papenfuse, et al., *New Guide,* p. 170.

series of builder's guides, how-to handbooks that explained the virtues (a word not to be taken lightly among Gothicists) of each style and that presented models to be copied. Nevertheless, despite this choice, most countians seem to have preferred (or were economically encouraged) to stick to their vernacular and Georgian traditions.

Of all the historicist styles to come to Talbot County, the Greek revival was the first. Here, again, Talbot is reflective of the rest of the nation. But the county's builders do not seem to have been overly enthusiastic about the style: there are one or two good houses and the inevitable (in Maryland) frame church, but the most pervasive examples of building in the Greek idiom are interior details—mantels, stairways, and door surrounds.

Fairview (T–60) is an exception. One of the great mansions of Talbot County, it began as a fairly modest Federal house, and, a generation or so later, became very grandly Greek indeed. It consists of a large, five-bay, two-story brick block and a four-bay, two-story kitchen wing which was standing in 1743. The period interior detailing and some exterior features suggest that the main building dates from the early 1800s. This assumption is further confirmed by the 1798 tax assessment, which lists no building of this size on the property.

Fairview's principal elevation faces north across a wide open lawn. Flanking this grassy sweep are groves of large trees; there was also, on the south, a large box garden, among the oldest and finest in the county until it was stricken with boxwood blight in the 1970s. A mid-nineteenth-century pedimented Ionic portico shades the central three bays of the north facade. Its frieze is carried across the facade of the building. In plan, Fairview has a central passage with double parlors on the west and two smaller rooms on the east divided by a narrow passage. There is an enclosed stair between the northeast room and the central passage. Both parlors were retrimmed in the mid-century with woodwork typical of that period. One original mantel is now housed at Lombardy nearby.

The Anchorage (T–52) south of Fairview, on the road to Easton at the Miles River Bridge, shows what could happen if you married a Lloyd. The oldest part of the house is the central, brick section, probably built by Thomas or Richard Bruff in the early eighteenth century. For several decades it was owned and occupied by a succession of people who were in no way greatly different from their neighbors. This state of affairs changed radically, however, after Edward Lloyd V—"the Governor"—bought the property in 1831.

Lloyd gave the house to his daughter, Sarah Scott, upon the occasion of her marriage to Lieutenant (later Commodore U.S.N.) Charles Lowndes, and the old Bruff house underwent a complete metamorphosis. Sarah Scott Lowndes clearly kept Wye in mind during the rebuilding, but she was also influenced by the Greek revival. The Anchorage was turned into a five-part composition with a large center section and small hyphens and wings. The main block has a two-story Doric projecting portico that shades the central double door. There is a one-story frame wing on each end of the main block, connected to the central section by a flat-roofed, stuccoed hyphen. The pedimented, templelike main block and end pavilions may safely be viewed as being reinterpretations of Wye. Whether the Lowndeses chose this style, or whether Governor Lloyd gave it to them as a not too subtle reminder of Mrs. Lowndes's past, could make an interesting matrimonial-psychological study.

Presqu'isle (T–86), another house with a Lloyd connection, sits serenely at the end of a long allée of trees overlooking the east branch of the Wye River with Wye Island, Bruff's Island, and Bennett Point in the distance. The house, circa 1820, is a two-and-one-half-story, three-bay, nearly square frame building. East and west facades are alike with shiplap sheathed pediment above the second story. Over the east and west entrances are handsome, original Greek revival porches of the Doric order. Most of the windows have six-over-six sashes and louvered shutters. Within, the house is divided into a central passage with double parlors on the south and three rooms to the north. With the exception of the dining room, all doors, trim, dado, mantels, floors, and stair are original and well maintained.

Presqu'isle: a small echo of Wye?

Yellow House (T–120), two miles south of Easton on Route 50, is a more modest, but no less fine, Greek building. The principal part of the dwelling is a three-story, three-bay, frame structure dating from the mid-nineteenth century. Probable Greek touches include the corner pilasters and the square posts that support the west porch. Above the first- and second-story windows are simple cornices and trim, painted white in contrast to the yellow body of the structure. All windows originally had louvered shutters. The entrance, with sidelights and transom, is centered on the first story, sheltered by a porch with a hip roof that reflects the roof on the house. The well-ordered interior consists of a central stair hall in the major portion, flanked by two rooms. Detailing is simple Greek revival style. The fireplaces on all three stories are located adjacent to the stair partitions; all mantels are plain and typical of the period except those on the third story, which are more reminiscent of the Federal style. The grounds contain a brick dairy built more or less contemporaneously with the house's small end (original) section. The dairy's east wall continues to the southwest corner of the kitchen, and the building has a low-pitch hip roof with wide overhang, with slats instead of a solid soffit, presumably for ventilation. East of the milk house is a brick meat house with a gable roof above a corbeled cornice. It has a cellar beneath and a carriage shed attached to the east gable. Its batten door, on the west gable, hangs on its original iron strap-hinges.

Londonderry: an exception.

All these structures might be viewed as an outgrowth of a nationwide mania for "the picturesque." The picturesque began as a Gothic movement, and if it is ever possible to pin down one factor as being pivotal in art or architectural history, the publication of Alexander Jackson Davis's *Rural Residence* in 1837 might be said to mark the beginning of the movement in American domestic architecture. Drawing literary inspiration from *Ivanhoe* and other novels by Sir Walter Scott, and self-styled as a means for "the improvement of American country architecture," *Rural Residences* was a "house pattern book" with hand-colored illustrations of "cottages, farm-houses, villas and village churches," arranged by architectural types and stressing volumetric form and plan.[8]

American rural domestic architecture in the colonial period and into the early nineteenth century had been dominated by one house form: the rectangular box with a door in the long side and regularly placed sash windows. Sometimes, as has been seen, large houses would adopt Palladian principles to create a three-, five-, or seven-part composition, but the basic module remained the box.

Davis introduced the term, and the concept, *villa* into American architecture, and this proved to be revolutionary. He argued that the villa (he was talking specifically about Gothic villas, but his arguments apply to all the picturesque, exotic styles) "admits of greater variety both of plan and outline, is susceptible of additions from time to time, while its bay windows, oriels, turrets and chimney shafts, give a pictorial effect to the elevation." He also favored integration of house and landscape, bemoaning what he felt was the "want of connection with site," and he encouraged attention to porches as one means of easing the transition from house to nature.[9] The porch, of course, was not new, but this idea of using it as a link between the parlor and the garden was.

Davis's Gothic villa is important because it was innovative, because it broke the box, not because it was ever very popular. William H. Pierson has noted that to most Americans "Scott's chivalrous knights . . . fantasy and philosophical reflections were out of touch with reality, and . . . they demanded levels of grandeur for which the profoundly organic Gothic style was inappropriate."[10] This is borne out in the decidedly non-Gothic Talbot County countryside. One exception, Londonderry (T–330), located to the east of Easton Point on a branch of the Tred Avon River, must be discussed. This Gothic revival house was designed by Richard Upjohn, the nationally prominent architect who also designed Christ Church Rectory (T–16; see p. 106). Solidly built of Port Deposit granite, the house, in its original form, was all that Davis—or Scott—would have wished. Unfortunately,

8.   This has been much discussed in many histories of American architecture; see, for example, William H. Pierson, Jr., *American Buildings and Their Architects*, vol. 2 (Garden City, N.Y.: Anchor Books, 1980), pp. 271–307.

9.   Quoted in ibid., p. 296.

10.   Ibid., p. 290.

Londonderry was nearly destroyed by fire in the 1960s, and one must look to the hyphen and wings (both escaped the blaze) to get an indication of the original, highly elaborate, exterior detail that once covered the structure. The hyphen has a steep gable roof with a highly ornate cross gable and cornice. This cornice continues around the wing, which is surmounted by a slate mansard roof. This in turn is topped by a finial. The main block is covered by a low gable roof with deep eaves. That 1960s conflagration also consumed the porches, which were replaced by the plain ones in place today.

But if Talbot's farmers were uncomfortable with whole Gothic houses, they sometimes liked certain Gothic details, as can be seen at the tenant house at Pickbourn (T-340) near Tunis Mills. Its central gable, scalloped trim on the eaves, delicate porch brackets, and large banded chimney combine to create an excellent example of a Victorian cottage in a restrained Gothic style. Moreover, the entire Pickbourn complex is noteworthy. As has been discussed, agriculture has underpinned the economy of Talbot County for three centuries and, if the importance of this way of life occasionally manifests itself in grand manors, it appears much more frequently in smaller-scale farms with their modest collections of outbuildings. At Pickbourn there is a fine example of such a grouping, including, besides the tenant house, a board-and-batten meat house, a 15-foot-square one-story slave quarters, and a dairy.

Davis's landscape designs were probably just as important as his architectural philosophy. His horticultural beliefs were paralleled in Britain, particularly in the work of the Scot John Claudius Loudon, who furnished early Victorian gardeners with several romantic theories, all of which followed a precept of the Scot philosopher Archibald Alison: beauty lay in the mind of the beholder; it was a human convention, not a matter of the intrinsic qualities of the object. It was the associations the viewer brought to a garden that determined its impact on him. Nature was an abstraction: the landscape garden obeyed rules just as arbitrary as any Tudor knot. Davis and Loudon and others reasoned from this that a garden should be thought of as a work of art and that it was bad taste to try to deceive the spectator.

This new emphasis on imaginative design created a choice of garden styles similar to the stylistic choices available to architects. In the 1830s, the pages of Loudon's *Gardener's Magazine* were filled with examples of layouts variously described by their authors as architectural, geometric, picturesque, Dutch, Elizabethan, Gothic, Italian, French, and ancient—not always for readily apparent reasons. Loudon distinguished four basic varieties of design: the geometric; the rustic, in imitation of cottage gardens; the picturesque, which imitated natural terrain and the studied irregularity of forms familiar in landscape painting; and the gardenesque, the style "calculated for displaying the art of the gardener."[11]

All these theories reached the shores of the Chesapeake and can still be seen in the gardens at Clifton (T-115) near Easton. The house was begun in 1741; about a century later Matilda Woodall Bartlett and her husband, John, members of prominent Talbot families, expanded the house and laid out the romantic gardens. Their landscape plan— now owned by the house's current owners—has curving lanes and reflects the taste for this informal garden design Davis advocated. The garden's spreading trees, now in full maturity, are particularly attractive.

Actually, Davis's Gothic theories were not his alone—a few years before *Rural Residences* appeared, beginning around 1830, England and America were caught up in the Ecclesiological movement. Superficially, this movement was motivated by the same romanticism that encouraged picturesque cottages, and, viewed in the broadest terms, "Ecclesiology was a reform movement within the Anglican Church which called for a return to traditional medieval forms both in ritual and in church building." More fully, however, "in the eyes of the Ecclesiologists themselves, Ecclesiology was the science of church architecture, a science, moreover, which was based on a careful and exhaustive examination of original Gothic buildings. Its first objective was to identify those features of the Gothic church and its furnishings which related to the liturgical and symbolic

11. Brent Elliott, "Victorian Garden Design," in *The Garden* (London: New Perspectives, 1979), pp. 56, 57.

Outbuildings at Pickbourn.

functions of the worship services; its second was to use that evidence for the formulation of rules which would govern church buildings.[12]

Colonial churches, as has been seen, were, like colonial houses, basically boxes. The venerable Third Haven Friends Meeting House, Old Wye Church, and the rest were simply four walls, a floor, a gable roof—the simplest building imaginable. But, as with domestic architecture, this changed in the nineteenth century. All Ecclesiologists agreed on one, basic, overriding principle—a "pure" medieval liturgy was only possible in a purely medieval space, one "rubrically" ordered and filled with the proper symbols and objects.[13] For true Ecclesiologists Gothic design was not picturesque; it was functional.

None of this, of course, is to suggest that Gothic revival churches had not been designed in America before the 1830s and '40s: Benjamin Henry Latrobe had submitted a Gothic alternative for the Baltimore Cathedral in 1805 and had designed Christ Church in Washington in the Gothic style in 1808; Maximilian Godefroy built St. Mary's Chapel in Baltimore in 1806. That last structure has been described as a charming confectionary, "as much Roman triumphal arch as Gothic Chapel,"[14] and none of the buildings had the rigor and discipline the Ecclesiologists demanded; they probably would have dismissed them as debased. Nonetheless, it is interesting to see that the Bay area was at the Gothic vanguard.

Talbot County had an early conversion to Ecclesiology. The first published work in America on the Gothic appeared in 1830 when an obscure scholarly periodical, *The American Journal of Science and Arts*, edited by the Yale professor Benjamin Silliman, ran a series of four articles on "Architecture in the United States." One was on "The Gothic Style." Re-enter the Lloyds. As has been discussed, Charles Lowndes married Sarah Scott Lloyd, a daughter óf Edward Lloyd V, and Governor Lloyd had given his daughter The Anchorage on the Miles River. In 1835 the Lowndeses donated some land a few yards from their house to St. Michaels parish. They and other Miles River Neck planters then gave money to build a church more convenient to themselves than the church in St. Michaels. They were successful, and in 1839 the Right Reverend George Washington Doane, Bishop of New Jersey, dedicated St. John's Protestant Episcopal Church (T–49), one of the first Gothic revival churches on the Eastern Shore. The Ecclesiological movement called for stone to achieve the proper aged and dramatic effects. Americans favored granite, a material not native to the middle Shore, but which was quarried near Port Deposit in Cecil

12. Pierson, *American Buildings*, vol. 2, p. 152.
13. Ibid., p. 153.
14. Ibid., p. 119.

St. John's Church: once pure Ecclesiology, now one of Maryland's most romantic ruins.

County. It was then easily brought down the Bay to Talbot County by ship. Attendance, fell off at St. John's, however, and the church was abandoned in 1900 when the building proved structurally unsafe. It has been deteriorating since, and now, with its vine-covered granite walls and its crumbling Gothic arches, is one of the state's most interesting ruins. Ironically, as such, it would probably be just as appealing to the Gothically minded, with their love of the eerie and the picturesque, now as when it was intact.

The Reverend Joseph Spencer, rector of St. Michael's parish, was the first to hold services at St. John's. It is not known how involved he was with Ecclesiology, but that can not be said of the Reverend Henry M. Mason, rector of Christ Church (T–15), St. Peter's parish, in Easton, a man thoroughly immersed in architecture and theology. He came to Talbot County from Salem, New Jersey, in 1838. There he had been closely associated with the Right Reverend George W. Doane, a builder of several churches in New England, a leader in the American Ecclesiology movement, and the dedicator of St. John's on the Miles.[15]

Mason chose William Strickland to design Christ Church. Strickland was a leading American proponent of Ecclesiological theory and had designed a church for Mason in Salem in 1836, a church he used as a model for Christ Church. The Easton building, constructed between 1840 and 1848, is a stylish product of the Gothic revival. Its pointed-arch windows and doors, heavy stone construction, and Gothic details make it an interesting contemporary to Trinity Church in New York. It was the first church in Easton to add a spire and church bell to its tower, which, originally, had four wooden pinnacles at its corners. These were removed in the late nineteenth century and the central window on the entrance facade was shortened. The three-part door was replaced in 1878, and the chancel was added in 1876 to respond to changes in liturgy; between 1871 and 1884 poppy headed pews replaced earlier seats. Despite these alterations, the church is of great significance to Talbot County architecture—indeed, to Maryland architecture in general.

After finishing the church, Mason commissioned Richard Upjohn to design the Christ Church Rectory (T–16). Of coursed granite, the house has a T-shaped plan and steep, slate-covered, gable roofs. Vertical and picturesque in feeling, its scale is somewhat reduced by the deep roof, but large dormers pierce the cornice line to permit tall windows. Consequently, the interior is spacious and light with a generous central hall and high ceiling. The rectory stands on a slight rise of ground enclosed by the L formed by the church

15. Ibid., pp. 177–79.

The Reverend Henry M. Mason hired Richard Upjoin to design Christ Church Rectory in Easton.

Christ Church in Easton in 1878, showing the original wooden pinnacles at the corners of the tower.

on the east and the parish house on the south; the dwelling is surrounded by clumps of handsome boxwood and is graced by intimate gardens with beds of herbs and flowers.

Upjohn, "a major rock in the foundation of the Gothic Revival in the United States,"[16] was born in England in 1802. Trained as a cabinetmaker, carpenter, surveyor, and draftsman, he emigrated to America in 1829. Although he was not schooled in architecture, "he did bring with him highly developed mechanical skills, a practical understanding of materials, and a sensitivity for three-dimensional construction. . . . In addition, through his environment and family connections, he brought a special awareness of medieval architecture and a personal involvement in the Anglican Church, neither of which would have been possible in America."[17]

Based in Boston, Upjohn built his first Gothic church—St. John's Church (1836–1839)—in Bangor, Maine. In 1839, he began his long involvement with Trinity Church in New York, his masterpiece. Upjohn's Trinity Church introduced into the American scene an authentic Gothic church functionally designed around liturgical principles. That Mason brought in such a distinguished architect as Upjohn to design the Christ Church Rectory—to say nothing of Strickland's church building—is evidence that Talbot County was trying to maintain its architectural sophistication. Upjohn's work "was specially influential in the spread of Ecclesiological ideas in American church architecture. . . . In 1849, he was invited to become an honorary member of the New York Ecclesiological Society; and in 1852, when the Society published its first list of approved architects, Upjohn's name was among them."[18]

Dr. Phoebe Stanton has written that "as soon as Trinity [in New York] was begun, many cities acquired at least one big church in its manner."[19] Trinity Cathedral (T–239) in Easton was built "in its manner" but was not begun until 1876, long past the height of the movement. It displays Gothic motifs in its pointed-arch windows, interior hammer beams, steep roof, and tower.

St. Michaels followed suit and in 1878 built its own Christ Church (T–260), or, rather, rebuilt Christ Church: the present building was the fourth on the site, services having been held here continuously since the seventeenth century. In fact, the town of St. Michaels evolved from the church. The first structure, of logs, was built in 1670 by Edward Elliott; the present handsome edifice was erected under the direction of Captain Daniel Feddeman. It is constructed of massive granite blocks that were brought by barge from Port Deposit.[20] There are several interesting memorials in the interior. Note, for example, the baptismal font, presented to the parish by Queen Anne in 1701; its handsome marble bowl bears symbols said to have been placed there by the direction of the queen. These symbols, carved on the bowl's eight sides, include a cross, the triangle of the Trinity, alpha and omega, a representation of the keys to the kingdom of heaven, and Greek words that translate, "I have conquered." The beautiful stained-glass windows of the porch at the south door remind parishioners to clothe the naked, feed the hungry, visit the sick, and be hospitable to visitors.

Talbot County's rural churches became Gothic, too. Often frame, these pleasant, often idiosyncratic, structures dot the county's landscape. All Saints Church (T–83), south of Longwoods, is one attractive example. Built on a brick foundation, the building's main section is six bays long below a steeply pitched gable roof. There is a two-bay, gable-roof apse on the east gable end; its exposed end has a triple lancet window, similar to the windows in the main block of the church. Several of the building's details are somewhat unorthodox: the walls' sheathing changes from horizontal clapboard to board-and-batten at the level of the window sills; the windows in the three-sectioned corner tower increase in size from the tower's first to second to third level; a curious gable projects from the north side to enclose a chimney. Still, these quirkish details give buildings personality. All Saints is no longer used as a church; it has been adapted for use as an art studio and private residence.

The village of Cordova has the small, Gothic-revival Emmanuel Lutheran Church (T–246). Five bays deep and one bay wide, it is built over a rusticated concrete-block cellar

16. Ibid., p. 201.
17. Ibid., p. 159.
18. Ibid., p. 201.
19. Phoebe B. Stanton, *The Gothic Revival and American Church Architecture* (Baltimore: Johns Hopkins Press, 1968), p. 225.
20. Tilghman, *History*, vol. 2, pp. 311, 312.

Talbot County's rural churches became Gothic: Emmanuel Lutheran Church near Cordova.

and below a steeply pitched roof with exposed overhanging rafters. The walls are covered in board-and-batten. In addition to the main body of the church, there are a vestibule and a sanctuary; two wings create a nearly cruciform building. Although the interior is now covered with sheetrock and beaverboard, originally there was diagonal board paneling and, in some places, lancet arched panels. The exterior of the old church is a smaller version of All Saints Church (T–83) and resembles the small churches at Hillsboro and Sudlersville. Built by Episcopalians, the church was later used by Lutherans; it now serves as a community center.

But not all of Talbot's Victorian churches were "Victorian." Or even Gothic. The Wye Mills Methodist Church (T–298) at Wye Mills is one example of continued use of traditional forms. It is a frame building constructed upon a brick foundation. The walls of the structure are covered with white weatherboard. It is three bays wide and three bays deep with four-over-four sash windows and green louvered shutters. Like most nineteenth-century Eastern Shore chapels, this building uses its gable end to create the main facade; this end has a small vestibule, whose door and unshuttered small windows have segmental arched heads similar to those on the openings in the main part of the building. Each opening has wide, bold trim. The cornice on both vestibule and chapel has curved brackets; turned pendants hang from the corners. The building's tranquil setting, high above Wye Mill pond in a grove of large white oak trees, encourages meditation.

If Talbot's landed citizens were reluctant to build Gothic cottages for themselves, her town residents seem to have been a bit more willing to experiment. Upjohn himself is popularly credited with 116–120 South Street in Easton, a picturesque group of Victorian Gothic cottages (T–20) which is outstanding in a neighborhood in which small frame houses predominate. The corner house, 120 South Street, is the largest. With its steeply pitched gable roof and triangular louvered inserts above the second-floor windows, the house does bear some resemblance to Upjohn's rectory (see above). The identity of the designer of these cottages is, however, uncertain, although there is much speculation on the subject.

At 220 South Street, the Trippe-Beale House (T–45) is a rectangular brick building, two-and-one-half stories in height. Its sweeping jerkin roof is pierced by wide jerkin-head dormers and by tall chimneys with flaring caps. This is a corner house; porches on the street

Richard Upjohn is locally credited with a group of cottages on South Street in Easton: shown, the Trippe-Beale House, 220 South Street.

Not all of Talbot County's nineteenth-century churches were Gothic: Easton's Methodist Protestant Church on Washington Street near Bay Street, photographed in 1878 (now demolished).

facades have wooden trefoil arches. Eaves of the roof and porches are edged with wooden ornament. Local sources state that the architect of this fine house was Richard Upjohn,[21] and the rooms have a spaciousness similar to that Upjohn achieved in the Christ Church Rectory. The house is two rooms deep and two rooms wide with double doors between the first-floor rooms. The stair has foliated step brackets, a bulbous newel, and turned balusters. This dwelling occupies the southwest corner of South and Aurora streets, and sits on grounds planted with magnolia, poplar, boxwood, and smoke tree.

These Gothic romances were the exception. Far more popular—but still by no means universally accepted in antebellum Talbot County—was the Italian Villa style. Characterized by a highly rhythmic, bracketed cornice, a square tower (or campanile) with a flat or low-pitched roof, ornamental rounded door surrounds and window hoods, the Italianate was the best of all possible styles because it managed to be respectably Renaissance (classicism never really died out in America), thus acknowledging the past, yet asymmetrically picturesque, thus recognizing the current fashion, all in all creating a vigorous picturesqueness that was expressive of the largeness, the energy, and the ambition of that era.

Perhaps the house in Talbot County that best embodies these ideals is Ashby (T–174), near Easton. The other Italianate houses in the county remained essentially symmetrical, self-contained Georgian blocks with Italianate frosting, but Ashby was designed in a rambling, expansive manner to take advantage of the views of the Miles River and to catch the prevailing breezes. Built in 1858 on the site of the original Goldsborough homestead, the house clearly followed Davis's precepts in using architectural elements to integrate house and terrain. The addition of the present portico in the 1940s marks a curious attempt to create a formal Georgian mansion out of the otherwise romantically sculptural Italianate villa.

21. Cynthia B. Ludlow, in conversation with Christopher Weeks, August 10, 1983.

Ashby: rambling, expansive, and designed to enjoy the views.

North Bend: some Greek, some Italianate, some Gothic influences.

Cherry Grove (T–308) was originally surveyed in 1812 out of parts of two earlier grants, Jamaica Point and Lowe's Ramble. Later in the nineteenth century the land was owned by William Hughlett, who built and owned the house Jamaica Point. Hughlett was a prosperous lumberman, shipyard owner, and farmer, a director of the Easton National Bank, and the probable builder of this fine Italianate Victorian dwelling overlooking the broad waters of the Choptank River in the Trappe district. It has five windows across both the southwest and northeast facades, and two windows on each of the other sides. The approach facade (southwest) has a small porch with chamfered posts and hip roof over the central entrance. The door is flanked by sidelights and rests below a louvered transom. The house is given a dignified importance by the low gable-roofed tower that pushes itself, and its thermal window, up out of the otherwise placid cornice line. The interior has a conservative four-square plan with central stair hall. The windows have bold trim, as do the panels of the six-panel doors. All the rooms have plaster cornices and medallions. A board in the cellar bears the inscription: "I painted this house 1863." The proud tone of this statement is thought to indicate that this was the first time the house was painted, and that 1863 is probably when it was built.

Telescope houses have been popular throughout the Eastern Shore for nearly 200 years; shown here is the Anne Parris Telescope House.

Stylistically, Cherry Grove is similar to nearby Ingleside (T–313), with which there is also a Hughlett family connection. Ingleside has a simplicity not found at other Hughlett houses, such as Cherry Grove or Belmont; it also stands as a reminder of the days when entertainment was an important part of the life of a country seat, an existence that slaves and servants made possible. This tall yet compact frame house is built on the banks of the Choptank River, and stands two stories on a brick basement. The main block is three bays long and two deep with a hip roof with four bold chimneys. The walls are covered with weatherboard; there are corner pilasters and a cornice. To the west is a long, two-story addition installed in the early twentieth century. The interior is very similar to Cherry Grove: both have a central stair hall with double parlors on the east and a dining room on the west. The original plan had matching double parlors, but later owners obviously felt the need for a large dining room. Most of the interior trim is original, as are the plaster cornice and ceiling medallions.

Later Italianate—or at least semi-Italianate—houses in Talbot county include Beverly (T–240) near St. Michaels, Doncaster (T–178) near Easton, and Knotts Farm (T–74) near Queen Anne.

Sometimes builders casually mixed their styles together, often with charming results. One house, the Marvel House (T–44) near Easton, is an interesting example of the two great farmhouse styles of the mid-nineteenth century: the trim belongs to the Greek revival, while the overall form is more Italianate. Many-sectioned North Bend is an even more exotic cross among these various styles: there are traditional, double-hung windows, Greek pilasters and columns, and an Italianate cornice with a Gothic peak!

Most of Talbot County's rural nineteenth-century farm houses, however, remained firmly in various vernacular traditions. One tradition, arguably the most entrenched on the Eastern Shore, is the so-called telescope house, which received its name because its external appearance resembled a small telescope, or spyglass, "of which the parts could slide one within the other, to be folded up compactly."[22] Forman has suggested that ever-growing families caused the form "although it is conceivable that there were some owners who merely wanted a large house for social eclat and easier entertaining." He further hypothesizes that a family would build one section; then, as the number of children increased, they would "add a large or small wing" to the gable end. "Then the telescopic form naturally came into being with the addition of a second wing—both sections being

22. Forman, *Old Buildings*, p. 113.

placed in line with the original house and rhythmically increasing or decreasing in size." Forman calls Myrtle Grove "Maryland's handsomest 'neo-telescope.' "[23]

Myrtle Grove, however, is not what usually comes to mind when "telescope house" is mentioned. One would more likely envision something like Claylands (T–190), near Royal Oak. Built on the edge of Irish Creek, Claylands is a telescopic vernacular dwelling, that, in appearance and location, resembles Vicker's Change in Dorchester County. The house, now agreeably weathered, is essentially unchanged from the early nineteenth century. As a telescopic house, it is composed of three sections: a three-bay, two-story part, a one-and-one-half-story, two-bay part, and a one-story, two-bay part.

The Anne Parris Telescope House (T–102), just north of Easton, is another typical, three-sectioned telescope. Built around 1830, the building is constructed on a brick foundation and the walls are covered with weatherboard. Its west facade has a late-nineteenth-century porch that shelters a Victorian entrance; there are two gables with Gothic arch windows.

Finally, three houses—Ennion's Range (T–212), Old Woman's Folly (T–196), and The Glebe (T–225)—serve to illustrate that many, perhaps most, Talbot countians built houses with no eye to any discernible style, but with a love of regularity: the balanced facades and symmetrical plans of the Georgian and Federal periods struck a responsive chord in Talbot's farmers.

Architecturally, Old Woman's Folly, near Royal Oak, is a typical, yet charming, mid-nineteenth-century clapboard farmhouse. Its simplicity, based on clean lines and unassuming folk woodwork, is the most important feature of the house. It has a three-bay, two-story section with a shorter two-story kitchen to the east and a modern two-story addition on the west. A two-story porch extends across the south side and is supported by simple square posts with a balustrade of jig-saw-cut balusters on the second floor. The floor plan of the main section consists of a center hall with a parlor on either side; the parlors have gable-end fireplaces whose mantels feature elongated, raised diamond panels.

Ennion's Range dates to around 1810 and is one of the most picturesque vernacular dwellings remaining in Talbot County. In several aspects it is similar to some houses in the Church Creek and Madison areas of Dorchester County, especially in its use of small one-room modules. Each of three single parts of this early-nineteenth-century, one-story frame dwelling includes a chimney, a stairway, and a dormer on either side of a gable roof. The central section appears to be the earliest part of the house. This room contains a six-panel door on the east, two, two-over-two sash windows on the west, a winding stair in the northwest corner, and an interior fireplace on the south wall. The varied moldings include a cavetto-astragal on the doorway, a small ogee on the chair rail, stair, and door panels, and small ogees (sometimes with an astragal) on the fine mantel. The north section's features are plainer and the south section is rougher still: its stair is actually a series of ladder-like steps built into the wall, similar to the one at the Chance Farm (T–176).

Built a generation or so later, the Glebe, near Easton, is a typical nineteenth-century farmhouse that has kept most of its original character and fabric. It is a two-story frame house with a two-room, two-story kitchen wing to the north and a 1920s garage to the east. The entire building is sheathed in German siding. A one-story porch supported by square columns wraps around the south, west, and north sides of the main house. The entrance door is flanked by sidelights and topped with a transom. The four-panel door's long upper panels have rounded tops and the panel molding is elaborate. In plan the oldest section has a central stair hall with a room to either side. There are fireplaces in the east room on both floors and in the west room on the first floor. The west fireplace on the first floor features a colonial revival mantel with decorative fluting. The two east mantels are each a different mid-nineteenth-century style; the one on the first floor has reeded engaged columns and oval insets edged in beads, while the one on the second floor has chamfered posts and raised panels shaped either as rectangles with cut-out corners or as shields.

23. Ibid.

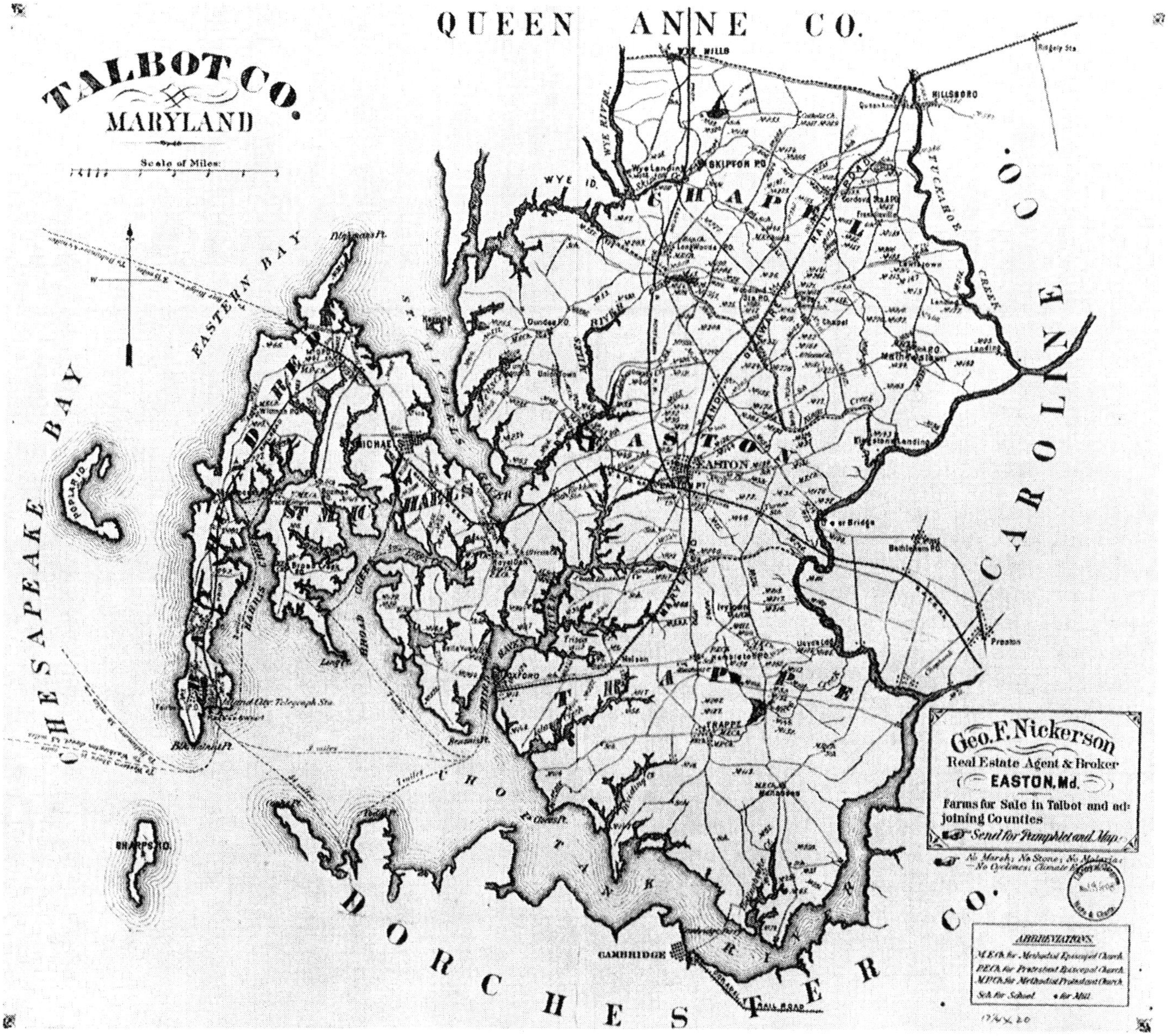

TALBOT CO.
MARYLAND

Scale of Miles:

QUEEN ANNE CO.

QUEEN ANNE CO.

WYE MILLS

RIDGELY Sta.

HILLSBORO

SKIPTON P.O.

CHAPEL

EASTON

EASTON

CAROLINE CO.

CHESAPEAKE BAY

EASTERN BAY

POPLAR I.D.

ST. MICHAEL

BAYSIDE

ST. MARY'S

BAY HUNDRED

OXFORD

TRAPPE

BAILEYS NK.

CAMBRIDGE

DORCHESTER CO.

DORCHESTER CO.

CHOPTANK RIVER

TRAIL R.ROAD

ABBREVIATIONS.
M.E.Ch. for Methodist Episcopal Church.
P.E.Ch. for Protestant Episcopal Church.
M.P.Ch. for Methodist Protestant Church.
Sch. for School.   • for Mill

CHAPTER 8

Victorian Talbot: Storm

After Appomattox, Talbot County's distinguished and dignified buildings were joined by the full range of extravagant revivalisms associated with the flamboyant years towards the end of the nineteenth century. Easton, in particular, had a burst of construction in the 1870s and '80s, explained by its expanding population, commerce, industry, and new modes of transportation.

What industry Talbot has experienced seems always to have been bound to her waters—the Bay and its broad tributaries. For example, as long ago as 1813, during the tumultuous years of the War of 1812, Talbot money helped start the steamboat era. Captain Edward Trippe of Dorchester, a friend of Robert Fulton, conceived the idea for the steamboat *Chesapeake*, developed the plans, and raised one-third of the money to build her with County funds. Built in Baltimore, in William Flanigan's shipyard, she measured 130 feet in length, 20 feet in width, and 7 feet in depth.[1] She operated across the head of the Bay and connected with her Delaware River–based sister ship *Philadelphia* to carry passengers from Baltimore to Philadelphia; coaches took care of the overland section of the route. Both *Chesapeake* and *Philadelphia* were luxuriously equipped with solid silver cutlery, imported china, and fine linens. A new era had begun, an era that was to make possible the transport of cargoes—fruits and vegetables and other perishables, such as fresh fish and soft crabs—regardless of winds and tides, to previously unavailable markets. And this is not to mention human passengers who sailed the steamers on business and pleasure.

Later, Talbot businessmen raised $40,000, formed the Maryland Steamboat Company, and built the *Maryland*. Nicholas Hammond was president of the company; William Clark, John Goldsborough, and Samuel Groome were among the directors. The *Maryland* had a hull very much like a schooner, broad with a flat bottom and full at the bow and stern; all her accommodations for passengers were below deck. Also below deck were the boilers and the engine, as well as miscellaneous freight and the wood—the only kind of fuel used for many years on steamboats.

The first steamship routes between Baltimore and Talbot County were all by way of the Miles River. It was not until about the time of the Civil War that the Tred Avon River was used and a steamboat landing established at Easton Point.

The success of the Maryland Steamboat Company led to the founding of rival companies to compete for the profitable traffic across the Bay. One competing company was the Wheeler Line. It stopped, on its way to Baltimore, at Wayman's Landing, New Bridge, Lloyd's Landing, Cambridge, and Trappe Landing. Wayman's Landing was named for the black family that lived along the Tuckahoe River near that point. From this family came Bishop A. W. Wayman, the first black to be consecrated a bishop in the Methodist Episcopal Church. Bishop Wayman, like many of his generation, achieved distinction with little schooling except the tutelage of his father. A prominent educator later heard Wayman preach and asked where he was educated. Wayman responded, "The University of Tuckahoe," and the educator then asked where it was. "On the banks of the Tuckahoe River on the Eastern Shore of Maryland," replied the bishop.[2]

OPPOSITE:
Nineteenth-century Talbot County: railroads and steamboat lines are prominent.

1. "History of Talbot County."
2. Ibid.

A. W. Wayman, the first black to be consecrated a bishop in the Methodist Episcopal Church.

If the black Bishop Wayman rose to religious prominence, it must be remembered that he was unusual in a slave-owning part of Maryland. In fact, many of Talbot's most prominent (white) citizens supported the Confederacy in thought, word, and deed.

Among these was Thomas Robson, editor of the *Star*. As was discussed in Chapter 6, the *Star* (today known as the *Star-Democrat*) is one of Maryland's oldest newspapers, and it was the heat of politics that caused the only real suspension in the paper's long history of publishing. During the Civil War editor Robson's uninhibited advocacy of the South's cause led to his arrest; he was paroled in 1862. A few months later, as a result of his hatred and continued denunciation of Lincoln's administration, his presses were damaged and his type cases emptied into the street. In May 1863 one of the Martins of Island Creek Neck wrote and editor Robson published a poem, "Noble Ashby," following the death of Confederate General Turner Ashby; this proved too much and Robson was arrested on (it is unofficially said) Lincoln's orders.[3] A newspaper friend wrote later, "they conducted the distinguished Maryland editor and his personal effects southward and eventually through the Federal lines and beyond into the broad and beautiful Shenandoah Valley. There they left him seated and cooling his heels on his trunk in the middle of a bare, winding road dust-filled and desolate." Two years and four months later, editor Robson returned, revived the *Star*, and before long it was flourishing again. When he died in 1888 the rival *Democrat* wrote, "Mr. Robson was a man of strong conviction and sense of duty. When he made up his mind about any question, he went to work to secure success for his side, and no matter whose toes he trod upon he went unswervingly to gain the desired end." Robson is celebrated in a commemorative stained-glass window in the Easton Cathedral. Eight years after Robson's death, his paper became known as the *Star-Democrat*, under which hyphenated name it continues to be published.[4]

Editor Robson was not alone in Talbot County in his support for the Confederate States of America. And, as was true in the Revolution, although no important action took place on Talbot's shores or lands in the Civil War, many of its citizens played active roles. Perhaps foremost was Admiral Franklin Buchanan of The Rest (T–339). One of the war's great naval officers, Buchanan's life embodies the split loyalties the conflict beginning at Fort Sumter caused.

From the age of fourteen, Buchanan was fortunate to be under the command of the foremost commodores of the early navy, and on famous ships such as *Hornet* chasing pirates in the Caribbean, on *Constellation* in the Mediterranean, and *Constitution* in the Pacific. Secretary of the Navy George Bancroft took note of Buchanan's brilliant naval record and appointed him to draw up rules and regulations for the establishment of a Naval School on the Severn River at Annapolis. Commander Buchanan not only drew up the rules and regulations but also served as the Naval Academy's first superintendent.

In 1861, thinking that Maryland was going to secede, Buchanan withdrew his commission in the United States Navy. When Maryland remained in the Union, he tried to withdraw his resignation, but the government did not accept the withdrawal. So he offered his services to the South, with whose armed services he had an interesting tour of duty: he was the first commander of the *Merrimac* and then fought in the battle of Mobile Bay. After the war, he returned to Talbot County. He had married Anne Catherine Lloyd, daughter of Edward Lloyd V, and a niece of Mrs. Francis Scott Key. The Buchanans rebuilt The Rest, which had been destroyed by fire during the war years. The relationship between Buchanan and his brother-in-law, Commander Charles Lowndes, U.S.N., has often been mentioned. These two men had married sisters, and they spent their last years in houses that faced each other across the Miles River: the Union veteran Lowndes at The Anchorage, appropriately on the north bank; Buchanan at The Rest, just as fittingly on the south. Each is now buried with his wife at Wye.

After the war, Talbot's steamboat lines were augmented in 1869 when General Joseph B. Seth of Easton founded the Baltimore and Eastern Shore Railroad while he was serving as speaker of the house of delegates. Seth developed the idea of connecting Baltimore and

3. Ibid.
4. The *Easton Star-Democrat*, August 7, 1959, Section A, p. 1.

The steamboat *Talbot*: a new era had begun.

The luxurious Bay steamboats remained in use well into the twentieth century.

Admiral Buchanan was commander of the *Merrimac* (known as the *Virginia* in the South) on her first voyage, when she sank the *Cumberland.*

Admiral Franklin Buchanan by Rembrandt Peale.

the Shore by direct route, and he secured a charter from the Maryland legislature. The first steamer used on this ferry system was the *Tockwah*, and she made the distance between Claiborne and Bay Ridge, at the mouth of the Severn River, on a schedule of 55 minutes, which—allowing 30 minutes from Easton to Claiborne by train, and one hour by train from Bay Ridge to Baltimore—made a total schedule of two-and-one-half hours from Easton to Baltimore. The railroad was completed in 1890. The schedule was so arranged as to give Talbot countians four or five hours in Baltimore before they made the return trip the same day. The line continued to Ocean City via Salisbury. In joint operation with the Baltimore and Ohio Railroad, the ferry system added the steamer *Thames*, with a capacity of ten railroad cars, to carry freight.

This expanded steamboat and rail business also helped Talbot County's watermen and farmers by connecting the county's seafood and farm produce with the markets of Philadelphia and New York. In fact, if railroads helped the Shore feed the citizens of the north, the Shore also fed passengers on the railroads: generations of Baltimore and Ohio Railroad riders to Chicago savored terrapin, oysters, and crabs. The improved transportation encouraged other industries as well, as the 1881 *History of Easton* was proud to note:

As before intimated, during the retrograde period of the town—from 1820 to 1865—some important industries were instituted, which however had but a feeble existence until a recent period. Steam was introduced as a motive power, there being a steam saw mill established at Easton Point by Joseph K. Neal, in 1836. The establishment passed through several hands, finally it came into the possession of Mr. John Tunis. The mill building having been destroyed by fire the business was removed to Easton in 1857, and with the addition of a grist mill, had a checkered experience until it came into the hands of Mr. Wm. Wilson. In 1860 the moulding and casting business was started by Messrs. Wm. and Jas. Oxenham, the foundry being the building now used by the Gas Company on West Street. When gas was introduced in 1857, the foundry was transferred to a small building at the extreme end of Washington Street. Here but little was accomplished until 1865, when Mr. N. Tuthill came into possession of the business, soon after associating with him Mr. D. C. Avery. These gentlemen rapidly built up an excellent iron enterprise; new and extensive brick buildings were erected; improved machinery introduced, and an enterprise of no little importance was ere long being successfully carried on.[5]

5. Garey, *History of Easton.*

If some of Talbot County's slave-owning farm families suffered after Appomattox many town residents seem to have prospered:

> Easton set out on a renewed growth. . . . Business of every kind improved, especially the mercantile. A lively competition sprung up among this fraternity. The usually low prices, and superior quality of the fabrics sold, attracted buyers from all the adjoining counties and even Delaware. The increase in business was sufficient to justify the enlargement of facilities, and in 1876, J. J. Jump & Co. led off by establishing what was claimed to be the handsomest store south of Wilmington. They were pioneers in the plate-glass fronts, and others were not loth to follow, until today there is scarcely a town in the land of equal size that possesses as handsome stores, which carry as large stocks and do as flourishing a mercantile trade as Easton.[6]

Another of these "handsome stores" is the North Building (T–40) at 110–112 North Washington Street. Built in 1870 as a residence, the building is three stories in height and is covered with a shallow hipped roof pierced by tall brick chimneys and supported by bold brackets. The building has Italianate verticality and detailing and has survived without substantial alterations. This is particularly true on the interior, where the stair is elaborate, well-proportioned, and grand; the ceilings are high, and door and window surrounds are wide. The rooms are still spacious and airy.

One of the first styles to appear in Talbot County after the Civil War (it appeared elsewhere during the war) was the Second Empire, a manner of building that dominated high-style American architecture in the 1860s and '70s. The most noticeable feature of this decidedly three-dimensional style is a mansard roof. Dormer windows are also common as is, in larger buildings, a projecting center pavilion. Talbot's Second Empire buildings include the so-called Mansard House (T–270) in St. Michaels, with its mansard roof finished in painted fish-scale shingles; two slightly less ornate houses (T–281 and T–284) in Trappe; and, in Easton, the house at 407 Goldsborough Street (T–292). The Easton building is a little, one-and-one-half-story structure. Its companion carriage house, one of the most elaborate in town, is a charming near-double of the main house and reflects the importance of outbuildings in this period.

Lodges and other fraternal organizations are an intimate part of small-town life, and freemasonry has existed on the Eastern Shore since the eighteenth century. The Easton

6. Ibid.

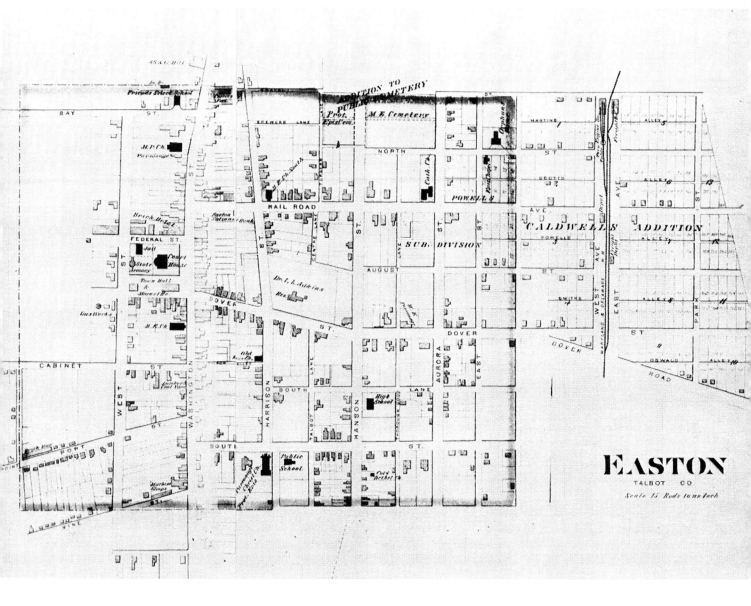

"Easton set out on a renewed growth": the city in 1877.

Lodge, number 102, was founded on May 12, 1855, and has met continuously since that time. The group first met in the Talbot County Courthouse; the present Masonic building (T–295), at 114 North Washington Street, was built in 1881.[7] It uses Italianate motifs to express the building's ceremonial functions. The three-story structure is of a lovely light orange brick with white-stone details. There is a shallow front gable with a single eye, a symbol of the order; tall chimneys rise at each side wall. The lodge room is on the third floor, and professional offices occupy the first and second floors. The lodge's position on the main street reminds the town of the popularity and importance of the organization that constructed it.

The Miller Lodge of the International Order of Odd Fellows is an even older organization, although its building (T–1) at 1 South Washington Street is slightly newer. The 1881 Easton *History* comments that the Miller Lodge "may be the handsomest structure on the Eastern Shore, and is undoubtedly the handsomest Odd Fellows' Hall in the State of Maryland." Perhaps. It is certainly one of the most aggressively symbolic structures: the four-story brick lodge is embellished with an eclectic combination of stylistic elements. The third-floor lodge room below its high, vaulted ceiling contains one of the most complete Victorian interiors in the town. Chartered in 1832, Miller Lodge has

7. Material in the library of the Maryland Historical Trust, Annapolis.

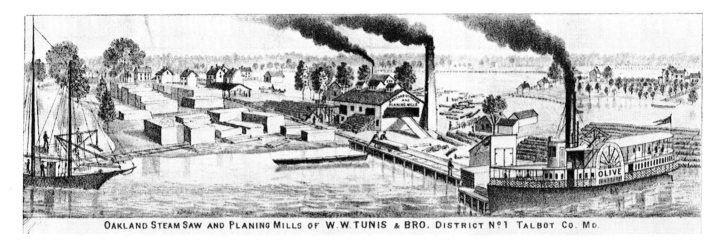

OAKLAND STEAM SAW AND PLANING MILLS OF W.W. TUNIS & BRO. DISTRICT N° 1 TALBOT CO. MD.

met at this site since 1854. Among the lodge's forty-three original members were Howes Goldsborough, who was largely responsible for the construction of Saints Peter and Paul Catholic Church in Easton, and Philip Francis Thomas, one-time governor of Maryland. The present building was dedicated on September 25, 1879.[8]

The age of steam brought new industries to Talbot County.

This Victorian vigor affected even the normally quiet Quakers, who erected a new building (T–47) near their ancient Third Haven Meeting House (T–46) when the practice of segregated meetings for men and women was discontinued in 1879; they dedicated their new "co-ed" building in 1880. Built at right angles to the old meeting house, it consists of a meeting room on the first floor with classrooms above. Its brick walls are red-orange, laid in common bond; mortar joints are smooth, narrow, and even. The main entrance to the east gable leads to a stair and entry hall, beyond which is the meeting room. The entire first floor is lit by tall, sixteen-over-sixteen windows.

The 1881 Easton *History* was pleased to note that new, post-bellum industries brought workers to Talbot, new shops attracted customers, and the railroads added "to those natural waterways that had proven so successful from the beginning. Northern and western settlers began to find homes in the county and its principal town." Many of these late-nineteenth-century houses are still standing.

Jump's store: "the handsomest store south of Wilmington" as depicted in 1877.

The Jumps' store was important enough to be singled out in the 1881 *History*, and their house at 107 Goldsborough Street (T–288) in Easton is also significant. A blending of two styles and two eras, the earlier Italianate and the Queen Anne, the house is an interesting transition piece.

Victorians loved variety and irregularity in their architecture, and in houses like the Chaffinch House (T–34) in Easton one can see the workings of their busy minds; structures like this building show that while their architecture was fanciful, it was also deliberate. The house's exuberance reflects the energy, inventiveness, and skill of its builder and designer. Basically a two-and-one-half-story, square building with a rear ell, it uses plastic elements —projecting windows and gables and a tower—to express interior functions. A dominant architectural idea in the late nineteenth century was that of volumetric expression. The interiors of buildings were seen as a composition of volumes, not as a series of rooms. The exterior walls were conceived more as "skins" covering these volumes than as structural elements carrying the roof and floors. Thus, in this building we can clearly see the interior volumes through the bulges of the exterior skin that encloses the volumes and holds them together. The builder made great use of the ceremonial idea of entry at the door; he also ingeniously used horizontal bands of texture—weatherboarding and shingles—as well as a porch to tie the composition together. All in all, a bravura performance.

The house at 9 North Aurora Street (T–293) is another of Easton's Victorian splendors. A frame house with hipped roof and tall flaring chimneys, it is beautifully detailed inside and out. Bay windows expand the front and side facades and the roof is broken by dormers. On the inside, the spacious rooms have well-proportioned golden oak

8. Garey, *History of Easton.*

Washington Street in Easton in the early
twentieth century: "There is scarcely a
town in the land of equal size that possesses as handsome stores."

The Chaffinch House in Easton: fanciful but deliberate.

trim; there is an oak stair with deeply carved newel and balusters. Some consider the house to be the finest of its period in town.

Farther up North Aurora Street is the McDaniel House (T–294), another of Easton's extravagant, towered, late-Victorian dwellings. Architecturally, all these buildings were designed with a concern for volumetric expression, asymmetrically balanced compositions, and delicately articulated exteriors. This building displays all of these elements, although it may not be quite as sophisticated or integrated in its design as 9 North Aurora or the Chaffinch House.

Another plump, exotic Easton Victorian house—these buildings seem frame versions of Lillian Russell—can be seen at 200 South Harrison Street (T–297). Built by Benjamin F. Parlett, a prosperous Easton merchant, it displays the free use of decoration and irregularity so favored during that period; its bold details make an interesting contrast to the delicately detailed Chaffinch House across the street.

Some of these late-nineteenth-century dwellings impress not through their size, but through their builders' skill. Note the Roberts House (T–290) at 211 Goldsborough Street. A showcase of the carpenter's artistry, the Roberts House was constructed by Captain Edward Roberts, a leading figure in Easton's volunteer fire department. Roberts was a carpenter by profession, which doubtless explains why this otherwise simple, center-hall building is adorned with fanciful wooden brackets, balustrades, and applied wooden

The Villa (now destroyed).

Llandaff, a rare example of Queen Anne style architecture in Talbot County.

ornament. The central porch is flanked by two pavilions covered by roofs with flaring eaves.

If Talbot's townspeople experimented with the more flamboyant Victorian styles—Gothic, Second Empire, Romanesque, and what historians throw up their hands and just call High Victorian—the county's farmers were less enthusiastic and such buildings are rare in the Talbot landscape. The reasons are probably twofold: first, Talbot County had, and has, a strongly developed conservative nature; second, the economic devastation wrought by the Civil War and Emancipation on the country's farmers left little local money to be spent on architectural fancies. Some of the most elaborate, fashionable houses were built by people who had made their monetary piles elsewhere and who moved to build their architectural piles in Talbot County. This phenomenon has certainly continued into the twentieth century.

Thus one finds only modest rural Gothicism. For example, Gaymcrest (T–194), near Bellevue, is a three-section farm house whose central section appears to have been built around 1880 in the Victorian Gothic style, but with touches typical of the vernacular dwellings of the period. (In the 1940s the boxer Gene Tunney owned the house and remodeled it to suit his taste.) Shipshead (Sheepshead) Farm (T–176) is a fine Federal house built around 1815 but remodeled—modestly—later in the nineteenth century: the roofline was extended by thin brackets, and low cross-gables with cut-out bargeboard trim were added. The Gothic peak of the cross-gable is reflected in the pointed casement window it accommodates. (For Talbot's antebellum Gothic structures, see pp. 105–9.)

The Villa (now destroyed but formerly at the end of Villa Lane at the confluence of the Miles River, Goldsborough Creek, and Glebe Creek) needs to be mentioned as another exception that proves the rule. Built by rich New Yorkers, the house's form must have shocked conservative Talbot countians because wild stories still rage about it and its occupants: Did Boss Tweed hide out here? And just what sort of gambling went on?

A more conservative style, conservative in the sense that it harkens back to the turn of the eighteenth century, made its presence known, in a superb manner, in Talbot County. The Queen Anne style, characterized by irregularity of plan and massing and by varied surface color and texture, was born in 1868 in an English house designed by the very successful architect Richard Norman Shaw. From the 1870s on, Shaw's houses were widely published in the architectural journals and grew to be admired on this side of the Atlantic. H. H. Richardson was probably the first American to design in this style, and his 1874 Watts Sherman House in Newport, Rhode Island, is an early, possibly the earliest, example of an American Queen Anne house. The Philadelphia Centennial Exposition in 1876 marks the real beginning of the style's popularity. There the British government put up two half-timbered buildings and the magazine the *American Builder* waxed ecstatic: "the most interesting . . . buildings erected by any foreign government on the Centennial grounds," it proclaimed. The article continued: "But the chief thing that will strike the observant eye in this style is its wonderful adaptability to this country, not to the towns indeed, but to the land at large. . . . It is to be hoped that the next millionaire who puts up a cottage at Long Branch will adopt this style, and he will have a house ample enough to entertain a Prince, yet exceedingly cozy, cool in summer, and yet abundantly warm in winter, plain enough, and yet capable of the highest ornamental development."[9]

Llandaff (T–231), a sprawling country house near Easton, is a significantly early (1878) example of the Queen Anne style. Built for John Robinson, a Wells-Fargo silver buyer and railroad magnate, it remains in the possession of his descendants. The main house has a hip roof partially concealed by broad, very Queen Anne gables. A particularly "ancient" touch is the entrance porch tower. Even though the house has undergone a remodeling that stripped it of several porches and much ornament, enough variegated details remain to give a hint of what it must once have looked like. In all respects Llandaff compares favorably with better-known Queen Anne houses, such as Theodore Roosevelt's Sagamore Hill (1884–85) on Long Island.

The Llandaff windmill.

9. Marcus Whiffen, *American Architecture Since 1780* (Cambridge, Mass.: M.I.T. Press, 1967), pp. 117, 118.

CHAPTER 9

Talbot Today: "It Is Still Vital"

The life that Talbot countians were enjoying at the end of the nineteenth century has continued into the modern era. If anything, the enjoyment has intensified. The Bay and the tidal inlets that form Talbot's aqueous borders have traditionally provided the county with a solid economic base. Oystering, fishing, and crabbing still bring in money, and they have been joined by the soft-clam industry. The waters, not incidentally, are a prime source of recreation as well.

Log canoes, built by the Indians centuries before John Smith came to the Bay, continue to be used in Talbot County. The canoe's history combines work (oystering) and war (Talbot County's southern sympathizers stealthily navigated them through the Union blockade to join Confederate forces); they now provide sport, and the beautiful log canoe sailing races draw thousands of spectators. The late Robert Dawson Lambdin, a well-known St. Michaels shipbuilder—"Captain Bob" to a generation of Talbot sailors—wrote a piece on "Shipbuilding on the Chesapeake" for the *Maryland Historical Magazine* of June 1941. In this article he described how to make a log canoe:

> In building a log canoe the first step is to locate suitable large pine trees. These are the kind grown as original pine trees as distinguished from second growth trees. The trees before felling are bored with an augur to ascertain the proportion of sap wood. Any tree containing a large proportion of sap wood is not felled. After felling the tree, it is stripped of branches, the bark removed, the logs roughly shaped and then hauled to the shipyard. All sap wood is removed.
>
> The bottom log is hewn out first. This is the bottom of the boat and is shaped at the ends in such a manner that the logs which form the bilge are practically fitted into it. After the bilge, the top log is fitted in a similar manner and shaped to give the desired shear to the deck line. The logs are then bolted together. The hull is shaped first on the outside, then holes are bored into the sides at various points and dark wood dowel pins of varying lengths driven in as gauges so that the appearance of their ends when hollowing the inside of the hull will indicate the desired thickness of the hull at various points.

Captain Bob Lambdin had this to say about the boat that skims like a swallow across the water:

> It may be noted that in most cases the canoes are sailed by others than the owner. This is because the sailing of a boat is a gift which very few possess. A good sailing captain has an instinctive feeling which tells him when all of the factors for getting the best out of the hull, sails, and crew are in harmony. It does not seem possible for one possessing this gift to impart it to another. Many instances can be cited where an expert sailing captain can win a race against a competing boat, and then transfer to the competing boat and beat the boat he originally sailed in. Recognizing this ability in this respect, all the boats belonging to me which were entered in races were sailed by Captain Giles W. (Bill) Jump.

In 1830 Captain Bob's father started his shipyard at Long Wharf and Mulberry Street in St. Michaels, where he later took in four of his five sons, George, William, Samuel, and Robert. They built schooners, sloops, pungies, and bugeyes. Captain Bob's father told him,

A log canoe race.

"The nearer you can keep a boat to the shape of an egg, the surer you can be that she will sail."

Captain Bob built sixty-eight canoes. When he was twenty-three years old, he bought a thirty-foot, three-log keel canoe, the *Mary*, which had been built by Thomas Kirby of St. Michaels. Against the advice of men whose opinion was noteworthy, Captain Bob installed the first centerboard ever put in a log canoe. "I had ideas of my own regarding the proper location of the centerboard with relation to the center of effort of the sail plan and also determined to use another idea of my own which was to make a well box in which the centerboard worked, one inch wider at the forward end than at the after end, in order to make the boat point higher into the wind," Captain Bob Lambdin said in relating the background of the innovation. *Mary* outsailed all competitors, and since that trial year, 1872, there have been no canoes built, it is believed, but the centerboard type. Among the "superior type of boat builders" (as Captain Bob called them) were Captain Lewis Farr, Samuel Blades, George Lambdin, John B. Harrison, and "Syd" Covington.[1]

In the Miles River Yacht Club Regatta of August 1962, celebrating Talbot County's 300th anniversary, ten log sailing canoes, the largest assemblage of this truly American craft in many years, met to race.

Another local institution is of more recent origin. In 1907 there was no hospital on the Eastern Shore. A Talbot countian with a ruptured appendix, for example, had the choice of being loaded on the night boat at Easton Point to arrive in Baltimore at 7 a.m., of leaving Easton by early morning train, changing at Clayton and again at Wilmington for Baltimore, or of staying home to die.

In February 1907, a forward-looking group of men rented the two upper floors of a vacant hotel (T–2) on South Washington Street in Easton, and the Emergency Hospital that serves four counties was born. Two surgeons and four general practitioners made up the staff. The elevator to the operating room rose thanks to a stout, hairy rope pulled by the doctor who was the anaesthetist for the day—the operating surgeon had to save his hands from rope splinters.

Extracts from the hospital's early constitution and by-laws might prove interesting in today's world of expensive medical sophistication:

No fee shall be charged for a person who is unable to pay, and such patients shall receive the same care and attention as pay patients. Patients who are able to pay shall be charged the minimum rates of $8.00, $12.00, and $15.00 per week for a private room, and from $2.00 to $5.00 per week for treatment in the wards. These charges to include board, fuel, lights and attention of the nurses. The laundry of a patient will not be attended to in the hospital except in special cases where the Superintendent so directs.

1. Robert Dawson Lambdin, "Ship-Building on the Chesapeake: Recollections of Robert Dawson Lambdin," in *Maryland Historical Magazine*, vol. 36 (1941):171–83.

The Emergency Hospital, circa 1910.

There must have been some complaints about these exorbitant costs, for there is a sort of apologia in the President's Report of 1909: "We are charging from $10.00 to $15.00 per week for private rooms, which is not as much as charged by the hotels where nothing is given but board and lodging."

A few other excerpts:

> The great bulk of our patients are accepted without any charge, or for small amounts such as the patients seem disposed to contribute. No one is denied admission because of lack of funds, consequently we find ourselves in a position, where the amount received from board and care pays about ⅓ of the expense of running the hospital, and the management have to look to charitable institutions to make up the remainder.
>
> Of the two hundred and sixty-eight patients admitted during the past year, one hundred and one were absolutely free; one hundred and twenty-six paid sums running from $1.00 to $5.00 per week and 41 paid the full charges for rooms $10.00, $12.00 and $15.00 according to situation—the $10.00 rooms being most in demand.[2]

Dr. William N. Palmer, who joined the staff in 1911, wrote a history of the hospital's first half century for the Maryland Historical Society. Dr. Palmer's reminiscences provide an unequaled account of how medicine was practiced in the early years of the century in a rural area.

> Compared to present standards the hospital of 1911 was primitive . . . but of 263 surgical cases (nearly all major) and 109 medical (including 44 typhoid) there were only 27 deaths and ten of those were within the first 48 hours of admission. The lack of room and the physical impossibility of expanding the buildings gave concern to everyone interested.
>
> An appeal was made for donations of linen, pillow case tubing, table cloths and napkins, towels of all kinds, bleached muslin for patient gowns, canned fruits and vegetables. As usual, the response was enthusiastic.
>
> The year 1916 was chiefly of interest in preparing for emergencies in case of war. I remember that this was the year "Birth of a Nation" was shown in this town of approximately 3,000 population and drew a crowd of 1,339 even though the projection room caught fire one evening. It was also the year that the hospital acquired a certain distinction across the Mason Dixon line when Mrs. Charlotte Varoter, a ninety year old cousin of Lincoln, was admitted for observation. This was the year that the nurses, even while receiving the magnificent sum of $25 per week for twenty four hour regular duty and $35.00 for contagion cases, began to talk of a possible twelve hour day.[3]

Another public institution, the Longwoods School (T–69) in the hamlet of Longwoods, is far more significant than its modest form might suggest: the little frame building represents the beginning of public education in Talbot County. Although not as aged as many structures in the area, the Longwoods School is one of the few remaining one-room

2. Material in files of the Talbot County Historical Society, Easton.
3. Quoted in "History of Talbot County."

Easton's beaux-arts bank under construction (above) and as it is today
(below).

schoolhouses on the Shore. The building is painted a bright red with white trim, and has recently been restored by the Talbot County Commissioners.

The present home of the Maryland National Bank in Easton, 32–36 North Washington Street (T–408), stands in direct contrast to the humble appearance of the Longwoods School. The bank's history actually began when the Farmers and Merchants Bank, the first of the Eastern Shore, opened its doors to depositors in 1805. The bank did well from the very beginning in its leased building on the west side of Washington Street near Bay Street: its first dividend, paid in October 1806, was 7½ percent. In 1810, the bank bought the southeast corner of Washington and Goldsborough streets and erected its own two-story brick building. This building no longer stands. Through prosperity, depression, and panic, the bank steered its conservative course, approving "foreign" loans only after much deliberation: it required some debate, for example, before the bank granted a $25,000 loan to the trustees of the Johns Hopkins Hospital. This attitude paid off and the bank prospered. In 1899, it steel-lined its vaults. In 1901, it erected a $4,000-building, which it rented to the post office, making a good return on its investment—$800 a year. In 1903–4, it built its own building at 32–36 North Washington Street. In February 1910, when the bank's deposits reached $1,000,000, bank president Robert Dixon gave a dinner for the employees to celebrate that happy landmark. This goal had actually been reached the previous August, but a terrapin dinner had been promised and the celebration was delayed until good terrapin could be had. In its more than 175 years of existence, the bank has paid its annual dividend without fail—a record that must be rare in the United States. It is the twenty-fifth oldest bank in the country and the second oldest in the state. In 1962, it merged with the Maryland National Bank.[4]

4. Ibid.

That Washington Street structure is one of the few in Talbot County to follow the dictates of the beaux-arts. The principles of this style were laid down by the Ecole des Beaux-Arts in Paris, an institution whose influence on nineteenth-century architecture was probably unmatched by any other organization anywhere in the world. By the end of the century, American architecture was dominated by men who had attended the Ecole.

Monumental is probably the best adjective to use to describe the style: monumental columns and/or pilasters; monumental flights of steps; monumental sculptural decoration; monumental cornices and parapets—beaux-arts architects wanted their buildings to be *noticed.* Students at the Ecole would compete for the Grand Prix de Rome, and their project

> was inevitably of a grandiose nature . . . and the program was written in those sonorous generalities to which the French language so readily lends itself. In the competition, which was judged by a jury, there were two requisites for success: first, a demonstration of expertise in the approved convention of planning, which demanded clear articulation of functions and a hierarchy of major and minor axes and cross axes; second, skillfully executed elevational drawings with plenty to look at in them.[5]

American beaux-arts buildings include many of the best-known public and quasi-public structures in the country, from libraries (such as the New York Public Library, 1895–1902), to railroad stations (Grand Central Terminal, 1903–1913), to museums (the Metropolitan Museum of Art, 1895). But the style was arguably more successful in "the plaster architecture of the exhibitions." And, again arguably, the most romantically successful of these exhibition structures is Bernard Maybeck's Palace of Fine Arts (1915) in San Francisco. Actually, the Palace of Fine Arts is not a building at all, but is, instead, a superbly sensuous stage set whose "crumbling stucco . . . gave eloquent if functionless expression to the mood of melancholy."[6]

The Maryland National Bank building (to use its current name) is more solidly architectural, but its debt to the Ecole is clear in its giant pilasters, medallions, festoons, parapet, and monumental arched windows with their console keystones. The generous use of plaster detail on the exterior is carried into the interior, which has a spacious, airy room with a ceiling supported by Ionic columns.

Twentieth-century domestic architecture in Talbot County has remained conservative and, if not as grand as the beaux-arts bank, relies just as strongly on the classically inspired past. At the same time, this century has seen an influence of "wealthy people from New York, Pittsburgh, and points West" who, in one writer's opinion, have given the county "a smarter and more sophisticated air." It is so "smart" and famous, in fact, that the same writer noted that "whenever people from outside Maryland refer to the Eastern Shore they are generally referring to Talbot County."[7] These men, having made their fortunes in the brusque world of corporate-industrial America, apparently have come to the Miles, the Wye, the Tred Avon to relax. They seem to like what they have found and have not tried to change Talbot's traditions: they shoot ducks; they net crabs; they sail ships; and they build their new country houses in the style of the past, seeking to achieve what V. Sackville-West called houses that seem to have grown "with the oaks and elms and beeches." Simply put, they embraced the colonial revival.

The colonial revival, a style extremely popular in the teens and twenties, suffered a long period of scholarly disinterest. The style and its great practitioners, McKim, Mead & White, John Russell Pope, Charles Platt, William Lawrence Bottomley, Delano and Aldrich, Baltimore's Wyatt and Nolting, are now just beginning to receive serious study.

This revival style—colonial, Georgian, or classical, they all grow from the same well-ordered roots—followed rules, and, it has been said, those rules were appealing in that troubled era because they allowed the architect "to strive for a perfection that was abstract and introspective, above the vicissitudes of his fellow man, and a hedge against the uncertainties he felt a new century might bring."[8] As the new century became more uncertain, bringing with it first the Great War and then the Great Depression, a retreat from "the vicissitudes of his fellow man" must have seemed desirous indeed.

5. Whiffen, *American Architecture,* pp. 150–51.

6. Ibid., p. 156.

7. Hulbert Footner, *Maryland Main and the Eastern Shore* (New York: D. Appleton-Century Co., 1942), p. 172.

8. Daniel O'Neill, *Lutyens, Country Houses* (New York: Whitney Library of Design, 1981), p. 94.

"They shoot ducks."

Fiske Kimball wrote a classic piece entitled "The American Country House" in *The Architectural Record* of October 1919. In it he noted the prodigious rise in the number of people financially able to build the sort of house he has in mind, people who were drawn to the shore of Miles and the Tred Avon: "[S]triking . . . is the large absolute number of 'millionaires,' and their rapid increases from the 4,027 . . . in 1892 to 15,190 in 1910 and 19,143 in 1917."[9] *Sunpapers* reporter Mary Corddry has recently written that "Talbot County has the unproven—but undisputed—reputation of having more millionaires per capita than any other county in the state."[10]

Kimball's article continued:

Foremost of the social conditions affecting the country house is the very impulse to its building, the great wave of renewed love of out-of-door life and of nature which swept over America in the last years of the nineteenth century and the opening years of the twentieth. Predominant in it, no doubt, is the fondness for out-of-door sports, which have had such an unparalleled development in the last generation; but beside this has come a fuller enjoyment of gardening and the quieter pleasures of country life. To permit the indulgence of these tastes even modern business has had to give way, adapting its organization to vacations and weekends, not only of the executives but of the whole sales and office force.[11]

Technological changes were important, too, and Kimball recognized that the "imperative demand for modern and American ideals of comfort" had, by the early twentieth century, been met by plumbing, electricity, central heating, fans, modern water system, rural mail delivery, telephones, and, most important of all, the automobile. "The result of these ideals and facilities has been the great decentralization of the more favored classes of towns and cities, whether by summer exodus to the seashore and mountains, or by life the year around on the borders of the country or in the country itself."[12]

Regarding what he called "Artistic Conditions," Kimball wrote that "while practical conditions determine the main types and the accommodations of our country houses, artistic conditions—the traditions and tendencies of style—have a decisive influence not only in fixing the character of the exterior and interior treatment, but even in determining the plan." And here is the stylistic key: "there have always been certain favored styles that have the advantage of conformity to practical needs or *cultural inheritance*" (emphasis supplied).[13]

The best practitioners of the colonial revival respected the architecture in the area in which they were building: they would not, for example, build a New England cottage in Florida. As Bottomley wrote in the May 1929 *Arts & Decoration*, a good revival house "should fit its setting. . . . Its character should reflect the best cultural traditions of its locality."[14] Bottomley and his fellow architects welcomed the "return to a simpler, more Anglo-Saxon tradition, combined with a strong American tendency," and deplored the nineteenth-century mansions that were "Italian, French, Japanese, anything! In this century, fortunately, we have come to realize the value—in fact the necessity—of a suitable artistic form for our American house."[15] The point was not to copy existing buildings but to absorb local building traditions and to create new houses within them.

This would be especially important in areas with a firm architectural past: New England, California, Philadelphia, and, to bring the focus back on Talbot County, the Chesapeake with its well-developed (and beloved) Georgian country houses: "We should do everything possible to preserve this old southern ideal of country house architecture because it is one of the finest things we have and it is still vital."[16]

Kimball ended his article on country houses on a curiously revolutionary note: "If the choice of forms is retrospective and dependent, we may quiet our artistic conscience by reflecting that our civilization itself is still fundamentally that of a passing era, and that a truly creative art can triumph only with a new social order."[17] No new social order was desired at Bonfield (T–161), near Oxford. It was built by John Lee Carroll Downes after Samuel Chamberlaine; Jr.'s, 1772 mansion burned in 1924. In 1918 Downes was elected

9. Fiske Kimball, "The American Country House," in *The Architectural Record*, vol. 46, no. 4 (1919):301.
10. Mary Corddry, "Easton," in *Maryland Magazine* (1983):38.
11. Kimball, "Country House," p. 310.
12. Ibid., p. 312.
13. Ibid., p. 329.
14. William Lawrence Bottomley, "The Country House and the Developed Landscape," in *Arts & Decoration*, vol. 32, no. 1:54.
15. Ibid., p. 98.
16. Ibid., p. 100.
17. Kimball, "Country House," p. 340.

an officer of the Philadelphia National Bank, and later joined with William C. Durant, then president of General Motors Corporation, to become vice-president of all the Durant Enterprises. He was at one time an officer and director of more than sixty large corporations.[18] His country house, now destroyed, was a seven-bay, two-and-one-half-story, H-plan house, complete with chauffeur's quarters in an old outbuilding.

In building their new country houses, Talbot's modern magnates have tended to follow one of two paths. Some, like Mr. Downes, built their mansions complete, intact, all-of-a-piece. This resulted in houses like Ellenborough (T–171), Locust Lane (T–232, notable as the residence of the sculptor Lee Laurie), Emerson Point (T–235), Hunting Hall (T–97), and Canterbury Manor (T–167). It also included Howell's Point (T–144), which has been destroyed. Others were able to find real, old houses and incorporate them into newer, larger structures. Houses with a bit of the old in them include Locust Grove (T–170), Harleigh (T–166), Lombardy (T–99), Forrest Landing (T–82), Cedar Point (T–208), Perry Cabin (T–206), Wye Heights (T–81), and Crosiadore (T–143).

Canterbury Manor, on Bailey's Neck overlooking Trippe's Creek, may stand as representative of the built-from-scratch group. It has a large, two-and-one-half-story section with wings on the east and a one-story porch on the west. The central portion of the dwelling has a pedimented Ionic portico complete with large lunette. The facade of the structure behind has a single architectural treatment composed of the door with side windows and a Palladian-style window above, connected to the door's architrave below. The opposite facade has double doors with sidelights, a central elliptical window above, and two flanking bay windows. There is a double porch with Chinese Chippendale balustrade. A small peninsula extends out from the lawn into Trippe's Creek and is planted in classic tidewater style with boxwood borders and flanking woodland. This charming and correct house was built in 1906 by Colonel F. Carroll Goldsborough and later expanded by Charles Wheeler, an Easton attorney, who owned the property from 1915 to 1945.

Perry Cabin, near St. Michaels, is an ambitious attempt to convert an eighteenth-century vernacular farmhouse to a stylish revival dwelling. The rambling, colonial revival, frame mansion has a large, six-bay, two-and-one-half-story section and two, flanking

Canterbury Manor when first built.

18. Material in the library of the Maryland Historical Trust, Annapolis.

one-and-one-half-story wings. Each main facade has a one-story porch, which on the east is interrupted in the center by an Ionic portico rising two full stories. The mansion's walls are sheathed in beaded weatherboard and the windows have paneled shutters on the first story and louvered shutters above. The original house consisted of the present north wing. Its stair was probably located in the position of the lower section of the new stair, its landing being a part of the new construction. Much of the original remains, but the mantels are probably most noteworthy. The hall mantel has delicate gougework, reeding, and rope moldings. The stair-hall mantel has, in addition to those moldings, pilasters with plinths. Most interesting of all, however, is the living room mantel with its reeded pilasters with plinths and ovals surrounded by beads. Both the old wing and the new house are associated with men of prominence. The original house was built by Samuel Hambleton, purser of the United States Navy during the first years of its existence. The remodeling was done by Charles H. Fogg, the owner and operator of coal mines and coke ovens in western Pennsylvania. Fogg lost the farm during the Depression, but not before it had served as the site for filming an early silent movie, *The First Kiss,* starring Gary Cooper and Fay Wray. Perry Cabin has recently been expanded, covered in aluminum siding, and now functions as a restaurant, inn, and bar.

Cedar Point near Easton is a large Georgian revival mansion that does Perry Cabin one better by incorporating two old dwellings: an early eighteenth-century farmhouse and a large eighteenth-century brick plantation house, both of whose measurements check out

Gary Cooper and Fay Wray in *The First Kiss,* shot in and around Perry Cabin.

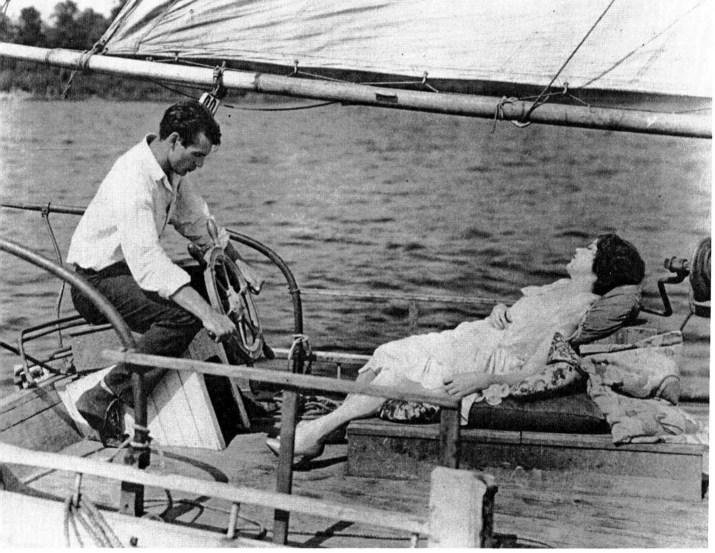

perfectly with the description of the house on this site listed in the 1798 tax assessment. These structures were remodeled circa 1830 to conform to Greek revival standards and again in the 1920s in the neoclassical tradition; the beautiful columns and portico were added in the second remodeling. Cedar Point's gardens, laid out in the 1920s, are now at their peak.

Wye Heights Plantation (T–81), situated upon a small peninsula at the juncture of four branches of the Wye River, is a 1,000-acre farm with a long, grand history through its association with the Lloyd family. The original house is a fine example of a Georgian-Federal dwelling, and, in this century, Wye Heights enjoyed a second burst of prosperity resulting in the great colonial revival mansion present today. It is composed of the original central portion with twentieth-century wings that tripled its size and a Doric portico that intensifies the overall effect of grandeur. The grounds are extraordinary. To the northeast of the house is a ten-acre walled garden extending to the river and Skipton Creek; a ha-ha allows an uninterrupted view from house to water. Closer to the dwelling are a series of outbuildings and subordinate houses extending in an easterly direction to a range of garages and barns.

Yet another way of incorporating an old building into a new one is seen at Forrest Landing, a five-part mansion near Longwoods. The house was built in the tradition of the great mid-Georgian mansions of Maryland, but not as a copy of any existing dwelling. The body of the Flemish-bond house is five bays longs and two-and-one-half-stories tall. The central bay of the approach facade contains the door with sidelights, with a balcony and a large arched window above. All of the windows of the main facade have segmental arches with three stone members set within the arch. There are five dormers across the broad gable roof with double chimneys rising at the gables. Opposite the service yard is a formal garden and on the southeast there is a broad lawn with a bell-shaped drive to the outer wall. The northwest facade enjoys an informal vista of the undulating lawn rolling down to the water. The incorporation of old and new is on the inside, which contains woodwork from the Tobias Rudolph House, a mid-eighteenth-century house in Elkton. The woodwork is of the quality of other houses of the period in that city, such as the Mitchell House, Partridge Hill, and Gilpin Manor.

Two of Talbot County's famous family seats, Gross' Coate and Myrtle Grove, were the recipients of two of the most interesting colonial revival projects in the area. The work at Gross' Coate has been discussed (see chapter 3). In 1927 Charles Goldsborough hired the

Wye Heights Plantation: an overall effect of grandeur.

Forrest Landing.

Baltimore firm Mottu and White to design a new kitchen for his ancestral house, Myrtle Grove. Samuel Chamberlaine, in 1881, while compiling a family history based on the manuscript of John Bozman Kerr, wrote of the Goldsboroughs and Myrtle Grove that "every relic of the past is carefully treasured by them, and all seem unwilling to part with anything that belonged to the olden time."[19] How much more important Myrtle Grove, that wonderful "relic of the past," must have seemed to Charles Goldsborough two generations after Chamberlaine's book.

Goldsborough had Mottu and White proceed with caution and care in designing the new kitchen. The first drawings, dated September 15, 1927, show that the architects intended to add the two-bay kitchen simply by extending the old frame house's roof and cornice lines and by duplicating the window and shutter treatment. This was quickly rejected in favor of a scheme dated October 21, and the difference is obvious: the first plan would have done a disservice to the venerable Myrtle Grove by making it unclear what was old and what was new. The second—and executed—plan is in sympathy to the old house, for the addition is differently scaled and made subordinate to the mid-eighteenth-century dwelling. An article in a 1916 issue of the magazine *American Architect* warns that "many so-called . . . remodelings of old places have ended disastrously."[20] Clearly Mottu and White's work at Myrtle Grove was not a disaster but a first-rate success.

Not all of Talbot's twentieth-century houses, however, followed the dictates of tradition. There is a superb art deco room in Tred Avon Manor and, near Oxford, there is a place that might best be called imaginative. Its name is Deep Water Point (T–165), and it is a 1926 dream house. Built by Oliver Grymes, a man at one time prominent in the world of ballet, the house's pavilions, towers, gables, turrets, and arcades create a structure that is beyond stylistic classification.

Norman Harrington, writer, photographer, and past president of the Talbot County Historical Society, has described Talbot County's development since World War II. The county has, he notes, managed to supplement and diversify its economic base by attracting varied "non-polluting industries such as Waverly Press, Black and Decker, Wheaton Glass Tubing, [and] Chesapeake Publishing." But, significantly, "citizens of Talbot County are . . . militant about preservation of their county's way of life."[21]

19. Chamberlaine, *Chamberlaine*, p. 91.
20. William Lawrence Bottomley, "Reclaiming the Old House," in *American Architect*, vol. 109 (1916):339.
21. Harrington, "Good Life," p. 147.

ELEV KITCHEN DRESSER   PANTRY   PANTRY   DRESSER   ELEVATION OF CLOTHES PRESS
DRESSER

FRONT ELEVATION
(Rear Elevation similar)

Mottu and White's original plan for the additions to Myrtle Grove.

The final version of the additions to Myrtle Grove.

Art deco in Talbot County: Tred Avon Manor.

137

"A heritage worth saving": Tilghman Island, showing Talbot County's fields and shoreline.

They have worked to maintain this way of life by statute and study. The county's planning department has been quick to experiment with agricultural zoning ordinances and with preservation laws to protect Talbot's fields and hundreds of miles of shoreline. And these edicts are not enacted by the whims of a heavy-handed bureaucracy: they are often responses to "petitions of landowners."[22]

Laws are not enough. Conservation must come from citizens working to keep a usable tradition alive. This does not mean forcing an obsolete past on people, it means studying to try to understand the past. In architecture it is nothing more complicated that trying to figure out why a building form has endured for 250 years.

The telescope house is a good example. These structures have been a part of the Eastern Shore since the mid-eighteenth century. Will they remain popular in the 1970s and '80s? Apparently they will, because new houses in that venerable vernacular style continue to be built, lived in, and enjoyed.

This appreciation of the value of the past is important in Talbot County, a county that is, as Harrington describes it, "a precious meld, unduplicated elsewhere in America . . . [with] a heritage to be proud of . . . a heritage worth saving."[23]

22. Ibid., p. 136.
23. Ibid.

PART II

HISTORIC SITES
IN
TALBOT COUNTY

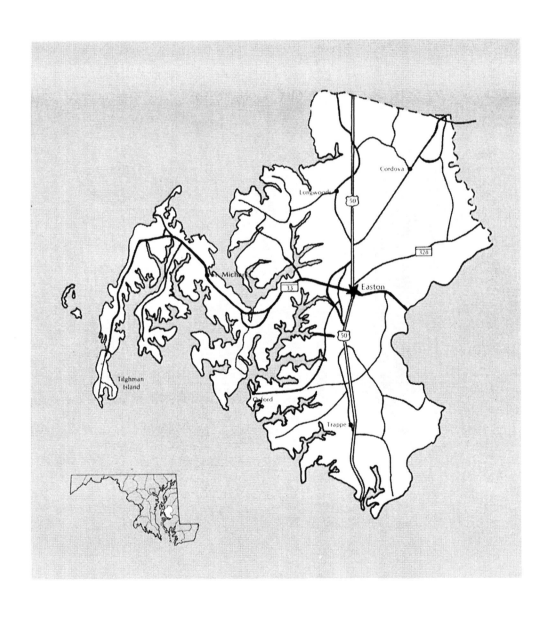

T-1

T-2

T-1
MILLER LODGE I.O.O.F.
1 South Washington Street, Easton
1879; Private

Chartered on July 29, 1832 and incorporated in March 1833, Miller Lodge is the oldest lodge in Talbot County. The original membership numbered forty-three, among whom were a governor of Maryland, Philip Francis Thomas and Howes Goldsborough, who was largely responsible for the construction of SS. Peter and Paul Catholic Church (T–448). The members first met in Washington Hall on Washington Street opposite Port Street. In 1839 they moved to the building that stood at Washington and Dover streets; this building was purchased in 1854 for $2,100, but it burned to the ground in a fire that broke out in Market Space on October 1, 1878. The lodge began immediately to rebuild, and the present structure was dedicated on September 25, 1879.

The four-story, brick Odd Fellows Lodge was built with a combination of stylistic elements and embellished by a number of symbols to express the ritual function of a meeting place for a fraternal order. The chimneys with their ornate caps show the influence of the Queen Anne style, whereas the lancet-arched windows, usually reserved for churches, reflect the Gothic revival; the asymmetrical arrangement of the windows is

a hallmark of Victorian architecture. Symbols tied to the lodge's purpose include an open hand, fasces, Celtic cross, and an open book. A small, towerlike gable marks the stair to the third-floor lodge rooms and lends a ceremonial quality to the entrance. The large meeting room has a high vaulted ceiling carried by huge scissor trusses and contains one of the most complete Victorian interiors in the town.

T-2
TRED AVON BUILDING
13 South Washington Street, Easton
Circa 1880; Private

This three-story, seven-bay, flat-roofed building is faced with red-orange, machine-made brick laid in common bond. The building is noteworthy because of its architecture and because it housed Easton's first hospital. (The house Webley [T–214] served as Talbot County's first hospital in the 1830s.) The Tred Avon Building is a typical commercial building of the late nineteenth century and is compatible in scale and materials with the other brick structures on this street. Probably constructed in 1879 or 1880, this building replaced an earlier one that burned in the fire of 1878. Although best known as the home of the Easton Emergency Hospital, the Tred Avon building might have been originally planned as a hotel.

The Emergency Hospital was incorporated by an elected board of directors in 1906, and in the same year it opened its doors. This hospital occupied the upper two floors. There were two surgeons, three general practitioners, and at least nineteen beds. During the first year, this staff treated two hundred patients, who otherwise would have had to go to Baltimore. Because of overcrowding and a fire that threatened the structure in 1913, the board authorized a fundraising campaign to finance the building of a new hospital.

T-3
OLD STAR-DEMOCRAT BUILDING
7 East Dover Street, Easton
Mid-nineteenth century; Private

Two brick buildings, one a three-story structure and the other a smaller, two-and-one-half-story structure, form the old Star-Democrat Building. Both parts illustrate the survival of an earlier, Federal-period building form into the middle of the nineteenth century. The gable roof terminating in brick (parapets and gable) end chimneys are architectural elements that may be seen in buildings constructed in the Federal style in Easton as early as the 1790s. On the other hand, the tall proportions of the building, as well as the robustly carved, wooden cornices and window hoods, follow the canons of

T-3

T-4

Victorian architecture. The diverse elements blend harmoniously to create a handsome building, which was for many years the home of the town's oldest surviving newspaper, the *Star-Democrat*.

T–4
WHEATLEY BUILDINGS
16–18 South Washington Street, Easton
Early nineteenth century; with alterations; Private

Although the Wheatley Buildings have undergone complex, numerous changes, both the two-and-one-half-story, three-bay brick section and the two-and-one-half-story, two-bay frame wing are recognizable as Federal-period structures. The three dormers, which cut through the cornice of the main building, are later additions, but beaded weatherboarding and early trim still remain on the frame wing. The buildings, which are now used as offices and apartments, have lost many original interior details, but there is an attractive Victorian stair with slender, turned balusters in the brick section and an early nineteenth-century fireplace with a mantle shelf, paneled frieze, and pilasters in the interior of the frame wing. The building has been extended in the rear with a series of brick and frame ells.

T–5
JUDGE THARP'S HOUSE
28 South Washington Street, Easton
Early nineteenth century; Private

Judge Tharp's House is a two-and-one-half-story, Federal-period townhouse with an added third floor, recognizable through the change in brick bonding. The earlier Flemish-bond wall is still visible, as is the outline of the original gable roof, which was more steeply pitched than the present one. Square, chamfered posts support a low, hip porch roof covered with raised-seam metal. Ornate brackets and the steps placed to the side make the porch resemble a delicate portico framing the sidewalk. The balustrade is of iron cast in an intricate, geometric pattern. Beautifully proportioned and skillfully crafted, this balustrade is a fine example of nineteenth-century cast iron work. Many interior features appear to date from the late nineteenth century. The stair has turned balusters and a heavy newel. A small portion of stair between the second and third floors may date from the earliest period of the building; it has a round newel and plain balusters and appears to be in its original position. There are several period mantels and doors, and there is vertical beaded board paneling in the basement. Additions form an ell to the rear.

T–6
MISS MARY JENKINS HOUSE
30 South Washington Street, Easton
Third quarter of the eighteenth century; Private

This two-and-one-half-story frame building dates from before 1783, and the house's mantels have shelves supported by consoles and door trim enlivened by crossettes, details common in the Georgian period. The tall, exposed chimney back, which reflects back-to-back fireplaces in the corners of the inside rooms, also suggests an early construction date. In addition, the uneven weatherboards, the wide, yellow pine floors, and the chair rails provide similar corroborating (if not conclusive) evidence. The rear hyphen, which connects the kitchen to the house, has a second-floor fireplace supported by a first-floor relieving arch, a feature necessitated by the lack of an underlying fireplace. Historical research shows that this property was for many years a tavern known by the name of the Seven Stars.

T-6

T-7

T-8

T–7
DOCTOR PACKARD'S OFFICE BUILDING
32 South Washington Street, Easton
Second quarter of the nineteenth century;
Private

This two-and-one-half-story frame town-house is related to the earlier side-passage double-parlor Federal-townhouse form, but it has bolder, simpler details. A long period of neglect has resulted in the loss of many details and outbuildings, but it retains some original elements and is greatly enhanced by a handsome two-story Victorian porch with decorative sawn-splat balusters.

T–8
GRYMES BUILDING
Easton
Early twentieth century; Private

The building complex at the corner of Dover and Harrison streets is an interesting combination of buildings from three periods. The earliest is the two-and-one-half-story, Federal-period dwelling on Harrison Street. It has a molded water table and segmental window arches of rubbed brick, an unusual detail also found on the Henry House (T–17). Between 1891 and 1895, a Victorian facade with a corner entrance was added to one gable end, and the structure is now connected to late-nineteenth-century,

brick commercial buildings on Dover Street and early-twentieth-century, masonry block commercial buildings on Harrison Street.

There are additional alterations on the interior, where trim from the Federal period has been replaced by late-nineteenth- or early-twentieth-century detail on all stories; the third floor, which appears to date from the late nineteenth century (possibly when the Dover Street facade was constructed), has trim from that period. In the block building, there is a small portion of balustrade, apparently from the Federal period; the slender turned balusters with flaring tops are unusual in the town and may have been moved to this location.

T–9
ASKINS HOUSE
105 South Washington Street, Easton
Late eighteenth century; Private

The Askins House is one of a number of brick row buildings constructed along Washington Street in Easton's early period. Like the others, this two-and-one-half-story, four-bay structure has a fine facade laid in Flemish bond and tall end chimneys. Its four-bay width is unusual, however, and suggests an unusual plan. The interior woodwork is intact and is a good example of Federal-style detail. Unlike most of Easton's Federal-style buildings, this one has not been greatly

changed on the first floor and is, consequently, one of the best-preserved, modest buildings of that period.

T–10
109 South Washington Street, Easton
Early nineteenth century; Private

This small, three-bay dwelling is one of Easton's finest buildings. The well-proportioned, two-and-one-half-story structure shows the influence of both the Federal and the Georgian styles, and it may be considered a transitional building. Its Flemish-bond facade is enriched with a beltcourse and double-keystone lintels above the window openings. The main entrance is outstanding; fluted pilasters carry an elaborate entablature, the frieze of which is decorated with Adamesque pineapples and sunbursts. The transom light has diamond panes, a detail also used in the building's exquisite interior woodwork. From the slope of the gable roof above projects a single dormer, and a partly exposed chimney rises along the south gable end. The interior has suffered very little alteration and consequently retains much original detail, including gouge-worked mantels, gouge-worked chair rails with alternating six-pointed stars and fluting, and doors with raised and beveled panels. In 1969 the house was carefully restored and converted into apartments.

T-9

T-10

T-11

T–11
TALBOT COUNTY WOMEN'S CLUB
18 Talbot Lane, Easton
Circa 1800–1805; with additions; Private

When constructed, the Talbot County Women's Club was a brick dwelling on the edge of the new town of Easton. The two-and-one-half-story building is restrained in design with a plain, almost austere, facade of beautiful, orange brick laid in Flemish bond. Set beside and somewhat in front of the brick house is a one-and-a-half-story frame wing with beaded siding and a steep gable roof with dormers.

The Women's Club bought the building in 1946. Among the earlier owners was the original builder, James Price, a public-spirited citizen, who, besides filling a variety of municipal offices, was Talbot County's register of wills in the early nineteenth century.

T–12
BULLITT HOUSE
108 Dover Street, Easton
1801; Private

Built by Thomas Bullitt, this elegant, well-proportioned home is among the best representatives of Federal-style buildings in Easton, and it is especially notable for its extraordinary brick work, carved front entrance, and wooden cornice. Recently re-

T-12

stored, this building retains many of its original details. The main house is three bays wide with the main entrance in the front, west bay. The gable roof has two dormers in each slope, and the upper window sash of these dormers is rounded with the muntins interlocking to form diamond-shaped lights. The double chimney, joined by a brick curtain, rises enclosed in the end wall and is finished with corbeled caps. The exterior detail is carefully executed, and the ornamental motifs are sophisticated and restrained. The main entrance door is set in a segmental arch filled with a transom light of petal design. The jambs are treated with three tiers of raised, beveled paneling, which corresponds to the paneling of the door. Flanking the entrance are slender, reeded engaged columns, which carry an entablature with a carved frieze and deeply molded cornice. Behind the main house is a one-and-a-half-story, three-bay ell that has a Flemish-bond east wall that continues from that of the main building, evidence that they are contemporaries. To the west of the house is a steeply roofed frame wing, reputedly built by Mr. Bullitt as a law office. Originally designed to be freestanding, the old office is now connected to the main house by a one-story brick hyphen. Window and door frames are beaded and decorated with backband moldings, and the box cornice has crown-and-bed moldings. The

showcase in the middle of the facade is a modern addition.

After Bullitt's death the house passed to a number of Bullitt descendants and remained in the Bullitt-Hayward-Chamberlaine family from 1801 until the Great Depression of the 1930s.

T–13
HILL'S DRUG STORE
30–32 East Dover Street, Easton
Circa 1880; Private

This two-story brick structure, now occupied by Hill's Drug Store, is a pleasing and picturesque example of late-nineteenth-century commercial construction. Although designed as a double store, its central pediment gives a unified and almost ceremonial quality to the strongly vertical facade. Pilasters are used at the corners of the facade and at both sides of the central, entrance bay. Emphasized by corbeled bases, these powerfully vertical elements support enriched bands of molded brick, a wooden cornice, and a central pediment. The pediment's tympanum is filled in with a sunburst design of molded tin, and tiny, triangular, modillion blocks with the same sunburst design surmount the end pilasters. A cresting of iron, cast in a delicate flower-like design, flanks the pediment, which is capped by a finely wrought weather vane, and cast-iron finials rest on the corner blocks.

T-13

T-14

T-15

T–14
HAMBLETON APARTMENTS
28 South Harrison Street, Easton
Circa 1794; 1850; Private

Hambleton Apartments is interesting for both its architecture and its identification with two of Easton's and Talbot County's important families. In 1790 Benjamin Stevens purchased city lots twenty-four, twenty-five, and twenty-six and began the construction of his new home. At the time of his death in 1794, Stevens devised the completed two-and-one-half-story, Georgian mansion to his father, John Stevens, the builder of Compton (T–146), a Georgian mansion of the 1770s near Trappe. Its belt-courses, water table, English-bond brick, keystone arches, and, above all, the proportions of the facade, betray a conservative, Georgian influence, unusual in this town. In 1845 Samuel Hambleton, a prominent Easton lawyer, purchased the property and presided over a remodeling that enlarged the building by the addition of the two southern bays and a two-story front porch.

T–15
CHRIST CHURCH
South and Harrison streets, Easton
Circa 1845; with additions; Private

In the mid-nineteenth century, the Episcopal congregation of Christ Church was fortunate in selecting as its pastor a man devoted to both theology and architecture. The builder of Christ Church and its rectory, the Reverend Henry M. Mason, came to Easton from Salem, New Jersey in 1838. There he had been closely affiliated with the Right Reverend George W. Doane, a builder of several churches in New England and a leading exponent of a High-Church movement that sought inspiration in the high Middle Ages. This movement, which started in England in the early nineteenth century, favored the English Gothic parish church as the paradigm for church construction. In the United States, William Strickland, a leading American architect heavily influenced by this movement, had designed a church for Mr. Mason in Salem, New Jersey, in 1836, and it was according to the plans of this church that Mr. Reynolds, a Talbot County builder, constructed Christ Church. The tower originally had four wooden pinnacles at the corners, which were removed in the late nineteenth century. The chancel, added in 1876, was needed to accommodate changes in the lit-

urgy and to reflect the common church form of the time; in 1878 a single opening replaced the original threefold door. Although histories of the church and local tradition attribute the chancel to Richard Upjohn, the designer of the rectory, it was in fact planned after the noted architect had retired. A stylish product of the revival of English Gothic architecture in the nineteenth century, Christ Church with its pointed arch windows and doors, heavy, stone construction, and Gothic details is an interesting contemporary of Trinity Church in New York and is similar to St. John's Chapel (T–49) and Trinity Cathedral (T–239).

T–16
CHRIST CHURCH RECTORY
12 South Street, Easton
1852; Private

After erecting the church (T–15) between 1840 and 1848, Mr. Mason commissioned Richard Upjohn to design a rectory. Built of coarse granite, the house has a T-shaped plan and steep gable roofs covered with slate. Influenced by the Gothic revival style, the picturesque building has a strongly vertical quality. Its scale is reduced by the deep roof, but dormers pierce the cornice line to permit the use of tall windows. Consequently, the interior is spacious and light

T-16

T-17

T-18

with a generous central hall and high ceiling. The rectory sits on a slight rise of ground, enclosed in the ell formed by Christ Church on the east and the parish house on the south. The dwelling is surrounded by rows of handsome boxwood with an intimate garden of flowering plants and herbs to the west.

T–17
HUGHLETT-HENRY HOUSE
10 South Street, Easton
Circa 1805; Private

The Hughlett-Henry House, a beautiful, brick townhouse, stands on a lot that once extended to the rear alley, where a one-and-one-half-story, brick carriage house still stands. Although constructed during the Federal period, this building has undergone such extensive alterations that its original form cannot be definitively established without further study. Virtually all of the original interior details have disappeared, and the stairs, hardwood floors, and the window and door trim date from the late nineteenth and early twentieth centuries. Flanked by gardens, the house consists of two blocks connected by a three-story hall and extended by porch additions on the west side and a rear ell. The main section of the building is three stories tall and three bays wide, and the gable roof is finished with

brick parapets, which tend to heighten the already towering mass. The cornice is of molded brick; its upper molding, a cyma recta, is separated from the lower one, a cavetto, by a plain, unmolded, brick course. The window openings have a flat arch of rubbed brick with a double keystone. Although damaged by time and inadequate repairs, the brick work of the facade is exceptional and bears comparison with the Neall House (T–32) nearby. The perfectly formed bricks laid in Flemish bond, the fine mortar joints, and the molded, brick cornice attest to the consummate skill of the bricklayers and masons and the high expectations of the builder.

T–18
BRICK ROW
124–130 South Washington Street, Easton
Circa 1850; Private

Almost certainly constructed as low-cost housing, this two-story, twelve-bay brick structure represents a type of row building common in many cities and towns, but unusual in Easton. Unlike the other row buildings on Washington Street, this single structure was designed to contain four units and may have been built as workers' housing. Today it is a pleasant, well-scaled addition to Easton's oldest and most urbane street.

T–19
ACADEMY OF THE ARTS
221 Harrison Street, Easton
Mid-nineteenth century; Private

The Academy of the Arts is composed of two frame buildings connected by a two-story frame hyphen. To the west stands a simple, two-and-one-half-story section with a centrally placed, jerkinhead dormer; on the east is a two-story building fitted with a square tower, which supports an open, hexagonal belfry. This structure has many elements of the Greek revival; the tower has double doors surrounded by a frame of Doric pilasters carrying a full entablature, and a row of blind windows immediately below the cornice suggests a frieze.

The history of the building is not clear. Although the east section would seem to be the earlier, the *Easton Atlas* of 1877 shows only the west block, and it is not until 1885 that both sections appear. Other historical records do not answer the question. According to school records, a frame schoolhouse, "forty feet long, twenty-eight feet wide, two stories high, with ceilings ten feet in the clear," was planned in 1835 to accommodate seventy-five pupils, but this description could apply to either wing. The structure cost $3,625.79 and served both male and female students. In 1865 school records refer to the school as the County School. Later it

T-19

T-20

T-21

was called the Male School of Easton and, still later, the Female School of Easton. Which changes required extending the structure, and whether a wing was constructed or moved in, are questions that need further research. Eventually the institution was called the Easton Primary and Grammar School. In 1933 the town sold the building, and it was used as a funeral home. Purchased in 1960 by the Academy of the Arts for use as a cultural center, it now houses classrooms, exhibition galleries, a concert room, and studios for painting, sculpting, and ceramics.

T–20; T–414; T–415
116, 118, and 120 South Street, Easton
Mid-nineteenth century; Private

Forming a picturesque group along South Street, these three Victorian Gothic brick cottages are outstanding in a neighborhood in which small frame houses predominate. They exhibit the same form and details, and the Pinkney House, 120 South Street, with its steeply pitched gable roof, miter-arched windows on the second story, and roof line dormers bears a resemblance to Christ Church Rectory (T–16), designed by Richard Upjohn in 1852. The architect of these buildings, however, remains unknown. The Pinkney House is the largest of the three. It is a one-and-one-half-story, two-bay struc-

T-22

ture with two brick wings on the rear which appear to be part of the original construction. The main entrance, with a transom and sidelights, is located in the west bay of the north gable end, and a hip-roofed porch with chamfered posts and brackets shades the first story of the facade. Distinctive features of the house are the miter-arched windows with triangular louvered inserts, the wide eaves supported by brackets, and the gable-roofed dormers that interrupt the roof line. To the west of this house is another Victorian cottage, the Bantum House (T–415). This house has many of the same features, including the main entrance with a transom and sidelights in the west bay of the north gable end, a hip-roofed porch, and miter-arched windows. Missing, however, are the side dormers and wide bracketed eaves. Completing this Victorian composition is the Blake House (T–414) on the west, which is almost identical to 506 Goldsborough Street (T–459). This is a two-story, two-bay structure laid in common bond, which repeats many features of the other two houses. Its main entrance is in the west bay of the north gable end, and it is equipped with a transom and sidelights. A hip-roofed porch shades the first story of the facade, but in this case it is supported by Doric columns. Further distinguishing features of this house include the flat and unmolded wood window sills and lintels and

the ninety-degree gable roof finished in ornate barge boards. An unusual feature of the interior is the arrangement of the dining room, which occupies the rear part of the house behind the living room and stair hall.

T–21
107 North Washington Street, Easton
Circa 1810; Private

Included in the construction that followed upon the building of the courthouse in 1794 was 107 North Washington Street. This brick structure, two-and-one-half stories by two bays, was probably built after a fire in 1808 destroyed several earlier buildings that stood along Federal Street and the southern portion of this block. Although the building has been greatly altered, it retains some features of its original, Federal-style construction, most notably the original cornice, finely molded parapet stop, and the superb pilastered dormer window with Adamesque sunbursts.

T–22
SHEARER JEWELER
111 North Washington Street, Easton
Circa 1795; Private

At 111 North Washington Street is an outstanding, Flemish-bond, two-and-one-half-story, five-bay building with double-keystone lintels above its window openings. A seg-

T-23

T-24

mental arch, partially concealed by a modern, pedimented door enclosure, marks the original, central door. The interior retains some original woodwork, including an elaborately carved archway in the stair hall on the second floor. This building is one in a row of Federal-period structures and is similar in detail to its two northern neighbors, T–23 and T–24.

T–23
HARRISON'S FLORIST
115 North Washington Street, Easton
Circa 1795; with additions; Private

In 1786 John Needles was appointed surveyor of a tract of land that by an act of the legislature was to become the town of Talbot. In December 1788 legislation was passed that not only located the court permanently within this tract but also changed its name to Easton; soon after, the Maryland General Assembly confirmed the city as the official capital of the Eastern Shore. Throughout the 1790s fine brick buildings appeared along Washington Street in response to the need for shops and houses to accommodate the immigrating merchants, lawyers, and tradespeople. The building now housing Harrison's Florist was erected during this early phase of construction. It is a two-and-one-half-story, four-bay structure covered by a gable roof with two dormers in

each slope. Double chimneys above the south gable end have corbeled caps and are joined by a brick curtain. Brick roof parapets rise above the gable ends and serve to distinguish the building from its neighbors. The facade is made of deep red, well-formed bricks skillfully laid in Flemish bond with narrow mortar joints. On the first floor a twentieth-century store front has replaced the original facade, and a bracketed cornice surmounts the twenty-four-pane store window. The interior possesses floors of wide, random-width, yellow pine boards. The first floor has an attractive tin ceiling, but alterations have all but stripped this story of its original detail. Fortunately, the second and third floors have not undergone such change, and much of the Federal-style detail remains. Two Federal-style mantels in the formal second-floor rooms have a rectangular opening flanked by reeded pilasters, which carry a frieze decorated with a shallow chain-and-star relief. Door frames are trimmed with narrow, composite moldings, and three-part chair rails are used in the major rooms. On the third floor no mantels remain, but other details, including chair rails, doors, and trim, are intact. All these details combine to produce a rich and elegant effect that suggests the prosperity of the building's original owners.

T–24
PERRIN SMITH HOUSE
119 North Washington Street, Easton
Circa 1795; Private

The architectural significance of the Perrin Smith House can hardly be overemphasized. Along with the Bullitt House and the Neall House, it is the most elaborate of Easton's Federal-period houses and is also among the best preserved. In every detail it displays the extraordinary craftsmanship and delicacy of detail so loved by builders of the Federal period. Intended to be a fine house, it is generous in its use of ornamental mantels, cornices, and door and window trim. If the Bullitt House is an example of a fine, freestanding Federal townhouse, the Perrin Smith House is its companion row house.

The building has played an equally illustrious part in the social and political life of the town. Although not the builder of the house, Perrin Smith, founder of the *Republican Star*, Easton's oldest newspaper (now the *Star-Democrat*), purchased the property in 1801 and used the location as his office for many years. The structure was purchased by The Chesapeake Bay Yacht Club in 1911.

T-25

T-26

T–25
HOLLYDAY HOUSE
131 North Washington Street, Easton
Circa 1820; Private

Number 131 North Washington Street, the Hollyday House, is a delightfully proportioned frame dwelling. Its unusually tall chimneys and steeply pitched gable roof give this two-and-one-half-story building a lively quality.

T–26
STEWART BUILDING
North Washington Street, Easton
Circa 1810; with alterations; Private

The Old Brick Hotel, as this building is commonly known, was probably constructed soon after a fire in 1808. A Federal-period building, its earliest appearance is unknown, but the structure was probably an L-shaped corner building, two-and-one-half stories high with a gable roof and dormers. Flat window arches and an attractive, deep red facade laid in Flemish bond are the major details remaining from this period. Midnineteenth-century photographs show a mansard roof with elegant cast-iron cresting. Fanciful Tudor revival elements such as beaded glass windows and parapet roof were added in the 1920s. Used as a hotel for many years, the building now houses apartments and shops.

T–27
118 North Harrison Street (site), Easton
Circa 1820; Private

This was a large, well-proportioned, boxlike structure that recalled earlier construction in New England. The four-by-three-bay house had a steeply pitched gable roof from which rose a chimney enclosed on the right end. The door, once covered by a Victorian porch of Moorish design, occupied the left front bay and had a fanlight and sidelight. The first-story, front windows had two-over-two sashes, those on the side had earlier nine-over-six sashes, while all second-story windows had six-over-six sashes; there were two small attic windows in each gable. In the rear was a small, one-and-one-half-story kitchen. Although it had not been well-maintained, this building could have been successfully refurbished before its demolition and would have made an attractive house. No photograph is available.

T–28
CEMETERY GATEKEEPER'S HOUSE
(site)
North Street, Easton
Circa 1875; Private

This building was a small, well-proportioned, Victorian Gothic cottage. The house, three bays wide by two bays deep, had a steeply pitched gable roof,

which was pierced by a large dormer decorated with cut bargeboards and a turned, wooden spire. Similarly treated were the gables. There was central door with a small fanlight, and a tall chimney with coping at each end of the house which was enclosed within the wall. This structure, set on the edge of the large Spring Hill Cemetery, had, with its weathered shingles and shabby condition, a picturesque, almost romantic, quality.

T–29
LUBY HOUSE
200 Goldsborough Street, Easton
Early nineteenth century; Private

Easton boasts few buildings that display Greek revival proportions and details so clearly as the two-and-one-half-story, frame Luby House. Corners are emphasized with flat pilasters and the low attic windows function as a frieze by setting the proportions of the facade. Inside, windows and doors are framed with pilasters carrying an architrave. The entrance porch and side addition are modern.

T-28

T-29

T-30

T–30
FOXLEY HALL
24 North Aurora Street, Easton
1794–1798; Circa 1889; Private

Foxley Hall represents a type of freestanding brick dwelling built in Easton during the Federal period. The building is impressive in its massiveness and interesting because of its many additions. The house's original owner was Deborah (Perry) Dickinson; she had married Henry Dickinson (d.1789) in 1787, and the structure was built shortly thereafter. It was later the home of U.S. Senator John Leeds Kerr (1780–1844), who called it Burnside. Still later Dr. Samuel A. Harrison altered the house for his daughter, Patty Belle, and son-in-law, Oswald Tilghman, who gave it its present name. Harrison and Tilghman are, of course, well known for their two-volume *History of Talbot County*. Their alterations include replacing the original stair and cutting a wide opening between the main house and rear wing. This stair is of oak and rises to the third floor around an open well. Newels are square and have octagonal caps. The balusters have lozenge-like turnings and rest on a closed-string course ornamented with reeding. Two spacious rooms on the first floor to the right of the stair hall also have late-nineteenth-century details. The window and door trim have bulls-eye corner blocks, which re-

semble details of the paneling of the stair spandrel. The present dining room, located in the rear wing, and the bedroom above have chair rails and mantels apparently from the Federal period. The mantels have rectangular openings, mantel shelves, and detailed reeding on the frieze. The building is now rented as a private dwelling.

T–31
MILLER'S HOUSE
23 Hanson Street, Easton
Late eighteenth and early nineteenth centuries; Private

Representing two early periods, this small, frame dwelling is made up of an early-nineteenth-century, two-story main house with a late-eighteenth-century, one-and-one-half-story wing. The wing with a steeply pitched gable roof has an enclosed corner stair and wide, beaded, exterior siding applied vertically, an unusual feature, now hidden by modern shingles. The simple exterior of the main house is enriched by a molded cornice above the windows and door, which is fitted with a transom. Whether the building ever housed a miller is moot; it is, however, next door to Barlett's old flour mill, now the Mill Place office.

T–32
TALBOT COUNTY HISTORICAL SOCIETY
27 South Washington Street, Easton
1804–1810; Private

The Talbot County Historical Society is developing a complex of four eighteenth- and nineteenth-century structures as headquarters and house-museums with gardens. The grandest of the structures, this Federal-period house, was constructed by James and Rachel Cox Neall between 1804 and 1810. The Nealls were Quakers, and some of the Nealls were cabinetmakers; predictably, their house was carefully designed and constructed.

Architecturally, the Neall House is significant as an example of a high-style Federal townhouse of exemplary detail. One of the largest and finest townhouses of its period on the Eastern Shore, it compares favorably with similar dwellings in Baltimore and Philadelphia. The exterior of the building is notable for the fine Flemish bond with unusual raised jointing, the reeded stone lintels, the molded brick cornice of the front facade, and the brick parapets that terminate the gable eaves. Similar masonry work and decorative details can be observed on a number of other contemporary buildings in Easton, which clearly suggests a possible connection in design and crafts-

T-31

T-32

T-33

manship. The most notable feature of the interior is the plan. The first floor plan is a relatively unusual and practical variation of the side-hall-and-parlor plan, featuring a narrow front-entrance hall at the east end of the south gable wall which opens into a larger stair hall to the rear. This arrangement minimizes lost space in the hall and allows a larger formal parlor in the front, adjoining the entrance hall. On the second floor, the front room extends the full width of the house, with a stair hall and a second, nearly square chamber to the rear. This plan variation creates an elegant front room that calls to mind the "piano nobile" of the Renaissance; this plan is particularly well suited to the Federal townhouse but is found only rarely in Tidewater Maryland. The decorative woodwork of the interior is typical of the Federal period in this region. Particular features of note include the pilastered arch with herringbone reeding between the front hall and the stair hall and the handsome open-string stair. The two-story rear addition is believed to date to the 1820s and may replace an original frame wing. The east end of the present wing originally had a "flounder," or shed room, similar to the early brick wing on the Old Inn in nearby St. Michaels. This form of roof is relatively common in larger towns and cities and was particularly popular in Philadelphia, but is relatively unusual on the Eastern

Shore. The entire interior of this fine house has recently undergone paint analysis and the original paint colors are being restored in accordance with analysis findings. The house is being furnished and run as a house-museum representing the Neall tenure.

T–33
JOSEPH'S COTTAGE
20 West Street, Easton
1797; Private

Joseph's Cottage was built by Joseph Neall, a cabinetmaker, to be used as his shop and residence. This one-and-one-half-story frame building has two rooms on each floor and a central entrance. Walls and ceilings are sheathed with boards, and there is an enclosed corner stair. The steeply pitched gable roof is complemented by the large, brick, exterior chimney. Owned by the Talbot County Historical Society, the house was restored for America's bicentennial and the interior has recently been repainted using its original color scheme as determined by paint analysis.

T–34
CHAFFINCH HOUSE
Easton
Late nineteenth century; Private

A dominant architectural idea in the late nineteenth century was that of volumetric

expression. A building's interior was seen as a composition of volumes, not as a series of rooms, and the exterior wall was conceived of more as a "skin" stretched over these volumes than as a structural element carrying the roof and floors. Thus, in this building we see the interior volumes clearly delineated by the thin, exterior "skin," which encloses and holds them together. The two-and-one-half-story house has many interesting features: the projecting windows, gables, and tower introduce an element of pomp and ceremony, while the porch and the horizontal bands of weatherboarding and shingles lend unity to the composition. Victorians loved variety, irregularity, and a picturesque quality in their architecture, and this structure exemplifies these qualities in a vivid fashion.

T–35
DYER ANTIQUES BUILDING
6 North Washington Street, Easton
Circa 1795; Private

The permanent location of the Talbot County Seat in Easton and the completion of the courthouse in 1794 guaranteed the survival of the town of Easton and stimulated commerce. Washington Street was soon lined with rows of brick buildings which provided for housing and business. The Dyer Antiques Building is an example

T-34

T-35

151

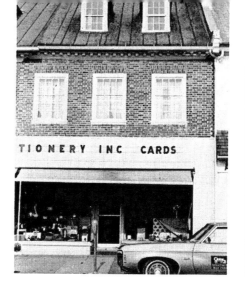

T-36

T-37

of the row house most commonly constructed, a two-and-one-half-story, three-bay structure, with a Flemish-bond facade, gable roof, dormers, and broad end chimneys. However, the delicate woodwork of the third floor and the gouge work of the cornice distinguish this building from the others and attest to its former elegance.

The probable builder, Lambert Hopkins, purchased this property in 1785. In the federal direct tax assessment of 1798, he is listed as owning and living in a house that may be this one. It remained a dwelling at least through 1818, during which time his daughter, Elizabeth Vickers, lived there. Little else is known of either Hopkins or the use of the building until the late nineteenth century. At that time it became a drug store; in 1969 it was remodeled into offices with its present front.

T-36
ROWEN'S ANNEX, SOUTH BUILDING
8 North Washington Street, Easton
Circa 1795; Private

Many Federal-style buildings were constructed along Washington Street after the present courthouse was built in 1794. These houses, shops, and stores formed the nucleus of Easton's commercial district, and, even though altered, this building is noteworthy because it is one of these early structures.

Built probably between 1791 and 1798, this two-and-one-half-story, three-bay, Flemish-bond structure with its molded brick parapet stop and fine cornice is typical of Federal-style construction. It is now connected to 10 North Washington Street, a similar structure, and a barrel-vaulted, covered walkway, now enclosed, runs between this building and 6 North Washington Street, indicating that they are contemporary.

In 1798 Bennett Wheeler bought the lease on the property from William Mebuy, who was probably responsible for the building's construction. Wheeler may have kept a store on the first floor, but to what use the building was put remains unknown. By the turn of the century, it housed a drug store, as did its neighbor, 6 North Washington Street.

T-37
R. ESTERSON AND CO.
Easton

Early nineteenth century; Private

Although greatly altered, this building is a notable example of a late, Federal-period row building. It belongs to a group of structures that, constructed as stores on the first floor with a fine residence on the second and third floors, have continued to function as such to the present day. The well-laid Flemish bond of its facade, the carefully

molded cornice, the eight-over-twelve-sash windows, and the particularly nice dormers represent the skilled craftsmanship of different periods felicitously combined. The structure adds to the evolutionary picture of building styles in the Easton commercial district, and it is interesting to compare it to a later, transitional structure, 7 Dover Street, (T–3). The structure served as the dry goods store of Edward Shannahan during the last quarter of the 1800s. He and his wife lived at 9 North Aurora Street (T–293).

T–38
McCRORY'S
24 North Washington Street, Easton
Circa 1805 and later; Private

Tall and well-proportioned, the McCrory's building adds to the interest of the Washington Street commercial district. Built before 1805, it is one of Easton's earlier structures and survives as an example of a Federal-period building erected to serve as a storehouse. Three-and-one-half stories in height, this building is laid in Flemish bond on the facade and has keystone window arches of tan sandstone. Major alterations carried out about 1920 introduced well-scaled, interesting additions, including the gambrel roof. The builder was probably Owen Kennard or Samuel Groome, promi-

T-38

T-39

T-40

nent figures in the early life of the town. Kennard owned several lots along Washington Street, including a lot with a house that stood on the site of the present Maryland National Bank; Groome's son, William, became president of the Easton National Bank.

T–39
OLD FRAME HOTEL
1 Goldsborough Street, Easton
1866; Private

Originally built as a hotel in 1866 by George Haddaway, this three-story frame building had a shallow hip roof and Italianate detail resembling the North Building, 110–112 North Washington Street (T–40). In 1897, the building was remodeled by its new owners, Nevius and Frampton, Inc., as a hardware store. The warehouse was also built at that time to house the horse-drawn farm machinery that the company sold. The structure has recently been renovated and is used for shops and offices.

T–40
NORTH BUILDING
110–112 North Washington Street, Easton
Circa 1865–1870; Private

Three stories in height, the North Building is covered with a shallow hip roof supported

by bold brackets and pierced by tall chimneys. A mid-nineteenth-century structure with Italianate verticality and detail, it is one of the few of its kind to survive with only minor alterations, which include the removal of a widow's walk from the roof and the addition of a store front. The massive quality of the exterior is carried through to the interior, where the ceilings are high and the rooms spacious and airy. Furthermore, the door and window surrounds are wide and decorated with broad, deep, composite moldings. The interior also retains many of its original details. The stair is elaborate with a heavy newel topped by an octagonal lantern; turned balusters and foliated step brackets are employed on the open-string course. Although this is a standard catalogue stair readily available in the mid nineteenth century, it is well-proportioned and built in a grand manner.

T–41
130 North Washington Street, Easton
Circa 1800; with alterations; Private

Constructed early in Easton's history, this house experienced major alterations in the late nineteenth century, which resulted in the addition of a flat-roofed third floor and a front porch. The brick structure has a deep, pierced-work wood cornice and elaborate wood detail on the porch. The orig-

inal part of the facade is laid in Flemish bond and the side elevations are in English bond; common bond, however, characterizes the brickwork of the later additions. The house is surrounded by grounds that are carefully planted in boxwood and crepe myrtle.

T–42
RATCLIFFE MANOR
Easton
1757; Private

Built by Henry Hollyday, Ratcliffe Manor is an impressive, well-maintained, two-and-one-half-story, plantation house of Georgian design. Five bays wide by four deep, the house has a gable roof with pronounced jerkinheads. A high basement with segmentally arched windows provides the foundation, and a water table of sloping brick girds the superstructure. A handsome cornice with a crown molding and row of carved modillions is carried across the front and rear facades. The gable-roofed porch, a modern addition, frames the segmentally arched main entrance. The windows have flat brick arches, and the sashes are twelve over twelve on the first floor, twelve over eight on the second, and six over six on each end of the house. Added during the Federal period, the three pedimented dormers, on the other hand, have nine-

T-41

T-42

T-43

T-44

over-six, segmentally arched windows with radiating muntins. Large, twin chimneys rise from the ends of the house. The garden facade is similar to the front save the absence of a porch. Northwest of the main building is a one-and-one-half-story, three-bay brick wing with six-over-six windows and an end chimney; there are two six-over-six, pitched dormers. The interior is beautifully kept and well-preserved. A stair with walnut balustrade and two turned balusters per step ascends to the second floor in three flights. The east room is stripped of paint to reveal the native, yellow pine paneling and has a diagonal fireplace flanked by fluted pilasters on paneled bases. The exquisitely decorated drawing room is fully paneled with a marble and double-crossette-trimmed fireplace. All these features combine to make Ratcliffe Manor an excellent representative of Georgian architecture. Surviving letters written by Hollyday show that in 1755 bricks for the house were baked, in 1756 more bricks were baked and planks were sawed, and in 1757 actual construction on the house began.

T–43
SPENCER-PLUMMER HOUSE
133 North West Street, Easton
Circa 1800; with additions; Private
On North West Street, just beyond the original boundaries of the town, is this three-bay, Federal-style house with flush gable chimneys and beautifully laid, Flemish-bond brick. Originally built by Perry Spencer, the house was enlarged in the mid-nineteenth century: a porch with heavily ornamented, scroll-like brackets and pendants was added to the front, and front windows and doors received deeply molded frames. An agreeable blend of two architectural periods, the building has an attractive garden at the rear and a small, brick outbuilding that probably served as a dairy.

T–44
MARVEL HOUSE
Easton
Mid-nineteenth century; Private
The Marvel House, once the residence of Raymond Marvel, a state senator in the late 1930s, is an elegant example of farmhouse construction combining elements of the two predominate styles of the mid-nineteenth century. The corner pilasters and dentiled cornice belong to the Greek revival, whereas the boxlike form is more characteristic of the Italianate style. The house has

a shallow hip roof, which accentuates the building's square lines. The resulting almost uncomprisingly square appearance is relieved by the one-story porch with wrought-iron posts which covers the south side and half of the west side.

T–45
TRIPPE-BEALE HOUSE
220 South Street, Easton
Mid-nineteenth century; Private
Situated on grounds planted with magnolia, poplar, box, and the *ethereal cotinus*, or smoke tree, the two-and-one-half-story, brick Trippe-Beale house was built in the mid-nineteenth century according to designs drawn up in 1851 by the noted architect Richard Upjohn. The sweeping jerkinhead roof is pierced by wide jerkinhead dormers and two tall chimneys fitted with flaring caps. Porches on the two street facades have trefoil, wooden arches, the design of which is echoed by a similarly carved ornament on the porch and roof eaves. Inside, the rooms possess a spaciousness and intimacy that Mr. Upjohn also achieved in his Christ Church Rectory (T–16).

T-45

T-46

T-47

T–46
THIRD HAVEN FRIENDS MEETING HOUSE
Washington Street, Easton
Circa 1683; Private

The Third Haven Meeting House was constructed in 1682–84 as a modified cruciform plan consisting of a rectangular building with a wing projecting from the facade and a smaller cross wing centered on the facade. The gable of the larger wing served as the front of the meeting house. Two interior doors opened from this front way into the main body of the building, which was evidently divided in half by a partition, possibly quite similar to the surviving one, which is believed to date to the end of the eighteenth or the early nineteenth century. A stair in the front wing allowed access to an unfinished room over the wing. From this room, two doors opened into a part of a pair of plastered rooms over the main body of the meeting house. These two rooms were divided by an unusual feathered panel partition. Narrow benches were carried around three walls of each room, suggesting that these rooms also served an important function. A small door in the wall of the room opened into an unfinished loft over the smaller cross wing. The church was dramatically altered in 1797. The two cross wings were demolished and a lean-to ad-

dition was made the full length of the facade. The principal entrance was shifted, a new enclosed winder stair was added, the elders' benches were extended, a new moveable partition constructed and the second-story partition and benches were removed. The original leaded casement windows were also removed at this time and replaced with the fifteen-light sash that survives to this day. With the exception of some moveable nineteenth-century replacement benches, few alterations have been made since this major remodeling. The meeting house survives as the oldest documented building in Maryland and is a landmark of national significance that has been maintained in an extraordinary state of preservation.

T–47
THIRD HAVEN FRIENDS MEETING HOUSE
Easton
1880; Private

The newer house of the Third Haven Meeting is a one-and-one-half-story, three-bay, brick structure erected to supplement the older, frame seventeenth-century building. The practice of sex-segregated meetings was discontinued in 1879, and the meeting moved to the new, "coed" building dedicated in 1880. The new house is perpendicular to the old one, and its walls are

red-orange, common-bond brick laid with smooth, narrow, even mortar joints. The exterior exhibits restrained, Italianate detail and reflects the simplicity of the Quaker way of life. The first floor is lit by tall, twelve-over-twelve, segmental-arched windows with segmental-arch-shaped upper sashes. The main entrance below the east gable leads to a stair and entry hall beyond which is the meeting room. The inside has a meeting room on the first floor with classrooms above.

T–48
CROOKED INTENTION
St. Michaels
Circa 1720; Private; National Register

Crooked Intention is an excellent example of an early-eighteenth-century, Tidewater Maryland dwelling. The one-and-one-half-story, brick main structure with its paneling and built-in cupboards is three bays wide and is flanked by brick wings on the east and west. The east wing is contemporary with the main building, but the west wing, dating from 1956, is a successful modern addition. Originally constructed with Flemish-bond brickwood, the house underwent alterations in the second quarter of the eighteenth century, which introduced common-bond walls and gable-roofed dormers. A porch supported by six chamfered posts ex-

T-48

T-49

T-50

tends the width of the main building and, like the roof, is covered with wood shingles. To the southeast stands an early brick smokehouse.

In 1681 Hugh Sherwood was granted a patent for a tract of 130 acres. According to one legend, Sherwood had planned to return to England but decided to settle in Maryland instead. Consequently, when he purchased land here he named it Crooked Intention in reference to his revised plans.

T–49
ST. JOHN'S CHAPEL
Near St. Michaels
1835; Private; National Register

St. John's Chapel of St. Michael's Parish, now a ruin, was probably the first granite Gothic revival church on the Eastern Shore. Basically a rectangular box with an end tower, St. John's is almost identical to a white, stuccoed Episcopal Church in Newark, Delaware and may have served as the model for later granite, Gothic revival churches in Talbot County, such as Christ Church, St. Peter's Parish (T–15); Christ Church, St. Michael's Parish (T–260); Trinity Church, Oxford (T–250); and the Cathedral (T–239) in Easton. This type of church is similar to some New England meeting houses, but here the New England steeple has been replaced by a crenelated

tower. Along with the tower, the windows' Gothic sashes and pointed arches gave the structure a medieval appearance. Reverend Joseph Spencer oversaw the construction, which was begun in 1835 on land donated by Charles Lowndes, and in 1839 the chapel was consecrated by the Right Reverend George Washington Doane, Episcopal bishop of the diocese of New Jersey.

T–50
TROTH'S FORTUNE
Possibly late seventeenth century (?);
Private; National Register

In 1686 William Troth bought a tract of 300 acres called Acton and built the house known today as Troth's Fortune. Probably constructed between 1686 and 1710, the structure is a well-preserved example of late-seventeenth/early-eighteenth-century, Maryland vernacular architecture. Its gambrel roof and dimensions, one-and-one-half stories by three bays by two bays, make this house a dwelling typical of the 1680s and '90s. Although small by today's standards, it would have been twice the size of numerous, contemporary dwellings of less wealthy planters. The unusual features of a medieval-looking stair tower, found also at Combsberry (T–156) in Talbot County, and Cloverfields (QA–2) in Queen Anne's County, and detailed, interior woodwork of

the early eighteenth century provide Troth's Fortune with interesting, distinctive elements. William Troth, the presumed builder of the house, is a good example of a successful merchant-planter, one of a group of entrepreneurs who augmented their agricultural income with mercantile activities.

T–51
WYE MILL
Wye Mills
Early eighteenth century; Public

The Wye Mill is of great importance on three counts: architectural, industrial, and historical. Architecturally, it appears to be the earliest extant mill on the Eastern Shore; from the point of view of industry it is representative of a major early industry in the rural Eastern Shore; and it has served as a landmark indicating the boundary between Talbot and Queen Anne's counties since 1706, when the Maryland General Assembly established the latter county. Wye Mill, now operated by the Society for the Preservation of Maryland Antiquities and students of Chesapeake College, has been in operation longer than any other mill on the Eastern Shore, even though it has not been in continuous use. It is a four-bay by two-bay, gable-roofed structure with an early, battened, Dutch door on the east facade. The waterwheel and sluice on the south are

T-51

T-52

modern replacements. In April 1779, Colonel William Hemsley of nearby Cloverfields received $10,000 to purchase supplies, including wheat ground at Wye Mill, for the Continental Army.

T–52
THE ANCHORAGE
Near Easton
Early eighteenth century; circa 1835;
Private; National Register

The Anchorage, a five-part house looking south to the Miles River, was originally a small, eighteenth-century, brick dwelling. In 1831, this simple structure was purchased by the Lloyds of Wye House (T–54), who presided over its metamorphosis into the estate known as The Anchorage. Using Wye House as a model, Sarah Scott Lloyd, a daughter of Governor Edward Lloyd, and her husband, Lieutenant Charles Lowndes, transformed a vernacular eighteenth century house into one of the great country seats of Talbot County. The main section is two stories tall and seven bays wide with a two-story, clapboard projection terminating in a two-story, three-bay, Greek revival porch supported by four Doric columns. In the central bay is the main entrance, fitted with double doors flanked by diamond-patterned sidelights and surmounted by a large, rectangular fanlight traced in delicate muntins.

Flanking this section are two one-story frame wings with two large, six-over-six sash windows in the pedimented ends overlooking the river; these wings are connected to the main structure by two one-story, flat-roofed hyphens.

T–53
MYRTLE GROVE
Near Easton
Circa 1724; 1790; 1927; Private;
National Register

Myrtle Grove, an excellent example of the successful combination of early- and late-eighteenth-century styles, is unusual in that it is still in the possession of the family that began its construction over 250 years ago. The first occupant was Robert Goldsborough II, a grandson of Nicholas Goldsborough and Margaret Howes, who settled on Kent Island in the late seventeenth century, and the eldest son of Robert Goldsborough, a respected lawyer, member of the Maryland General Assembly, and chief justice of the provincial court. Three parts constitute the present house: a 1724 frame structure flanked by a 1790 brick section and a 1927 frame wing. The oldest section, five bays wide and one-and-one-half stories high, sits on a brick foundation laid in English bond and is covered with beaded clapboard. In the central bay is the main entrance with a

ten-panel door framed by a simple, molded architrave with a five-light transom. Each of the other bays contains a nine-over-nine sash window with thick muntins and three-panel shutters. Three dormers with four-over-four sash windows project from the shingle-covered roof. On the northwest is a large exterior chimney, now enclosed by the frame wing, and on the southeast rises a tall end chimney. In 1790 the house was enlarged to the southeast by the construction of a large two-and-one-half-story three-bay brick addition with a side-passage double-parlor plan. This building is constructed in Flemish bond and has a molded water table on the southwest and northeast. A modillioned cornice, which continues along the gable-end bargeboards, surrounds the wing and forms pedimented gable ends. The beautiful doorway is framed by fluted pilasters with a full entablature. The major facades of both structures are identical except for the addition of a back porch, which extends only the width of the original house. The interior contains some superb paneling and plaster work and a delicate stairway, which, along with the overall sophistication of the structure, reflect the position of its owners. The third section is sympathetic to the other parts and was designed by the Baltimore architecture firm Mottu and White.

T-53

T-54

T–54
WYE HOUSE
Easton vicinity
Circa 1784; Private; National Historic
Landmark

By any standard, Wye is a phenomenon.
Home of the Lloyd family since the 1660s,
the estate's many extraordinary features form
a unit whose importance and romantic
charm are unsurpassed in Maryland. The
best summation of Wye was probably written by the late J. Donnell Tilghman in 1953
for the *Maryland Historical Magazine:* "Wye
House is outstanding among the old estates
of Maryland and perhaps of the nation.
There are colonial and early Federal houses
of greater beauty and better architectural
design. There are old gardens more extensive and more imposing. There are families
who have served their states and their country in higher and more important offices
than those held by succeeding generations of
the Lloyds. But in no other colonial residence in Maryland are these qualities combined in so great a degree as at Wye
House." For a full discussion of Wye House
see chapter 5.

T–55
OLD WYE CHURCH
Wye Mills
Circa 1717; Private

Old Wye Church, or St. Luke's, Wye Mills,
is one of the earliest churches on the Eastern Shore and the only eighteenth-century
Anglican church remaining in Talbot
County. It is a small, one-story, brick structure covered by a gable roof. The walls
above the chamfered water table are laid in
Flemish bond while those below are in English bond. Brick buttresses mark each of
the four bays on both sides of the building.
Alternating glazed headers are used in the
semicircular arches above the windows,
which have nine-over-twelve sashes below a
four-pane, fanlight transom. The entrance,
with its double doors and Doric pilasters and
architrave, is built upon a projecting plane
of the west gable. In 1949 a renovation and
partial restoration, carried out through the
generosity of Arthur A. Houghton by the
Boston architectural firm of Perry, Shaw
and Hepburn, resulted in the addition of a
large, round window in the west gable and a
large, Palladian window in the east gable of
the sanctuary. The interior is also the result
of this work, but many of the details are
based upon evidence of the original construction. The building is notable especially
for its Flemish bond with glazed headers in
its west gable end, and for its buttresses.

T–56
WICKERSHAM
Near Easton
1750; Private

This plantation was originally known as
Harwood's Hill and was the property of
Robert Harwood, whose ancestors came to
Talbot County to escape persecution because of their Quaker faith. The house is of
a design far more sophisticated than other
early Quaker dwellings, however, and this
may reflect Harwood's desire to flout Quaker
conventions in the face of his expulsion
from the meeting after his marriage to a
young heiress. The one-and-one-half-story,
large-scale, brick house, known today as
Wickersham, is not only a fine, mid-
eighteenth-century dwelling, but it also
carries the most ambitious glazed brickwork
in Talbot County. A chamfered water table
girds the structure, which is laid in Flemish
bond on the facade with English bond from
the grade to the water table. The facade has
a wide central entrance with double doors
flanked by two windows on each side.
Above the entrance and to the sides of the
immediately flanking windows, traces of a
porch are still visible. Two end chimneys
rise from the gable roof, and three dormers
project from the roof plane above the facade. Under the west gable is a bricked-in
door that led to the kitchen, now located in
the two-bay, two-story, frame wing on the

T-55

T-56

T-57

T-58

northeast. On the east there are two bricked-in windows on each story flanking a large, diamond design in glazed headers similar to, but more sophisticated than, Orem's Delight (T–193) in Ferry Neck. Wickersham also boasts three bricks dated 1750 in the east gable.

T–57
WYE OAK SCHOOL
Wye Mills
Circa 1800; Private

Beneath the long limbs of the Wye Oak stands a one-and-one-half-story, one-room, brick building said to be the first public school on the Eastern Shore. The three-bay facade, laid in Flemish bond above the un-molded water table, has a central door approached by wood steps. There is a dormer on each side of the steeply pitched gable roof and a casement on the south gable. On the west there appears to be a bricked-in door. One curious feature is the use of glazed headers in the original brickwork of the south gable. The interior has simple period trim and a ladder to the loft. This structure is almost identical to the building called Tilghman's Fortune (T–247) near Easton on Route 50, now used by the chamber of commerce.

T–58
WYE OAK
Wye Mills
Circa 1540; Public

The Wye Oak, standing in Wye Oak State Park, first came to public attention in 1909 when a state forester found it to be the largest specimen of Maryland's state tree on record in the Eastern United States; eventually Dr. Charles S. Sargent, one of America's noted tree botanists, catalogued the Wye Oak as the largest and finest white oak in the entire United States. Fifty feet in circumference at its widest and 95 feet tall with a 165-foot branch spread, this umbrageous tree is, owing to the foresight and efforts of a few individuals, in remarkably good health. In 1914, DeCourcey W. Thom of Blakeford, Queen Anne County, engaged the services of a tree expert, H. Stevenson Clopper, for general repair work. Mr. Clopper returned in 1930 to trim the tree and brace several large limbs, and in 1947, J. Russell Smith of Columbia University donated and applied 800 pounds of fertilizer. On October 6, 1953, a severe storm tore off a large limb, but Theodore R. McKeldin, then governor of Maryland, used the wood to make gavels for a number of state judges.

T–59
SAN DOMINGO
St. Michaels
1805; Private

San Domingo, a two-and-one-half story, five-bay brick structure, built by Joseph and Mary Harrison, is one of the best preserved Federal-style farmhouses in the St. Michaels area. Common bond is used in the majority of brickwork, but Flemish bond adorns the main facade near its central bay. The main entrance is flanked by pilasters carrying an architrave and open pediment. There is a brick kitchen to the east. In the farmyard the dairy and corncrib with thick, horizontal, plank walls and a deep roof overhang are good examples of early-nineteenth-century agricultural buildings. Stylistically San Domingo is similar to several of the best houses in St. Michaels and was undoubtedly built by the same craftsmen. The interior architectural features—including trim, doors, mantels, staircase, and room proportions—are as highly refined as the exterior architectural features.

T-59

159

T-60

T–60
FAIRVIEW
Easton vicinity
Circa 1729; circa 1800; with additions;
Private

Fairview is one of the great, Federal-style mansions in Talbot County, the architectural importance of which is increased by the substantial, mid-nineteenth-century additions in the Greek revival style, a style not otherwise well-represented in the county. From the original interior detail, as well as the masterful laid and struck joints of the Flemish-bond walls, which lack both a water table and a beltcourse, the main building appears to date from the early 1800s. The attribution is corroborated by the 1798 tax assessment, which fails to list a building of this size on the property. Fairview consists of a large, two-and-one-half-story, five-bay, brick building to which is appended an early eighteenth-century, two-story, four-bay frame wing; the wing matches the dimensions of a structure listed in the 1798 assessment. Looking north across an expansive lawn, the main facade is framed by clusters of large trees, and on the south there was a large box garden, believed to be the oldest in the county. In the mid-nineteenth century, Fairview witnessed a massive, Greek revival reconstruction, the results of which include the addition of the

Ionic portico with its architrave, frieze, and cornice continued along the facade and the alteration of the roof slope to accommodate this classical structure. Characteristics of the Greek revival style are also seen in the side-lights and transom of the main entrance and in the lengthened first-floor windows; window frames, sashes, and shutters also appear to date from this work.

The interior consists of a central passage with two large rooms on the west and two smaller rooms divided by a narrow passage on the east. Both parlors were retrimmed in the mid-century rebuilding with woodwork typical of that period. The original, Federal-style mantels were removed in 1929 and installed in nearby Lombardy; these were later replaced by other Federal-period mantels. For many generations Fairview was the house of the Skinner family.

T–61
CANNONBALL HOUSE
St. Michaels
Circa 1805; Private; National Register

A two-and-one-half-story, three-bay brick dwelling, the Cannonball House is a fully articulated, Federal-style structure. The facade and street elevations are laid in Flemish bond with extremely thin mortar joints and have nine-over-six sash windows topped by flat splayed arches. The main entrance,

approached by modern brick steps and porch, is surrounded by a modern frame of engaged Ionic columns that rest on paneled plinths and carry a pedimented Ionic entablature; the immediate door surround (transom, soffit, and reveals) is original. Two dormers project from each roof slope, with those above the facade fitted with engaged, fluted Doric columns elevated on plinths and supporting an entablature with broken pediment. A brick kitchen wing of the same age as the main building is attached to the east elevation, and on the south is an enclosed porch with a modern door and windows. The house acquired its unusual name during the British siege of St. Michaels in 1813, when a fleet of ships threatened to destroy the thriving, commercial port. Tradition has it that the citizens hung lights in the treetops and blacked out the buildings in order to confuse the British, who consequently overshot their mark. A lone cannonball, however, grazed the chimney stack of this house, ricocheted, and entered the southwest dormer window, leaving burn marks on the stair.

T-61

T-62

T-63

T–62
WYE CHURCH VESTRY
Wye Mills
1949; Private

Wye Church Vestry is a reproduction of the vestry erected in 1763. Standing on the original site, this building was reconstructed when the church underwent restoration. A small, three-bay frame structure, the building sits on a brick foundation. The main entrance is flanked by two tall windows with nine-over-six sashes and paneled shutters. A chimney exposed to the level of the ceiling rises from the south gable. The interior, with its paneled wainscot and chimney breast, is finished in a style more characteristic of Virginia than of Maryland.

T–63
JAMAICA POINT
Trappe
1838; Private

Jamaica Point is one of the finest representatives of late-Federal-style construction in this part of Talbot County. It comprises a two-and-one-half-story, three-bay brick main building and a two-story, four-bay brick wing. The main building, the principal facade and northeast side of which are laid in Flemish bond, is raised above a basement. A modern millwork entrance of pilasters with architrave and open pediment has

replaced a larger, original door frame, the outlines of which are still visible. The jack arches above the shuttered windows splay widely, thus becoming a conspicuous architectural element. Three dormers interrupt the steep pitch of the roof, from which rise two chimneys connected by a curtain. This curtain gives the northeast gable a massive appearance relieved only by a large attic lunette. The wing, in addition to displaying many of the same architectural elements as the main house, exemplifies an arrangement often employed in vernacular construction: a door framed by two windows leading into a middle room with a door and window opening into the kitchen. Beside the kitchen door is a brick marked with W. R. H. 1838, which refers to William R. Hughlett, the builder of Jamaica Point, who was a prosperous shipbuilder and director of the Easton National Bank from 1847 until 1875. Interesting interior features include the plaster ceiling medallions, which were probably executed by the same artisan who made the medallions for Judith's Garden (T–172).

T–65
TALBOT COUNTY COURTHOUSE
Easton
1794; Public

Noteworthy for both its architecture and its history, the Talbot County Courthouse is one of the most important buildings in Easton because the location of the court here was largely responsible for the establishment of the town. Research conducted for the National Historic Landmarks Commission in 1970 outlines the physical history of the building:

The first brick Talbot County Courthouse, constructed in 1710–12, was replaced by the second and existing structure in 1794. A lithograph of Easton, made in 1835, indicates that the second courthouse was a two-story brick structure with a gable roof surmounted by an octagonal open cupola. The main facade was five bays wide and three of these bays were located in a projecting central pavilion. The pavilion was pedimented and there was a circular opening with four keystones and a clock located in the center of the pediment. The windows were topped by flat arches of gauged brick. The courthouse was Victorianized by the nineteenth century and "rebuilt" by the city fathers in 1898. If the 1835 lithograph is accurate, two bays were added at that

T-65

T-66

time to the width, thus increasing the main facade from five to seven bays. The two first-floor windows flanking the entrance, in the center pavilion, had their flat arches replaced by round brick arches and an elaborate pedimented "colonial" door with an elliptical fanlight was inserted. The roof was changed from gable to hip and the octagonal open cupola was replaced by an octagonal closed cupola of different design. The clock was also removed from the face of the pavilion pediment and inserted in the new cupola.

The 1794 courthouse was further remodeled and restored in 1958 and at that time the two-story brick hyphens, with arcaded open first stories, and two large two-story rectangular brick wings were added. The simple courthouse of 1794 is now the central block of a large and elaborate five-part composition.

Cornelius West was the contractor for the 1794 courthouse, the total cost of which was £3,099; the county paid £599, and the state made up the difference.

T–66
MOUNT PLEASANT
Easton
Nineteenth century, many periods;
Private

Mount Pleasant has undergone several additions and alterations, and its three central Flemish-bond bays represent the original, Federal-style house. The first alterations appear to be the remodeling of the original entrance into a window and the addition of two bays, an entrance and window, in common bond to the south. To this was attached a two-story frame wing with a shed roof. Further work resulted in the addition of a cornice of closely spaced modillions, which spans the entire facade, and the three northern bays on the southern side, one of which has replaced the main entrance. Finishing the major alterations is a porch, supported by square posts with ornately carved brackets and covered by a shallow hip roof, which embraces the six central bays. Still retaining its character as a late nineteenth-century farmhouse, Mount Pleasant has been converted into apartments, and its cow pastures have yielded to suburban cul-de-sacs.

T–67
SAINT AUBINS
105 Willis Avenue, Easton
1803; Private

Constructed in the early nineteenth century as the main house of a large farm that extended for many acres north of Easton, Saint Aubins now stands on a shady block in a suburban neighborhood. The farm was founded by Nicholas Hammond, a state senator and the first president of the Farmers Bank of Maryland, Eastern Shore branch, who named it after his ancestral home on the Isle of Jersey. Although considerably altered in the third quarter of the nineteenth century, the original Federal-period form can still be distinguished. The two-and-one-half-story, three-bay, brick house has a Flemish-bond facade with double-keystone arches above the windows. Dormers project from the hip roof, at the ends of which rise two exterior chimneys, which, although extensively rebuilt, are in their original positions. Victorian alterations include the three-bay front porch with square, chamfered posts and ornamental brackets, an addition to the original rear ell, and on the stair landing the addition of a small, stained-glass window.

T-67

T-68

T–68
HAMPDEN
Trappe
Early eighteenth century; Private

In plan similar to Compton (T–146) and Boston Cliff (T–122), and in detail much like Boston Cliff, White Marshes (T–105) and Troth's Fortune (T–50), Hampden is one of the best representatives of early-eighteenth-century construction in Talbot County. The L-shaped brick house is five bays long and has a three-bay, brick kitchen wing attached to the north wall. The foundations are built of stone to the grade, English-bond brick to the water table, Flemish bond to the second floor, and common bond in the gables. Rubbed-and-gauged brick lintels are employed on the main facade, but segmental arches surmount the windows on the garden elevation. The principal entrance has its original molded frame and wide-paneled door, above which is a good, nineteenth-century porch, recently remodeled. North of the west door is the ell, covered by a shed roof. Between the ell and the south gable is a glass porch, above which project only two dormers because the roof of the ell extends high into the gable roof of the house. Beyond the ell stands a recessed brick kitchen apparently of late-eighteenth-century construction. Porches on this addition extend the width of the garden

elevation and two-thirds of the facade. The north gable has been completely rebuilt, and the east and west facades have undergone partial reconstruction. A dwelling of a well-to-do planter, Hampden is an interesting combination of vernacular form and early Georgian interior design. The house was probably built by the second of a long line of Thomas Martins who occupied this farm.

T–69
LONGWOODS SCHOOL
Longwoods
1900; Public

Representing the beginnings of public education not only in Talbot County but also in the United States, Longwoods School is one of the few extant, one-room school-houses in the county (see T–57). Although not so old as many of the county's buildings, the school is a good example of early-twentieth-century construction, which not only reflects the tastes of the era, but also illustrates the abilities of the craftsman. The school is a frame building set on a brick foundation, three bays wide and three bays deep with a shed addition to the rear. A shed roof supported by four chamfered brackets extends from the entrance facade to protect the door and window bays. On the apex of the roof above the entrance is a small, open belfry with a copper roof and

weathervane. Behind the building are two privies and fencing for privacy. Recently painted red with white trim, Longwoods School is now maintained by the Talbot County Commissioners.

T–70
MILLER'S HOUSE
Wye Mills
Circa 1750; Private

Constructed for Edward Lloyd III of Wye House as his miller's residence, this structure is a fine example of a mid-eighteenth-century vernacular dwelling and exemplifies the quality architecture commensurate not only with the position of the Lloyds, but also with the position enjoyed by the miller in the community. Although now in poor condition, the two-and-one-half-story, three-bay brick building resembles White Marshes (T–105). The house, built over a basement, is laid in Flemish bond save the west gable, to which a one-story wing was originally attached. It has a water table, and a three-brick beltcourse that is elevated to the attic floor level in the east gable end girds the structure.

T-70

163

T-71

T–71
LLOYD'S COSTIN AND PART
OF GRANTHAM
Wye Mills
Circa 1780; with additions; Private

On the Lloyd's Costin and Part of Grantham tracts near Wye Mills is a large farmhouse that combines the construction of two periods. The original house, still distinguishable, was built by the prominent Elbert family. It is a two-story, three-bay brick structure erected in the fourth quarter of the eighteenth century. The facade and west elevation are laid in Flemish bond, but the south wall is done in all-header bond, an unusual feature which in Talbot County is repeated only at Combsberry (T–156) and Cedar Point (T–208). All of the walls rise from a stepped water table. The windows, frames, and sashes (which are replacements) are tall and narrow with segmental arches one brick in depth. In the late nineteenth century the house experienced major alterations. A large frame wing with a porch was added, and the facade was remodeled with the installation of a large gable above the main entrance and a porch with ornate brackets extending across the original bays. The main entrance, with sidelights and transom, is also a result of the Victorian remodeling.

T–72
WYE LANDING FARM (King Hayes Farm)
Wye Mills
Mid-eighteenth century;
with additions; Private

Situated on a hill overlooking Wye Landing and the Wye River, Wye Landing Farm is one of the great houses of upper Talbot County; few telescopic buildings in the county are built on such a large scale, and far fewer have such a beautiful location. The house is composed of three brick sections, the smallest of which appears to be the earliest because of its Flemish bond brickwork. Constructed in the mid-eighteenth century as a one-and-one-half-story, two-bay cottage, this section was enlarged by the addition of a second floor after the construction of the other two sections. These two, two-and-one-half-story, three-bay structures as well as the addition were built by William Hindman, a wealthy state senator. The larger structure rises on a basement, and two dormers with pilasters and entablature with broken pediment pierce each roof slope. The central section, on the other hand, lacks a basement, and while there are two dormers above the facade, only one dormer projects from the roof slope above the garden elevation. Since there is no seam in the common wall, these

sections must have been constructed at the same time. Contrary to expectation, the facade does not look out on the water. Instead, the open gable end of the largest section faces the Wye River at its junction with Skipton Creek and Wye Narrows. This elevation is fitted with ten windows, two in the gable and two flanking each of the four fireplaces on the first and second floors, an instance in which the designer of an early house was conscious of a superb view. Behind the original cottage stands a brick milkhouse with the customary wide overhang.

In 1669, Thomas Emerson, a cooper by trade, began to put together a vast plantation on the east branch of the Wye River and just below what is now the village of Wye Mills. By 1715, Emerson held all the patents, warranties, deeds, and surveys for Buckingham, Whetstone, Hambleton's Park, and Keilding. His son, Major Emerson, left these holdings to his widow, Elizabeth, and his two young sons. In the evaluation of the plantation for the two minor boys, the dwelling and outbuildings were described as being in very bad repair. The elder of these sons, Philip, was in court in 1749 when his right to title was challenged, in part by Edward Trippe of Dorchester County, and in part by William Goldsborough of Talbot County. By the Act of Recovery, Emerson was awarded ownership of all his lands,

T-72

comprising nearly 1100 acres. His dwelling house then was on the original Harwood's Lyon and Stevenson's Purchase tract. It seems probable that he built the earliest brick portion of what is now the present mansion. Philip Emerson ran a big business operation here. At the landing on Wye River then called Emerson's Landing he had warehouses, tobacco storage houses, and, of course, wharves for vessels.

T–73
SAINT JOSEPH'S ROMAN CATHOLIC CHURCH
Cordova
1782; 1843; 1903; Private

Saint Joseph's is one of Maryland's few extant Roman Catholic churches from the eighteenth century. Although it is now composed of three sections from three periods, the original building, dating from 1782, can still be traced by the color of the brick, its Flemish bond, and the chamfered water table. Outlines of a bricked-in opening partly corresponding to the central bay on the east side of the nave may indicate the original main entrance. In 1843 a two-story addition was built on the south side to provide better accommodations for the parish priest, and in 1903 three semicircular additions were made on the north side, which gave the church a Latin cross plan with apse.

T–74
KNOTTS FARM
Queen Anne
Late nineteenth century; Private

Knotts Farm, located in the northeast corner of Talbot County near the town of Queen Anne, is a locally rare survival of an Italianate frame farmhouse. Like many of the houses of the period in this area, Knotts Farm is composed of two major sections: a main block with a rear ell. Its two-story, five-bay facade is partially shaded by a one-story, three-bay porch. The main entrance has sidelights and transom, an arrangement echoed by the three-part window above. This window in turn is topped by a plain pediment that repeats the outline of the gable in the roof. Windows on both stories have four-over-four sashes, although the upper sashes are uniformly smaller. A wide cornice supported by brackets overhangs the house on all sides. Above the gable ends rise two brick chimneys with small, recessed panels in each side, similar to Memory Lane in Caroline County (CAR–46). The four-bay ell lacks ornament except for a small porch on its north side, near which is a smokehouse.

T–75
JAMES F. MOORE FARMHOUSE
Near Queen Anne
Site; Private

The James F. Moore Farmhouse was demolished after the photo was taken in 1970. Nothing above the ground remains on the site.

T–76
BEHRENS HOUSE
Cordova
Site; Private

The Gordon Behrens House was demolished after its inclusion in the 1970 list of historic sites. Nothing above the ground remains, and no photo is available.

T–77
RICHLAND
Queen Anne
Circa 1740; Private

Noteworthy not only because of its early construction date, Richland is also important because it illustrates how early building styles progressed inland up the Choptank River. Situated on a peninsula in Tuckahoe Creek north of Covey Landing, the house is a one-and-one-half-story frame structure of five bays between two large chimneys and a two-bay extension that is appended on the west. The facade, resting

T-78

T-79

on a brick foundation, has four windows of nine-over-six sashes and a main entrance fitted with a paneled door. Three asymmetrically placed dormers, corresponding to the asymmetrical arrangement of the bays, pierce the steep gable roof above the facade, while only two dormers light the upper floor on the garden elevation. The two-bay extension has a door and window on the facade, and two windows in the west gable light its upper floor. On the north side of this extension is attached a four-bay lean-to with a one-bay porch, which extends across the two western bays of the main building. The interior has a central stair hall flanked by two large rooms with a third room behind the hallway, a plan that suggests Hampden (T–68), Compton (T–146), and Anderton (T–155). In the living room the fireplace, which is framed by vertical panels and surmounted by horizontal ones, recalls that of Troth's Fortune (T–50).

T–78
BUCKINGHAM
Skipton
Circa 1820; with additions;
Private

Important because it retains most of its original woodwork and trim, Buckingham is also important as a unique combination of forms, materials, and building sequence. The one-

and-one-half-story, five-bay, main building has a gambrel roof from which rise two end chimneys within the gables. The southwest gable end is done in stuccoed brick, whereas a frame wall of weatherboards extends from the southwest gable end to the far side of the main entrance. From this point to and including the northeast gable the structure is brick, laid in common bond and painted red. On the northeast is attached a two-story, frame wing, on the southeast of which is an addition with a catslide roof and dormers. The former appears to date from the late nineteenth century while the latter, designed to be compatible with the earlier structures, was added in the mid-twentieth century.

T–79
SKIPTON FARM
Skipton
Circa 1800; with additions; Private

Skipton Farm is composed of two sections, both of which are of frame construction built on a brick foundation. From examination of the plan, woodwork, and materials as well as stylistic elements, it is evident that the one-and-one-half-story section is not only the earlier but itself consists of two building stages. The major facades of this section have two doors and three windows and are shaded by a porch with a shed roof.

Two dormers project from each slope of the steep gable roof, and an exterior chimney of uniform dimensions from ground to cap rises against the south gable end. To the north of this structure is a two-story, two-bay kitchen addition. Its west facade has a jettied second floor, evidence that the wing was originally one story. A wide, stuccoed chimney rises from the apex of the roof near the juncture of the two sections. On the west near the old section projects a small lean-to with a shed roof similar to that of the porch. The interior still possesses a large amount of original trim; of particular interest is the east room with its original mantelpiece and closet with battened doors and wood locks.

T–80
SKIPTON LANDING
Skipton
Circa 1820; Private

Just above Skipton Landing is this small, one-and-one-half-story, one-room frame house, which, despite its early-nineteenth-century date, stands as a reminder of the typical, modest dwelling of the seventeenth and eighteenth centuries. It has serviced farmers, hired help, and slaves. The main section has a three-bay facade with a central entrance and a single dormer in the steep gable roof. On the west is a lean-to from which rises the original chimney. In the

T-80

T-81

T-82

1960s the house underwent a substantial remodeling; a lean-to containing a kitchen, bath, and bedroom was added to the rear, and most of the interior was renewed, although there are still some original, exposed, ceiling joists.

T–81
WYE HEIGHTS
Longwoods

Circa 1721 (?); with additions; Private

Wye Heights, 1,000 acres situated 1.5 miles north of the village of Longwoods, commands an impressive site on a small peninsula at the junction of four branches of the Wye River. The mansion is composed of the original, three-bay, central section with later wings that nearly tripled its size. The main facade is laid in common bond and may originally have been covered by scored stucco, some of which remains. A grand, Doric portico covers the original section and bears the date 1721, the source for this date being unknown. The porch probably dates to one of the house's remodelings. Flanking this structure are two, two-story, three-bay wings recessed from the original section's plane. The wings maintain this subservience even in their details, save the segmental arches above the windows of the east wing and the jack arches of the west wing. The garden elevation is differentiated from the

main facade by the addition of a large Ionic porch with full pediment including a lunette in the tympanum; there are three central French doors surmounted by fanlights. To the northeast is a ten-acre enclosed garden extending to the river and Skipton Creek. An interesting feature of these extraordinary grounds is the ha-ha, a low-lying construction designed to prevent the farm animals from wandering into the manicured lawns of the estate without sacrificing the view.

Notable historically because of its association with the Lloyd family of Wye House, Wye Heights is also important architecturally, both as a superior example of an early plantation house and for its additions and alterations which give it grandeur nearly comparable to Wye House (T–54) itself. Furthermore, the outbuildings, garden, driveway, and ha-ha are of great importance in the history of landscape gardening in Talbot County.

T–82
FORREST LANDING
Longwoods

Early twentieth century; Private

Standing at the headwaters of Pickering Creek, a tributary of the Wye River, is Forrest Landing, a five-part brick mansion. Although built in the early twentieth century,

it is a synthesis of the great mid-Georgian mansions of Maryland and not a copy of any building of that style. The two-and-one-half-story, five-bay main house is laid in Flemish bond. The main entrance flanked by sidelights is located in the central bay and is surmounted by a large, arched window and balcony. Each of the eight windows has a brick segmental arch accented with three stone members. Five dormers stretch across the broad gable roof, and double chimneys rise at the gables. From the gable ends extend one-and-one-half-story hyphens and pavilions, which are perpendicular to the main house. The interior has some woodwork taken from the mid-eighteenth-century Tobias Rudolph House in Elkton, which is equal in quality to other houses of the period in that city, such as Mitchell House, Partridge Hill, and Gilpin Manor. The grounds include a formal garden, a broad yard with a bell-shaped drive, and an undulating lawn, which rolls down to the creek on the garden elevation.

T–83
ALL SAINTS CHURCH
Near Easton

Late nineteenth century; Private

All Saints Church displays the heavy massing usually found in revivalist church architecture. This massing is relieved, however,

T-83

167

T-84

by the variation in frame construction, which also provides a measure of ornament representative of American building in the late nineteenth century. Built on a brick foundation, the main section of the church is six bays long below a steeply pitched gable roof. Each bay is opened by a narrow lancet window. Interesting features include the exterior sheathing, which has a flared, wood water table directly above the brick foundation, and the horizontal clapboards, which rise to the level of the lancet window sills where the clapboards become board-and-batten. Another curiosity is the chimney stack on the north side, which is tied into the roof by a small gable and bargeboard. Also on the north side is a large, square tower with a shingled spire. This former religious edifice has been deconsecrated and has found a new adaptive use as a residence and art studio.

T–84
PLEASANT VALLEY
Near Easton
1774; Private

Architecturally Pleasant Valley is clearly among the great, Revolutionary period houses of Talbot County; not only was it constructed with superior materials by able craftsmen, but most of these materials are still intact. Built for Howes Goldsborough and his wife, Rebecca, on part of a tract of

T-85

land called St. Michael's Fresh Run located near the headwaters of the Miles River between the towns of Longwoods and Easton, Pleasant Valley is mentioned in the 1783 tax assessment as a "large brick dwelling house and kitchen" with subordinate quarters, barns, and shops. The 1798 federal direct tax describes the home in detail and notes the presence of a schoolhouse, quarters, and smokehouse. The main house is a two-and-one-half-story, five-bay brick building with a one-and-one-half-story, three-bay brick wing. Constructed with uniformly colored brick, the house is laid in Flemish bond above the cyma-reversa, English-bond water table. The major facades are identical and have their main entrance in the central bay topped by semicircular fanlights and flanked by twelve-over-twelve windows with widely splayed jack arches; the Doric porches with balustrade are twentieth-century additions. The five second-story windows also have twelve-over-twelve sashes, but their arches are partially obscured by the bold, plaster cove cornice. A rubbed, four-brick beltcourse girds the structure and divides the two main floors. Two twentieth-century dormers project from each slope of the gable roof and serve to light the attic. The interior has appropriately elegant paneling and woodwork, and of particular interest is the walnut stair, which rises gracefully three stories.

T-86

T–85
KRECH TENANT HOUSE
Near Longwoods
Circa 1810; Private

This house may have been built by a small-scale farmer or by one of the Lloyds as a tenant dwelling. In either case, the building is of interest owing to its early date and to the similarity it has to the kitchen wings of several dwellings on the Eastern Shore. In plan it is identical to Lyford Landing, Caroline County (CAR–135).

T–86
PRESQU'ISLE
Longwoods
Circa 1820; Private

Presqu'isle sits serenely at the end of a long alley of trees and overlooks the east branch of the Wye River with Wye Island, Bruff's Island, and Bennett's Point in the distance. Built by the Lloyds, the house is a two-and-one-half-story, three-bay, box-like frame building. The major facades are sheathed in weatherboard, which contrasts with the shiplap covering the tympanum of the pediment. Over the east and west entrances are handsome, original Doric porches with hip roofs. A dormer projects from the gable roof between the twin chimneys on the south. On the north the same arrangement existed until the northwest chimney was removed

T-87

during the remodeling of a small, first floor room into an enlarged dining area. The interior is divided into a central passage with double parlors on the south and three rooms to the north. With the exception of the dining room, the doors, trim, dado, mantels, floors, and stair are original and well-maintained. The late Rogers C. B. Morton, congressman, secretary of the interior, and ardent Eastern Shoreman, made his home here. Presqu'isle is one of four existing Lloyd houses with a gabled primary facade, the other three being Wye House (T–54), Wye Heights (T–81), and The Anchorage (T–52).

T–87
GROSS' COATE
Near Easton
Circa 1760; with additions; Private
Gross' Coate is important on several counts. The original, mid-eighteenth-century structure is noteworthy as a survival of a building plan resembling that of Avonville (T–168) and Ratcliffe Manor (T–42). The late-eighteenth-century additions include fine examples of auxiliary structures such as the kitchen wing, milk house, and meat house. In 1914 an ambitious remodeling was undertaken in an attempt to tie these additions and those of the nineteenth century into a unified composition and link the service

yard to the house and garden. The Tilghmans built the house and lived here until 1983; they are buried in the family cemetery located to the east not far from the mansion. Gross' Coate is more fully described in chapter 3.

T–88
BRUFF'S ISLAND (site)
Tunis Mills
1888; Private
Built by Charles Howard Lloyd in 1888, the house on Bruff's Island was a large, gambrel-roofed, stuccoed dwelling designed (or remodeled) in the colonial revival style. Across the facade stretched a screened porch covered with a kick of the exaggerated gambrel roof. On the second story there was also a porch; it was recessed into the roof and enclosed by a balustrade. The house has been razed.

T–89
WYE TOWN FARM HOUSE
Near Easton
Circa 1800; with additions;
Private; National Register
Wye Town Farm is located on Woodland Creek near the site of the early-nineteenth-century town Doncaster or Wye Town. The original section of the structure is of common bond brick, one-and-one-half stories

T-88

tall, three bays wide, with a relatively usual plan: two rooms with back-to-back corner fireplaces at the gable end. The relatively plain exterior belies an interior that has retained much of its original details including a handsome Federal mantel, molded two-piece chair rail, baseboard, and architrave trim. It is speculated that Edward Lloyd V probably built the house as the residence of a supervisor or overseer of his vast agricultural activities.

The original house gained a one-story brick kitchen to the east in the mid-nineteenth century and a two-story addition to the west after 1900.

T–90
HOPE
Near Easton
1805 (restored); Private; National Register
Hope is one of the great mansions of Talbot County. Not only was it the home of several illustrious members of the Tilghman and Lloyd families, but it is also an excellent example of twentieth-century restoration. When built, Hope resembled Mt. Clare, Baltimore, the home of Charles Carroll, Barrister. This resemblance may not be accidental, because Mrs. Carroll was a cousin of Peregrine Tilghman, the builder of Hope. Its original configuration consisted of the present central section, the roof of

T-89

T-90

T-92

T-93

which was not so tall as it is now, and two one-and-one-half-story frame wings connected to the main building by ogee-roofed hyphens; it was a dramatic composition. The house had fallen into disrepair by 1907, when it was purchased by Mr. and Mrs. William Starr, who hired local craftsmen to restore the brickwork and the interior as well as to rebuild the hyphens and wings. The Starrs retained most of the original material of the main section, but new porches were added to the major facades. The landscaping, walls, allees, formal gardens, and driveway were laid out chiefly by Mrs. Starr; she and her husband successfully devoted themselves to bringing Hope back to its former glory.

T-92
NEW DESIGN FARM
Tunis Mills
Circa 1830; with additions; Private
New Design Farm is located at the headwaters of Leeds Creek on Miles River Neck. The house is a small dwelling composed of a one-and-one-half-story, three-bay brick structure with a one-and-one-half-story, two-bay frame wing. The south facade is arranged with a central door flanked by two windows and two dormers projecting from the gable roof. The north elevation, on the other hand, has a second door. Because

common bond has been used throughout this section and both facades have doors, it is difficult to determine the principal entrance. Appended to the east gable end is a wing, which has an asymmetrical roof and a two-story tower adjacent to the brick section.

T-93
GEORGE OLDS'S BRICK HOUSE
Near Easton
Circa 1820; with additions; Private
The original section of George Olds's Brick House forms the central section of the present home. It is a two-story, three-bay structure laid in common bond with interior chimney stacks at each end of the gable roof. The east and west facades have central doorways and large-paned sash windows in the other bays. The windows have flat-arched, marble lintels with keystones, wood sills, and shutters. The west facade has a one-bay, one-story entrance porch with a gable roof. There is evidence that the east facade had a similar porch, but now a full, modern portico runs along this elevation. There are two, two-story frame wings flanking the original structure. Attached to the south wing is a one-story, screened porch while the north wing has a modern, one-story service extension.

T-94

T-94
KNIGHTLY
Tunis Mills
Circa 1820; Private
Overlooking Leeds Creek, Knightly is a two-story, three-bay, Federal-style brick house built by Edward Lloyd V as a wedding gift for his daughter, Elizabeth Tayloe Lloyd, and her husband, Edward S. Winder. It is laid in Flemish bond on the facade and has a hip roof. On the north gable end is attached a two-story, brick service wing, and a one-story, glass porch is appended on the south. The facade has a central entrance covered by a one-story, one-bay, gable-roofed porch with chamfered posts and flat, hourglass-shaped balusters. The interior has a small foyer with a staircase in the northeast corner. A small room is located south of the foyer, and two large rooms are on the west side of the house. The interior woodwork dates to the mid nineteenth century and is probably original.

Lloyd retained title to Knightly, but allowed the Winders to receive the farm's income. Edward Winder bred, sold, and presumably bet on race horses: by 1831 he was heavily in debt, and a chattel mortgage to his father-in-law provides a vivid description of Winder's lavish lifestyle. The house was eventually sold out of the Lloyd-Winder family in 1880.

170

T-96

T–96
MARENGO (Site)
Near Easton
1891; demolished 1979; Private

Marengo was situated on Miles River Neck between Leeds and Hunting creeks and overlooked the Miles River with St. Michaels in the distance. The house was a simple building of the 1890s, the ornate trim of which mitigated the otherwise severe appearance. Designed as a Victorian Gothic structure, Marengo consisted of a large, two-and-one-half-story, five-bay, rectangular, frame section with a two-story kitchen. Off this wing was a two-story servants' quarters. In the early twentieth century the house underwent some alterations, including the addition of a dining room in front of the wing and adjacent to the screened porch. It was during this time that Thomas Sears, a landscape architect from Providence, Rhode Island, designed and laid out the gardens, which were maintained until the house was razed in 1979.

The land on which Marengo was built originally belonged to Jacob Gibson, a prominent farmer and outspoken observer of the early republic, who was the associate judge of the Talbot County court from 1802 until 1806. It was Gibson who named the plantation after Napoleon's great victory over the Austrians in 1800 in northern

T-98

Italy. The property eventually passed into the hands of Harold Wheeler, the builder of Marengo, and in 1917 Homer Williams, a former president of Carnegie Steel and Pittsburgh Steel, purchased the estate.

T–97
HUNTING HALL
Tunis Mills
Early twentieth century; Private

Located on a bank of Hunting Creek, Hunting Hall is a frame building designed in the colonial revival style popular during the late nineteenth and early twentieth centuries. The house sits on a brick foundation and has a gambrel roof, from the south end of which rises a single, exterior chimney. The main section is two-and-one-half stories by five bays, and its facade has a central entrance with a semicircular door frame and fanlight; three dormers pierce the slate roof. To the south is a one-story screened porch with a balustrade on the flat roof, whereas to the north lies a one-and-one-half-story service wing with an arcade on its facade.

T–98
STILL WATERS
Near Easton
Mid-nineteenth century; Private

Overlooking Hunting Creek, Still Waters is a late Federal-style frame dwelling raised on

T-97

a brick foundation. Like Presqu'isle (T–86), the gable end faces the water and serves as the principal facade. This elevation has five six-over-six windows and a central entrance framed by sidelights and transom. A small, four-pane, round window is centered in the upper gable below deep eaves supported by scroll-shaped brackets. Across the facade runs a one-story porch of simple design. On the northeast is a small, two-story kitchen wing, which is balanced on the southwest by a two-story, enclosed porch.

T–99
LOMBARDY
Near Easton
Circa 1830; circa 1930; Private

There are two noteworthy buildings on this land. The larger, known as Lombardy, is an ample, two-and-one-half-story, five-bay colonial revival structure of the 1930s with a Mt. Vernon porch. The five-part house has superior details and is obviously the product of a thorough academician and skillful craftsmen. To the northeast is an early-nineteenth-century, one-and-one-half-story, three-bay brick house with a T-shaped plan. Its facade is laid in Flemish bond and opened by two windows and a late-nineteenth-century entrance with sidelights and transom; two dormers project from the gable roof. On the rear is a three-bay exten-

T-99

171

T-100

T-101

sion that forms the stem of the T. An interesting feature of the interior is the basement kitchen. Much of the rest of the interior detail has been lost through later alterations.

T–100
WHEATLANDS
Near Easton
Late eighteenth century;
circa 1860; circa 1960; Private

Situated on Miles River Neck, Wheatlands overlooks the Miles River. The house is composed of a two-and-one-half-story, five-bay main section and a one-and-one-half-story brick wing of the 1960s on the west. Apparently Wheatlands began as a late-eighteenth-century dwelling when the property was in the possession of the Benson family, a prominent member of which was Perry Benson, a captain in the continental army and major general in the Maryland militia. It was remodeled in the mid nineteenth century with Italianate features, and the brick, old as well as new, was covered with stucco scored to simulate ashlar masonry. A second remodeling carried out in the 1960s eliminated the Italianate characteristics and removed both the stucco and brackets supporting the eaves. The interior is divided into a central stair hall with a large living room on the west and a dining

room and corridor on the east. The dining room faces the river and still possesses a fine marble mantel appropriate to the period of the first remodeling. This mantel, however, is not original to the house; it was brought in from another building, as was the Federal-style mantel that graces the living room fireplace. Near the house is a fine, shingle style, five-bay stable. It has a tall hip roof and a projecting, second-story, towerlike extension.

T–101
SPRINGWOOD FARM
Near Easton
Circa 1800; with alterations; Private

Despite its present appearance, Springwood Farm was built either in the late eighteenth or early nineteenth century as a typical frame farmhouse. The building rests on the original bond cellar. Apparently the two long facades were identical: they had a central entrance flanked by two windows and either two or three dormers on each side of the gambrel roof. In 1937 the house was shingled and the shed dormers installed. Further remodeling took place between 1971 and 1972, which resulted in the addition of the aluminum siding and the wing on the south and the removal of the chimney stacks.

T–102
ANNE PARRIS TELESCOPIC HOUSE
Near Easton
Circa 1830; Private

Standing on a knoll north of Easton between Route 662 and Route 50 is an early-nineteenth-century, telescopic frame farmhouse. Like other telescopic houses of the period, the Anne Parris House is composed of three sections diminishing in height from two-and-one-half stories to one-and-one-half stories to one story. The building is constructed on a brick foundation, and the walls are covered with weatherboard. The main facade of the largest section has a late-nineteenth-century porch with a Victorian entrance and two cross gables with Gothic-arched windows. The east elevation has three dormers, which predate the cross gables, and a chimney rises within each gable end. The middle section has a door with transom and a single window on each facade. A small dormer with four-over-four sash pierces each slope of the gable roof. The kitchen wing is of less sophisticated construction. It is longer than the middle section, but its entrance and window bays are arranged in the same fashion. A chimney, the back of which is exposed, rises within the open gable end.

T-102

T-103

T-104

T–103
MANOR HOUSE (site)
Near Easton
Private

This site is occupied by a new car agency.

T–104
GALLOWAY
Near Easton
Circa 1773; Private

Galloway, one of the many fine, Georgian country houses in Talbot County, was built by William Nicols, who married Henrietta Maria Chamberlaine in 1760. The estate eventually passed into the Goldsborough family, who in 1841 sold it to William Hughlett. Although smaller, Galloway resembles nearby Pleasant Valley (T–84) in exterior design and both Pleasant Valley and Caroline County's Willow Grove (CAR–3), in interior detail and floor plan. The house consists of a two-and-one-half-story, three-bay, brick main section and a two-story, frame kitchen wing. The walls are laid in Flemish bond above the chamfered water table and English-bond foundation, while the gables are finished in common bond; the foundation below grade is stone masonry. The basement windows not obscured by porches have segmental arches, as has the central entrance of the southeast facade. Lying immediately above the first-story

windows is a three-course beltcourse that divides the two floors. A lean-to porch runs across the northwest facade, in the central bay of which is located the main entrance; this has been enlarged to accommodate a transom and sidelights. Three dormers project from each slope of the gable roof, and a chimney rises from each gable end. The irregular fenestration on the southeast facade indicates the position of the original kitchen mentioned in the federal direct tax of 1798. This was replaced in the nineteenth century by a two-story frame wing appended to the east gable end. The interior has elegant woodwork throughout the first floor and plainer paneling and simpler trim on the second. Paneled dado and diagonal fireplaces with paneled chimney breasts and fluted pilasters characterize the first-floor rooms save the dining room, the chimney breast of which lacks the pilasters. The stair, which ascends to the third floor, has fluted newels and turned balusters.

T–105
WHITE MARSHES
Near Easton
1735; Private

White Marshes is located near the headwaters of Kings Creek about four miles east of Easton. The house is a two-and-one-half-story, three-bay brick structure with a one-

story, frame kitchen wing dating from the 1960s. The original part of the house is essentially unchanged from the eighteenth century, when it appeared in the federal direct tax of 1798. It is laid in English bond except the west facade, which is laid in Flemish bond with glazed headers. In this facade is a central door flanked by two windows with rubbed-and-gauged brick jack arches. A narrow string course runs across both gable ends at the attic level in addition to a two-brick beltcourse that girds the entire structure. Each gable has a line of glazed bricks running parallel to the bargeboards, and in the north gable is a brick dated 1735. The east facade has a central entrance flanked by two windows and sheltered by a small, finely detailed porch, on top of which is a Chinese Chippendale balustrade. An outline in the whitewash and the door on the second story suggest that there was a two-story wing appended to this facade. This was the home of the wealthy Quaker Berry family; the exciting architectural detail of the house demonstrates that not every Friend built a simple, somber dwelling. William Berry (d. 1685) established the Tuckahoe Meeting House on the Choptank. In 1775 the Berry family sold the house to Henry Johnston of Dorchester County. Johnston presumably is responsible for much of the present interior.

T-105

T-108

T–106
SHADY SIDE FARM
Near Easton
1759; with additions; Private

The home of Dr. Ennalls Martin, a surgeon in the War for Independence, Shady Side Farm is located on Route 328 across the road from White Marshes. The building is composed of a two-story, three-bay brick structure with a two-story, two-bay frame wing to the east, to which is attached another wing of the nineteenth century and a modern carport. Although illustrating the continuation of the telescopic form well into the nineteenth century, the nineteenth- and twentieth-century structures are of little architectural importance. The main house is, however, extraordinary because, unlike any other house in Talbot County, the facade is two full stories while the rear elevation has only one story with a single dormer. A beltcourse spans only the main facade, which alone is laid in Flemish bond; the other elevations are finished in common bond. A bulkhead cellar entrance on the asymmetrical gable end has been replaced with a small cellar window. Seams in this gable end suggest the location of a demolished wing. The interior, similar in plan to Harrington (S–108) in Somerset County, retains the original close-string stair with paneled spandrel, turned balusters, and bold

handrail; some original fielded paneling still survives on the fireplace wall of the dining room.

T–108
BEAVER NECK
Near Easton
Date uncertain; Private

From the exterior it is not possible to determine the age of Beaver Neck, but this type of dwelling was built on the Eastern Shore from the seventeenth to the late eighteenth century. Research shows that William Berry (see T–105) owned this land in the late seventeenth century. In 1705 Berry's heirs sold 600 acres of the tract for £140 sterling, a figure that has led some to date the house to circa 1700. Further work, possibly using dendrochronology, might help solve the mystery. The house is a one-and-one-half-story, three-bay brick structure that is one-room deep with a one-and-one-half-story, one-bay frame wing. White paint obscures the fine, glazed-header Flemish bond above the stepped water table on the facade and open gable end. An entrance marks the central bay of the facade, and three dormers pierce the gable roof. The rear elevation has the same arrangement but lacks the dormers. Although the exterior has experienced only minor alteration, the interior has undergone considerable change and has lost almost all of its early paneling.

T-109

T–109
MIDDLESPRING
Matthews
Circa 1824; Private

Built by the Mackay family, the brick farmhouse called Middlespring is composed of a two-and-one-half-story, three-bay section and a one-and-one-half-story, five-bay wing. The existence of a brick house in an area where frame is more common is testimony to the prosperity of the builders. The facade of the house is laid in Flemish bond, but the other elevations are of common-bond construction. The building lacks both a water table and a beltcourse, and except for the two-brick corbeled cornice on the lower part of the wing, it presents a simple appearance. The ground-floor plan consists of a living room and stair hall in the main section with a dining room, bath, and kitchen in the wing. Most of the interior trim is original except in the kitchen, which has undergone rebuilding to correct deterioration. The living room mantel is of good proportions and is notable for pilasters with herringbone reeding. Other interior details include the two-piece chair rail, the complex architrave trim, and the stair with delicate balustrade and paneled soffit.

T-110

T-111

T–110
KINGSTON LANDING
Near Easton
Early nineteenth century; Private

This landing served as a shipping point from at least as early as 1706, when the village of Kings Creek was formally recognized, until the close of World War I. This house dates to the early nineteenth century when maritime trade reached its peak in this area, because of the growth of river transportation. The building is notable architecturally for its telescopic form and because it is one of only a few Talbot County buildings of the early nineteenth century with a two-story porch. Built of frame, the house is now covered with aluminum siding. The main section is two-and-one-half stories tall and three bays wide with two dormers on each slope of the gable roof. The two-story middle section also has three bays, but it is slightly narrower. On the east gable end is attached a one-story wing with a vestibule on the facade and a lean-to addition on the south.

T–111
MOUNT HOPE FARM
Near Easton
1822; Private

Located east of Easton near a branch of Kings Creek is Mount Hope Farm. On the farm is a large brick house, nearly square in plan, which was built by Mary Bullen Benny, the great-great-granddaughter of William Catrop, who bought part of Mount Hope in 1686 and whose descendants still own the property. The main facade of the farmhouse is laid in Flemish bond and is three bays long with a central entrance. Across the facade is a late-nineteenth-century porch with a hip roof. The five windows on this elevation have nine-over-six sashes and original louvered shutters. From each gable rises a large chimney partially projecting from the plane of the gable end. On the rear is a large, two-story, brick shed addition, which was later enlarged to complete the square plan. To the south of the house is a small brick carriage house with the date 1843 carved in a wood lintel over the original entrance. On the west, snuggled among later outbuildings, is the original dairy, with a widely overhanging pyramidal roof rising to a pinnacle; to the north is the original meat house.

T–112
JOHN TRAX HOUSE
Near Easton
Early nineteenth century; with additions; Private

The John Trax House began as a one-and-one-half-story, two-room vernacular dwelling. When it was built, an exterior chimney rose against each gable end, and there was possibly a central door with two flanking windows on the facade. The original form with two dormers on each slope of the gable roof is still discernible between the now-enclosed chimneys. In the early twentieth century two, two-story, two-bay wings were added, and the entire structure was covered with brown wood shingles.

T–113
CEDAR GROVE
Near Easton
Early nineteenth century; 1929; Private

Cedar Grove, located at the Eastern Shore Nurseries east of Easton, is an early Federal-style brick farmhouse with later frame wings and porches. The brick structure, probably built by John Bennett, an Easton merchant, is two-and-one-half stories by three bays with the entrance in the northeast bay. The main facade is laid in Flemish bond while the rest of the brickwork is common bond. The windows have six-over-six sashes and are surmounted by jack arches. Two dormers project from the slope of the gable roof above this facade, and a chimney rises from the southwest gable end. In 1929 a two-story, two-bay wing with a one-story porch was added on the northeast. This wing was built in the same style as the earlier house and blends harmoniously with it.

T-112

T-113

T-114

T-114
FERNWOOD
Near Easton
Circa 1740; circa 1870; 1960;
Private

Fernwood is a large, two-and-one-half-story brick house, five bays long and one room deep, with brick chimneys rising from within the gable ends. The main facade is laid in Flemish bond above a plain water table and English-bond foundation. English bond is also used in the south elevation; common bond is found in the west gable end. Although slightly altered, the main facade has segmental arches surmounting the two cellar windows of the main facade and all its ground floor openings, a two-course beltcourse, and a twentieth-century porch that shelters the central main entrance and two of the four flanking windows. On the south elevation a two-story, brick wing was added about 1870, when the roof was altered and a stair to the attic was installed. Evidence from the west gable end— including four bricked-in windows and seams reflecting the dimensions of the chimney as well as bricks from different periods— suggests the original roof was hipped. This hypothesis is corroborated by details of the interior structure and the lack of a period stair to the attic. In 1960 a wing set back from the facade was added to the east gable

end and an addition and porch were attached to the rear wing.

The interior of the early house consists of a central stair hall with a single room on each side. The stair dates to the second quarter of the eighteenth century. Its open-string course has three turned balusters per step and a bold continuous handrail that curves over the intermediate newels; a paneled spandrel matches the raised paneled dado. The doors and trim appear to date from the nineteenth-century reconstruction. The living room, however, contains eighteenth-century raised paneling on the chimney breast, which was taken from the old Dover Ferry House and installed in 1960. This room also has original, paneled wainscot, window sections, and jambs. Peculiar to Fernwood are the curved, fluted corners of the window seats.

T-115
CLIFTON
Near Easton
Circa 1741; with additions; Private

Clifton stands east of Route 50 in a romantically landscaped garden. Built by the Denny family, the house was originally a one-and-one-half-story, three-bay brick structure laid in Flemish bond on the main facade and in English bond on the other elevations. Like most houses of this period,

Clifton has a central main entrance; but on the south elevation the door is asymmetrically placed owing to the rise of the stair. Peter Denny bought the land in 1741 and brought his bride, Lucy Richardson, here in 1747. An evaluation in 1774 shows that, besides the usual outbuildings, the place boasted a "new logged schoolhouse," a large enclosed garden, an orchard, and three nurseries for the cultivation of many kinds of fruit. In the mid-nineteenth century the house was brought to its present form by Matilda Woodall Bartlett and her husband, John C. Bartlett, a member of one of the founding families of Talbot County. They added the second story and attic and wings on the west gable end. A two-story brick wing runs perpendicular to this gable end and is recessed from the facade. To the south of this wing is attached a two-story, frame lean-to with a lean-to porch and on the west is an enclosed area, which extends across the juncture of the two wings for one story. The landscape plan, with its curving lane and large trees, is rare in the county and reflects the taste for informal gardens popular in the mid-nineteenth century

T-115

T–116
PRATT FARMHOUSE
Near Easton
Circa 1820; with additions; Private

Once representative of the type of building constructed to house successful farm families in the early nineteenth century, Pratt Farmhouse was enlarged later in the same century. Laid in Flemish bond on the main facade and in common bond on the north and west, the dwelling began as a two-story, three-bay structure with a one-story brick kitchen. The main house eventually acquired a two-story, frame wing to the east under a gable roof perpendicular to the roof of the house, and the kitchen was raised a floor by the addition of a frame second story. One-story, frame shed additions were made on the north and west sides of the wing, which extends beyond the north elevation. A one-story porch now covers the enlarged facade and east elevation. Interesting features of the interior include a mantel on the west wall and a complex architrave framing the main entrance to the stair hall.

T–117
EDMONDSON'S FRESHES (Stoney Ridge)
Near Easton
1763; Private

Located at the headwaters of the Tred Avon River, Edmondson's Freshes was patented to

John Edmondson in 1666. He soon sold the property to Emmanuel Jenkinson whose grandson of the same name began construction of the present house in 1763. He died shortly thereafter, but a series of initials and dates carved in a number of bricks shows that his son John, among other members of the family, continued the work, constructing a two-story, three-bay brick house, which was later enlarged by a frame kitchen wing that projects from the southeast gable end. The brickwork includes a variety of bonds: Flemish bond is used on the main facade; English bond is on the rear and northwest elevations; and common bond is on the southeast gable end. The foundation is constructed of stone below grade. A water table runs along the exposed elevations, but the two-brick beltcourse is restricted to the principal facade, which has a central entrance. An exterior chimney rises along the southeast gable end, and above the northwest gable end rises an interior chimney. The interior is arranged according to the basic hall-and-parlor plan with an enclosed winder stair in the western corner. The story-and-loft kitchen is of undetermined age. It has entrances on the southeast and northeast, and, in the eastern corner, a boxed winder stair similar to that found in the main house.

T–119
SPRINGFIELD (site)
Near Easton
Private

This important, early-nineteenth-century farmhouse was razed despite local efforts to save it, but some materials from the well-constructed building were rescued by the Talbot County Historical Society. Until its destruction, Springfield was composed of a two-story frame main house with a one-story brick wing on the north and a two-story frame wing on the south. To the north of this complex stood a brick smokehouse.

T–120
YELLOW HOUSE
Near Easton
Circa 1810; mid-nineteenth century;
Private

Situated on the northeast corner of Route 50 and Schwaninger Road, two miles south of Easton, Yellow House is a large, three-part farmhouse with a three-bay Greek revival principal section. Its Greek revival features include the corner pilasters, third-floor casement "frieze" windows, and the square posts that support the porch. Above the windows of the first and second stories are simple cornices and trim painted white to contrast with the yellow of the building. The central main entrance has double doors

T-121

with sidelights, transom, and beveled glass in the upper panels. From the apex of the low hip roof rise twin chimneys. This farmhouse is not the oldest building on the site, however. To the south is a two-story, one-bay, frame and brick wing that dates to the early nineteenth century. It is recessed from the facade, but extends beyond the rear elevation. The west and south elevations are finished in frame, but the north and east are laid in brick. There is also a one-story, one-bay wing that, with the brick walls of the middle section, appears to be the remains of the early-nineteenth-century dwelling, a one-story, two-bay structure with a steeply pitched gable roof. In the mid nineteenth century half of that building was raised to two stories, extended on the west, and finished in frame. Connected to this on the south by a brick wall is a brick dairy with a hip roof; it is contemporary with the original house. To the east is a brick meat house with a gable roof and corbeled cornice. The batten door on the west gable end hangs on the original, iron strap hinges.

T–121
PEACHBLOSSOM MEETING HOUSE
Near Easton
Circa 1870; Private
Peachblossom Meeting House is located across the creek from the seventeenth-

century Robins patent, Peachblossom. In the third quarter of the nineteenth century four Protestant denominations, Swedenborg, Lutheran, Methodist, and Brethren, built this hexagonal meeting house on the north bank of Peachblossom Creek south of Easton. The Peachblossom Meeting House is raised on piers, between which is brick-fill in a basket-weave pattern. Six-over-six windows pierce the weatherboard walls, except on the west where an entrance with double doors is located. A small chimney projects on the north, and a hexagonal, corrugated tin roof rises from the plain box cornice. Still open for religious services, the meeting house now is solely in the possession of the Church of the Brethren. The meeting house's building may have been influenced by Orson Fowler's 1848 book *The Octagon House: A Home for All.* Fowler, a phrenologist, marriage consultant, and sex scientist, used his book to encourage people to use the octagonal form in domestic architecture. The cogent rhetoric of his work resulted in the construction of thousands of octagonal buildings, not only houses but also churches, schoolhouses, barns, pigsties, and seance chambers.

T–122
BOSTON CLIFF
Near Easton
1729; Private
Boston Cliff has the most carefully executed early Georgian interior in Talbot County. Moreover, a chimney brick marked 1729 makes it the earliest dated example. The splendid interior is divided into a stair hall, living and dining rooms, and a bedroom in the lean-to off the dining room. Original woodwork remains in many of the rooms, but the most noteworthy feature is probably the open-string stair with its turned balusters and continuous handrail; the carved flowers on the step-ends are similar to those on the stair of Otwell (T–164). The house is a one-and-one-half-story, five-bay brick building with a one-and-one-half-story, three-bay twentieth-century brick wing on the east. All four elevations are laid in Flemish bond with random glazing. A stepped water table jogs above the basement windows on all four facades. The exposed gable end has a belt-course at the second floor level, a casement window on the first story, and two casement windows above. The first story of the main facade has a central door with a jack arch and twelve-over-eight windows with row lock arches; above, five-over-six dormers project from the gable roof, at the ends of which rise two chimneys with plaster-banded caps.

T-122

T-124

T-125

T–124
LLOYD'S LANDING
Trappe
Circa 1720; 1950; Private

Architecturally, Lloyd's Landing is a superior example of the type of dwelling most often constructed by prosperous families in the first half of the eighteenth century. It was built by James Lloyd for his son James, "the Mariner," so that the latter could be conveniently near the warehouse at the landing and the deep anchorage on the Choptank River. There is a 1720 letter in the archives of the Maryland Historical Society from "the Mariner" to a cousin in London in which Lloyd mentions how much he and his wife are enjoying their newly finished home. By 1798, the estate had grown to include a frame kitchen, a log meat house, a frame milk house and a fowl house. The one-and-one-half-story main house is remarkable because all elevations are laid in English bond above and below the stepped water table, and because the joist ends remain exposed in the facade eave, in a manner similar to the original treatment at Cloverfields (QA–2). A porch extends across both the north and south facades, and two dormers project from each slope of the gable roof. Two large chimneys rise partially enclosed within the gable ends, although the west chimney now rests in the

T-126

center of the building because of the additions made in 1950, which doubled the size of the original house. Of particular interest is the living room, which still possesses much original woodwork. There are two large, horizontal panels above the bolection-molded fireplace opening, and paneled dado and window seats are used throughout. Moreover, a two-piece cornice runs around the room, and an ovolo molding is found on the edge of the window jambs. There is also original trim in the dining room, but it has not fared as well as that in the living room.

T–125
PARROTT HOUSE
Trappe
Early nineteenth century; Private

This early-nineteenth-century, vernacular farmhouse is located between Wright's and Tarbutton Mills. It is composed of two three-bay, frame, one-room sections. The two-story section of the house appears to be later than the one-and-one-half-story wing, but both date from the early nineteenth century. The taller section has an entrance with sidelights and transom in its northern bay and two windows on both stories of the south gable end, with a chimney between. The wing has a central entrance with two dormers above, and a chimney rises from each gable end.

T–126
GIBSON WRIGHT MILL HOUSE
Trappe
Circa 1750 (?); Early nineteenth century; Private

The Gibson Wright Mill House's excellent details, both exterior and interior, attest to the prosperity of millers in this area of Maryland. The large brick house is composed of an early-nineteenth-century, two-story, three-bay section and a one-and-one-half-story, three-bay wing believed to have been built about 1750 by Samuel Abbott, a miller. The Abbotts sold their house in 1837 to Wright. Others suggest that Samuel's great-grandson built the entire brick house early in the nineteenth century. The main building has extraordinarily fine brickwork of uniform color with convex joints. The main facade has a central entrance flanked by two nine-over-six windows with three six-over-six windows above. All of the openings are surmounted by rubbed-and-gauged widely splayed brick jack arches. From the gable ends rise two chimneys with corbeled caps. The wing has a partially enclosed, lean-to porch across its front. Two dormers project from each slope of the gable roof, and a large chimney rises exposed along the open gable end. The Wrights continued milling until 1885; H. Chandlee Forman describes their operations in his *Old Buildings, Gardens, and Furniture of Tidewater Maryland*.

179

T-128

T-130

T-127
GIBSON WRIGHT MILL (site)
Trappe
Private

Representative of early Maryland industry, Gibson Wright Mill stood well into the 1960s. H. Chandlee Forman recorded the building between 1956 and 1964 and describes it fully in *Old Buildings, Gardens, and Furniture of Tidewater Maryland,* including in his account several photos and drawings. (See also T–126.)

T–128
SAULSBURY (properly called Nomini)
Trappe
Circa 1705; Private

The house known today as Saulsbury, located east of Trappe south of Miles Creek, is a fascinating example of eighteenth-century, vernacular architecture. It is sometimes dated to the 1660s, but this date probably refers to the patent date or to an earlier building on this site. It is known that in 1704 Peter Sharp bought the land where the present-day house now stands and in the same year erected a house thereon. There is a somewhat remote possibility that today's Saulsbury is the same hall and parlor house described in Sharp's 1732 inventory. The dwelling consists of a large, three-story brick section with a twentieth-century frame

wing. The gambrel-roofed main house is unique in the county because the south gable end forms the principal facade, the fenestration of which is markedly asymmetrical. The walls are laid in Flemish bond above the water table and in English bond below, and a course of stretchers runs between the first and second stories on the facade. Segmental arches surmount the window openings. In addition to the gable-end entrance, Saulsbury's floor plan consists of a central vestibule with a stair against the chimney. One each side of the vestibule, partitioned off by raised paneling, is a single room with a fireplace. In the living room the fireplace is treated with bolection molding and surmounted by a raised panel similarly treated. The dining room resembles the living room in its details, but is smaller and the woodwork plainer.

T–129
KNAUER HOUSE (site)
Trappe
Private

This house was a one-and-one-half-story frame dwelling with a two-story frame wing. In appearance it was typical of the nineteenth century. The building was destroyed after 1969. No photograph is available.

T–130
EBERHARD HOUSE
Trappe
Circa 1800 (?); with addition;
Private

The Eberhard House is an example of the vernacular building form common in the county from the seventeenth through the nineteenth century. The smaller one-and-one-half-story, three-bay section with a steeply pitched roof appears to be the earlier section of this two-part house. It is joined by a large, two-story, three-bay structure. Both sections are built on brick piers and covered with brown wood shingles added in the early twentieth century. A small brick chimney rises between the sections. Across the main facade of the larger structure is a one-story porch, which shelters the central entrance and its flanking windows.

T–131
BELMONT
Trappe
Circa 1845; with additions; Private

William Hughlett of Jamaica Point, one of the most prosperous merchants and shipbuilders of Talbot County in the mid-nineteenth century and builder of several houses in the county, was responsible for the construction of Belmont. The oldest section of the house is the two-and-one-

T-131

T-132

T-133

half-story frame structure now flanked by additions. The west wing is from the 1930s or '40s, but the east one was built sometime between 1850 and 1900. The building is raised about three feet off the ground by a masonry foundation and is covered by clapboards. A widow's walk cupola rises from the roof.

T–132
BRYAN HOUSE (site)
Trappe
Private

The Bryan House was a gambrel-roofed frame dwelling, three bays long by two bays deep with a long, two-story, nineteenth-century wing on the north. Unusual features of this building included the exposed brick backs of the fireplaces and a broad roof. An outbuilding, pictured, was moved to Harrington (S–108) in Somerset County.

T–133
A. B. HIGHLEY HOUSE (site)
Trappe
Private

The A. B. Highley House, which now stands behind the Robert Morris Inn (T–249), Oxford, once occupied this site. It is a small, one-and-one-half-story, four-bay frame structure with exterior chimneys on the gable ends. On the east was an addition

T-134

that was removed at the time of relocation. The removal of plaster revealed that the building is composed of two sections, which were built at different times. The first structure was twenty feet square and was built in the early nineteenth century. Shortly after its completion, a fourteen-foot addition was made on the west, and the house assumed its present form.

T–134
TOP MARK FARM
Trappe
First quarter of the nineteenth century; with additions; Private

Top Mark Farm is an interesting structure that has been allowed to fall into ruin. It is composed of a two-story, three-bay brick section and a smaller-scale, two-story frame wing on the north, to which is attached a one-story hyphen and a two-story wing. Although the brick main house dates to the early nineteenth century, the frame constructions appear to have been built around the turn of this century. The brick structure is laid in common bond and lacks both a water table and a beltcourse. The long facades are identical with a central entrance sheltered by a porch and flanked by two windows. There are also corbeled cornices below the lines of the gable roof. The difference in brickwork above the second

floor and outlines of a gambrel roof in the gable ends are evidence that Top Mark underwent a major remodeling. The date of this work is not known for certain, but corbeled cornices are usually associated with buildings of the 1820–50 period. The interior is divided into a small stair hall with a single room on each side.

T–135
BOUNTIFUL FARM
Trappe
Circa 1770 (?); circa 1850; Private

Bountiful Farm is a good example of the combination of early vernacular structures, similar to the nearby Eberhard House (T–130), and, like Eberhard House, its progression of buildings indicates the continued prosperity of its owners. It may, however, be a finer building than the Eberhard House, because the one-and-one-half-story structure has dormers and two rooms on each floor, and the two-story addition exhibits a sophisticated treatment of its main entrance. This addition appears to date from the second half of the nineteenth century, but the smaller east wing has many features characteristic of eighteenth-century masonry construction. These include the drip cap of the chimney and the fat muntins in the windows on the east.

T-135

T-136

T-137

T–136
MAYNADIER HOUSE
Trappe
Circa 1810; Private

Maynadier House is architecturally notable because it is a good example of the Federal-style rural housing of the upper middle class in the nineteenth century. It consists of a two-and-one-half-story, three-bay main house and a one-and-one-half-story, four-bay wing, the east half of which is covered with aluminum siding. The main house is laid in common bond save the main facade, which is laid in Flemish bond. The principal entrance is in the east bay and is surmounted by a transom. The rear elevation has similar features, but its entrance lacks a transom and the window above is placed at the stair-landing level. Partially exposed chimneys rise along the gable ends, and two dormers pierce each slope of the roof.

T–137
OLD WHITEMARSH CEMETERY AND CHURCH RUIN
Trappe
First attended circa 1665; Private

Old Whitemarsh Cemetery and the ruins of Old Whitemarsh Church are tangible remains of the early history of the Episcopal Church in Maryland. Located on the main public road halfway between Oxford and the now-defunct town of Dover, an early county seat of Talbot County, the original church is believed to have been built between 1662 and 1665, but the first date mentioned in the parish records is 1690, when Joseph Leech was acting minister. There is, however, a courthouse record in Talbot County for June 21, 1687, which authorizes road repairs "from Cooleys' gate to the Church at Whitemarsh." When the Maryland General Assembly made the Church of England the state church in 1692, it designated St. Peter's Parish, whose parish church was Whitemarsh, as one of the thirty original parishes in the colony. In 1751 the church was remodeled and enlarged to nearly double its size; the membership, however, continued to decline. After 1795 services were alternated between Whitemarsh and Easton, which by then had become the county seat and center of commerce in the area. By 1847 the rector had moved to Easton, where Christ Church (T–15) had been built, and still fewer services were being held at Whitemarsh. At this time the old Bible, the silver communion service received from England in 1738, and the wood alms box were taken to St. Paul's Church (T–282) in Trappe, where they have remained. In 1851 Holy Trinity (T–250) in Oxford became the parish church, and Whitemarsh was almost completely abandoned except for occasional services. One day in January, 1897, the de-

T-138

teriorating church was being prepared for services when it caught fire. The conflagration destroyed the building, leaving only the brick walls that stand today. In 1974, the site was reconsecrated along with four acres to be used as a cemetery, operated by the Episcopal Church in Trappe.

T–138
HOLE-IN-THE-WALL
Trappe
Circa 1780; with additions; Private

This frame house, to which tradition assigns a date in the seventeenth century, actually began as a late-eighteenth-century, one-and-one-half-story, three-bay dwelling with a side-hall-and-parlor plan. It is covered with a gable roof, each slope of which is pierced by two dormers. From the north gable end extends a kitchen wing added not long after the completion of the main house. Originally covered with a gable roof, this wing now has a flat deck roof surmounted by a railing. In the mid nineteenth century a two-story frame wing perpendicular to the main house was added on the south gable end. Interesting features of the interior include a boxed stair, the original mantel with cyma-recta moldings in the parlor of the main house, and a boxed stair with a fine chamfered newel topped by a cap with cavetto-astragal moldings in the large wing.

T-139

T-141

T–139
CASTLE RACKET FARM
Trappe
Circa 1800; Private

Castle Racket stands on a farm northwest of Trappe. It is a handsome, two-story, three-bay vernacular farmhouse, with a Flemish-bond main facade that lacks both a water table and a beltcourse. A three-bay, twentieth-century porch shelters the central entrance and its flanking windows. The house is topped by a moderately pitched gable roof and an exposed chimney along each gable end in a manner similar to that at Maynadier House (T–136). The interior plan consists of a stair hall flanked by two rooms, all of small scale. The original mantels, doors, and paneling (if any) have long since disappeared, and the crossetted moldings around the doors and the fine chair rail were stolen in the late 1970s.

T–141
MONKTON
Trappe
Early nineteenth century; Private

Illustrating the prosperity that Talbot County enjoyed in the early nineteenth century, Monkton is a fine period building similar in date, plan, and detail to Middlespring (T–109) and Maynadier House (T–136). The two-story, three-bay brick house has a

Flemish-bond main facade; its entrance is located in the west bay. On the west gable end is a one-and-one-half-story wing with a modern porch, and attached to this on the west is a catslide-roofed kitchen wing. An interesting feature is the placement of the original kitchen in the basement of the main house.

T–142
WELSH FARM
Trappe
Late nineteenth century; Private

The Welsh Farm is one of the many well-known, small landmarks in Talbot County. It is a two-part farmhouse composed of a two-story, three-bay frame section and a one-story, three-bay frame wing, both of which are built on brick foundations. The main house has a central entrance, a moderately pitched gable roof, and two chimneys that rise within the gables. The wing exhibits fenestration altered in order to accommodate a modern kitchen arrangement and a newly constructed fireplace on its open gable end. To the south of the wing is an early smokehouse.

T–143
CROSIADORE (site)
Trappe
Private

Architecturally Crosiadore illustrated the tastes of several generations of the Dickinson family, who maintained the estate for over two hundred years and only relinquished title in the late 1950s. From the eighteenth-century vernacular dwelling to the dramatic, Victorian Gothic manor of the 1880s, to the noble colonial revival mansion of the 1930s, Crosiadore was built in major styles successfully articulated and harmoniously combined. The five-bay, two-story section to the west represented the earliest structure; tradition has it that the room in which the Revolutionary War hero John Dickinson was born in 1732 was incorporated into it. Around 1880 a large, two-and-one-half-story, five-bay, Victorian Gothic wing was added on the west along with a one-bay, secondary stair hall between these structures. This wing had a very steep gable roof with dormers and a towerlike extension on the south. The tower was partially obscured by the addition in the 1930s of a two-story, three-bay porch supported by fluted Doric columns and surmounted by a full entablature with pediment. This colonial revival reconstruction also saw the addition of a Mt. Vernon–style porch to the

T-142

T-143

T-144

T-145

facade. Further remodeling done at this time included the addition of a living room and bedrooms on the south elevation of the vernacular structure, the alteration of its original gable roof into a gambrel roof to accommodate these additions, and the addition of a lean-to roof to shelter the second-story porch. In 1976 Crosiadore was razed by its new owner who used the site to build a modern house.

T–144
HOWELL'S POINT (site)
Trappe
Circa 1920; Private

Howell's Point was one of the finer Georgian revival structures in Talbot County. It had very fine wood details—the interior was well appointed with paneling, Corinthian pilasters, and a superior stair. The primary timbers of the house, however, suffered from extensive termite damage and water rot during the 1950s and '60s and the house was demolished in 1976.

T–145
BOSTON
Near Trappe
Circa 1800; circa 1820–1840; Private

The land on which Boston is situated was first taken up by Thomas Powell in 1663. At his death it passed to his daughter, Ann, who married Nicholas Goldsborough. The couple settled here and began to build their home, which, in the hands of their descendants who retained possession of the property well into the twentieth century, became the estate known as Boston, a name borrowed from one of the family's sloops. The two-and-one-half-story, four-bay common-bond wing appears to be the earliest part of the present house. It was originally a one-and-one-half-story building; both its long facades had a central entrance flanked by windows. When the two-and-one-half-story wing was added on the south, the old dwelling was raised another story. That newer wing is laid in Flemish bond and has a convex molded water table. Its south gable end has two triple-sash windows; once doors leading to a porch, the windows have jack arches with rubbed brick.

T–146
COMPTON
Near Trappe
Circa 1740; circa 1810; Private;
National Register

An allee of maple and cedar provides the approach to Compton, the home of Samuel Stevens, eighteenth governor of Maryland (1822–1825). Stevens's tenure is best remembered for the enfranchisement of the Jews, the abolition of a religion test for Maryland office holders, and the incorporation into state law of the civil liberties guaranteed by the Bill of Rights. The house he chose to make his residence was a simple, one-and-one-half-story, L-plan building of the second quarter of the eighteenth century that he had inherited from his father in 1794. Stevens began to remodel the old structure, probably around 1810. He added the second story to the main house, changed the floor plan, renewed the woodwork, and added the one-and-one-half-story wing on the southeast gable end. In transforming Compton into a residence befitting his station, Stevens created a beautiful combination of eighteenth-century vernacular architecture and early-nineteenth-century additions.

T-146

T-147

T–147
BEAUVOIR
Trappe

Late eighteenth century; Private

Beauvoir, the birthplace of Daniel Martin, governor of Maryland (1828–1829; 1831), is located on Island Creek Neck west of Trappe. The first mention of a house on this site is in 1745 when Thomas Martin II stipulated that his sister was to have a life estate in the "home where she now lives." How much of this house has survived is uncertain. The 1798 tax assessment describes the house here as one story, frame, with a frame addition, a large passage, and a kitchen. The present house is a two-and-one-half-story, three-bay frame main structure with a one-and-one-half-story, six-bay frame wing (possibly the part standing in 1798). It is one of Talbot County's fine houses. That Beauvoir is such a sophisticated dwelling is not immediately evident because of the plain exterior and plan, but the interior possesses woodwork characteristic of the great country seats in the county. Especially notable are the walnut stair with turned balusters and the raised paneling in the dining room. To the north of the house is a large, square smokehouse with battened siding and a steep pyramidal roof; it is among the best outbuildings in the county. The name Beauvoir was applied in the twentieth century.

T-150

T–149
THE WILDERNESS
Near Trappe

Circa 1785; circa 1815; Private;
National Register

Located on a large farm overlooking the Choptank River is the Wilderness, the home of Governor Daniel Martin (see also T–147). In 1808 Martin inherited from his father a two-and-one-half-story, four-bay brick house. To this he added a larger-scale, two-and-one-half-story, three-bay, Federal-style brick wing. The walls of both structures are laid in Flemish bond; chimneys rise from the gable roofs—two from the gables of the earlier section and twin chimneys, connected by a curtain, from within the open gable end of the main house. Both sections have two dormers on each slope of their gable roofs, and the original dentil cornice is intact. Early in the twentieth century the four-bay wing was widened six feet, and the whole house was painted white. To the east are two early outbuildings, a smokehouse and a dairy.

T–150
BULLEN'S CHANCE
Trappe

Circa 1780; with additions; Private

Located on a small inlet of Island Creek on Island Creek Neck, the small house known

as Bullen's Chance was probably built by the Martin family. It is composed of a very tall one-and-one-half-story frame main house with a lower two-story frame wing on the west and a small one-story wing on the east. The main facade originally had a central door, but today it presents a side entrance with a twentieth-century architrave. Two dormers pierce each slope on the gable roof, and a chimney rises within the east gable. The west wing, built in the nineteenth century, is recessed from the entrance facade and extends toward the inlet.

T–151
WALNUT GROVE FARM
Trappe

Early nineteenth century; Private

The architectural importance of Walnut Grove Farm lies not in its farmhouse, which was built in the 1930s to replace a seventeenth- or early-eighteenth-century dwelling, but in its two early-nineteenth-century outbuildings. The one-and-one-half-story, two-bay frame building served as quarters. It is raised on a brick foundation and is covered with modern weatherboard. Partitions now divide the interior into two sections with exposed joists and girder, but originally there were at least three rooms. A fireplace is located at the rear of the building and services the larger room. A shed

T-151

T-152

addition on the rear gable contains the kitchen. Next to the quarters is a spring-house or dairy sunk halfway into the ground with a modern bulkhead entrance. To the west is a graveyard with stones dating from 1794 to 1912, bearing the names of the Martin, Clayland, Lloyd, and Stevens families.

T–152
LOCUST GROVE (Island Creek)
Trappe
Early nineteenth century; Private

Locust Grove, built by the Mullikin and Stevens families, is an early-nineteenth-century frame dwelling with a two-story frame addition. The gambrel-roofed main house is one-and-one-half stories tall and five bays wide; its principal facade has a central entrance sheltered by a three-bay, hip-roofed porch. An unusual feature is the placement of dormers in the gambrel roof; the only other example of such an arrangement is at the nearby Dickinson House. Also unusual is the very low profile of this section owing to the gambrel roof and the lack of a visible foundation. This squatness is emphasized by the vertical quality of the addition and its gable roof that rises above the roof of the main house. Many original details remain, but wood shingles have replaced the weatherboard.

T-154

T-153

T–153
CATLIN'S PLAIN
Trappe
Late eighteenth century; Private

Catlin's Plain may be unpretentious in appearance, but it displays the builder's great care in construction and attention to detail. The house consists of a two-story, three-bay brick section and a two-story brick kitchen wing, which was originally one-story. The main block has a central entrance with a crossetted architrave and doors of beaded, diagonal battens on the interior and six raised panels on the exterior. Flemish bond rises from the common-bond foundation. Common bond is also found on the gable end above the second floor and on the re-built southwest wall of the wing. The reconstruction has been limited, however, and the exterior of Catlin's Plain presents itself today as it did when it was built. The interior is similarly intact and exhibits the same attention to detail and expert craftsmanship in its mantels, paneling, and stair. The house is associated with the noted Stevens family (see, for example, T–146).

T–154
SAILOR'S RETREAT
Near Oxford
Circa 1834; Private

South of Trappe Station on the north bank of Island Creek stands Sailor's Retreat, a small frame dwelling probably built by Captain John Stevenson, a seafaring merchant of Oxford, who acquired the property in 1834. The frame house is composed of a one-and-one-half-story main section raised on a brick foundation and flanked by one-story wings. The main facade has asymmetrical fenestration around a central entrance sheltered by a one-bay, gable-roofed porch. Three symmetrically arranged dormers project from the gable roof, and exterior chimneys rise along the gable ends. The east wing is original; its exterior chimney indicates that it was probably designed to serve as a kitchen.

T–155
ANDERTON
Oxford
Circa 1740; circa 1880; Private

In the 1680s Anderton was the home of Colonel Nicholas Lowe, a nephew of Lady Baltimore. The property remained in the Lowe family until 1740 when it was sold to William Thomas, who probably built the oldest section of the present dwelling. This

T-155

T-156

T-157

section is discernible in the three bays of the one-and-one-half-story, five-bay main house nearest the two-and-one-half-story wing. It is covered with beaded shiplap siding, while the two bays to the west of what is today the central main entrance are finished with beaded weatherboard. The interior is similarly differentiated; yellow pine floors are found throughout the shiplap section whereas white pine flooring is used in the part covered with weatherboard. Furthermore, the trim and several early four-panel doors are clearly distinct from the later-style doors and trim that characterize the weatherboard section. An interesting feature of this part is a four-foot door on the north facade; it is perhaps the smallest outside door in Maryland. On the south gable end is a two-and-one-half-story, three-bay wing built in the second half of the nineteenth century, reputedly by Alexander Stewart. He may also be responsible for the two-bay weatherboard addition, because its woodwork is typical of his era.

T–156
COMBSBERRY
Oxford
Mid-eighteenth century; with additions; Private
One of Talbot County's extraordinary vernacular dwellings, Combsberry is situated on

T-158

Oxford Neck near a small branch of Island Creek. The two-and-one-half-story, five-bay main house is framed by a brick wing of the 1870s on the east and a brick wing of the 1930s on the west. The house is especially notable for its brickwork. The house is laid in English bond except for the main facade above the stepped water table, which is laid in all-header bond, a feature found elsewhere in Talbot County only at Lloyd's Costin (T–71) and Cedar Point (T–208). This type of bonding normally dates to the 1750–80 period and was popular in Annapolis's grand houses (such as the Brice House) of that time. The windows on the first story have segmental arches, whereas a fanlight and semicircular arch surmount the central main entrance. A unique feature of this facade is the use of glazed headers in recessed panels below the windows. Furthermore, the second-story central bay has a panel that is wider than the window opening and equal to the bay containing the main entrance below. The north facade has an unusual element, a stair tower, which is characteristic of seventeenth-century, English vernacular construction and unusual in Maryland (but see Troth's Fortune T–50). The floor plan consists of two rooms separated by a passage leading from the entrance to the stair tower. The interior contains period fireplaces, a wall of rearranged period paneling, and a stair with a paneled

soffit and a late-eighteenth-century close-string balustrade. The land and house are associated with the Oldham and Martin families.

T–157
FOSTON
Oxford
1862; Private
Foston, located on Oxford Neck overlooking Island Creek, is a two-and-one-half-story, three-bay house raised on a brick foundation and covered with weatherboard. On the east gable end is appended a two-story wing, and to this is attached a one-story addition of the twentieth century. The exterior is remarkably plain for its period, but this may be due to the absence of porches, which frequently carried the majority of ornament in the mid-Victorian era. The interior retains its original (late) Greek revival woodwork; the scrollwork on the mantels is particularly interesting. On the back of one mantel is the name and date: Mr. Baker, 1862.

T–158
ATTICA
Near Oxford
Early eighteenth century; 1920; Private
Originally an early colonial one-and-one-half-story brick dwelling, Attica was re-

T-160

T-161

modeled and is today a large house typical of the colonial revival style popular in the 1920s and '30s. Insofar as its original form can be discerned, however, it represents the important survival of an early-eighteenth-century building comparable with Beaver Neck (T–108) and the wing on Cedar Point (T–208). Evidence for the early structure is seen in the west gable end, which contains the outline of the original roof north of the chimney. The house is raised on a stone foundation, and a stepped water table runs along the exposed elevations. The south facade is laid in Flemish bond with random glazing, but both the north facade and the west gable end are finished in a combination of English and common bonds. In the 1930s a two-story, three-bay wing was added on the east, and a one-and-one-half-story wing recessed from the facade was attached to this, giving the whole structure a telescopic appearance when viewed from the south.

T–160
BONFIELD (site)
Oxford
1773; with additions; Private

In 1924 a fire destroyed this mansion, which was built by Samuel Chamberlaine (1742–1811) to mark his marriage. It was a three-bay, nearly square frame dwelling. On the east the basement was at ground level, but

elsewhere a man-made knoll rose about four feet to cover the foundations. Across the main facade was a two-story, three-bay Greek revival porch with full entablature in the Ionic order. The central entrance was surmounted by a pediment, and there appears to have been a small gallery on the second-story level. In the jerkinhead roof were two twentieth-century dormers, and a balustrade stood between the chimneys. Across the south facade was a one-story glass porch. Noteworthy features of the interior included three revolutionary period mantels and the six-panel doors flanking the fireplaces. With its jerkinhead roof and two-and-one-half stories, Bonfield was a unique frame house in Talbot County, but its interior was comparable with the best of the county's Revolutionary period houses, such as Pleasant Valley (T–84) and Galloway (T–104). There is an attractive modern residence on the site (see T–161).

T–161
BONFIELD
Oxford
Circa 1924; Private

After fire destroyed the eighteenth-century house (T–160), John Lee Carroll Downes, vice-president of Durant Enterprises and president of the Liberty National Bank in New York City, built the present structure.

Standing on part of the original foundations and basement, this colonial revival dwelling is one-and-one-half stories tall and seven bays wide. The main entrance is located in the center bay; all three center bays are recessed. Three dormers project above this recess. A balustrade encloses the large flat roof, from which rise two chimneys; dormers pierce the open slopes of the gable roofs that cover the two-bay sections flanking the entrance recess. East of the house is an interesting outbuilding with a steeply pitched gable roof and wide overhang. Its original use has been obscured by its conversion in the 1920s into an office with chauffeur quarters above. Today Bonfield is remembered as the residence in the 1930s of Hervey Allen, author of the best-seller *Anthony Adverse*.

T–162
PLIMHIMMON
Oxford
Mid-eighteenth century; with additions; Private

Plimhimmon is an important vernacular dwelling with stylish detail that is in almost pristine condition. Matthew Tilghman acquired the property from Thomas Coward in 1787 and gave it to his daughter Anna Maria, widow of Washington's aide-de-camp, Lieutenant Colonel Tench Tilghman. Here Mrs. Tilghman entertained Lafayette

T-162

T-163

during his 1824–25 visit to America. Like Bonfield (T–161) across the road, Plimhimmon is situated on a man-made rise. The house today is composed of the original two-story, two-bay brick structure, a two-story, five-bay frame wing, and a two-story, three-bay frame kitchen wing. These wings were built in the 1870s by William Myers, grandfather of the present owner, to replace an earlier one-and-one-half-story wing. The brick section, late Georgian in design, is included in the 1798 tax list; it remains nearly intact. Its first story is covered by a porch with pierced balustrades, square posts with small brackets, and a low hip roof; the garden elevation is identically arranged. The cornice with dentils and triglyphs is carried around the building to form a pediment on each of the gable ends. The interior is divided into a stair hall and parlor and contains much important woodwork. Its open-string stair has a walnut balustrade and turned newels. On the wall adjoining the wing immediately before the stair is a large arched recess with fluted pilasters, paneled soffit, and keystone trim. The focal point of the parlor is the mantel. It has fluted pilasters supporting the shelf with a course of triglyphs and fluting and a Wall-of-Troy molding. The surround of the fireplace and hearth is marble. The windows are recessed from the interior wall, and their trim rests

upon pilasters. There are recessed paneled jambs and panels with applied molding below the windows. A chair rail composed of a cap and a course of triglyphs beneath protects the walls. Most of the woodwork retains early paint, including the grained door, black baseboards, and gray trim.

T–163
JENA
Oxford
Circa 1800; with additions; Private;
National Register

Jena, situated on an inlet of Goldsborough Creek near Oxford, is a superior example of early-nineteenth-century Federal-style architecture. The name comes from Napoleon's victory over the Prussians in 1806 and may have been suggested to the owner, Perry Spencer, by his friend, Jacob Gibson. Gibson, an admirer of Napoleon, named his own estates after battles which Napoleon won (note Marengo [T–96]). Jena was probably built by Richard Robinson (whose family had owned the estate since the early eighteenth century) to replace a frame dwelling. It is a one-and-one-half-story, three-bay brick structure laid in Flemish bond on the main facade and common bond on the gable ends; the bonding on the west has been obscured by the kitchen wing that completely covers this elevation. A boxed

cornice with complex crown molding extends across the facade, as does a water table, which continues around the south gable end. Two dormers project from each slope of the steep gable roof, and a chimney rises from the open gable end. The interior is divided into a side hall and double parlors; except for two doors with surrounds and a fine window sash and surrounds, it retains little of its original woodwork. In the second quarter of the nineteenth century, a two-story, two-bay frame wing was added to the north gable end and the main stair with its Greek revival trim was installed. Building has continued into the twentieth century; a two-story, one-bay frame wing has been attached to the north gable end, and the paneling on the chimney breasts (while appropriate in style) is a modern replacement.

T–164
OTWELL
Near Oxford
Circa 1720; with additions; Private;
National Register

Otwell is one of the best-known architectural landmarks in Talbot County and is an outstanding example of an early eighteenth-century plantation house that has grown, in a leisurely manner, over a 250-year period. The land on which Otwell stands was surveyed in 1659 for William

 T-164

T-165

Taylor and served as the site of the county court in 1662. In 1721 Sarah Turbutt Goldsborough and her husband, Nicholas Goldsborough III, inherited the property from her father, Foster Turbutt. The Goldsboroughs, in whose family the estate remained until 1946, probably built the original T-plan structure. The gambrel-roofed west section is one-and-one-half stories tall and three bays wide. It has two asymmetrically placed dormers above the facade and two flanking the extension on the east. Two chimneys with corbeled caps rise flush with the end walls, and ventilators flank each stack. The main entrance, which is sheltered by a modern porch with a pedimented entablature, is located in the gambrel-roofed section that extends to the east. Dormers project above the two windows framing the entrance, and a chimney with a corbeled cap rises from the east end wall. In 1811 Nicholas Goldsborough VI acquired Otwell and added the three blocks in linear succession to the east end. The first of these is a one-and-one-half-story, one-bay, gambrel-roofed stair hall. To this is attached a two-story, three-bay, gable-roofed kitchen wing with an entrance on the main facade, and finally, a one-and-one-half-story, two-bay bedroom addition extends from the east gable end of this wing. Evidence that these were erected at the same time includes the

similar brickwork and the fact that they are bonded together. Very late in the nineteenth century the original gable roof of the westernmost section of the house was raised to its present gambrel shape. In 1958 a fire swept through Otwell, destroying most of the eighteenth-century interior. Fortunately, drawings had been made of the woodwork during a 1946 remodeling. These were used in the reconstruction to ensure authentic replications, which included the dogleg entrance stair with its tulip-carved step-ends. This carving resembles the flowers found at Boston Cliff (T-122); according to H. Chandlee Forman, they were executed originally by the same woodcarver.

T-165
DEEP WATER POINT
Near Oxford
1926; Private

Built for Oliver Grymes, Deep Water Point is a 1926 dream house that defies stylistic classification. It is essentially a rectangular, gable-roofed, one-and-one-half-story brick structure with applied pavilions, towers, turrets, gables, and arcades. On the south is a kitchen, built in 1935, set behind the wall that connects a garage–guest house to the main building. Two large round towers, separated from the main house by gable-roofed pavilions, flank this central section: the

walls are laid in common bond; the turrets have corbeled cornices. The irregularly placed windows are equipped with steel casements; some have stained glass, which adds to the house's picturesque nature.

T-166
HARLEIGH
Near Easton
Mid-nineteenth century; with alterations;
Private

At first glance Harleigh seems to be a Georgian revival mansion built during the second and third decades of the twentieth century. From an examination of the basement, however, where older brick walls are easily distinguished from newer ones, it is clear that the apparently modern structure has incorporated a nineteenth-century, three-bay dwelling. Today the mansion stands two-and-one-half stories tall and five bays wide, covered by a hip roof with a deck enclosed by a balustrade. Three dormers pierce the roof above the facade, and two chimneys rise from the center of the deck. The interior is divided into a central corridor with two flanking rooms. A few features from the old house remain: the stair with its tapered balusters and mahogany newel and rail, and some doors and trim. In 1983 an addition was made to the north end

T-166

T-167

of the structure, thereby improving the balance of the design of the west facade of the house.

T–167
CANTERBURY MANOR
Near Easton
1906; Private

Canterbury Manor is a colonial revival mansion on Bailey's Neck, overlooking Trippe's Creek. The land on which it stands was originally a 100-acre parcel called Graves granted to Samuel Graves in 1659. The tract adjoined Richard Tilghman's 1659 Canterbury Manor grant of 1,000 acres. One of Tilghman's descendants, Colonel F. Carroll Goldsborough, built the main block of the present mansion. The mansion consists of a large two-and-one-half-story main section with wings on the east and a two-story porch on the west. The entrance facade has a two-story, three-bay Ionic portico with a pedimented entablature and a large lunette in the tympanum. Behind this is the central entrance, a single architectural treatment composed of a door with sidelights and a Palladian window above the entablature of the door frame. Following a principle of Georgian architecture, ground-floor windows are nine-over-six, while those on the second story are six-over-six. The rear facade has a central entrance with

double doors and sidelights, an elliptical window above, and two flanking bay windows. A small peninsula extends from the lawn into the creek and is planted in classic tidewater style with boxwood borders and flanking woodland.

T–168
AVONVILLE
Easton
Circa 1760; with additions; Private

The original part of Avonville was built by William Trippe in the third quarter of the eighteenth century, as a brick dated 1760 near the first-story central bay attests. Trippe's Creek, onto which Avonville faces, is named for the family. The house has grown for 200 years and is today a large gable-roofed brick structure. Trippe's house is still discernible as the two-and-one-half-story, three-bay section located in the center of the long composition. Its principal facade is laid in Flemish bond with both a water table and a beltcourse. The main entrance, originally located in the central bay, has a small Doric portico with a pedimented entablature. The door is flanked by sidelights and is surmounted by an elliptical fanlight; these are probably the result of a modern remodeling. Around 1840 Avonville underwent reconstruction that relocated the entrance and changed the floor plan; until

T-168

that time Avonville's floor plan resembled those of Ratcliffe Manor (T–42) and the original Gross' Coate (T–87). In the 1880s a large, four-bay frame wing was added on the east, and in 1937 a two-story brick wing with the characteristic Georgian elements of a beltcourse and a water table was appended on the west. Also at that time the frame wing was faced with brick, and its roof was raised. The interior, like the exterior, has experienced much alteration, and, although some trim remains from the earliest building period, most of the details have been replaced at least once.

T–169
AVONDALE (Hambleton's Neck)
Near Easton
Circa 1770; Private

Built by Freeborn Banning in the late eighteenth century, Avondale commands a superb position at the end of Bailey's Neck, overlooking the Tred Avon River. The house today stands two-and-one-half stories tall and five bays wide, but in its original three-bay form it was a good example of the vernacular architecture favored by the well-to-do families of colonial Talbot County. The main facade of this early section is laid in Flemish bond but lacks both a beltcourse and a water table. The main entrance was located on the south, and in plan the house

T-169

T-170

T-171

was similar to that of Jamaica Point (T–63). In the early twentieth century a two-bay extension was added on the south, converting the moderate-sized dwelling into a large five-bay house with a central entrance. To this extension was attached a one-and-one-half-story hyphen and a one-and-one-half-story wing. These modern additions were designed by Henry Powell Hopkins and built of bricks from the ruins of Old Whitemarsh Church (T–137). The door frame, with its fluted pilasters and ornate entablature, dates to the Hopkins remodeling. The interior has lost all of its original detail save the stair with its panel soffit and three balusters per step.

T–170
LOCUST GROVE
Near Easton
Circa 1865; with additions; Private

The oldest part of Locust Grove was built by Frank Johnston, probably at the time he married Anna Goldsborough. Today the house is a three-part frame structure composed of a two-and-one-half-story, five-bay house and flanking one-and-one-half-story wings; the east "wing" was Johnston's original house. The center section is a 1940s attempt to simulate a southern colonial mansion by adding to the facade a two-story, three-bay Doric portico with a pedi-

mented entablature and an elaborate door frame with pilasters and broken pediment. A balustraded portico was also added along the rear elevation. The interior of the old house has not undergone much alteration, and it retains much original detail, including some four-panel doors, bold trim, plaster cornices, and the stair. Locust Grove is also the site of William Hayward's house; he was one of the last provincial judges of Maryland. The parlor mantel, which has MDCCLXXXI incised on the back, was salvaged from his house and installed in Avonlea, the residence to the west of Locust Grove, built by Tilghman Johnston in the 1920s.

T–171
ELLENBOROUGH
Easton
1928; Private

Designed by Emory Ross for Mrs. Margaret Chaplin, Ellenborough is a superior composition and a fine, late, academic example of the colonial revival. It occupies the site of an earlier plantation house built by Matthew Tilghman Goldsborough about 1860 and named for his daughter, Eleanor. This house was razed in 1928 to make way for the present mansion, which consists of a central, two-and-one-half-story, five-bay brick block flanked by frame hyphens and

wings covered with beaded weatherboard. The principal section is laid completely in Flemish bond; its main facade is shaded by a three-bay Ionic portico with fluted columns supporting a pedimented entablature. The garden elevation is more simply arranged, with a pedimented door frame surrounding the central entrance. The three dormers that project from the slope of the gable roof above this facade are interesting and have details that resemble those found on Federal-period houses in Easton.

T–172
JUDITH'S GARDEN
Near Oxford
Circa 1788; circa 1837; Private

The earliest record of Judith's Garden dates from 1693, when it was patented by John Paddison, but the oldest structure standing on the land is the one-and-one-half-story, two-bay frame kitchen wing built by Samuel Turbutt. In the second quarter of the nineteenth century, Turbutt's son-in-law, Benjamin Bowdle, one of the founders of the Maryland Military Academy, built the frame main house. This has five bays, but the dining room on the east has only one window; irregular fenestration also appears on the rear elevation. The interior is distinguished by a wealth of original detail, especially in the parlor: a Greek revival mantel, a plaster

T-172

T-173

T-174

medallion with grape motifs in the ceiling, corner blocks, trim, and doors with graining in imitation of tiger maple. The stair, with its cherry rail and newel, is also of this period, as is the bell pull in the dining room. Furthermore, there are several good examples of iron-rim locks and other early nineteenth-century hardware throughout the house. The grounds contain many fine outbuildings, masses of daffodils, huge boxwood bushes, and the second-oldest known American beech tree.

T–173
WAVERLY
Near Easton
First and second quarters of the
nineteenth century; Private

Waverly, located on Edmonson Neck in the Tred Avon River, is composed of a tall, two-and-one-half-story, two-bay section with a two-story, two-bay wing and one-story porch on the northwest, a one-story garage on the southeast, and a one-and-one-half-story wing on the northeast. Both the principal section and the two-story wing date from the first half of the nineteenth century, but the former predates the latter by several years. The main entrance is located in the southeastern bay of the older house, which appears to retain its original beaded siding. Two dormers pierce the gable roof,

and a chimney rises within the northwest gable end. Waverly is particularly noteworthy for the quality of the original fabric used in both the exterior and interior of the Federal-style main house and the excellent woodwork in the wing.

T–174
ASHBY
Easton
1858; 1941; Private

Ashby is noteworthy as the only genuinely Italianate dwelling in Talbot County. The other structures designated Italianate, such as Cherry Grove (T–308) and Ingleside (T–313), are essentially symmetrical, almost self-contained, Georgian blocks, but Ashby was designed in a rambling fashion to afford panoramic views of the grounds and the Miles River and to catch the prevailing breezes. The addition of the Doric portico with pedimented entablature in 1941 was a curious attempt to create a formal Georgian mansion out of the otherwise romantically informal Italianate house. In the basement the foundations of the original seventeenth-century dwelling are still visible. Behind the house is the Goldsborough family cemetery, a notable seventeenth-, eighteenth-, and nineteenth-century private burial ground, similar to those at Gross' Coate (T–87) and Wye House (T–54).

T–175
OLD BLOOMFIELD
Near Easton
Circa 1711; with additions;
Private; National Register

Old Bloomfield was built about 1711 by John Bartlett and his wife, Mary Townsend, of Germantown, Pennsylvania, when Bartlett inherited this property from his father. The Bartlett home, one of the oldest extant buildings in Talbot County, now forms a wing on the northwest of the present dwelling. It is a brick, one-room, story-and-loft structure. Its pent roof—an overhang cantilevered from the loft floor joists—is typical of Philadelphia architecture from that period. The brickwork, Flemish bond on the first story, English bond above, is visible only on the exposed sections of the southeast gable end. Two dormers project from each slope of the gable roof, and a chimney rises from the northwest gable end. On the southwest is a one-and-one-half-story addition with brick gable ends and brick-nogged frame sides. On the south corner of this addition a two-story frame kitchen wing was added at right angles in the late nineteenth century. At the juncture of these two sections is a small, square, one-and-one-half-story brick addition. Just off the back porch of the kitchen stands a frame milk house or dairy, and to the northwest of the

T-175

193

T-176

T-177

house stand a nineteenth-century corn crib and barn. The property is still owned by descendants of the builders.

T–176
SHEEPSHEAD POINT (Chance Farm)
Near Easton
Circa 1819; Private

The house on Sheepshead Point (later corrupted to Shipshead Point and today known as Chance Farm) is a rarity. While it has undergone some exterior alteration, the building, probably constructed by William Hayward, Jr., in the early nineteenth century, still presents an intact interior of the late Federal period. The two-story, three-bay main block sits on a deep cellar with a brick floor. Above the brick foundation the house is finished in brick-nogged frame. Sometime after the original construction, the gable roof was altered both by the addition of cross-gables with cut-out bargeboard trim and by the extension of the actual roof line. This exterior is supported by thin brackets. On the east gable end is attached a two-story frame hyphen that connects the one-and-one-half-story, frame kitchen wing to the main house. Outbuildings of particular interest include the two-part tenant house, the board-and-batten barn, and the seven-hole privy.

The interior of the main house is divided

into a side hall on the east and two parlors on the west. The parlors are joined by doors that slide into the walls. Each room has a highly ornate, plaster ceiling medallion and a fireplace with a simple marble mantel. There are deep cove cornices, and a quirk-ogee is the dominant molding. The stair has a heavy turned newel, slender turned balusters, and decorative step ends. The second floor includes the interesting feature of four original closets, two of which have built-in, waist-high, lidded chests.

T–177
NORTH BEND
Near Easton
Mid-nineteenth century; Private

Built by James Dixon and his wife, Mary Ann Bartlett of Old Bloomfield (T–175), in the mid-nineteenth century, North Bend is an elegant frame house composed of three, three-story sections. The most prominent is the three-bay block on the north. The main entrance is located in the southern bay of its east facade and is sheltered by a two-story, three-bay Ionic porch, which extends around the southeast corner and covers one bay of the middle section. An identical porch shades the north facade. The roof is a low pyramid capped by a widow's walk. The middle section extends from the south elevation of the main block. It also has three

bays, but they are built on a scale smaller than the principal section.

T–178
DONCASTER
Near Easton
Circa 1870; Private

Doncaster is a fine late-nineteenth-century dwelling that still has most of its original disparately styled details. In addition, when alterations have been made, they have been executed with sensitivity and attention to detail. The main house is three stories tall and three bays wide above a brick foundation and basement. The walls are covered with German siding to the third story, which is finished in plain shiplap. There are pilasters at the corners rising to the change of siding. These pilasters are fitted with panels that terminate in Gothic arches. The third story has small openings in a form characteristic of the Greek, not the Gothic, revival, and a Georgian-style beltcourse that girds the structure at the third-floor level. Brackets support the overhang of the gable roof, and two chimneys at right angles to each other rise from the center of the structure. There is a frame wing to the east, and to the east of that wing is a small addition sheathed with board-and-batten and covered by a steep gable roof.

T-178

T-180

T-181

T-182

T–180
SUNNYSIDE
Near Easton
Early nineteenth century; Private

Sunnyside is located in the development called Traveller's Rest, south of Kirkham on a silted inlet of the Tred Avon River. The house is composed of three small sections in a row and maintains its original form. Inside, however, the floor plan and most of the original work have been altered or covered.

T–181
AVONWOOD
Near Kirkham
Early nineteenth century; with additions; Private

Like Perry Hall (T–186), Avonwood has undergone such extensive exterior alteration that its original appearance has been almost completely obscured. The original two-story frame house with a side-hall, single-parlor plan was probably built in the early nineteenth century. Sometime later a two-story, three-bay frame addition was attached on the west. The house, once covered with brown shingles, is now finished in clapboards.

T–182
RIGBY'S LOTT
Royal Oak
Circa 1800; extensively remodeled; Private

The original part of Rigby's Lott, the middle and kitchen sections, was built by Jonathan Rigby, to whom 221 acres were patented in 1797. This original part is still visible among the accretions, but most of the original material has been either altered or removed. The property stayed in the Rigby family until the late nineteenth century.

T–183
HALCYON
Royal Oak
Mid-nineteenth century; with additions; Private

Halcyon began as a mid-nineteenth-century, one-story frame dwelling with an interior chimney at each gable end. Various small alterations have completely changed the original fenestration, added a second story, and attached wings on the east and west and porches ~~ ~ the north and south. The interior is also now very different from the way it was when built, but on the second floor there are two old mantels featuring Greek revival ovolo moldings. In 1972 the owner made repairs to check deterioration and renovated the late-nineteenth-century tenant house to the east.

T–185
LOVE'S FOLLY
Royal Oak
Circa 1800; with additions; Private

Love's Folly, once known as Shrigley's Fortune, was built by Major John Dawson to replace the frame structure listed on this site in the 1798 tax assessment. This important house is composed of a three-bay long, two-and-one-half-story brick section with two modern brick wings. The original house is laid in Flemish bond with glazed headers on the south, an unusual feature at this time. The main entrance is located in the northern bay of the facade and is equipped with a transom. Rusticated stone lintels with keystones surmount both the entrance and window bays, and the dormers have a semicircular opening under a gable. An interior chimney rises above the south gable end, and a later exterior one rises on the north. The interior has been altered, but some notable original work remains. The open-string stair, with its delicate turned newels, two balusters per step, and shaped rail, is typical of the early Federal period. Paneled doors and window jambs and three-part trim adorn the parlor, and the second and third stories retain their yellow pine floors. The fireplaces were fitted with magnificently carved and highly ornate Federal-period mantels, but these were removed in the

T-183

T-185

T-186

T-187

1940s. All three are now in Easton: one has been installed at 133 South Harrison Street, and two are in storage.

T–186
PERRY HALL
Near Easton
Circa 1820; Private

Perry Hall is believed to have been built by John Rogers and his wife, Maria Perry, to replace an early Georgian dwelling of the 1740s which was erected by Jacob Hindman. The present house is a four-part telescopic structure covered by gable roofs. In the 1970s the exterior as well as some structural details were reworked to such a degree that the original appearance has been completely obscured. There are, however, some original interior details remaining, including a mantel with cyma-recta moldings and gouge-worked trim and the stair with its slender, turned newel. The grounds, which were once elaborately landscaped, contain a family burial plot and a number of outbuildings, including a brick smokehouse, slave quarters, and a barn with early shed additions.

T–187
FERRY FARM HOUSE (Aker's Ferry)
Trappe
Circa 1730; with additions; Private

Ferry Farm is situated near the northern end of the Choptank River Bridge overlooking the broad waters of the Choptank, with Cambridge in the distance. It consists of an early-eighteenth-century, gambrel-roofed frame house, one of Talbot County's earliest examples of this type of roof, and a large, twentieth-century, gambrel-roofed frame wing. The early structure is one-and-one-half stories tall and three-bays wide. It is built on a brick English-bond basement, and its walls are covered with plain weatherboard. Each facade has a central entrance, and the one on the south is fitted with a transom. An interior chimney rises above the east gable end, and a twentieth-century exterior chimney rises on the west. From the location of the original chimney bases in the cellar, it is clear that the interior was arranged with a single room on the east and two rooms with corner fireplaces on the west. Today the central hall is flanked by a living room on the west and a dining room and kitchen on the east. The stair is a good example of early-eighteenth-century woodwork, and the east rooms retain some period detail. In these rooms the major posts protrude from the walls and are treated to simulate fluted pilasters.

T-189

T–188
PLAINDEALING (site)
Royal Oak
Private

The home of Samuel Chamberlaine (1697–1773), an important eighteenth-century figure in the county, once occupied this site, as did a house built by General E. L. Hardcastle in the mid-nineteenth century. Today nothing remains above grade. No photograph is available.

T–189
CLAY'S HOPE
Bellevue
Circa 1790; Private; National Register

Clay's Hope was patented to Henry Clay in 1662. In 1664 it was repatented to James Colston, whose descendant of the same name built the house that stands today as one of the finest late-eighteenth-century dwellings in Talbot County. Colston owned the property in 1783, but lived in a frame house. The present brick house is described in the 1798 tax assessment, so it was built between those dates. The property eventually was acquired by Alexander B. Harrison, grandfather of Oswald Tilghman, the compiler of the *History of Talbot County, Maryland*. The house is a vernacular structure of excellent, although simple, craftsmanship and reflects the plans of great houses of this

T-190

period, such as Pleasant Valley (T–84), Galloway (T–104), and, in Caroline County, Willow Grove (CAR–3). It consists of a large, two-story, three-bay brick structure with a two-story, three-bay frame wing on the west. The brick is laid in Flemish bond on the front and in common bond on the sides and rear. The main facade has a chamfered water table and a beltcourse, both of which continue around the other exposed sides. There is also a beltcourse at the attic floor level on the east gable end. Two dormers project from the slope of the roof above the facade, and a chimney rises within each gable end. The interior still possesses some original detail, including the stair, chair rail, and trim. The wing is as long as the main house, and it also has chimneys at the gable ends. Its fenestration has been altered by the addition of a bay window on the first floor. Located between the house and the road is a large frame barn originally used for tobacco, but later adapted for hay storage and livestock shelter. This may be the earliest surviving tobacco barn in the upper Eastern Shore and is a rare survival of a once-common building type.

T–190
CLAYLANDS
Near Royal Oak
Early nineteenth century; Private

Claylands, situated on the edge of Irish Creek, is a telescopic, vernacular frame dwelling, which in appearance and location resembles Vicker's Chance (D–239) in Dorchester County, although the latter was not a telescopic building. The house, now agreeably weathered, remains almost unchanged. As a telescopic building, it consists of three sections, a two-story, three-bay main house, a one-and-one-half-story, two-bay wing, and a one-story, two-bay wing. With the exception of the kitchen, which is built on a solid brick foundation, the house is raised on brick piers like many Dorchester County homes.

T–193
OREM'S DELIGHT (Fox Hole)
Royal Oak
Circa 1725; Private; National Register

Orem's Delight is one of the few small, eighteenth-century dwellings that has survived without being incorporated into a larger building. Fox Hole, the land on which it stands, was purchased by John Morris from William Smythe in 1676. It was Morris's grandson, Morris Orem, who built the brick cottage in the early eighteenth

century. Later in that century a descendant of Orem, Andrew Orem, had the tract resurveyed and patented as Orem's Delight. The house is a one-and-one-half-story structure measuring 20 by 25 feet. It has a stepped water table and is laid in Flemish bond. The main facade and north gable end have glazed headers, and in the north gable itself there are a two-brick beltcourse and a pattern of two interlocking diamonds in glazed headers. The south gable, however, is finished in shiplap. The principal facade has a slightly off-center main entrance flanked by one window on the south and two on the north, the northern one of which has been bricked in. All of the openings have been altered, but there are the remains of a segmental arch above the entrance.

The interior is divided into two rooms by a vertical beaded partition. The fireplace, which is flanked by a cabinet and enclosed stair, has some late-eighteenth-century fielded paneling above it. The second floor consists of one large, unfinished room. Originally the house had a huge fireplace with mitre-arched recesses in the cheeks and a large wood lintel. Furthermore, the floor was ten inches lower. The 1798 tax assessment shows that by the end of the eighteenth century, Orem's Delight was the size it now is; it also records the presence of a spinning house, kitchen, and smokehouse.

T-193

T–194
GAYMCREST FARM
Bellevue
Circa 1880; circa 1940; Private

Gaymcrest Farm is a three-part, late-nineteenth-century farmhouse with a frame central section flanked by two brick wings. The main section appears to have been built in the Victorian Gothic style while maintaining touches typical of the vernacular dwellings of the period. Its two-and-one-half stories are covered by a gable roof, which has a large cross gable rising above the center of the main facade. This gable is pierced by a semicircular window and is flanked by two dormers. Both wings are two stories by two bays. The north wing has a central gable with a semicircular window corresponding to the main house and may be part of the original construction, save its 1940s brick facing. In the 1940s the famous boxer Gene Tunney owned Gaymcrest and, presumably, remodeled it to suit his tastes.

T–195
CLARKE CROFT
Bellvue
Circa 1850; Private

Clarke Croft is a mid-nineteenth-century frame house, one-and-one-half stories tall and three bays wide. The east facade has a central entrance and two small windows on

the upper story. Interior chimneys rise from the gable ends with backs exposed to the first-floor ceiling level. A porch supported by chamfered posts covers the southern two bays of the west elevation, and a one-story kitchen wing extends from the south gable end. The house has two rooms per floor, each with its own fireplace. The south mantel shelf has deep Greek ovolo moldings; there is a stair alongside the central partition in the south room. There are three buildings on the grounds: a barn, a large shed, and a small storage building with an overshot second story on the south and a plastered interior with built-in shelves.

T–196
OLD WOMAN'S FOLLY
Royal Oak
Mid-nineteenth century; Private

Old Woman's Folly is a pleasing, period, clapboard frame house. Its simplicity, achieved through clean lines and unassuming, folk woodwork, is the most important feature of the house. It has a two-story, three-bay main section with a shorter two-story kitchen wing on the east and a modern two-story addition on the west. A two-story porch supported by simple square posts and fitted with a balustrade of jigsaw-cut balusters on the second story extends across the south facade. The floor plan of the main

house consists of a center hall with flanking parlors. The parlors have fireplaces with elongated, raised diamond panels on their mantels. The stair has a large, squat newel and rises in three straight flights interrupted by two landings.

T–198
ORA ET LABORA (Woodlawn)
Royal Oak
Late eighteenth century; with additions; Private

Ora et Labora (the phrase is the motto of the Benedictine Order), formerly Woodlawn and originally part of Yafford's Neck, is a late-eighteenth-century structure that has undergone major additions and extensive remodeling. The house was built possibly by the Aldern and Royston families and was later in the possession of the Skinner family. The 1798 tax assessment shows a two-story brick house measuring 30 by 20 feet and belonging to Mordecai Skinner. It is still discernible as the two-bay section on the west with a beveled water table, a three-course beltcourse, and facades laid in Flemish bond. When first built, this section was two-and-one-half stories high and three bays wide. There was a central entrance on both facades. These doorways have now been bricked in, and the interior has been remodeled into one room. In the early nine-

T-199

T-201

teenth century a two-story, two-bay brick addition was added on the east gable end. It shares the same roof line as the original house, but does not repeat the water table or beltcourse. Together these structures vividly illustrate changes in brick construction and how late-eighteenth-century houses were altered in the nineteenth century to keep them architecturally fashionable.

T-199
DEEP NECK
St. Michaels vicinity
Circa 1810; circa 1850

Deep Neck consists of a three-bay, two-and-one-half-story brick house probably built circa 1800 by the Skinner family, to which was added in about 1850 a five-bay two-and-one-half-story frame addition. The entire structure has been painted in order to provide unity. The brick section has Flemish bond on the main facades, but lacks a water table and beltcourse. It nevertheless has a number of noteworthy interior features, including six-panel doors, period mantels, and the original flooring and staircase.

T-201
SOLITUDE
St. Michaels vicinity
Circa 1820; 1943; Private

Solitude is a large two-and-one-half-story frame structure probably built by the Spencer family in the first quarter of the nineteenth century. In the 1840s Dr. John Spencer conducted here his "Academy for Young Men." In 1846 the property passed to the Hammond Family, who held the property for about one hundred years and who made additions to the house. Although most of the interior woodwork is of recent construction, the largest section of the house still retains its original staircase and some trim.

T-202
BELLE-AIRE
St. Michaels vicinity
Undetermined age; Private

Belle-Aire is a two-and-one-half-story five-bay frame house with a one-and-one-half-story frame wing, both of undetermined date of construction. Thomas Goldsborough, who owned the property in the late eighteenth century, named the estate Belle-Aire. His son-in-law and daughter, Dr. and Mrs. John Barnett, who moved to the property immediately after 1808, are usually given credit for beginning construction of at least

part of the present house some time after 1808. The kitchen wing is probably older than the large block of the house.

T-203
MAIDEN POINT
St. Michaels
1866; Private

Enjoying a fine site on the Miles River, Maiden Point is a well-constructed Victorian farmhouse built for Richard S. Dodson. Like many houses in Talbot County, Maiden Point has been remodeled and enlarged. Today the house consists of a two-and-one-half-story, three-bay frame main section with a two-story, one-bay hyphen and a lower two-story, three-bay addition with an enclosed porch, all of which extend eastward from the principal section. On the west is a twentieth-century, two-story, three-bay wing with a two-story enclosed porch. There are also covered porches along the river elevation and in front of each entrance. In composition it resembles Love's Folly (T-185), which was built fifty years earlier.

To the east of the house, overlooking Little Neck Creek and the Miles River, is a small, early-nineteenth-century dwelling probably built for the farm manager. It is a vernacular structure covered with brown shingles and composed of three parts: a two-

T-202

T-203

T-204

story, two-bay section, a one-and-one-half-story addition, and a one-bay lean-to. A photograph in the collection of the owners shows a two-story dwelling of the nineteenth century; this may be a house that formerly stood to the northwest, whose foundation piers can be seen on the river bottom from a boat.

T–204
TARBUTTON MILL HOUSE
Trappe
Eighteenth century; mid-nineteenth century; Private

Tarbutton Mill House, located between Easton and Trappe, is one of three Talbot County dwellings of early date known to have belonged to a miller. In the early nineteenth century Robert Bartlett of Old Bloomfield (T–175) owned the property, which was eventually acquired by James C. Tarbutton, Jr., from whom the mill derived its name. The original house is the one-and-one-half-story, two-bay section on the north of the present four-bay-long dwelling. Adjacent to the second bay window on the west elevation is a seam in the brickwork that clearly marks the end of the early house. The north gable end is the principal facade and is laid in Flemish bond, while the other elevations are finished in a rare type of common bond with only two courses of

stretchers for each course of headers. The central door is sheltered by a one-story, three-bay, twentieth-century porch. In the mid nineteenth century a two-bay wing was added on the south gable end, and a one-bay, partially detached kitchen was added to this. Within, the house is divided into three rooms and a stair passage. The north room's massive chimney on the south wall has been removed, although its base is still visible in the cellar. This north room and the loft above it formed the original eighteenth-century house. The north parlor is now separated from the middle room by large double doors. Immediately to the south of the kitchen was a three-bay frame building, the cellar of which remains. To the west of the house stands an early brace-framed barn with remnants of original beaded siding attached with wrought nails and other hardware. One original tilted false plate survives; this same feature may be found at Wye Mill (T–51).

T–205
RAY'S POINT
St. Michaels
Circa 1801; with additions;
Private

Ray's Point, for many generations a seat of the Hopkins family (descendants of the Ray family), was constructed in two sections at

different times during the early nineteenth century. The earlier section is the one-and-one-half-story brick structure now functioning as a service wing. Its large bricks are laid in Flemish bond on the main facade and in common bond on the other elevations. The main facade has four bays with an entrance in the third bay from the west. The brickwork shows that several alterations have been made to the fenestration. Similarly, the rear facade underwent alteration when the interior was remodeled to accommodate a modern kitchen and study: to the east is the main section, a two-story, three-bay brick structure built not long after the original construction. Its facade is laid in Flemish bond and has a central entrance with a transom and sidelights. Shading this elevation is a two-story, five-bay porch with late-nineteenth-century trim consisting of square posts with molded capitals on the first story and double columns with ornamental trim on the second. The interior is divided into a central stair hall with flanking parlors. The woodwork is simple: note the square newel-post and thin balusters of the stair. In contrast, the six-panel doors were originally grained and stenciled to imitate mahogany and inlay; they have been painted over. The 1798 tax assessment lists a frame house on this site, but the 1804 tax list mentions a "new brick house" whose dimensions match Ray's Point perfectly.

T-205

T-206

T–206
PERRY CABIN
St. Michaels
Circa 1800; circa 1920; Private

Perry Cabin today is a rambling, colonial revival frame mansion, but it started as a vernacular, Federal-style farmhouse built by Samuel Hambleton, purser of a nascent U. S. Navy. This early house now forms the north wing and contains the hall, stair hall (each with a corner fireplace), and living room of the present mansion. While the exterior has been altered, the interior retains many original details. Especially noteworthy are the mantels. The hall mantel has delicate gougework, reeding, and rope moldings. In addition to these features, the mantel in the stair hall has pilasters raised on plinths, and the living room mantel has reeded pilasters on plinths and ovals surrounded by beads. In the 1920s Charles H. Fogg, the owner and operator of coal mines and coke ovens in western Pennsylvania, oversaw the transformation of this house into a stylish revival mansion. He added a large, two-and-one-half-story main house with a two-story, pedimented Ionic portico and a wing on the south. The mansion's walls are sheathed in beaded weatherboard and the windows have paneled shutters on the first story and louvered shutters above. This house was the site of an early Gary

Cooper movie, *The First Kiss*. Recently it was extensively remodeled and converted into an inn and restaurant.

T–207
MT. MISERY
St. Michaels
Circa 1804; Private

In 1804 Edward Covey bought this property at a bankruptcy sale and built the brick house that stands today. It is two-and-one-half stories tall and three bays wide and has a hall-and-parlor plan, rare in a two-and-one-half-story house. The parlors have chair rails and fireplaces with simple, but attractive, mantels. Mr. and Mrs. Richard Tennant hired Dr. H. Chandlee Forman to save the house, and Forman's restoration either preserved or reproduced the house's best features. The estate's unusual, but perhaps well-deserved, name suggests an unhappy past. In 1834 Frederick Douglass, the great abolitionist, was sent as a slave to Edward Covey, a slavebreaker, to be broken.

T–208
CEDAR POINT
Near Easton
Eighteenth century; with additions and alterations; Private

Cedar Point, a large Georgian revival mansion of the 1920s, incorporates a very large eighteenth-century brick plantation house of the Edmondson family, which was remodeled in the mid-nineteenth century by Dr. Joseph R. Price. The grounds and gardens, also done at the time of the revival reconstruction, are now reaching maturity and are particularly beautiful. The main block of the mansion is two-and-one-half stories tall and five bays wide. Its facade is laid in Flemish bond and is shaded by a large pedimented portico with fluted columns. Of the early details only a Federal-style mantel and the stair with its massive mahogany newel and rail and maple balusters remain. On the southeast is the most important part of Cedar Point, a one-story, three-bay dwelling with a modern gable roof. It now serves as a wing. Dr. H. Chandlee Forman, in his *Old Buildings, Gardens, and Furniture in Tidewater Maryland*, has suggested that this structure might be the seventeenth-century home of John Edmondson, who in 1672 hosted George Fox, the founder of the Religious Society of Friends. Its all-header-bond facade and common-bond brickwork, how-

T-207

T-208

201

ever, are features normally associated with the third quarter of the eighteenth century. All-header bond may also be found at Lloyd's Costin (T–71) and Combsberry (T–156). The central entrance is flanked by windows on both facades, and a chimney rises above the southeast gable end. The interior has been reworked completely and has consequently lost its early appearance; of the eighteenth-century fabric only the walls remain. Charles Todd added the wing that contains the kitchen and dining room. The next owner was W. Alton Jones, builder of the Colonial Gas Pipeline from Texas to the East Coast.

T–209
ROLLES RANGE
St. Michaels
1751; Private

Situated on the upper reaches of Broad Creek north of St. Michaels is this mid-eighteenth-century dwelling with a twentieth-century wing. The early house is one-and-one-half stories tall and five bays wide below a gambrel roof. The main facade is laid in Flemish bond above a stepped-bond water table and English-bond foundation. The main entrance is in the central bay and is fitted with an eighteenth-century door and nineteenth-century transom and sidelights. Since the brick jambs are un-

altered, the original entrance must have had double doors with a wide frame. Three dormers project from each side of the gambrel roof, and interior chimneys rise at the ends. In the north end glazed headers form the date 1751 as well as the builders' initials, F.L.R. for Feddeman and Lydia Rolle. This glazed brick date, rare in itself, makes Rolles Range the only dated gambrel-roofed structure in the county. Inside, the plan consists of a hall, stair passage, and parlor. Some early paneling in the hall may be original to the house. Its design is unusual and is unlike any other in Talbot County. The stair itself is probably early, but its balustrade and trim are nineteenth-century replacements. All of the roofing appears to be original. There is a common rafter system with mortise-and-tenon and peg joints at the apex. Two braces nailed onto the underside of the rafters are still in place.

T–210
MARTINGHAM
St. Michaels
Seventeenth (?) and early nineteenth centuries; Private

In the mid-seventeenth century a tract of 500 acres was granted to Robert Martyn for bringing his wife and five children to the province. Eventually a 200-acre area of the original tract was assigned to William Ham-

bleton of Scotland. Hambleton was high sheriff of Talbot County by 1663 and was also a justice of the peace. One of his descendants, Samuel Hambleton, born at Martingham in 1777, was purser of the U. S. Navy in its early years and served under Commodore Perry at the battle of Lake Erie. The estate remained in the Hambleton family for 200 years, and its members built the house that stands today. Evidence of an early brick chimney, visible in the crawl space below the first floor, has led some to speculate that Martingham was built around 1700 as a small dwelling with a two-room plan and central chimney. Later alterations included the addition of rooms on the rear, the extension of the roof to cover these, the removal of the central chimney, and the placement of interior chimneys at the gable ends. A kitchen wing was later added on the east. In the 1940s this wing was converted into a living room, and a wing was added on the west to create a balanced composition. Thus, today Martingham presents itself as a three-part dwelling, of uncertain age, composed of a one-and-one-half-story, three-bay central section with flanking one-story wings. An early photo shows that in the twentieth century two dormers were added to the single central dormer projecting from the south slope of the gable roof and the door in the east gable end was

T-210

T-211

made into a window. On the grounds are two interesting frame outbuildings. The dairy is a small, square structure with a pyramidal roof and a lean-to porch. Next to this is a smokehouse raised on brick piers and covered with white pine weatherboard.

T-211
RICH NECK MANOR
Claiborne
Eighteenth century; circa 1824; with additions; Private

Rich Neck Manor was patented to Colonel Henry Fox in 1649; this is the earliest known grant in Talbot County. In the course of the next 200 years the property passed through the Murphy, Ward, Tilghman, and Harrison families. Around 1824 Samuel Harrison, a lawyer and owner of vast acreage in the county, built the main section of the present house. It is two-and-one-half stories tall and three bays wide. The brick is laid in Flemish bond on the facade, but elsewhere it is finished in common bond. A twentieth-century, two-story porch shades the main facade, which is fitted with a central entrance. This entrance is surmounted by a semicircular fanlight and flanked by fluted pilasters. The interior is divided into a central stair hall with four rooms on both stories. The trim throughout the house, moldings and turned corner

blocks, is typical of the Greek revival period. On the north extends a three-bay, gambrel-roofed wing perpendicular to the long axis of the main house and connected to it by a two-story wall. This is a remnant of the home of Matthew Tilghman, "The Patriarch of Maryland," president of the Maryland Provincial Convention of 1776, and father-in-law of Washington's aide-de-camp Tench Tilghman. This part may even date back to the time of Matthew Tilghman Ward, who died here in 1741. East of the main block and south of the wing is a small, rectangular building. Its main facade has a bricked-in central entrance surmounted by a quatrefoil panel and flanked by ogee-arched windows. Inside, the building has plastered walls and a semicircular brick, vaulted ceiling. One local tradition maintains that this was built as a chapel; another suggests it was a powder house. Whichever, Forman has called the structure "the strangest piece of architecture in Talbot County" (*Early Manor and Plantation Houses of Maryland*, 176).

T-212
ENNION'S RANGE
Claiborne
Circa 1810; Private

Ennion's Range is one of the most picturesque vernacular dwellings in Talbot

T-212

County. In several aspects, but particularly in its development through the addition of self-contained, one-room structures, it resembles some houses in the Church Creek and Madison areas of Dorchester County. Each of the three one-room sections of this early-nineteenth-century, one-story frame dwelling is equipped with a stair and a chimney and with a dormer on each slope of the roof. The central section appears to be the earliest. It has a six-panel door on the east, a winding stair in the northwest corner, and a fireplace in the south wall. The detail has a wide variety of moldings— cavetto-astragal, cyma recta, and cyma recta-astragal. The section on the north is plainer and that to the south, plainer still. In fact, its stair is actually a series of ladder-like steps built into the wall, similar to the steps at Chance Farm (T-176).

T-213
WADE'S POINT
Claiborne
Circa 1820; 1850; 1898; Private

Until recently this was one of the few properties in Maryland still owned by descendants of the original seventeenth-century patentee. The main house was built by Thomas Kemp, an important shipbuilder. It is a two-and-one-half-story, five-bay brick block with a two-story brick kitchen wing

T-213

T-214

built of material from an earlier structure and added in 1821. The principal facade is laid in Flemish bond and has a central entrance. Three dormers project from the slope of the gable roof: the central one is the result of a late-nineteenth- or early-twentieth-century remodeling. Interior chimneys rise above the gable ends, and a frame lookout is built against the interior wall of the west chimney stack. This undoubtedly allowed Kemp to view the Chesapeake and Eastern bays and to watch the ships, perhaps some built by him, traveling the busy commercial lanes between St. Michaels and Baltimore. After Kemp's death his son, John, added the wing on the bay side, the two-story porches across its main facade, the exposed bays of the rear elevation, and three bays of the wing. The front porch, one of the finest examples of mid-nineteenth-century work, has a pierced-work balustrade and a bracketed cornice. In 1898 John's son, Joseph, raised the wing to two-and-one-half stories and added a captain's walk to the mansard roof. This wing was probably designed to function as a guest house. A detailed account of the building is included in Thomas Kemp's diary, and a study based on it and prepared by M. Florence Bourne, a descendant of Mr. Kemp, appeared in the December 1954 issue of *Maryland Historical Magazine*.

T–214
WEBLEY (Mary's Delight)
Claiborne
Circa 1805; 1925; Private

In 1798 Impey Dawson died, leaving his fortune to his only child, Mary Lamdin Dawson, and her husband, John Kersey. With this money the couple financed the building of what is today the main section of a five-part mansion. The name, Mary's Delight, is an obvious reference to the heiress. In 1826 one of the Kerseys' sons-in-law, Dr. Absalom Thompson, purchased the property, and in 1830 he converted the house into the Eastern Shore's first hospital. This Federal-style structure is laid in Flemish bond on the principal facade and in common bond on the other elevations. Extending from the center of the facade is a pedimented pavilion that contains the main entrance. This door is surmounted by a transom and flanked by two narrow windows, a composition echoed by the window treatment above and similar to the main entrance of Bloomingdale (QA–4) in Queen Anne's County. Sheltering this entrance is a well-executed, 1920s Doric portico with a pedimented entablature. Now hidden behind white paint, the house once exhibited rusticated stone jack arches, contrasted with the even colored brickwork, a refinement rare in Talbot County at that time. (See

also Hope, T–90.) The rear elevation, overlooking the Chesapeake Bay, is plainer, lacking both the Flemish bond and the stone arches of the entrance facade. In 1925 a segmental-arched architrave above the central entrance and a two-story, three-bay Doric portico with pedimented entablature were added to achieve a more monumental effect. Also added in 1925 were the Georgian-style hyphens and wings designed by Arthur Blakeslee. The interior of the Federal-period house is in a fair state of preservation and presents many original features. The stair has a delicate walnut balustrade with turned newels, two balusters per step, and a shadow-rail above the paneled wainscot. The soffit is plain, but the step-ends have fretwork scrolls. The parlor has a finely executed mantel with pilasters supporting a decorated frieze. As in most late, great Georgian homes, the window trim continues to the floor, and there are recessed paneled jambs. Furthermore, the doors were originally stained and stenciled to imitate mahogany with inlay.

T–215
BRIDGES (Hebron)
Near St. Michaels
Circa 1802; 1932; Private

Bridges, known today as Langdon, was built by Daniel Lambdin sometime prior to 1804.

T-217

T-218

The tax assessment of that year describes "Bridges Chance" as being improved by a "new brick dwelling with brick kitchen adjacent." In 1809 Lambdin devised the property to his daughters, Sarah Seth and Ann Winchester. The Seths took up residence here and renamed it Hebron after the biblical city south of Jerusalem. The original house, now the central section of a five-part composition, is a late-Georgian-style, two-story, three-bay brick structure. The main facade is laid in Flemish bond, and has a central entrance. Following Georgian architectural principles, the first-story windows are longer than those on the second story. A bold cornice runs along the roof line, and two large chimneys rise flush above the gable ends. In 1932 the Gillespie family of Pittsburgh converted the house into the present mansion through the addition of hyphens and wings. Today the house, grounds, and Seth family graveyard with its ornamental brick wall are in a good state of repair and well maintained. No photograph is available.

T–217
KIRK'S COVE
Bozman
Circa 1800; with additions; Private
Kirk's Cove is located on a narrow neck of land overlooking the northeast branch of

Harris Creek. The central section of the three-part, one-and-one-half-story, frame house dates from the late eighteenth or early nineteenth century. It has four bays asymmetrically arranged in an attempt to accommodate a central entrance; there are three symmetrically placed dormers above. Interior chimneys rise from the gable ends, to which lower, one-and-one-half-story, three-bay frame wings were added in the 1940s. The interior of the early house retains the original stair with its round rail and square balusters. The molding and trim are typical of the early Federal period, but the living room chair rail appears to have been added when the house was remodeled in this century. While Kirk's Cove may lack great architectural refinement, its straightforward simplicity achieves a dignity that escapes some grander homes.

T–218
LOSTOCK
Bozman
Late eighteenth century; Private
Lostock, built by Major William Caulk on a tract originally surveyed for John Anderton in 1659, is a fine example of the hall-and-parlor plan vernacular house. It is a two-and-one-half-story, three-bay brick structure with a one-room frame addition. This addition may be a remnant of the previous

house, dating from before 1706. It is interesting that the principal doors are placed on the end elevations, and that Flemish bond, a water table, and a beltcourse make the north wall the most refined elevation. Lostock boasts its original staircase, some original paneling, and, on the northeast facade, a magnificent dentil cornice.

T–219
GRACE CREEK FARM
Bozman
Early nineteenth century; Private
Overlooking the confluence of Grace and Leadenham creeks, Grace Creek farmhouse is typical of the early-nineteenth-century frame dwelling found in the remote regions of Talbot, Dorchester, and Caroline counties. It is composed of a one-and-one-half-story, three-bay main section with a lower one-and-one-half-story, one-bay wing. The central entrance, located in the northwest facade, has an 1840s six-panel door and is sheltered by a gable-roofed porch. Two dormers pierce the gable roof and interior chimneys rise above the gable ends. Since the original construction, various owners have built seven additions to create a very long, low dwelling with an extensive water view.

T-219

T-221

T-222

T–221
RILEY FARM
Bozman
Circa 1850; Private

This cottage is a one-room, one-and-one-half-story, two-bay frame structure with a one-story, one-bay addition. Its long facades are identical, with a modern door to the north and a shuttered six-over-six sash window to the south. A dormer projects from each slope of the gable roof, and an interior chimney rises above the south gable end. The exterior is sheathed with wood shingles painted white; the doors and windows have plain trim, consisting of unadorned flat boards. Within, a winding boxed stair with a closet beneath rises alongside the chimney in the southeast corner. The fireplace is framed by the original mantel of simple form with ovolo molding. Today the cottage serves as a guesthouse. The name comes from its appellation in an 1878 deed.

T–222
WOODSTOCK
Near Easton
Circa 1835; Private

Dr. Samuel Harrison, a Talbot County physician and historian from whose studies his son-in-law, Oswald Tilghman, compiled the *History of Talbot County, Maryland,* built

Woodstock in the second quarter of the nineteenth century. Located between Goldsborough and Glebe creeks on a neck of land known originally as "The Ending of Controversie" (T–223; T–299), the house is a three-part dwelling composed of a two-bay, two-and-one-half-story, central block, flanked by a two-and-one-half-story, three-bay wing on the east and a late-nineteenth-century, two-story, two-bay wing on the west. (The west wing is a late-nineteenth-century addition.) The building is constructed on a brick basement and covered with plain weatherboard except where the porches were affixed. The central block has a townhouse plan with a generous side hall and double parlor. The east wing now houses the dining room and kitchen, but when built, the kitchen was located in the basement below the main section. Unfortunately, many of Woodstock's details have suffered damage through lack of repair and vandalism.

T–223
THE ENDING OF CONTROVERSIE
Near Easton
Circa 1800; with additions; Private

This rambling, telescope house, located on part of the original Ashby tract, overlooks Glebe Creek. Today frame siding completely covers the building, but the smaller two-

and-one-half-story section is actually a brick structure. From an examination of the limited exposed areas, the wing appears to date to the second half of the nineteenth century. An absence of original interior detail, however, prohibits any definitive dating. The largest section contains woodwork of the early nineteenth century, and may have been the oldest part. The plan resembles several period dwellings in the county: there is a living room and stair hall in the largest (oldest?) section, a den is the second block, and a dining room is the third. The kitchen is now in the hyphen. Attractive paneling was brought to the house from New Hampshire, altered, and is now installed in the den. The house's name, "The Ending of Controversie," has been erroneously applied to this house; it actually belongs to the tract of land to the east on which Woodstock (T–222) stands. In 1670 Dr. Peter Sharp gave "The Ending of Controversie" to Wenlocke Christison, who built a small cottage on the land. In the 1940s Christison's house was destroyed, but a replica (T–299) was built by Dr. H. Chandlee Forman in 1970.

T-223

T-224

T-224
FAUSLEYWOOD
Near Easton
Early nineteenth century; Private

Situated at the head of Glebe Creek, Fausleywood is a deceptive, two-story, three-bay dwelling. It is deceptive because, while it appears to have been built in one period, it is actually composed of two early-nineteenth-century structures. Moreover, although today covered by aluminum siding, the building is not entirely of frame construction; the west bay is actually a brick structure. Further, although both parts have a common roofline, the west section's windows are smaller and higher than those to the east, reflecting a change in floor level within. The interior, like the exterior, has been greatly remodeled and exhibits few original details. The brick west room, placed two or three steps higher than the east room and hall, has a stair in the southeast corner. It has two-panel doors with a bolection chair rail between: the chair rail may have been taken from Fausley (T–338), the birthplace of Colonel Tench Tilghman; the handsome, Victorian, painted-slate mantel was taken from Woodstock (T–222).

T–225
THE GLEBE
Near Easton
Circa 1875; Private

The Glebe is a typical late-nineteenth-century farmhouse that retains its character and much of its original fabric. It is a two-story, three-bay frame dwelling with a two-story, three-bay wing on the north and a 1920s garage on the south; all three sections are sheathed with German siding. The main facade has a central entrance with sidelights, transom, and an elaborately paneled door. A porch supported by square posts with ornate brackets runs along the first story of the facade and continues—screened in—around the gable end and the west bay of the north elevation. The floor plan consists of a center stair hall with a room to each side. There are three noteworthy mantels. The west parlor features a colonial revival mantel with decorative fluting. Those in the east rooms, one on each floor, illustrate two mid-nineteenth-century styles: the ground story's has reeded engaged columns with beaded oval insets; the one above has chamfered posts and raised panels.

T–226
THE COVE
Near Easton
Circa 1830; with additions; Private

About two miles from Easton, situated on the banks of Glebe Creek, is The Cove, a two-and-one-half-story, five-bay brick farmhouse with flanking brick wings. The second quarter of the nineteenth century was not Talbot County's most prosperous period, and the central block of the cove is one of the few dwellings built here in toto (not as the result of a remodeling) in that era. All the walls are laid in common bond, and there is neither a beltcourse nor a water table. The main entrance is fitted with a modern door and elliptical fanlight and is shaded, along with the immediately flanking windows, by a modern three-bay porch supported by Doric columns. The wings date to the twentieth century and are recessed from the front facade of the original sections. They are well designed and do not compromise the integrity of the original construction.

T–228
BARNABY HOUSE
Oxford
1770; Private

A deed made July 28, 1770, between Edward Oldham and Richard Barnaby records "the lot whereon the said Richard is about

T-226

T-228

T-229

T-231

T-232

to build a dwelling home"; a stone in the cellar of the present structure is carved with the date 1770. Although the exterior is basically indistinguishable from its more recently built neighbors, this one-and-one-half-story, weatherboard and shingle covered cottage has the unusual feature of a door set sideways to the street. Further, the interior retains much original detail including the stair, corner fireplaces, pine paneling, and a hand-carved corner cupboard. The carving on the mantel is especially interesting because it incorporates copies of details from some of this area's early sailing craft.

T–229
RICH BOTTOM FARM
Easton
Circa 1830; with additions; Private

The two-part frame house on Rich Bottom Farm is situated on a knoll overlooking the farm, with the Choptank River beyond. The one-and-one-half-story, two-bay structure dates from the first half of the nineteenth century, whereas the two-story, three-bay section is from the second half. The house is covered with aluminum siding, but some original fabric is visible in the chimney that rises on the south gable end.

T–231
LLANDAFF
Near Easton
1878; Private

Llandaff is one of the few buildings in Talbot County built in the nationally popular Queen Anne style. It was the home of John Robinson, a Wells-Fargo silver buyer and railroad magnate, and remains in the possession of his descendants. The main house has a hip roof partially concealed by the gable roofs of the wings. The entrance is located beneath the front wing, which resembles the porch tower of seventeenth-century English vernacular construction. Also recalling this style is the overhang of some second-story sections. The house underwent a remodeling that stripped it of several porches and much exterior trim and renewed the main supports of the front wing. Some degree of ornament, however, is still provided by the plain and patterned shingles used to sheath the exterior. On the grounds, laid out in 1878 by the New York landscape architect Thomas Hogan, stands a windmill covered in the same manner as the house, as well as a barn, a farm manager's house, and a boathouse; are all in good repair.

T–232
LOCUST LANE
Longwoods
Early twentieth century; Private

The sculptor Lee Laurie lived at Locust Lane for the last 23 years of his life. The frame house is composed of a two-story, five-bay main section with a one-story addition running perpendicular on the east. This addition, originally a kitchen and a garage, was recently modernized. The main house is covered with white shingles; notable features of its facade include the colonial revival enclosed entrance, which is surmounted by a fanlight and flanked by double pilasters and the Greek revival window trim.

T–233
LOWE'S POINT
Sherwood
Eighteenth century; Private

Lowe's Point is important because, unlike most early dwellings, which come down to us altered by remodelings, it still presents its original eighteenth-century appearance. It is a small, one-and-one-half-story, three-bay house, whose brickwork exhibits a variety of bonds: Flemish bond is employed on the east (main) facade, English bond is used on the west elevation, and common bond is found on the gable ends. The interior has a hall-and-parlor plan.

T-233

T-234

T-235

T-236

T–234
UPHOLLAND
Bozman
Mid-nineteenth century; Private

Situated on land patented in 1667, Up-holland is a fine example of mid-nineteenth-century construction. It consists of a two-and-one-half-story, five-bay main house with a two-part, one-story kitchen addition on the south gable end. The main facade, shaded by a two-story porch, has a central entrance with a transom and sidelights en-cased in a frame of pilasters carrying a pedi-ment. This simplified Greek revival treat-ment of the entrance is carried through to the interior, which has many examples of restrained Greek revival decoration.

T–235
EMERSON POINT
Claiborne
1928; Private

This large Georgian revival mansion domi-nates an estate that is dotted with many outbuildings, including an overseer's house, several barns, a boathouse, and two frame structures said to have served as "boarding houses" in the late nineteenth century. There is also a mid-nineteenth-century cem-etery with inscribed stone markers for white burials and unmarked fieldstones for black burials. The extensive landscaping of the

property features hundreds of ornamental trees and shrubs.

T–236
ELBERTON
St. Michaels
Early nineteenth century; Private

Elberton is a one-and-one-half-story frame dwelling that today consists of a tall central section with two lower wings of nearly equal size. The east wing appears to be original, but the west wing was added during the twentieth century. On each section the dormers have been connected by a shed roof addition covered with shingles, which cre-ates more headroom while allowing the house to maintain its one-and-one-half-story appearance.

T–238
ACADEMY HOUSE
Oxford
1848; Private

Also known as the Bratt Mansion, this Greek revival, three-story, five-bay house was built in 1848 as the officers' quarters for the Maryland Military Academy, the pre-paratory school for the U.S. Naval Acad-emy between 1849 and 1855. The house is raised on a high basement and is covered with clapboard. Two-story pilasters give rhythm to the facade, and a widow's walk

surmounts the low hip roof. An 1850 fire consumed most of the important academic buildings, and today the Academy House stands as the lone remnant of this institution.

T–239
TRINITY CATHEDRAL
Easton
1876; Private

Built in imitation of an English Gothic par-ish church, Trinity Cathedral joins St. John's Chapel of St. Michael's Parish (T–49) and Christ Church (T–15) as prod-ucts of an architectural style that sought its inspiration in medieval forms. The plan of the church is cruciform, and its nave ter-minates in an apse. Many Gothic motifs characterize the construction, including the pointed arch windows, interior hammer beams, steep roof, and heavy buttressing. The tower, also dictated by this style, was originally flat-roofed, but it was recently raised as a memorial to a parishioner. Stone was considered the appropriate building ma-terial, and granite, not found on the mid–Eastern Shore, but mined near Port Deposit in Cecil County and brought by water, was used to fashion the exterior. The interior relies almost exclusively on structural fea-tures, such as trusses and beams, for decora-tive effect. The pews are not original, but

T-238

T-239

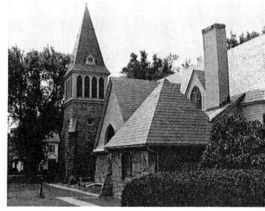

T-240

T-241

T-242

the altar and chairs of the bishop and dean along with the stained glass combine to give Trinity Cathedral a good late-Victorian interior.

T–240
BEVERLY
St. Michaels
Circa 1880; Private

Beverly is a well-appointed Victorian frame dwelling with vernacular form and Italianate details. The house, beneath the colonial revival additions, is composed of a two-and-one-half-story section with an L-plan, and a one-and-one-half-story kitchen wing, which turns the original L into a T, and a two-story addition parallel to the kitchen. The main entrance, located near the base of the L, has a transom, sidelights, and double doors set within a bolection-molded rectangular frame. The section that lies adjacent to the entrance is heavily ornamented with paneled corner pilasters, molded window cornices, and a full pediment. The cornice on the pediment is composed of brackets with raised diamond-shaped panels, and the tympanum is pierced by two round windows. A single chimney rises from each gable end of the main house.

T–241
THE BRUFF HOUSE
St. Michaels
Eighteenth century; with additions; Private

The Bruff House is a small, one-and-one-half-story, three-bay frame structure set on a brick foundation. The main entrance is located in the central bay of the principal facade, and interior chimneys rise above the gable ends. There is one one-bay wing on the west, and around 1970 the owners added another on the north and restored the house.

T–242
HIGGINS HOUSE
St. Michaels
1854–1855; Private

The Higgins House was built between 1854 and 1855 after Navy Point was subdivided into town lots in 1851. Until that time the point was part of Perry Cabin (T–206), owned by Samuel Hambleton. The house is a two-story, two-bay frame structure with a smaller two-story, two-bay wing of the 1890s. There have been many owners, but the last private owner, John Higgins, gave his name to the building. Today it houses the curatorial offices of the Chesapeake Bay Maritime Museum.

T–243
HARRISON FUNERAL HOME
St. Michaels
Eighteenth century; with additions; Private

This three-part structure is in excellent condition and serves as a fine example of the telescope house. The small one-story section is probably the oldest and reputedly dates from the early eighteenth century. The interior has undergone much alteration, and very little original interior woodwork remains in any of the three sections.

T–245
WHITE MARSH TRACT (site)
Near Easton
Private

White Marsh Tract is located at the headwaters of Kings Creek. Until the early 1970s there was a nineteenth-century frame farmhouse on the property. This was composed of a one-and-one-half-story section probably dating to the second quarter of that century, a mid-century, two-story, three-bay main house on the west, and a wing on the east dating to the second half of the century. It was a simple combination of vernacular and Italianate styles. The house burned in the 1970s, but when it stood, the modest house resembled the Holland House (CAR–50) near Bethlehem in Caroline County.

T-243

T-245

T-247

T–246
EMMANUEL LUTHERAN CHURCH
Cordova
Late nineteenth century; Private

This small, Gothic revival church is five bays long and one bay wide raised on a rusticated, concrete block basement and covered by a steeply pitched gable roof with exposed overhanging rafters. The frame walls are sheathed in board-and-batten and pierced by lancet windows. In each gable are structural brackets; a belfry and spire rise above the entrance gable. The main body of the church is rectangular, but with the additions of two wings, a vestibule, and a sanctuary, the plan approximates a Latin cross. The interior is covered with sheetrock and beaverboard, but originally diagonal boarding (and, in some places, lancet-arched panels) decorated the walls. Built by an Episcopal congregation, the church was for a time used by Lutherans; today it serves as a community center.

T–247
TILGHMAN'S FORTUNE
Route 50, Easton
Circa 1800; with additions; Private

The Talbot County Chamber of Commerce moved Tilghman's Fortune from Easton Point to this location in 1969, placed it on a brick foundation, and adapted it as their

office. Architecturally the one-story, two bay structure is representative of the better-quality one-room-plan houses in the late eighteenth and early nineteenth centuries. The main east facade is laid in Flemish bond, with common bond on the other elevations. The two long facades both have a central entrance. A chimney rises above the north gable end. The interior has a mantel and trim of the late eighteenth or early nineteenth century; an enclosed stair rises beside the fireplace to the loft above. There is a one-story, two-bay frame wing on the north.

T–248
1780 HOUSE (Grapevine House)
Oxford
1780; Private

This handsome, two-story, five-bay frame house is one of the few eighteenth-century houses still standing in Oxford. It is raised on a foundation covered with concrete and stucco and is sheathed in narrow clapboard. The main facade has a central door with a transom and sidelights in the style of buildings from the second quarter of the nineteenth century. The interior detail also appears to date from this period. Extending from the north gable end is a modern one-and-one-half-story wing with a bell-cast gambrel roof and a porch supported by Doric

columns. The house is often called the Grapevine House after the large grapevine that was brought from the Isle of Jersey and planted in the front yard in 1798.

T–249
ROBERT MORRIS INN
Oxford
Second half of the eighteenth century; Private

It is not known for whom or when this building, which today houses the Robert Morris Inn, was erected. Some interior detail, however, suggests a mid- to late-eighteenth-century date. The inn is named for Oxford's most prominent citizen, Robert Morris, Sr., who arrived in the town in 1738 as an agent for the firm of Foster Cunliffe, Esq., and Sons. It is certain that he did not live in what is today the early part of the inn, since it was built after his death in 1750. Consequently his connection with this property remains unknown. The eighteenth-century house was eventually converted into an inn and is referred to in several nineteenth-century sources as the Riverview House. In the 1870s the owner, Albert Robins, added much of the interior fabric and recast the entire exterior in the Second Empire style. The interior, however, retains the stair (with its exceptionally fine balusters and rail) and the raised pine paneling of the early house.

T-248

T-249

T-250

T-251

T–250
THE CHURCH OF THE HOLY TRINITY
Oxford
1853; 1892; 1947

The cornerstone for this Episcopal church was laid in 1853 upon lands skirted by the Tred Avon River. The first vestry, consisting of General Tench Tilghman of Plimhimmon (T–162), Benjamin M. Bowdle of Judith's Garden (T–172), John H. Allen, James G. Thomas, and John W. Cheezum, engaged Richard M. Upjohn of New York as the architect. The stone walls were erected, but the building was not completed. In a historical sketch, Mrs. Virginia S. G. Ritter writes: "Forty years passed, during which time the walls became overgrown with vines; trees sprang up and attained full size within the enclosure." In 1892 an appeal for completion was made and the church was completed with the exception of the tower called for in Upjohn's original plan. In 1945 the church was destroyed by fire, leaving only the stone walls standing. The church was reconstructed with two changes in the design: the entrance was relocated from the north to the west facade with a circular window above; and the chancel was enlarged.

T–251
OLD PENN-CENTRAL STATION
Conrail Tracks at Goldsborough Street, Easton
Circa 1900; Private

Typical of many period railroad stations throughout the United States, the Easton Station is distinguished by widely flaring eaves supported by heavy knee braces and shaped rafter ends. A hip roof covers this rectangular structure, and the walls are finished halfway up in brick with a shingle section above. This station fell into disuse and was abandoned, but it was recently restored and converted into a farmers' market.

T–252
ST. MARY'S SQUARE MUSEUM
St. Michaels
Late seventeenth century (?)
1860s; Public

This small frame building was moved to St. Mary's Square in the 1960s from a site (T–267) on land originally patented to John Hollingsworth in 1659. Constructed of timbers hewn with a broadax and joined with mortise-and-tenon, it is a fine example of early construction techniques in the St. Michaels area. Behind the old two-part house is a one-story frame hyphen and a three-bay "teetotal" building. This structure derives its name from its resemblance to an

old-fashioned top. It was built in the 1860s and moved to its present location from Willow Street.

T–253
THE COTTAGE
St. Michaels
Early nineteenth century; Private

This one-and-one-half-story frame house was built by the Lambdin family, who lived here for several generations. Members of the family were successful merchants and probably found it advantageous to live near the water. Much of the charm of the house, now expanded far beyond its original cottage size, derives from the diamond-patterned muntins of the sash windows; even the bay window on the first story possesses this distinctive sash pattern.

T–254
AMELIA WELBY HOUSE
St. Michaels
Late eighteenth century; Private

This one-and-one-half-story, three-bay house is an unusual example of brick-nogging construction of the late eighteenth century. The brick east gable end shows the line of an addition that raised the roof and permitted greater use of the second story. Amelia Welby, a local poet whose work is said to have earned the praise of Edgar Allan Poe, once lived here.

T-252

T-253

T-254

T-255

T-256

T-257

T–255
DR. MILLER'S FARMHOUSE
Talbot and Chestnut streets,
St. Michaels
Circa 1845; Private

Dr. Miller's Farmhouse is a rambling, composite dwelling of brick and frame. Laid in all-stretcher bond with flat arches above the windows and doors, the two-story, three-bay brick section was built as a townhouse. The main entrance, located in the northern bay, is equipped with a transom and sidelights. A stepped brick cornice runs along the roof line, and chimneys rise flush with the gable ends. A one-story porch extends from the south gable end; on the north is a two-story, three-bay frame wing, a two-story porch, and a round corner tower.

T–256
114 East Chestnut Street, St. Michaels
Mid-nineteenth century; Private

This two-and-one-half-story, three-bay house is a mid-nineteenth-century dwelling with a number of smaller, undistinguished wings extending from the rear elevation. The most notable feature of the house is the "Steamboat Gothic" trim on the porch and cornice.

T–257
OLD INN
St. Michaels
1816; Private; National Register

Along with the Cannonball House (T–61), the Old Inn is one of the more interesting buildings in St. Michaels. It was built in 1816 by Wrightson Jones, who operated a shipyard at Beverly (T–240). The building is a two-and-one-half-story, four-bay Federal style structure with a two-story, two-bay brick kitchen wing on its south gable end and a frame wing on the east. The main facade, laid in Flemish bond and reworked in several places, has two entrances on the first story and a door leading to a two-story porch shading the facade; the porch is set under the gable roof of the house and within the north wall, the lower half of which has been removed. Both this porch and the one on the rear elevation appear to be original. Three dormers with arched upper sashes project from the slope of the roof above, and chimneys rise flush with the gable ends. The kitchen wing has a flounder roof, which slopes from two stories on the facade to one on the rear and resembles the kitchen wing of the Cannonball House.

T–258
MARYLAND NATIONAL BANK BUILDING
St. Michaels
1806; Private

A large two-and-one-half-story brick structure, this handsome building was built in 1806 on land purchased by William Sears from Christ Episcopal Church. It was originally built to face Church Cove, but the orientation was changed later in the nineteenth century by the addition of the imposing two-story porch. In 1963 the former residence was acquired by the Maryland National Bank and carefully renovated to serve as the bank's St. Michaels office.

T–259
ST. LUKE'S METHODIST CHURCH
(Sardis Chapel)
St. Michaels
1871; Private

Constructed in 1871, St. Luke's is the third Methodist church in St. Michaels (see T–274). The ornament and trim of the eaves and steeple are among the best examples of Victorian gingerbread in the area. The parish house, designed in a similar style, dates from the 1960s.

T-258

T-259

T-260

T-261

T–260
CHRIST CHURCH
St. Michaels
1878; Private

Although this is the fourth church building on this site, services have been held here since 1670, when the congregation worshiped in a log church built by Edward Elliott. The second church was built of clapboard in the eighteenth century, but by the time of the War of 1812, the construction of a brick church was already underway. This structure was replaced by the present church, which was built in 1878 under the direction of Captain Daniel Feddeman. It is a Gothic revival structure constructed of stone brought by barge from quarries near Havre de Grace. It has a front tower with corner buttressing and a high vaulted ceiling under the steep gable roof. The interesting interior features include the baptismal font in the northwest corner, presented to St. Michaels Parish by Queen Anne in 1701, and, above the main altar, a five-panel stained-glass window depicting Christ and the evangelists.

T–261
TARR HOUSE
St. Michaels
Circa 1800 (?); 1870s; Private

This house, reputedly one of the oldest in St. Michaels, is locally believed to have been built in the 1670s by Edward Elliott. It was Elliott who built the first Episcopal church in St. Michaels on the site of Christ Church (T-260). While it is likely that Elliott's house was on this lot, the present house probably dates to the 1790–1810 period. The house today is composed of an original brick section with a late-nineteenth-century frame wing. The early part, one-and-one-half stories tall and three bays wide, has a central entrance. One dormer pierces the slope of the steep gable roof above the main facade, and a large chimney rises flush with the open gable end. This chimney contains separate flues for the cellar fireplace, which was used for cooking, the parlor fireplace, and the bedroom fireplace on the second floor. The interior retains some original features, including the fireplaces, flooring, and beams. In the 1870s Benjamin Blakes built the wing for the owner, Captain Thomas. This is a smaller version of the brick section, and supposedly was constructed out of flood debris picked up in the Chesapeake Bay.

T–262
BRUFF-MANSFIELD HOUSE
St. Michaels
Late eighteenth century; Private

The Bruff-Mansfield House is a one-and-one-half-story frame dwelling built on land that James Braddock purchased from John Bruff in 1778. The early date of the house is most conspicuously borne out by the interior, which still contains many of its late-eighteenth-century details. These include two large fireplaces, unusual paneling, and hand-hewn floor joists showing marks of the broadax. Remarkably, many of the wood dowels used to peg the flooring are still in place.

T–263
HELL'S CROSSING
St. Michaels
Mid-nineteenth century; Private

The name "Hell's Crossing" refers both to this small frame house and to the intersection on which it stands. Legend has it that during St. Michaels's raffish years as a center of navigation and commerce, this area accommodated grog shops and houses of ill repute. The merrymaking and fighting that usually took place in the late hours earned the intersection its name.

T-262

T-263

T-265

T-266

T-267

T–265
DR. DODSON'S HOUSE
St. Michaels
Late eighteenth century; with additions;
Private

Dr. Dodson's House is a three-part brick structure, the early sections of which are of late-eighteenth-century origin. The south section, which is the earliest, is two-and-one-half stories tall and two bays wide. Its brickwork is laid in Flemish bond on the main facade and in common bond on the other elevations. Perhaps built at the same time, the small one-and-one-half-story wing on the east is laid in common bond and reputedly was used as a U.S. post office in 1788. In the mid nineteenth century a second wing approximately the size of the oldest structure was added. At this time a two-story porch was constructed across the street facade, and the first-story windows were lengthened to match the ones in the new wing.

T–266
SNUGGERY
St. Michaels
Mid-nineteenth century; Private

Although possibly dating from the early eighteenth century, this small cottage owes its present appearance to a mid-nineteenth-century remodeling. This work was carried

out in the English Gothic cottage style, and the result recalls Washington Irving's famous "Snuggery" at Sunnyside beside the Hudson River in New York. Whether that cottage served as an inspiration for the one in St. Michaels is uncertain, but the latter is an imaginative interpretation of a rural English cottage. Elements of this cottage style include the steeply pitched roof, dormers set close to the roof line, and the use of decorative shingles.

T–267
LOG HOUSE
St. Michaels
1819; Private

Although now covered with brown wood shingles, the Log House is constructed of hand-hewn timbers, mortised and tenoned with wood pegs. It was built low to the ground and is similar to many simple one-and-one-half-story cottages in St. Michaels. The oldest section of St. Mary's Square Museum (T–252) stood next to the Log House until the museum was moved in 1960s.

T–268
SENATOR DODSON HOUSE
St. Michaels
1850s; Private

Between 1851 and 1861 Thomas Dyott built this brick house, the largest residence on

Navy Point. In 1855 it was purchased by Richard Dodson, a member of a distinguished family of shipowners and captains who settled in the county in the 1700s. He probably added the two-story porch with pierced-work balustrade. His son, Richard Slicer Dodson, was a well-known state senator who retired to St. Michaels and lived in this house until 1961. Today it is owned by the Mariner's Museum and will eventually house the museum's library.

T–269
EAGLE HOUSE
St. Michaels
1893; Public

A steam saw and grist mill occupied the site of the Eagle House in the middle of the nineteenth century. It burned in 1860, was rebuilt, and exploded in 1864. In 1893 the Dodson family acquired the lot and built this Victorian house. It is now covered with asbestos siding and houses the steamboat exhibits of the Mariner's Museum. The steamboat eagle on top of the tower is a reminder that steamboats were once moored at the wharf in front of the house.

T-268

T-269

T-270

T-271

T–270
MANSARD HOUSE
St. Michaels
Mid-nineteenth century; Private

The Second Empire style, whose hallmark is the revival of the mansard roof developed in the seventeenth century by the French Renaissance architect François Mansart, was inaugurated by the enlargement of the Louvre under Napoleon III (1852–1870) and dominated French architecture through the end of the nineteenth century. Its influence spread to the United States, and the Mansard House illustrates one of the most elegant expressions of this style in Talbot County (see also T–281; T–284). The house, situated on a slight rise overlooking Navy Point, is a five-bay frame building with one-story porches supported by Ionic columns. The mansard roof is the most outstanding feature of the house. It has an elaborate cornice at the eaves and the roof itself is finished with fish-scale shingles; painted shingles between the segmental-arched dormers add a decorative touch.

T–271
GINGERBREAD HOUSE AND SHOP
St. Michaels
Late nineteenth century; Private

Within only a few yards of each other are three of St. Michaels's most imaginative

buildings: Snuggery (T–266), the Mansard House (T–270), and the Gingerbread House. This otherwise ordinary frame house is transformed by an explosion of carved woodwork on the porch, cornice, and window trim. The detail includes ornate brackets; turned, Eastlake-style spindles arranged in a ray pattern; and a pierced work, "Steamboat Gothic" balustrade. The shop next door, at 101 Talbot Street, is a smaller, three-bay structure that has undergone alteration. That the buildings are contemporary and by the same builder is suggested by the similarity of the decorative woodwork running along the eaves.

T–272
112 West Chestnut Street, St. Michaels
Eighteenth century; Private

This one-and-one-half-story frame house stands on part of the property patented to John Hatton in 1695. It has undergone many alterations, but it retains some features of the original construction, including beams and timber, an enclosed stair, and wide pine flooring on the second story.

T–273
108–110 East Chestnut Street,
St. Michaels
Mid-nineteenth century; Private

This double-numbered house was probably intended to be a single dwelling, but it was built in at least two stages. The west section of the building, number 108, is two stories tall, three bays wide, and resembles a small townhouse. The main facade has a side entrance and a single double-unit window instead of the customary two windows. The wing, number 110, is a simple rectangular two-story frame structure distinguished by some unusual features: adjacent to the main house is a bay window that accommodates the entrance, and at the open corner of the facade is a three-story octagonal tower with delicate snowflake-patterned jigsaw work on the third story.

T–274
GRANITE LODGE
St. Michaels
1839; Private

In the midst of St. Michaels's Victorian exuberance and colonial refinement, Granite Lodge stands as one of the town's most pristine examples of Greek revival architecture. It is a two-and-one-half-story, three-bay brick structure designed to resemble a classical temple. The gable end serves as the

T-272

T-273

T-274

T-275

principal facade and takes the place of the pediment required by Greek and Roman temple architecture. A small porch with a pedimented entablature supported by two Doric columns shades the central main entrance and echoes the roof line of the gable. The land on which Granite Lodge stands was given to the Society of Friends by James Braddock, a London merchant who laid out St. Mary's Square, in 1771. In 1782 the first Methodist Church in Talbot County was erected here, only to be replaced in 1832 by the present building. In 1871 the members of the congregation left this church and moved to their new home, St. Luke's (T–259), on Talbot Street, where they continue to worship today.

T–275
CHESAPEAKE BAY MARITIME MUSEUM
St. Michaels
1879; late nineteenth century; Public
The Hooper Strait Lighthouse and the Old Canning Shed are notable exceptions to the many buildings in this museum complex which are either reconstructions or were specifically built to house the museum's collections. The lighthouse, built in 1879 off the shore of Dorchester and Somerset counties, was moved to this location in 1966. It is a screw-pile lighthouse similar in

construction to Drum Point Lighthouse in Calvert County and Thomas Point Lighthouse off Anne Arundel County. Today it contains exhibits on the history of lighthouses in the Chesapeake Bay area. The Old Canning Shed was originally a freight shed built in the late nineteenth century in Claiborne by the Baltimore, Chesapeake and Atlantic Railway Company, which provided steamship and rail service between Baltimore and Ocean City. In 1932 the building was acquired by the St. Michaels Packing Company; the next year it was moved to its present location, where it was used as a warehouse for finished products. In 1970 the museum purchased the building along with a quarter acre of waterfront property.

T–276
208 East Chestnut Street, St. Michaels
Mid-nineteenth century; Private
This house is composed of two, two-bay sections. The west section is deeper and has a taller roof. Like many houses in St. Michaels, this house has a two-story gallery, but here the first story on the east is enclosed. The simplicity of design and fabric is relieved by the ornate, pierced-work Victorian balustrade on the second story.

T–277
210 Talbot Street, St. Michaels
Late nineteenth century; Private
This Queen Anne style house is one of the most unusual in Talbot County. The main facade is divided into three sections recessed from one another. There is a two-story, one-bay section followed by a two-story, one-bay entrance tower topped by a pyramidal roof with flaring eaves and mouse-tooth brick dentils. Finally a three-bay polygonal section projects toward the street from the tower. A paneled chimney runs up the center of this section and is flanked by windows on both stories. The brickwork throughout is enlivened by herringbone and diaper-worked patterns. On the tower and one-bay section is a one-story porch, with elaborate, well-preserved, Eastlake-style carved woodwork.

T–278
204 Talbot Street, St. Michaels
Mid-nineteenth century; Private
This two-story, three-bay brick house is one of the many in St. Michaels that carries Italianate detail. In this case the large bracketed cornice that runs along the facade at the roof line is characteristic of the Italianate style. Less Italianate and more Greek revival is the porch supported by Doric columns which shades the first story.

T-276

T-277

T-278

T-279

T-280

T-281

T–279
SMITHTON INN (Colonel Kemp's House)
St. Michaels
1805; Private

This two-and-one-half-story, five-bay late Georgian style house was built by Colonel Joseph Kemp, a Revolutionary War soldier and hero of the War of 1812. Kemp, in fact, commanded a horse patrol along San Domingo Creek during the Battle of St. Michaels. Another noted military man, General Robert E. Lee, once spent two nights in this house as the guest of Mr. and Mrs. Oliver Sparks, descendants of Colonel Kemp. The house has been carefully restored and converted into an inn, and it retains much original interior detail, including the mahogany doors, mantels, and stair.

T–280
201 Mill Street, St. Michaels
Late nineteenth century; Private

This house is a two-story, two-bay frame structure with a one-bay frame wing. The wing runs perpendicular to the main house and, consequently, presents its gable end as part of the principal facade. The most interesting features of the house are the polygonal bay on the wing, which has panels and an ornate cornice, and the two-story

porch with jigsaw-worked balustrade on the main house.

T–281
MANSARD HOUSE
Trappe
Mid-nineteenth century; Private

Like the Adams House nearby (T–284) and the Mansard House in St. Michaels (T–270), this house was built in the Second Empire style and has the characteristic mansard roof. Its form is particularly interesting because of the addition of a two-story bay projecting from one of its facades. The house is less ornate than its companion in St. Michaels, but it is, nonetheless, a fine expression of this internationally popular style.

T–282
ST. PAUL'S EPISCOPAL CHURCH
Trappe
1858; Private

The present austere appearance of St. Paul's Church is very different from that designed by its builders in 1858. Originally there were ornately carved brackets along the eaves of the roof and steeple tower, and above the central entrance was a round-arched hood also with carved brackets. Furthermore, carved finials topped the corners of the main block as well as the steeple. It

is not known when these decorative features were removed. When Old Whitemarsh Church (T–137) was abandoned in the 1850s, the silver communion service received from England in 1738, the wood alms box, and the Bible were given to St. Paul's.

T–283
BRICK HOUSE
Trappe
Early nineteenth century; Private

This is one of only a few brick houses in Trappe. It is a tall two-and-one-half-story dwelling with two dormers projecting from the steeply pitched gable roof. The off-center main entrance is equipped with a three-pane transom.

T–284
ADAMS HOUSE
Trappe
Mid-nineteenth century; Private

The Adams House is an impressive example of the Second Empire style (see also T–281 and T–270). An outstanding feature of this house is the fine cornice with dentils which runs along the eave from which rises the characteristic mansard roof. Shading the five bays of the main facade is a one-story porch supported by Doric columns.

T-282

T-283

T-284

T-285

T–285
ANTIQUE SHOP
Trappe
1830s; 1870s; Private

This large three-bay frame house stands in the center of Trappe's commercial district. It was built in the second half of the nineteenth century and was enlarged to the rear in the 1870s. Corner posts in the interior mark clearly the extent of the original building. The main facade is enriched by a finely executed dentiled cornice.

T–286
QUEEN ANNE HOUSE
Trappe
1880s; Private

This house is the most exuberant example of Victorian–Queen Anne style architecture in Trappe. Interesting features include the many gables that form an unusual skyline and the Chinese Chippendale railing on the large porch.

T–287
BYEBERRY
Oxford
Early eighteenth century;
Mid-nineteenth century; Private

This rambling, one-and-one-half-story shingled house, probably the oldest residence in Oxford, has undergone extensive remodeling

T-286

on several occasions and retains little of its colonial appearance or fabric. Originally it stood at the corner of Market and Morris streets, opposite the town park. In 1929 it was moved to this site and renamed Byeberry.

T–288
JUMP HOUSE
107 Goldsborough Street, Easton
Mid- and late nineteenth century; Private

This house illustrates the blending of two architectural styles. The two-story, three-bay main house was built or possibly just remodeled in the Italianate style in the mid-nineteenth century, when that style was popular. To this was added in the late nineteenth century a three-story, octagonal Queen Anne style tower. At this time the house was in the possession of the Jump family, who ran one of the largest dry good stores in Easton.

T–289
FOUNTAIN HOUSE
117 Goldsborough Street, Easton
1854; Private

The Fountain House is a two-and-one-half-story, three-bay, gable-roofed dwelling with a central-hall plan. The merchant Alexander Washington Fountain built the house and his descendants still own it. Wide

T-287

weatherboards and a two-story porch with square columns and bracketed cornices lend a grandness to the basically simple structure.

T–290
ROBERTS HOUSE
211 Goldsborough Street, Easton
Circa 1880; Private

A showcase of the carpenter's artistry, the Roberts House was built by Captain Edward Roberts, a leading figure in Easton's Volunteer Fire Department. Roberts was a carpenter by profession, and it is to him that we owe the rich exterior and interior wood detail. He decorated this simple, central-hall plan dwelling with ornate brackets, balustrades, and applied wood ornament. The porch on the main facade has a pediment with an ornately carved tympanum over the entrance. Flanking the porch are one-story, one-bay pavilions with flaring eaves and bold cornices and returns. On the interior, Roberts enriched his house with parquet floors, heavily carved moldings, and a highly ornate cove cornice in the parlor.

T-288

T-289

T-290

T-291

T-292

T–291
BISHOP'S HOUSE
214 Goldsborough Street, Easton
Circa 1880; Private

Philip Francis Thomas, a former congressman (1839–41), governor of Maryland (1847–49), and secretary of the treasury under President Buchanan, built this house after he had retired from public life. In 1891 his widow sold the property to the diocese of Easton as a residence for the bishop, but, in 1956, it reverted to private hands. Thomas's house is characterized by tall, narrow, gable-roofed pavilions that project from the central rectangular block. The roof terminates in wide eaves, which are finished in plain, narrow fasciae. The pavilion on the west of the facade has two projecting bays. The bay on the first story is polygonal and has three windows with a pierced-work band. Above this is a rectangular bay with four windows, on top of which runs another pierced-work band; this one has a vine-like motif. The interior has very deep cornices in the first-floor rooms, and doors and windows have wide frames trimmed with deep composite moldings.

T–292
407 Goldsborough Street, Easton
1890–1893; Private

This small, one-and-one-half-story frame house and its companion carriage house stand in a neighborhood of modest late-nineteenth-century dwellings. Covered by mansard roofs, these fanciful structures illustrate a Victorian interpretation of the Second Empire style (see T–270; T–281; T–284). The carriage house, nearly a double of the main house, is elaborately treated and reflects the importance of outbuildings in this period—it even has a belvedere atop the roof.

T–293
J. E. SHANNAHAN HOUSE
9 North Aurora Street, Easton
Circa 1890; Private

The J. E. Shannahan House is a two-and-one-half-story structure with three bays, one of which contains a projecting gable-roofed pavilion. The frame house is covered by a tall hip roof from which extend dormers and chimneys with flaring caps. On the main facade is a beautifully detailed one-story porch. It has a pierced-work skirt below the cornice and a balustrade made up of lozenge-like turned balusters. The most notable feature of the interior, which is divided into commodious rooms by the central

stair hall, is the oak stair with a square newel and deeply carved balusters. The J. E. Shannahan House has escaped alteration, and many considered it the finest of its period in Easton.

T–294
McDANIEL HOUSE
14 North Aurora Street, Easton
Circa 1890; Private

McDaniel House is one of Easton's extravagant, towered Victorian dwellings. Architecturally these structures were designed with a concern for volumetric expression, asymmetrically balanced compositions, and delicately articulated interiors. This house displays all of these elements, although it is not perhaps so sophisticated or integrated in its design as the J. E. Shannahan House (T–293) or Chaffinch House (T–34), two of Easton's outstanding Victorian dwellings.

T–295
COATES LODGE NUMBER 102
(Masonic Temple)
114 North Washington Street, Easton
1881; Private

Freemasonry was brought to the Eastern Shore in the eighteenth century, and by 1787 there were five active lodges. Coates Lodge, number 102, the third of Easton's fraternal organizations, was founded in 1855

T-293

T-294

T-295

T-296

and has met continuously since that time. The lodge members first met in the Talbot County Courthouse; then in 1881 they moved to this temple on North Washington Street. By 1930 the membership had outgrown the building, and a new three-story addition was made to the rear. The nineteenth-century building has an elaborate facade that uses a number of devices to achieve a ceremonial appearance. Framing the central main entrance is a porch supported by fluted Doric columns carrying a full entablature. The flanking double windows are surmounted by segmental arches with stone keystones and corner blocks; pierced work fills in the space between these arches and the sash. On the second story the end bays have two windows separated by recessed ornamental brick panels. These windows have jack arches with stone corner blocks, and a segmental arch traced by a row of headers spans each pair. In the central bay is a double window equipped with the same features as those of the first story. The third story, which contains the lodge room, has a double window topped with a jack arch and a tripartite window with a segmental arch interlarded with stone members. The gable immediately above is elaborately finished with ornamental bands of brick, either molded in a floral design or laid to form slots in the

brickwork. In the center of the gable is a semicircular opening with a stone slab carved with an eyeball, the emblem of the Masonic Order. Other iconographic details are found framing the tripartite window. The brick is of a light orange color and makes an attractive contrast with the stone blocks of the window arches. Further contrast is provided by the facade's numerous beltcourses.

T–296
18 West Street, Easton
Circa 1815–1835; Private

This two-and-one-half-story, three-bay house was restored in 1973 and now forms part of the Talbot County Historical Society complex. The house is raised on a brick foundation, is covered with wide, random-width weatherboard, and is so situated that it presents its west gable end to the street, while its long facade looks out on a side garden. Shading the entrance, which is located in the west bay of the garden facade, is a one-bay porch with a shallow gable finished in a cornice and return and supported by chamfered posts with lamb's-tongue stops. A single dormer pierces each slope of the gable roof, and above the east gable end rises a large chimney, which services both the main house and kitchen wing. This wing is two stories tall, one bay wide, and is

covered by random lapped siding. The interior of the building, like the exterior, is simple but well constructed. The parlor is distinguished by a mantel with reeded pilasters and a fluted frieze and a chair rail made of composite moldings. The kitchen has a floor of old brick, exposed ceiling timbers, and a fireplace with a segmental-arched opening and a brick shelf and trammel bar.

T–297
PARLETT HOUSE
200 South Harrison Street, Easton
Circa 1890; Private

The Newnam Funeral Home now occupies the Parlett House, one of Easton's grandest Victorian buildings. It was designed by the Baltimore architect T. Buckler Ghequier for B. F. Parlett, a prosperous Easton merchant. (Ghequier also remodeled Foxley Hall, T–30, for the Harrison-Tilghman family.) The main house is composed of a hip-roofed square block; three of its elevations have gable-roofed pavilions radiating from them; on the east is a two-story wing. Noteworthy features of the exterior include a three-story tower and an elaborately detailed porch. The main entrance is located on the first story of the tower and is fitted with a paneled oak door. The third story consists of an enclosed belfry with segmental-arched openings; from this rises a pyramidal roof topped

T-297

221

T-298

T-299

by a delicate cast-iron weather vane. The porch, which wraps around the main facade to meet the pavilions on the north and south, is equipped with turned posts and a skirt decorated with wood balls. The interior, like the exterior, is of grand design and richly detailed. The main parlor has a deeply carved white-marble mantel; marbleized slate distinguishes the fireplaces of the other rooms. The stair has circular inset decorations on its closed-string course; the balustrade is made up of quarter-round openings. In overall design Parlett House is an excellent example of the irregularity and free use of decoration so favored during this period.

T–298
WYE MILLS METHODIST CHURCH
Wye Mills
1880; Private

An architectural remnant of rural Methodism, Wye Mills Methodist Church is a one-story, three-bay-by-three-bay, rectangular structure raised on a brick foundation and sheathed in white weatherboard. Like many of the Eastern Shore's nineteenth-century chapels, this building has a gable-end facade to which is attached a small gable-roofed vestibule. Ornamental features are restricted to the wide eaves, which also extend over the gables. They are supported by brackets,

have pendants at the corners, and end in cornices that continue around the gable ends to form returns. The vestibule is identically treated and echoes in miniature the form of the church.

T–299
THE ENDING OF CONTROVERSIE
Behind 538 Aurora Street, Easton
1970 reconstruction; Private

Dr. H. Chandlee Forman designed this reconstruction of Wenlocke Christison's seventeenth-century house, which stood near Woodstock (T–222). Christison was a Quaker who had been severely persecuted in New England and sought refuge in Maryland, where he became one of the province's foremost champions of religious freedom. The replica of his home is a one-story structure with a steep gable roof. It has brick gable ends laid in English bond with random stretchers in the header course, and its sides are finished in palisaded board-and-batten siding. The small cottage is used as a studio.

T–301
LANGSDALE HOUSE 1
220 West Bay Street, Easton
Third quarter of the nineteenth century;
Private

This mid-nineteenth-century dwelling was one of four structures that formed a lively block along North Washington Street until the mid 1970s, when one was razed and two of them, this one and its neighbor, 218 West Bay Street (T–302), were moved and restored by Historic Easton, Inc. Locally known as the Langsdale Houses, these small frame buildings were built as detached row houses with exterior decoration limited to the facade. This house has a two-story porch with brackets and pendants and a gable, which is finished in a cornice and return and covered with ornamental shingles. Although legend claims that this house was modeled on houses of Caribbean island villages, it resembles other Eastern Shore dwellings, notably several in nearby St. Michaels.

T–302
LANGSDALE HOUSE 2
218 West Bay Street, Easton
Third quarter of the nineteenth century;
Private

The second Langsdale House saved from demolition (see T–301), this structure is two

T-301

T-302

T-304

T-305

stories tall and three bays wide, covered by a shallow hip roof. It is raised on a brick foundation and sheathed with German siding on the front facade and weatherboard on the side and rear elevations. The main facade, which carries the architectural ornament, has a side entrance with the transom and sidelights secured in a narrow frame. Shading its first story is a three-bay porch with a balustrade of slats that are slotted and pierced with round and four-sided holes; the posts are made of an elegant pattern of sticks. The cornice is very deep and decorated with scalloped double brackets; the roof is embellished with a band of diamond-shaped shingles.

T–304
LANGSDALE HOUSE 3;
(Talbot Banner Building)
124 North Washington Street, Easton
Circa 1875; Private

This is the only Langsdale House that stands on its original site (see T–301; T–302). It is two stories tall and three bays wide, covered by a low hip roof. Designed as a detached row house, this structure, like its companions, carries architectural ornament only on its front facade. Across this elevation runs a two-story porch, which is interrupted on the second story by a turretlike projection in the two northern bays. This poly-

gonal section has three windows, is covered with fish-scale shingles, and is surmounted by a conical roof. The porch has ornate brackets extending from its posts; consolelike brackets with pendant drops support the cornice on both stories. The first story of the porch has a pierced splat balustrade; on the second story the balustrade is composed of slender turned balusters. This house has a side-hall plan; it is one room wide and two deep. There is a dog-leg stair at the end of the hall and an entrance to the rear addition (1976).

T–305
TRED AVON (Oxford-Bellevue) FERRY
Oxford and Bellevue
1683; Private

A ferry has been in operation between the towns of Oxford and Bellevue continually since 1683. In that year the Talbot County court prevailed upon Richard Royston to run a ferry service at an annual subsidy of 2,500 pounds of tobacco. Power has been variously provided by sail, oar, steam, and diesel fuel, making this the oldest cableless ferry in the United States.

T–306
MACGEE METHODIST EPISCOPAL
CHURCH
Longwoods
1830; renovated 1945; Private

MacGee Methodist Episcopal Church is a fine, late Federal style chapel. The building is composed of a single volume two stories tall and three bays wide. It has a central entrance in a vestibule projecting from the central bay of the facade. Brick piers with brick fill support the superstructure, which is sheathed in asbestos siding; a cornice girds the building and forms pediments in the gable ends.

T–307
MONEY MAKE FARM
Trappe
Circa 1870; circa 1880; Private

The house on Money Make farm is a frame telescopic dwelling. The largest section, two stories tall and three bays wide, is the most recent and dates from the last quarter of the nineteenth century. It has a central entrance with sidelights and transom, and a gable projects from the roof directly above, adding a touch of ceremony to the door. The middle section is one-and-one-half stories by two bays with a single dormer in each slope of the gable roof. On the south is a small, shedlike appendage, which creates

T-306

T-307

T-308

T-309

headroom for the stair. The third section is one story by three bays with a central entrance. The interior of the largest section is composed of a center stair hall with a single room to each side. There is original detail throughout, including some grained woodwork and a slate mantel with marble graining. The stair is typical of the 1880s, except for the newel, which, although period, seems much too large for the small hall. The interiors of the other sections have undergone remodeling, and their original work has been covered. To the south of the house is a nineteenth-century meat house.

T-308
CHERRY GROVE
Trappe
Circa 1860; Private

Overlooking the broad waters of the Choptank River, Cherry Grove was originally surveyed out of Jamaica Point (T-63) and Lowe's Ramble. The house dates from the third quarter of the nineteenth century, when the property belonged to William Hughlett, the builder of Jamaica Point. It is a fine Victorian Italianate dwelling, two stories by five bays, raised on a brick basement and covered by a hip roof. There is a central entrance equipped with a transom and sidelights and flanked by full-length windows; a hip-roofed porch supported by

chamfered posts shades this story. The bracketed eaves are interrupted above the main facade by a low-pitched gable with a semicircular window. This projection may have been intended to simulate a ceremonial entrance tower. The interior is divided into a stair hall with two rooms to each side, all of which is equipped with plaster cornices and ceiling medallions. In the cellar is a board with the inscription, "I painted this house 1863." Stylistically Cherry Grove is similar to nearby Ingleside (T-313), also built by the Hughlett family.

T-309
BUNKER HILL FARM (Bullen)
Trappe
Early nineteenth century;
with additions; Private

While seemingly a twentieth-century frame dwelling, this house is actually an early-twentieth-century telescope house that is engulfed by the present two-story sections of the modern structure. The farm was formerly called Bullen, and from 1852–80 it was in the possession of Thomas J. Chaplain, son of the William Chaplain who built Reed's Creek (T-314). Since then the house has had many owners and has undergone a number of remodelings; several modern features of the house were designed by Dr. H. Chandlee Forman.

T-310
CRAIG'S POINT (Readly)
Trappe
Second quarter of the nineteenth century;
with additions; Private

This one-and-one-half-story, four-bay frame dwelling stands on the south bank of Reed's Creek near the Choptank River. It is composed of three sections built on brick foundations. The three bays on the west constitute the main house. To this was added a one-bay addition on the east; it is the same height as the main house, but its dormers and first-story openings are lower. Affixed to the east gable end of this addition is a one-story, two-bay kitchen wing with a modern lean-to on the north. The floor plan consists of two rooms in the largest block and one in each of the other two parts. The interior of the earliest section is distinguished by original mantels: those on the first story have columns and are in the Greek revival–Empire style; those on the second are simpler and recall the Federal period.

T-311
CHANCELLOR'S POINT
Trappe
Third quarter of the nineteenth century;
Private

The Chancellor's Point tract was given to Philip Calvert, brother of Cecil, the second

T-310

T-311

T-312

T-313

Lord Baltimore, in the mid-seventeenth century. He did not settle here, however, and eventually the land passed into the hands of William Hughlett (see T–63). Hughlett built the present house and lived here until his death in 1885. The house is a simple vernacular structure composed of a two-story, three-bay main section with a wing on the west and a twentieth-century wing on the north. The original entrance was located in the central bay and was equipped with a transom and sidelights. This bay now accommodates a window, and the entrance is in the northern bay. The interior retains its original generously proportioned floor plan with a living room to the north; other original features include the stair, with typical late-nineteenth-century detail, and the door and window trim.

T–312
MIDDLEVILLE
Trappe
First half of the nineteenth century; with additions; Private

Although Middleville has been completely remodeled on both the exterior and interior, its proportions are those of a farmhouse of the first half of the nineteenth century. It is a large house composed of a two-story, three-bay central section with flanking one-and-one-half-story wings. The wing on the

southeast appears to be the earliest section of the three-part house. On the grounds is an early-nineteenth-century tenant house (T–324).

T–313
INGLESIDE
Trappe
Mid-nineteenth century; Private

Ingleside is another of the great antebellum houses built by the Hughlett family (see T–63; T–131; T–308). The tall Victorian Italianate frame house is situated on the banks of the Choptank River and stands two stories on a brick basement. The walls are covered with weatherboard with corner pilasters below the eaves of the hip roof. The three-bay main facade has a central entrance fitted with a transom and sidelights and shaded by a gable-roofed porch with a cornice and returns. Four chimneys rise from the roof in a manner similar to the chimneys at Cherry Grove (T–308), and a widow's walk surmounts the apex. On the west is a two-story, twentieth-century wing. The interior, too, resembles Cherry Grove. Both houses have a central stair hall with a double parlor to the east and a large dining room to the west. (The original plan had matching double parlors, but later owners felt the need for a larger dining room.) Most of the interior decorations—plaster cornice

and ceiling medallions—are intact and resemble details at Cherry Grove.

T–314
REED'S CREEK FARM
Trappe
Late eighteenth century; Private

This land was first patented to Thomas Reed in 1659. Later in that century Nicholas Holmes bought the tract, and it remained in his family until 1765, when William Chaplain purchased the property. Chaplain's son, also named William, probably built the present house before his death in 1813. The house is composed of a two-story, three-bay brick main block with a one-and-one-half-story, four-bay brick kitchen wing with a modern garage. The principal section has a double-struck joint above the quarter-round English-bond molded water table. Its long facades are laid in Flemish bond; the side elevations are common bond. The central bay of each long facade accommodates an entrance, but only that on the south is fitted with a transom. The windows are surmounted by jack arches and framed by louvered shutters. The west chimney is partially exposed but the east chimney rises flush with the gable end. From this elevation extends the kitchen wing, which is laid in common bond and has a tall chimney on its east gable end.

T-314

T-315

T-316

The interior is arranged according to the typical central-hall plan and retains many of its original details. These include the stair with raised paneling beneath an open-string course and the mantels with gouge work in the living and dining rooms. The fireplaces are of special interest today: their shallowness and widely splayed sides are the result of a conscious effort to conserve heat. Two terraces on the south extend toward the water. To the west of the lower terrace is the private cemetery of the Chaplain and Stevens families.

T–315
KIRBY'S WHARF
Trappe
Nineteenth century; Private

Overlooking the Choptank River, Kirby's Wharf is a three-part dwelling exhibiting a variety of styles. The two-story, three-bay central section has Italianate windows, corner pilasters characteristic of the Greek revival, a Georgian hip roof, and, on the southeast, an earlier, one-and-one-half-story vernacular structure with a gable roof and lean-to porch. An unusual feature of the early section is the balustrade around the entrance to the cellar. On the northwest of the central section is a modern, one-and-one-half-story addition.

T–316
THE ANCHORAGE
Trappe
Circa 1800; with additions; Private

The Anchorage and the estate of the same name near Easton (T–52) are similar only in that they both sit on knolls overlooking rivers. This Anchorage overlooks the Choptank River. It is a frame, three-part telescopic dwelling of the early nineteenth century. The exterior has been obscured by the addition of aluminum siding and the remodeling of several bays to accommodate picture windows. The plan consists of a parlor and stair hall in the tallest part, a dining room and corridor in the middle section, and a den and kitchen in the smallest block. While the interior has been altered, a few early details are intact, including the mantel in the parlor (now a bedroom), which has pilasters and reeding, and the stair, whose balustrade was replaced in the mid-nineteenth century.

T–317
SANDAWAY
Oxford
Late nineteenth century; Private

Sandaway, now part of the Robert Morris Inn, is one of the largest and most unusually composed structures in Oxford. The main block is two-and-one-half stories with a bell-

cast gambrel roof pierced by dormers. There is a two-story porch across the riverfront facade; its ground story continues with a bracketed cornice around to the street elevation. To the rear are a two-story, three-bay addition, surmounted by a Second Empire style mansard roof, and a one-story wing.

T–318
BAKER BIRTHPLACE
Trappe
Circa 1850; Private

This house, the birthplace of Frank "Home-run" Baker, an early twentieth-century baseball player, is a mid-nineteenth-century dwelling clearly based on vernacular structures in its form and simplicity of line. It is composed of a two-story, three-bay main house with a two-story, two-bay wing, both raised on a brick basement and covered with asbestos siding. Baker was born here March 13, 1886, and later starred with the Philadelphia Athletics and New York Yankees. He led the American League four times in home runs (1911--14) and in 1955 was elected to the Baseball Hall of Fame. He died in Trappe in 1963.

T-317

T-318

T-319

T-320

T–319
MARSHLAND
Near Easton
Circa 1800; mid-nineteenth century; Private

The one-and-one-half-story section of Marshland has a side entrance, two first-story windows, and dormers, which make this vernacular structure resemble the early section of neighboring Hole-in-the-Wall (T–138). Marshland is raised on a low brick foundation and is covered with asbestos siding. Similarly constructed and sheathed is the taller two-story addition on the east. The house is a structure that embodies the modest aspirations of the Victorian working class.

T–320
CHLORA'S POINT
Trappe
Circa 1800; circa 1830; circa 1875; circa 1920; Private

Chlora's Point is located at the tip of Island Neck and enjoys a panoramic view of the Choptank River and Chesapeake Bay. The house has grown through the addition of several wings and stands today as an interesting combination of different styles and materials. The earliest structure is that on the south, which has a brick first story. It was built as a one-and-one-half-story vernacular dwelling. The original brickwork is

intact on the first story, and the bases of the original chimneys are still visible in the basement. The second building phase saw the addition on the west of a two-and-one-half-story, three-bay frame section. This wing, which contains the entrance–stair hall and parlor, has undergone little alteration, and still contains its late Federal style interior. Activity continued a generation later when an addition was made to the brick section, and its height was raised to a full two stories. Around 1920 a two-story portico was added on the west of the frame section, and a large kitchen was added to the east. Eventually the second story of the portico was enclosed and the first story screened in. Recently a room has been added to the north of the kitchen. To the north of the house is a small meat house covered with vertical siding.

T–321
317 Morris Street
Oxford
Late nineteenth century; Private

For such a small town, Oxford possesses a large number of Second Empire style buildings: Sandaway (T–317), the Robert Morris Inn (T–249), and this house on Morris Street, whose tall mansard roof, punctuated by gable-roofed dormers, and chimneys, is particularly dramatic.

T–322
ALMSHOUSE (site)
Near Oxford
Private

The Talbot County Almshouse was located on the road between Hole-in-the-Wall (T–138) and Trappe Station at the head of Island Creek. Old photographs show a substantial brick structure with two large frame wings. The corbeled brick cornice suggests a construction date in the 1820s, but that detail may have been the result of the remodeling of an earlier structure. It stood well into the third quarter of this century, when it was razed and its bricks salvaged for use in other buildings.

T–323
PEACHBLOSSOM (site)
Near Easton
Private

Patented in 1669, Peachblossom was, in the late seventeenth and early eighteenth centuries, the seat of the powerful Robins family. In the late eighteenth century it was the residence of Henry Nichols, Sr., a prominent figure in Talbot County politics. Nothing of the structure remains, but a pencil sketch at Myrtle Grove (T–53) records its appearance. The late H. Robins Hollyday often commented that the house had a porte-cochere—a canopy of some sort built

T-321

T-322

T-323

T-324

over the courtyard so that carriages could drive in and let guests disembark or embark without being exposed to the weather. The ancient Robins and Goldsborough tombstones at Peachblossom were removed and placed in the graveyard at Ashby (T–174).

T–324
MIDDLEVILLE TENANT HOUSE
Trappe
Circa 1820; with additions; Private

The Middleville Tenant House (see T–312) is a simple dwelling of the first quarter of the nineteenth century. The house began as a typical Federal period, two-story, three-bay frame structure and was enlarged by a two-story, one-bay addition and two shed additions. The single-bay addition, although it has the same roof line, is easily distinguished from the main house by its smaller and lower windows.

T–325
PILGRIM HOLINESS CHURCH
Oxford
Late nineteenth century; Private

This church, located at the entrance to Oxford, exhibits several elements of the stick style, particularly in the decoration of the entrance and steeple. It has a T plan and, unlike most churches, the entrance is located between the transepts at the top of

the nave where the chancel is normally found. The entrance is treated in an elaborate fashion, with a gable-roofed vestibule surmounted by an ornate pinnacle, behind which rise a gable with rose window and a pyramidal steeple. It served as the Methodist church in Oxford until 1948, when it became the Pilgrim Holiness Church.

T–326
WATERLOO (site)
Near Easton
Private

Waterloo, named by a political enemy of the Bonapartist Jacob Gibson (see T–96; T–163), was a three-story, five-bay Italianate farmhouse, which, even before it was burned by developers in 1978, had lost many of its distinguishing exterior features. Above the central bay was a projecting gable, which, along with the canopy on the second story, suggested a tower and lent a ceremonial aspect to the entrance. The interior, unlike the exterior, retained many of its original details, including fine mid-nineteenth-century mantels, stair, and ceiling.

T–327
WILLIAMSBURG FARMHOUSE (site)
Williamsburg
Circa 1800; Private

The Williamsburg Farmhouse, located at the upper reaches of Trippe's Creek, was a good example of a simple vernacular dwelling of the late eighteenth or early nineteenth century. It was composed of a one-and-one-half-story, four-bay main section with a one-story, three-bay wing, both of which were covered with shingles. The house was razed in 1982, but the (former) main section's stone- and brick-walled cellar, only four-and-one-half feet deep, still remains.

T–328
ENNISKILLEN (Marshy Point)
Near Easton
Circa 1825; with additions; Private

Enniskillen, named after the principal town of County Fermanagh in Ulster, is a large frame dwelling composed of a two-and-one-half-story, three-bay vernacular structure with two modern wings. The main house is raised on a brick cellar with one original wood window grill and is covered with beaded weatherboard applied with cut nails. Three gable-roofed dormers project from the slope of the gable roof above the facade, and exterior chimneys, now enclosed by the wings, rise against the gable ends. In the

T-325

T-326

T-327

T-328

T-329

late nineteenth century the exterior underwent some alteration, with the addition of pilasters and a wide fascia. In the 1930s a Georgian style entrance was installed, with a recessed door framed by fluted pilasters carrying a broken-apex pediment. The interior is divided into a central hall with flanking rooms. The detail is simple and appears to date from around 1830. On the grounds there is a fine brick smokehouse with a corbeled cornice and gable roof.

T–329
ROCK CLIFT (High Banks)
Near Matthews
Circa 1785; with additions; Private;
National Register

Despite the establishment of the High Banks subdivision, the house on Rock Clift farm retains its bucolic setting thanks to a field that separates it from the development. It is an important vernacular structure in that it possesses much of its early fabric. During the eighteenth century, Rock Clift was the plantation of the Needles family, several of whom were prominent Quakers. The house is composed of a two-and-one-half-story, three-bay brick section with a two-story, four-bay frame wing built in two sections. The brick is laid in Flemish bond on the principal facade and in common bond on the other elevations. The main entrance is

flanked by two windows, but it is off center in contrast to the symmetrical arrangement of the second story. A three-brick beltcourse runs between the two main stories. Two dormers project from the slope of the gable roof above the facade, and partly exposed chimneys rise above the gable ends. The interior of both sections has a two-room plan, but that of the brick section is more elaborately finished: the living room has a fine mantel with crossetted trim, consoles, and dentiled molding, and the dining room has a wall of raised paneling and cupboards across the fireplace wall and paneled wainscoting. The easternmore room in the frame section boasts beaded board paneling on three walls, and a wooden door hinge.

T–330
LONDONDERRY
Easton
1860s; Private

To the east of Easton Point on the south bank of the Tred Avon River is Londonderry, a Gothic revival house built of Port Deposit granite (see T–16; T–239). Its design is attributed to Richard Upjohn, the prominent architect who also designed Christ Church Rectory (T–16) and the Trippe-Beale House (T–45). The facade has a projecting, polygonal two-story entrance bay framed by a window on each story on

the west and one window between stories on the east. This extension, as well as the main block, is covered by a low gable roof with deep eaves. These roofs were installed after a fire destroyed the third floor in the 1960s. The conflagration also consumed the porches, which were replaced by the plain ones seen today. An indication of the original, highly elaborate, exterior detail that once decorated the house is provided by the hyphen and wing, both of which escaped damage. The hyphen has a steep gable roof with a highly ornate cross gable and cornice. This cornice continues around the wing, which is surmounted by a slate mansard roof. This in turn is topped by a finial.

T–331
PICKWICK
St. Michaels
Circa 1835; circa 1865; Private

Pickwick, located at Little Neck Creek, a small tributary of the Miles River, is composed of a one-and-one-half-story, five-bay vernacular structure with a lean-to shed and frame kitchen to the north and a two-and-one-half-story, three-bay wing to the west. The interior detail in the long section dates to the second quarter of the nineteenth century; the wing appears to be from the third quarter of that century. The early section is raised on a brick foundation and covered

T-330

T-331

T-332

with plain weatherboard. It has a central entrance shaded by a porch with a steeply pitched gable roof. Originally there were chimneys at both gable ends, but the east end's chimney disappeared. On the rear is the lean-to shed, and beyond this is the frame kitchen. Because of its size, the wing is now the principal part of the dwelling. It is covered with weatherboard like the early section and has a bracketed cornice. Outbuildings from the first period of house construction include a slave quarters and a dairy.

T–332
DOUBLE MILLS
Near Royal Oak
Circa 1800; with additions; Private

Now large and late Victorian in appearance, Double Mills began as an early one-story frame house. It had a hall-and-parlor plan with exterior chimneys on the gable ends. In the late nineteenth century the house was raised by two stories, and a two-story wing was added on the west. This wing has a gable roof perpendicular to that of the main house, but a cross gable carries through the line of the original roof. In the second quarter of the twentieth century a balanced composition was achieved through the addition of a wing on the east. At this time the original east chimney was removed.

The roof of the east wing, like that on the west, runs perpendicular to the roof of the main house, but instead of a cross gable an exterior chimney rises along its east elevation. The house, now covered with modern siding, was once entirely sheathed in the decorative rectangular shingles that today are seen on the gables. The property still has an old wharf, originally a landing for steamboats traveling between Baltimore and the Eastern Shore.

T–333
FERRY NECK CHAPEL
Royal Oak
1856; Private

Recently converted into a private residence, this small frame chapel is raised on a brick foundation and covered with weatherboard. Exterior detail, as on many Eastern Shore chapels, is restricted to the entrance facade, which carries Greek revival elements. The entrance itself is composed of paneled double doors enclosed in a frame of pilasters carrying a full entablature of architrave, frieze, and cornice. The pilastered corners and cornice returns suggest pedimented gable(s). In the center of the gable directly above the entrance and double window is a sign with the date of the building: Anno Domini 1856. The interior, besides containing the main room for the congregation,

had a vestibule, closet, and slave gallery (now a bedroom). The most outstanding feature of the interior is the arched ceiling; now covered with wallboard, the ceiling is still painted with original colors that range from light blue, rose, and lavender to tan and gold.

T–334
SHERWOOD FOREST
St. Michaels
Circa 1810; circa 1865; Private

Sherwood Forest is a two-and-one-half-story, five-bay frame structure with a two-and-one-half-story frame kitchen wing. Although in some respects it appears to be a single antebellum composition, tradition maintains that it is a product of two periods, and there is evidence to corroborate this view; the interior, with the exception of the living room, which is finished with detail characteristic of the 1860s, has Federal-style woodwork. The main facade has a central entrance with a transom and sidelights. Across three bays, (the entrance, and two bays on the east) runs a two-story porch with a highly rhythmic second-story balustrade composed of overlapping segmental-arched balusters. The two bays on the west are located in a Greek revival pavilion the depth of the porch. The pavilion has corner pilasters with a full entablature, which continues

T-333

T-334

T-335

T-336

across the gable, forming a pediment. On the grounds is a fine Victorian ice house. It is of square plan with a gable-roofed entrance. The main section is topped by a pyramidal roof, which rises to a large louvered cupola surmounted by a tall finial.

T–335
LONG POINT (Elston)
Neavitt
Circa 1720; with additions; Private

Built by the Ball family, prominent Quakers, Long Point is an early-eighteenth-century gambrel-roofed dwelling similar in form to Troth's Fortune (T–50) and in detail to Orem's Delight (T–193). The original section is one-and-one-half-stories tall and three bays wide with a central entrance. The entrance facade is laid in Flemish bond with glazed headers; the rear elevation is English bond. On the exposed gable end are interlocking diamonds of glazed headers and chevrons along the rake of the roof. Two dormers pierce each side of the roof, and chimneys rise within the ends. In the crawl space under the house, ruins of the brick foundation of a still-earlier house are visible. A series of modern additions extends to the southwest.

T–336
BOLTON
Near Sherwood
Early nineteenth century; Private

Today Bolton, formerly the home of the Kemp and Dawson families, is a two-and-one-half-story, three-bay brick dwelling with a one-story, one-bay brick wing, but originally there were two two-story telescoping wings. The house is laid in Flemish bond on the main facade and in common bond on the other elevations. There are widely splayed jack arches above all the openings and an entrance on each facade. A corbeled cornice runs along the roof line, and two dormers pierce each slope of the gable roof. Above the south gable end rises a double chimney connected by an access way to the roof. The outline of a two-story porch can still be seen on the east facade. Although the interior has undergone alteration, original woodwork remains on the upper stories. Today Bolton serves as a residence and office.

T–337
GOWE-BROOKS HOUSE
Sherwood
Late eighteenth century; twentieth century; Private

The Gowe-Brooks House retains some details from the eighteenth century—raised

paneling in the main rooms on the first floor and an enclosed stair in the southwest corner of the house—but its appearance today is the result of a remodeling carried out in the 1930s. The cornice and roof line of the original dwelling can still be seen on the principal facade and exposed gable end respectively.

T–338
FAUSLEY (site)
Near Easton
Private

Although nothing above grade remains, this site is noteworthy as the birthplace of Tench Tilghman, aide-de-camp to General Washington during the Revolution. The federal direct tax of 1798 describes Fausley as a "one story brick dwelling 55 by 22 with two adjoining brick kitchens 22 by 19 and 22 by 17." Also listed were a brick study, wood smokehouse, and brick slave quarters. No photograph is available.

T–339
THE REST (site)
Easton
Private

In the nineteenth century, the home of the Confederate admiral Franklin Buchanan and his wife, Ann, the third daughter of Governor Edward Lloyd, was located on these

T-337

T-340

T-341

grounds. Buchanan sailed on the *Constellation*, was the first superintendent of the Naval Academy, served with Perry in the Mexican War and in the Orient, and eventually commanded the *Virginia (Merrimac)* in the Civil War. In this century The Rest was owned by Charles T. Owens. Commander Owens supervised the construction of the Panama Canal and served in the Atlantic theater in World War II. No photograph is available.

T–340
PICKBOURN OUTBUILDINGS
Tunis Mills
Nineteenth century; Private

Agriculture has underpinned the economy of Talbot County for three centuries. The importance of this way of life has sometimes manifested itself in grand manors, but, more frequently, it can be seen in small-scale farms with their modest collections of outbuildings. At Pickbourn there is a fine example of such a collection, composed of a board-and-batten smokehouse, a 15-foot square, one-story slave quarters, a dairy, and a tenant house. Of these, the two-story frame tenant house is probably the most noteworthy: its central gable, scalloped trim on the eaves, delicate porch brackets, and large banded chimney combine to create an excellent example of a Victorian Gothic cottage.

T-342

T–341
LONGWOODS STORE
Longwoods
Late nineteenth century; Private

The Longwoods Store represents a type of building that was very common in the towns and villages of the Eastern Shore until the advent of mass-marketing and chain stores. It is a two-story, three-bay structure with a one-story, one-bay lean-to affixed to the south and an addition on the north. The exterior is finished in German siding, and a gable roof tops the building. The main facade has a central entrance with double doors and a one-story, three-bay porch with a hip roof. Architecturally the Longwoods Store is similar to the Woolford Store and Post Office (D–233) in Dorchester County.

T–342
SCHOFIELD HOUSE
St. Michaels
Circa 1730; with additions; Private

Schofield House was built in the early style of Tidewater Maryland architecture. Its form, two-room plan, and frame construction are characteristic of early-eighteenth-century building, and the interior woodwork corroborates the attribution of such an early date. The original house, now obscured on three sides by twentieth-century wings, is the one-and-one-half-story,

T-343

three-bay structure in the center. It is covered in clapboard and has a central entrance. Two dormers project from each slope of the gable roof, and wide interior chimneys rise above the gable ends. The interior has paneled end walls, corner stairs, and original hardware. The room on the south has ovolo moldings on its panel and mantel, a molded shelf, paneled overmantel, and a molded chair rail. The north room has a paneled cupboard, and a dog-eared ovolo-molded mantel with a cove shelf. The upper story has small fireplaces with shelves and painted designs.

T–343
RIVERSLIE
Easton
Circa 1870; with additions; Private

Riverslie, a two-story, three-bay frame house with a modern two-story wing, is situated on Hunting Creek with a view towards the Miles River. A precursor of the prefabricated house of today, Riverslie's parts were formed elsewhere and then assembled on site. The house is built on a granite foundation, covered with aluminum siding, and surmounted by a hip roof. Its front facade has a central entrance shaded by a porch.

T-344

T-346

T–344
SNUG HARBOR
Easton
1920; Private

In 1920 Charles E. Humphreys built the nucleus of this colonial revival frame house on the site of a house that had burned. It is composed of a two-story, three-bay main section with wings extending from the gable ends. The facade has a central entrance framed by an elliptical fanlight and sidelights and sheltered by a delicately executed porch made up of columns supporting a pedimented entablature. The broken pediment and tympanum echo the door's elliptical fanlight. The windows have molded frames and paneled shutters on the first story and louvered shutters on the second. Three dormers project from each slope of the slate-covered gable roof; chimneys rise within the gable ends. The east wing is perpendicular to the main house and presents a gable end fitted with pilasters and a pediment as the facade. A two-story pedimented portico with a second story Chinese trellis balustrade extends from the south elevation of the wing.

T–346
WILLIAM C. KNIGHT HOUSE
Easton
Early nineteenth century; Private

Located at the head of navigation on the Tred Avon River, Easton Point was marked by many vernacular structures connected with its mercantile activities well into the twentieth century. With the coming of heavy industry most of these dwellings and small businesses were displaced by oil and concrete companies. The William C. Knight House, however, stands as a reminder of Easton Point's early years. Tradition assigns 1779 as the date of construction, but all available evidence points to the early nineteenth century. The house is a one-and-one-half-story, three-bay frame and brick structure raised on a brick foundation. Except for part of the east gable end, the structure is covered with aluminum siding. The front facade has a central entrance, and its first story is shaded by a lean-to porch. A single dormer projects from the slope of the gable roof above, and a chimney rises within the east gable end. The interior has undergone some alteration, but two handsome Federal-style mantels, some door and window trim, and a stair in the northwest corner of the north room remain. To the northeast stood Tilghman's Fortune (T–247) before it was relocated by the Talbot County Chamber of Commerce.

T–347
PRATT-HOFFMAN HOUSE
Easton
Early nineteenth century; Private

The Pratt-Hoffman House is a two-story, three-bay structure covered with wood shingles. The street facade has a side entrance with its original six-panel door and Federal style transom. The second story's three windows retain their original nine-over-six sashes, and above these runs a cornice with crown-and-bed molding. The interior still has much of its Federal-style detail: the living room mantel has herringbone pilasters raised on plinths, the cupboard next to the fireplace is equipped with recessed-panel doors, and a three-part chair rail encircles the entire room.

T–348
BELLEVILLE CEMETERY
Easton
Eighteenth and nineteenth centuries; Private

The Belleville Cemetery contains several interesting monuments erected to the memory of members of the Bozman and Kerr families. One such reads:

Col. Thomas Bozman of Talbot County son of John Bozman and Grandson of William Bozman the last named among

T-347

T-348

T-350

T-353

the early Protestant settlers on the Chesapeake in 1629. He marked out this place for his family.

T-350
DOLVIN
Wye Mills
Early nineteenth century; 1884; Private

Dolvin began as an early-nineteenth-century, vernacular brick dwelling, but today that structure forms only part of a much-enlarged house. This early house can still be distinguished as the two-and-one-half-story, three-bay section to the northwest. It has a side entrance and a one-story, three-bay porch across its main facade. In 1884 a two-and-one-half-story wing was added on the southeast, perpendicular to the early house and extending beyond it on both the northeast and southwest. A two-story polygonal bay with ornate brackets supporting cornices on both stories projects from the facade. The gable above is elaborately treated with diagonal boards and heavily carved triangular panels. From this wing extends a brick kitchen and service wing, also built in the late nineteenth century. At the time of this construction the main facade of the early house was refaced; this work was probably done not only to add some Victorian sophistication to the early structure but also to unify the composition.

Many generations of the Rathell family occupied this farmhouse.

T-353
ST. PAUL'S METHODIST EPISCOPAL CHURCH
Cordova
Late nineteenth century; Private

St. Paul's Methodist Episcopal Church is a typical, late-nineteenth-century church structure built in the Gothic revival style. It is supported by a brick foundation and covered with asbestos siding. The elevations and entrance tower have Gothic-arched windows, as does the double-door entrance. The tower also has a round window and is topped by a hip roof truncated to accommodate a belfry. The belfry has two lancet arches on each side, a balustrade, and a pyramidal roof topped by a finial.

T-354
ST. PAUL'S ON THE HILL
Cordova
1901; Private

St. Paul's on the Hill is one of the many small, attractive, rural churches that decorate the Talbot County countryside. Like St. Paul's Methodist Episcopal Church (T-353), it is a product of the Gothic revival style, and the churches bear a strong resemblance to each other. The elevations

have Gothic-arched windows, as does the entrance in the partly engaged tower. The tower has a belfry crowned with a cross.

T-355
LEE HAVEN QUARTERS
Easton
Mid-nineteenth century; Private

This outbuilding is a small two-story structure, approximately 16 feet deep, raised on a brick foundation. Its walls are covered with vertical boards and battens and are punctuated by several six-panel casement windows. From the center of the gable roof rises a chimney with a corbeled cap. The interior has been remodeled with a narrow board floor, a sheetrock ceiling, and an enclosure around the stair. Although the building has only one room on the first story, the fireplace, which opens to the east, indicates that there were originally two rooms. The second story is divided into two rooms by roughly sawn boards at the head of the steep stair.

T-356
HOPKINS HOUSE (Bronson House)
Wye Mills
1881; Private

The Hopkins House is a two-story frame dwelling with a T-plan, German siding, and Victorian details. On the southwest is a

T-354

T-355

T-356

three-bay section with a side entrance adjacent to the northeast part. The entrance is fitted with a transom and sidelights, and the window bays are surmounted by pediment-shaped lintels. There is a very steeply pitched gable above the central bay with a round-arched window and jigsaw work at the apex. The perpendicular northeast wing presents its southeast gable end as the facade. A two-story bay window projects from this elevation; the window is polygonal on the first story and rectangular on the second. Each window's upper sash is fitted with colored glass.

T–357
CROWE POINT
Easton
Circa 1829; twentieth century; Private
Crowe Point is located near Easton on the Choptank River. The frame house is composed of an early-nineteenth-century dwelling with twentieth-century additions on its gable ends and rear elevation. The exterior of the early section has been remodeled and covered with wood shingles. It has a central entrance with two dormers above and exterior chimneys at the gable ends. There is a large ventilator, seemingly more appropriate for outbuildings, in the center of the gable roof; it was presumably added as a decorative element at a much later date. The

interior contains many original details, including the enclosed stair, beaded baseboards, a two-piece chair rail, and two mantels, one of which is trimmed with pilasters.

T–358
MT. PLEASANT
St. Michaels
Late eighteenth century; with additions; Private
Mt. Pleasant is a two-story brick house believed to have been built by William Harrison in 1791. It has been enlarged several times. There are new wings on the gable ends, and the main facade has a projecting, two-story, gable-roofed entrance bay. The Greek revival entrance is framed by columns and topped by pedimented entablature. All this adds refinement to an otherwise simple dwelling.

T–359
PLUGGE FARM
Cordova
Circa 1785; with additions; Private
The house on Plugge Farm is a late-eighteenth-century, two-story, three-bay brick structure similar to Hassett Farm and Clay's Hope (T–189) in form and fenestration. The entrance is located in the center bay of the principal facade and is shaded by

T-357

a one-bay, gable-roofed porch. The walls are laid in Flemish bond above the stepped water table and English-bond foundation. A three-brick belt course runs across the three exposed elevations. In the nineteenth century a two-story frame wing was appended to the east gable end.

T–360
BLESSLAND
Easton
Circa 1750; circa 1777; Private
Blessland, built for Joseph Darden, is a two-part dwelling nestled in the lowlands along the Choptank River. The one-and-one-half-story, three-bay brick section dates from the mid-eighteenth century and has a cooking fireplace in the basement. The east facade, which has a central entrance, is laid in Flemish bond with glazed headers; the other elevations are laid in English bond. The west facade is similar to the east, but its entrance is offset to the south and is shaded by a porch. A dormer projects from each slope of the gable roof, and two chimneys rise within the north gable end. From the south gable end extends a one-and-one-half-story, two-bay brick wing of the late eighteenth century. It is laid in Flemish bond on the west facade and has gauged jack arches above the windows and doors. A single

T-358

T-359

T-360

T-361

dormer pierces the west slope of the gable roof, and a central chimney rises from the apex. A lean-to addition conceals the east facade.

T–361
MAPLE HALL
Claiborne

Late nineteenth century; Private

Resort hotels were once a conspicuous feature not only in Talbot County but throughout rural Victorian America. Maple Hall, now a private residence, is one of Talbot County's few remaining buildings of this type (see also T–213 and T–368). The central rooms make up the original house, which was expanded in all directions in several stages, ending in 1927. These additions include two-and-one-half-story gambrel-roofed wings on three elevations and a one-and-one-half-story gambrel-roofed service wing to the rear. The interior has dining and socializing rooms on the first floor and thirty bedrooms on the second.

T–362
WAKEFIELD
Easton

1786; with additions; Private

Wakefield, an early Bartlett property, is composed of a late-eighteenth-century brick section and brick kitchen wing to the north

T-362

with a larger Victorian frame addition to the south. The early, two-story, two-bay house has a side entrance in the north bay of the west facade, which is shaded by a one-story, three-bay, hip-roofed porch. The kitchen's attic is lit by a gable window, and a chimney rises from the north gable end; a brick in the kitchen is dated 1786. The gable-roofed frame addition is perpendicular to the early sections and has an entrance and porch on the south. Early interior details in the early house include a fine mantel with cyma-recta and cavetto moldings and an open stair framed in simple beaded boards with one baluster per step.

T–363
ITALIANATED-ON-THE-BAY
Wittman

Eighteenth century; mid-nineteenth century; Private

Many serviceable but plain eighteenth-century buildings were given face-lifts during the nineteenth century by the addition of Greek revival or Italianate decorative features. This is an example of such a house. In fact, all that remains of the eighteenth-century structure is a brick cellar and four partly stuccoed and plastered walls on the first and second stories. In the mid-nineteenth century the old house was raised to two-and-one-half stories, and a gable roof

T-363

with deep bracketed eaves was added to give the building its present appearance. Within, the rooms were rearranged into a side-hall-and-parlor plan, and the floor levels were altered. At one time additions extended from the south and west elevations, and a hipped-roof porch shaded the east elevation. Today the house is in ruins.

T–364
HATTON FARM
McDaniel

Circa 1810; Private

This one-and-one-half story, three-bay structure was originally the service wing of a late-Federal farmhouse that was torn down in the late 1960s. It has an off-center entrance with flanking windows. The gable roof is pierced by a dormer and by an interior chimney. There are back-to-back fireplaces, a boxed stair, and simple moldings in the two-room interior of the house and an early barn (constructed with large, roughly chamfered posts) on the grounds.

T–365
JONES HOUSE
Tilghman

Mid-eighteenth century; Private

The Jones House was moved to this site from Virginia during the 1970s. It is a good vernacular dwelling of the mid-eighteenth

T-364

century, and its resemblance to other similar structures of the same period illustrates the architectural unity of the Bay area. The house is one-and-one-half stories tall and three bays wide with a modern one-story porch on the north and a one-story, two-bay frame wing on the west. The long facades are finished in weatherboard and have central entrances. Three dormers project from each slope of the gable roof, and partly exposed chimneys rise from the exposed-brick gable ends. The interior has retained much of its original detail.

T–366
TILGHMAN ISLAND VICTORIAN HOUSE
Tilghman Island
Late nineteenth century; Private

This is a late-nineteenth-century structure whose peculiar design resembles some other, unsurveyed, houses elsewhere on the island. The form follows an L-plan with two equal gable-roofed sections placed perpendicular to each other. From their intersection projects a three-sided entrance bay. The first story accommodates a central entrance framed by a transom and sidelights and flanked by windows in the side bays. The arch in the gable's window echoes the lines of the apex of the roof above. There is a three-sided, one-

story porch with ornate brackets and posts on the main facade between the wings.

T–367
ROYAL OAK CHURCH
Royal Oak
Circa 1875; Private

According to local tradition this church was built by Southern-sympathizing Methodists after the Civil War. It is a frame structure with corner pilasters. The walls have Gothic-arched windows of opalescent glass; the north gable end has an engaged entrance tower. The entrance has double doors with a transom and sidelights framed by pilasters and an entablature. Above this are two rectangular windows of colored glass set below a dentiled cornice. The interior consists of one large room with a vestibule in the tower. Elaborately patterned pressed tin covers the ceilings of the main room; the wainscoting in both rooms is of the same material pressed into lancet arches. Originally both rooms were plastered, and the ceiling of the main room was painted with a floral design.

T–368
PASADENA INN
Royal Oak
Late nineteenth century; Private

Pasadena Inn, like Maple Hall (T–361), is a late-nineteenth-century resort hotel, but, unlike Maple Hall, it is still in operation. According to the owners, an earlier frame structure exists within the building but is concealed by the various alterations and additions made in the early twentieth century. The three-and-one-half-story, two-bay gable end on the west serves as the entrance facade, a use emphasized by a two-story Doric portico with double columns at the front corners supporting a pedimented entablature. The central entrance has a small columned porch, and the doorway is framed by a transom and sidelights. The many porches and red trim provide an open and cheerful atmosphere appropriate to vacationing.

T–369
LOWE'S FARM
Kirkham
Circa 1800; Private

Now undergoing restoration, this early-nineteenth-century frame cottage is one of the smallest and latest examples of the hall-and-parlor plan in the area. The one-and-one-half-story, three-bay house has been

T-366

T-367

T-368

T-369

T-371

stabilized by a new concrete-block foundation and sheltered by a new roof. There is a central entrance surmounted by a transom. Two dormers project from each slope of the gable roof, and chimneys rise within the gable ends. The interior retains original features. Each mantel is finished with cavetto-astragal and small cyma-recta moldings and reeded pilasters. A cupboard with glass doors is set in the northwest corner alongside the chimney, and in the northeast corner a boxed winder stair ascends to the second floor.

T-371
DULIN HOUSE (site)
Cordova
Mid-nineteenth century

In the 1970s this small nineteenth-century farmhouse was stripped and burned. Originally it consisted of a two-story, two-bay section with a one-and-one-half-story, two-bay wing on the north. Eventually a shed was added to the north gable end of the wing to cover the large, pyramidal brick pile of the kitchen fireplace.

T-372
HADDAWAY'S FERRY
St. Michaels vicinity
Circa 1820; Private

This one-and-one-half-story farmhouse has recently been restored to its original appearance through the removal of late-nineteenth-century accretions. The roof lines of still earlier structures can be discerned in the gable ends of the present restored house. Investigations have shown that this first house was composed of two wings joined by a hyphen. The hyphen and the foundations of the wings are almost completely encased in today's house. No photograph is available.

T-373
LANCASHIRE
St. Michaels vicinity
Circa 1783; circa 1920; Private

Lancashire was probably built by William Haddaway circa 1783 on land patented to his great-grandfather in 1678. The property has never been sold out of the family, now in the tenth generation of ownership. The old section of the house is a one-and-one-half-story structure of brick laid in Flemish bond on the two primary facades and common bond on the gable ends. It has yellow pine flooring and some original eighteenth-century paneling in the parlor. The 1798

federal tax assessment describes the house as having an attached log kitchen. The present frame section of the house was added in the twentieth century. Near the house are a frame dairy built in the second quarter of the nineteenth century and an ancient family burial ground. Lancashire is the setting for many of the stories related in General Joseph B. Seth's *Recollections*; General Seth was born and raised on this farm.

T-374
TANYARD
Trappe vicinity
Circa 1810; Private

Tanyard, probably built by Charles Bowdle, consists of a two-story brick section, and two frame additions that form a telescope design. The brick section's symmetrical approach side is laid in Flemish bond and has the unusual feature of two six-panel front doors. The east wall has random glazed headers, but none of the walls has a water table or beltcourse. The central and west frame sections have undergone great remodeling, but an early photograph shows a one-and-one-half-story frame kitchen wing connected to the brick section by a small one-and-one-half-story hyphen. At one time tan was made from bark on this property.

T-373

T-374

T-375

T-377

T-376

T–375
HOLLY HOUSE (Belleville)
Easton vicinity
Circa 1840; Private

Holly House, a two-story frame columned structure, was built as a modest late Greek revival farmhouse circa 1840 and was later enlarged. The frame house's interior features original refined Greek revival doors and mantels in well-proportioned large rooms with high ceilings.

T–376
LITTLE OTWELL
Oxford vicinity
Circa 1840; with additions; Private

Little Otwell consists of an almost square two-story central section of brick laid in common bond, flanked by two twentieth-century brick wings. The central section, which has original flooring and several Greek revival doors, was constructed by George Washington Melson, who is buried near the house.

T–377
EAST BONFIELD
Oxford vicinity
1852; Private

East Bonfield is a telescope house built for James H. Willis in 1852, consisting of a two-and-one-half-story five-bay frame sec-

tion, a smaller two-and-one-half-story frame wing, and a new one-story kitchen wing. The interior has an early Victorian staircase and original floors, doors, trim, and mantels. East Bonfield still belongs to descendants of its builder.

T–378
DEFENDER HOUSE
Trappe vicinity
Circa 1815; Private

This recently restored frame one-and-one-half-story building was probably originally the home of an early nineteenth-century artisan. The original interior consists of one large room on the first floor and a sleeping loft on the second story, each with fireplace. The original flooring and staircase survive. A shed kitchen has been added at the structure's west end. Today the building houses a hand-stenciling and design business.

T–379
ISLE-OF-RAYS
Trappe vicinity
Circa 1835; Private

Also called "Caulk Farm," the present-day structure known as Isle-of-Rays is a handsome two-and-one-half-story brick residence with a two-story service wing built by Joseph Caulk circa 1835. The brick is laid in 3-1

common bond on the south (approach) facade and 5-1 common bond on the other facades. The interior of the house is well preserved with original pine flooring, doors, mantels, trim, and staircase intact. The interior architectural features are well crafted in a simple Greek revival style. The exterior design remains Federal, however, with five bays: the front door is flanked by two windows on either side on the first story, there are five windows on the second story, and two balanced dormer windows on the third story. Several period barns and other outbuildings still survive, as does the tombstone marking Joseph Caulk's grave near the creek bank.

Isle-of-Rays is important as illustrating top quality craftsmanship in a house that is a fine late representation of the transition from the long-favored Federal style of architecture to the later prevailing Greek revival style.

T–380
BEARFIELDS
Oxford vicinity
Circa 1794, circa 1820; Private

Bearfields, a one-and-one-half-story frame house with a gambrel roof, beaded clapboard siding, and a flush chimney, to which was added a frame kitchen wing with a gable roof, was moved to its present location in

T-378

T-379

T-380

T-400

1976 from its original location in northern Queen Anne's County. The present dining room is the oldest section of the house, built in 1794 by George Primrose, and boasts a vertical beaded board paneled wall and a handsome mantel with reverse dog-ear molding. The stair hall and parlor were added circa 1820, as was the kitchen wing. Other noteworthy features include a number of period six-panel doors with large carpenter locks, and the original staircase.

T–400
CORKRAN-PONEY HOUSE
113 South Hanson Street, Easton
Circa 1810; with additions; Private

A late-Federal, two-and-one-half-story, three-bay structure, the Corkran-Poney House is laid in Flemish bond on the street facade and in common bond on the other elevations. The main entrance, equipped with a transom and shaded by a gable-roofed porch, is located in the south bay; the windows on this elevation have gauged brick jack arches and modern paneled shutters. Two dormers, which appear to have been rebuilt, project above the facade, and a chimney rises above the north gable end. Much of the interior detail is intact, including chair rails, window trim, and a second-floor mantel with paneled pilasters. There is a two-story, two-bay mid-

nineteenth-century shingled frame addition to the west. In the second and third quarters of the twentieth century the house was the residence of Theodore and Gertrude Poney; Mrs. Poney was a popular and respected caterer in Easton for many years.

T-401
MATTHEWS YOUNG CO-ED STORE
2 North Washington Street, Easton
Circa 1880; Private

The earliest building known to have stood on this site was the office of Dr. Theodore Denny. It was a two-and-one-half-story, two-bay brick structure that may be the building pictured in photographs taken before the fire of 1878. (In any event, it was not consumed in the conflagration, but was torn down afterwards). The present three-story structure, once called the Daylight Building, and its neighbor, 4 North Washington Street (T–402), are examples of the type of brick commercial building constructed in the decade after that conflagration and illustrate the movement toward taller, more asymmetrical structures which characterizes late-nineteenth-century architecture. For example, while these buildings still retain the flat, boxlike form of their Federal-style neighbors, they have lost the gable roof. Instead, the roofs slope gently to the rear, and delicate, pierced work

cornices supported by brackets form a strong horizontal silhouette against the sky. Both buildings are laid in common bond with narrow mortar joints. The bricks are smooth, dark orange machine-made blocks similar to those used in the construction of the Tred Avon Building (T–2). Little remains of the late-nineteenth-century interior of this building, but a simple marble mantel on the second floor may be original and may indicate that the room served as a parlor.

T–402
4 North Washington Street, Easton
Circa 1880; Private

Like its neighbor (T–401), this building replaced an earlier structure that was razed after the fire of 1878 although it was not a victim of the blaze. It is likely that the owners of both buildings were inspired by the general construction boom and were attracted by the variety of available architectural styles at that time. This building is two stories tall and four bays wide with a modern ground-floor storefront. The chief decorative feature is the elaborate cornice with pierced decoration: supported by large brackets carved to simulate the triglyphs of a frieze, the cornice has a series of panels with a fan motif. Both buildings, although products of the late nineteenth century, blend in well with their earlier Federal-style neigh-

T-401

T-402

T-403

T-404

bors and enhance the Washington Street skyline.

T-403

10 North Washington Street, Easton
Late eighteenth century; with additions; Private

This two-and-one-half-story, three-bay Flemish-bond brick house and store is a typical row building of the middle of the Federal period, erected in response to the growth of commercial activity after the courthouse was established in Easton. Although today it is fitted with a modern storefront, the street facade may have originally accommodated an elegant entrance with a fanlight similar to that on the Perrin Smith House (T-24). The original box cornice with crown-and-bed moldings is still intact on the rear, but the cornice on the main facade is a replacement put on when the building was joined to its neighbor, 8 North Washington Street (T-36). The two dormers above the facade have been stripped of some original detail, including round-arched upper sashes and pilaster capitals, but their former refinement is suggested by the reeded pilasters and crown moldings. Double chimneys joined by a brick curtain on the south gable wall were later demolished. There is much original detail inside despite several alterations. The open-string stair has

slender, turned balusters and newels with square bases and molded tops. There are parts of a delicately executed chair rail on the third floor.

T-404
SHANNAHAN AND WRIGHTSON BUILDING

12 North Washington Street, Easton
Circa 1800; 1877; 1881; 1889; Private

The basement arches supporting the fireplace and the Flemish bond on the first story of the main facade provide ample architectural evidence that part of the Shannahan and Wrightson Building dates to the middle of the Federal period. There is much documentary evidence to corroborate this: the venerable Shannahan and Wrightson Hardware Company was once Easton's best-known commercial establishment. As it stands today, however, the building is a product of the late nineteenth century. Its upper levels were added in three stages from 1877 to 1889, as the dated blocks on each story indicate, and from the completeness of the design it appears that the work was carried out by the same hand. The cornice has dentils and end brackets, and above it rests a signboard typical of the late nineteenth century, but unique in Easton.

T-405; T-406

16 and 18 North Washington Street, Easton
Circa 1900; Private

These two buildings are late-Victorian structures typical of the commercial construction in Easton around the turn of the century. Each has a storefront with an elaborate pressed-tin cornice on the first floor. The brick is laid in all-stretcher bond save three English-bond pilasters. These pilasters have recessed panels and three marble bands, the lowest of which corresponds to a beltcourse of the same material. There are segmental arches of long, narrow Roman bricks above the windows; there is a series of recessed panels with a chain motif in the pilasters at the intersection of the sash. A frieze of raised brick with recessed panels decorated with egg-and-dart moldings tops the facade of each building. Above this is a pressed-tin cornice with fleurs-de-lis and arabesques on the projecting corner blocks and fan and floral patterns on the panels between the brackets.

T-407

20 North Washington Street, Easton
Circa 1880; Private

This small, brick commercial building resembles in detail its neighbors, 16 and 18 North Washington Street (T-405; T-406), but it predates them by at least twenty

T-405

T-407

T-408

T-411

T-412

years. Its first story is taken up by a modern storefront, but its original second story still rises intact. This story is finished in dark red brick laid in all-stretcher bond and has a plethora of detail. The facade has three windows topped by segmental arches and is framed by corner pilasters with recessed panels, marble bands, and corbeled blocks. The cornice is extremely elaborate and may be the best example of ornate brickwork in Easton. It begins with bands of egg-and-dart molded bricks, which rise to a frieze of recessed panels. Above this is a band of highly ornate shields and a band of yellow brick. The cornice is finished in molded red brick and a thin cove of marble. The interior has been completely reworked and little original detail remains.

T–408
32–34–36 North Washington Street, Easton
1904; Private

Now the home of the Maryland National Bank, this structure is the only commercial building in Easton that displays beaux-arts classicism. The aesthetic principles of this style, as enunciated by the Ecole des Beaux-Arts in Paris, were formality, symmetry, and monumentality; these were to be articulated by a wealth of detail including a variety of moldings, colossal columns, medallions, arched openings, and festoons. These princi-

ples—and the required superabundance of detail—are manifest here. The street facades, laid in Roman brick, are divided by two-story pilasters with molded capitals displaying medallions and are punctuated by tripartite windows on both stories. The first-story windows are fitted into round-arched frames and surmounted by fanlights with delicate tracery; in the center of the arches are consolelike keystones decorated with acanthus leaves. The second story rises above recessed panels of brick and a molded cornice. Its tripartite windows have rectangular frames and transoms, all of which display elaborate tracery. There is a wide band filled with festoons immediately above the windows and the tops of the pilasters' capitals. This is finished by two cornices: a lower one with egg-and-dart moldings and, above, a second cornice with lion heads. The height of the building is increased by the addition of a parapet with rich moldings. The vertical line of the pilasters, although interrupted by the band of festoons, is continued by the raised panels with cartouches that project from the parapet. The generous use of plaster detail in relief found on the exterior is carried into the interior, which has a spacious room with a coffered ceiling carried by Ionic columns with exaggerated entasis.

T–411
25 South Washington Street, Easton
Circa 1880; Private

The Historical Society of Talbot County has acquired this two-story, three-bay structure for use as a museum and office. The society has preserved the exterior appearance of the building as an example of a simple Victorian store.

T–412
BETHEL A.M.E. CHURCH
112 South Hanson Street, Easton
1877; Private

This simple, Gothic revival church, founded in 1877, has played an important part in the religious life of many of Easton's black residents for over a hundred years. The congregation itself predates the church by almost sixty years and is thought to have been formed by an itinerant preacher who spoke from a cart on South Street. The members had no permanent home for decades and experienced much hardship. This was particularly true during the years before the Civil War, when laws prohibited them from meeting and their pastors were frequently harassed with the threat of being sold into slavery. Finally a Quaker named James Cochran arranged for them to meet in a small carpenter shop on South Hanson Street; this property eventually passed into

T-413

T-414

T-415

the hands of the congregation's trustees, who built the present structure. In 1878, shortly after the church had been completed, Frederick Douglass addressed the congregation. The church is a simple two-story common-bond structure. Its west gable end, with corner buttresses, serves as the main facade and has Gothic-arched windows and a tudor-arched central entrance. There is a large tripartite window with deep muntins forming patterns of interlocking pointed arches above the entrance, a treatment that the smaller windows echo. A stone in the gable is inscribed with the name and date of the building. Above this is a round opening filled with louvers. The interior is divided into an anteroom with a double stair and a large room for the congregation with the sanctuary in the east.

T–413
PARRIS HOUSE
520 Goldsborough Street, Easton
Mid-nineteenth century; Private

The three-story, four-bay Parris House, a duplex built in the middle of the nineteenth century, shows the influence of two styles popular at that time. The Second Empire style can be seen in the shingled mansard roof. Italianate influences are clear in the three-story, flat-roofed central section with its large brackets and emphasis on the vertical.

T-416

T–414
118 South Street, Easton
Mid-nineteenth century; Private
See T–20.

T–415
120 South Street, Easton
Mid-nineteenth century; Private
See T–20.

T–416
BECK-HIGGINS HOUSE
127 North Washington Street, Easton
Mid-nineteenth century; Private

This house is one of four mid- to late-nineteenth-century structures near the north end of the Washington Street commercial district. Although very simple, its verticality, shallow pitched roof, and large cornice are notable. The three-story, three-bay structure is covered with weatherboard and has a side-hall plan. The main entrance has a transom and sidelights and fills the north bay; a modern, three-bay porch with a balustrade shelters the ground and second stories. Interesting interior features include an open-string stair with geometric step brackets and a fireplace with marbleized slate mantel, tile hearth, and flanking turned posts. In the early twentieth century the house was the home of Martin Higgins, Easton's first elected mayor and author of

T-421

The History of the Reincarnation of Easton, Maryland, a study of how the mayoralty and town council were established here in the first quarter of the twentieth century.

T–421
ASBURY METHODIST EPISCOPAL
CHURCH
127 Higgins Street, Easton
1876; with additions; Private

According to a history written in celebration of its 118th anniversary in 1954, the Asbury Methodist Episcopal Church was founded in 1836 with both white and black members and met in a building called the Old Carriage Shop. By the late 1840s, however, the congregation separated along racial lines, and, in 1849, the black members purchased a lot at Higgins Street and South Lane. The first house of worship was frame, but in 1876 this was replaced by the present common-bond brick structure. It is two stories tall, three bays wide, and four bays deep. The main facade is punctuated by pointed-arched windows with opalescent glass and by corner pilasters. There is a central bay entrance tower built between 1893 and 1898; further additions date to the early twentieth century: a chancel (between 1901 and 1903), a choir loft (between 1901 and 1913), and a metal ceiling (between 1919

T-422

T-423

and 1923). The church is named in honor of Francis Asbury, the first Methodist bishop in the United States.

T–422
LITTLE BROTHER HOUSE (site)
Hammond Street near Bay Street, Easton
Circa 1800; Private

Before its demolition in the late 1970s, the two-story, three-bay Little Brother House was among the earliest structures in Easton. Little is known of the house's early history, but at one time it served as an addition to one of the Langsdale Houses (T–302). A one-story shed addition contained the main entrance. The interior possessed early pine flooring and a well-preserved stair enclosed with vertical boarding.

T–423
GORDON-STARTT HOUSE
410 Goldsborough Street, Easton
Circa 1875; Private

The Gordon-Startt House is an elegant example of a common architectural form that emerged in Easton after the mid-nineteenth century and continued to be built well into this century: a three-bay, gable-end facade, and a side-hall plan. These houses are usually two stories tall, one room wide, two rooms deep, and have a rear ell and three-bay front porch. Details may be derived

T-424

from the Italianate, Greek, or other styles, but the form is essentially a vernacular one. This particular house is built of all-stretcher brick; its main facade is finished with fine joints of white mortar tooled into a bead. The wide eaves and molded cornice with returns suggest a pediment and contrast strongly with the deep red-orange of the smooth brick. Originally a three-bay porch with a deep cornice, delicate scrolled brackets, and slender posts covered the first story. The interior has unusually high ceilings and elaborate window and door trim. The spaciousness and formal quality achieved by these elements are reinforced by the tall windows and their molded panels.

T–424
LITTLETON-LYONS HOUSE
408 Goldsborough Street, Easton
Circa 1885; Private

The Littleton-Lyons House is a good example of a simple vernacular form often chosen by families of moderate means in the last quarter of the nineteenth century. Located in a neighborhood of other simple, late-nineteenth-century houses, this building is a two-story, three-bay frame structure with a steep gable roof. The exterior ornament is almost exclusively restricted to the decorative sticks and a pinnacle on the central gable.

T-426

T–426
SHORTALL HOUSE
409 Goldsborough Street, Easton
1890–1893; Private

This two-story, three-bay weatherboard frame dwelling is, like its neighbor (T–424), in an area where moderate-income families built their homes in the late nineteenth century. The street facade has a side entrance with a transom and sidelights, and a three-bay porch with chamfered posts, ornate brackets, and dentiled cornice. This cornice echoes the house's main cornice. Although simple, this house is sophisticated in design and detail.

T–427
MARKER FROM THE 1786 SURVEY
South Harrison Street and South Lane, Easton
1786; Private

By an act of March 12, 1786, the state legislature approved the establishment of the town of Talbot (later Easton). The act authorized a group of men, including Jeremiah Banning, Hugh Sherwood, John Stevens, Greenbury Goldsborough, and Alexander McCallum, to purchase land and lay out the town "in the best and most convenient manner into lots not exceeding one-half acre each." John Needles was hired to survey the land, which was to be divided into

T-427

T-428

118 lots. This marker with the Roman numerals XXIII designates lot twenty-three. According to the survey map, lot twenty-three was located at the northwest corner of South Harrison Street and South Lane, and, therefore, this marker may be in its original position. There is a similar but unmarked granite stone at the northwest corner of Goldsborough Street and Thoroughgood Lane; it appears to be a marker, but without numerals, it is impossible to be certain.

T-428
CHILDREN'S HOME OF THE EASTERN SHORE
313 North Street, Easton
1871; Private

Near Easton's original northern boundary, in an area set aside for public facilities, the Orphans' Home Benevolent Society built this large, simple structure to serve as the orphanage for the Eastern Shore. The house is made of frame covered with stucco and is composed of a two-and-one-half-story, three-bay main block and a two-and-one-half-story, six-bay addition on the rear; two wings extend from the rear parallel to the main block. The principal facade has a central entrance equipped with a transom and is shaded by a one-bay porch with fluted Doric columns. The front slope of the steep gable roof is pierced by three pedimented, gable-roofed dormers. Like the exterior, the interior is plain. The catalogue stair, identical to one advertised by the George O. Stevens and Co. in Baltimore, has turned balusters and an octagonal newel. In 1959 the orphanage closed its doors; today the building contains a number of apartments.

T-431
SPRING HILL CEMETERY
North and Hanson streets, Easton
Private

Occupying a slight rise of ground at the north end of Hanson Street, Spring Hill Cemetery was first used as a burial ground over 150 years ago. This land was purchased in 1802 by subscription for the use of "several denominations of Christians, strangers, and people of color." In 1827 a plot was given by Dr. Ennals Martin to the Vestry of Christ Church to be used as a cemetery, and in 1847 a lot near that owned by Christ Church was purchased by the Methodist Church as their burial ground. By 1877 these two areas had been enlarged and joined, as the History of Easton, published in that year, notes. The cemetery was then expanded by the annexation of the north end of Hanson Street and several acres owned by Colonel Samuel Hambleton. This whole area was enclosed by a fence and received the name of Spring Hill. This tract also figured in an interesting episode in the political life of the Eastern Shore. During the presidential campaign of 1840, a large Whig meeting was held here. Invitations were sent to the leading Whigs, including Henry Clay, who declined. The fifteen to twenty thousand people who attended the meeting, roused to enthusiasm, contributed to the Whig landslide that elected General William Henry Harrison to the presidency.

T-433
DODD-CLAGUE HOUSE
105 Goldsborough Street, Easton
Mid-nineteenth century; Private

This two-story, three-bay frame house shows how the Greek revival influenced even simple domestic architecture. The severe regularity of the lines, the boldly molded cornices, and the returns that suggest a pediment are characteristics of this style. The house has a side-hall plan with the main entrance in the west bay of the gable end facade; the door's rectangular transom is in accord with archless classical Greek architecture. The porch, with Doric columns and plain balustrade, shades the first story of the main facade and extends along the west elevation to a rear addition.

T-431

T-433

T-435

T-436

T–435
WIGHAM HOUSE
109 Goldsborough Street, Easton
Circa 1895; Private

After the first quarter of the nineteenth century, many of Easton's prosperous merchants developed Goldsborough Street, making it one of the city's more fashionable neighborhoods. This L-plan, frame house is two-and-one-half-stories tall and four bays wide, covered with German siding. The main facade is formed by a three-bay gable end with a one-bay section perpendicular on the west. The principal entrance is located in the west bay of the gable end and is fitted with double doors. The gable forms a pediment whose tympanum is covered with shingles and is pierced by an oriel window.

T–436
TURNER-LOVE HOUSE
111 Goldsborough Street, Easton
Third quarter of the nineteenth century;
Private

A good example of a mid-Victorian dwelling, the Turner-Love House is a two-story, four-bay, L-plan structure covered with German shiplap. Like the Wigham House (T–435), this house incorporates a gable end into the main facade. The entrance, located in the corner of the L, has a fanlight and sidelights and is shaded by a mod-

ern pedimented and gable-roofed porch with Doric columns. This porch replaced a two-story porch that ran across the facade to the gable end. There is a two-story bay projecting from the gable end: polygonal on the first story and rectangular on the second, the first story of the bay has three nine-over-nine sash windows separated by fluted pilasters, and the second story has one-over-one sash windows and a cornice with small brackets and scalloped wood ornament. The east yard is enclosed by a cast-iron fence with a bronze sign that reads "Iron Fence. Dickey & Davis. Ox/Pat. Sep. 1877/Frank Turner." J. Frank Turner owned the house in the late nineteenth century. He was a successful lawyer who served as the clerk for the Talbot County Court and the State Court of Appeals and as comptroller of the treasury.

T–438
EASTON WATER COMPANY STANDPIPE
Hanson Street and Mill Place, Easton
1886; Public

A concern for fire protection generated by Easton's great 1878 Market Space fire and the desire for improved delivery of water for domestic use were met when the Easton Water Company erected this 100-foot tall water standpipe. Inspired by the com-

memorative columns of Trajan and Marcus Aurelius in Rome, the designer, Isaac Cassin, provided Easton with a useful structure, as well as an impressive monument and landmark. The 14-foot-diameter shaft rests on a wrought-iron base, which is fastened with huge bolts to a 9-foot foundation.

T–439
EASTON CREAMERY BRICK HOUSE
23 Creamery Lane, Easton
Circa 1900; Private

This simple, two-story, three-bay brick house is the sole remnant of the Easton Creamery Company. The creamery itself stood on the north bank of Tanyard Creek to the west of this house and was a brick and frame structure with rooms for churning, separating, and storing. This house probably served as the residence of the company's overseer. It is finished in common bond and covered by a gable roof. The main facade has a central entrance with a hood and modern door; the window openings, fitted with modern sash and framed by modern louvered shutters, have projecting brick sills and jack arches. A corbeled brick cornice tops this facade, and a small chimney rises above the west gable end. The interior still retains its original pine flooring and stair with round oak balusters and square newel.

T-438

T-439

T-440

T-442

T–440
16 Locust Street, Easton
Circa 1800; Private

This small, one-and-one-half-story, frame house represents the type of dwelling popular in Easton's early years. The west gable end is covered with random-width weatherboard and serves as the main facade. There is a central door, one window to the north, and another placed in the gable directly above the entrance. The steep gable roof is shingled and terminates in barge boards and an unmolded box cornice. From the east gable ends extends a one-story gable-roofed wing; it originally had vertical beaded siding, but it is now covered with wide weatherboard. The interior of the house is divided into two rooms by a partition of beaded boards. Chair rails remain in all rooms and appear to be original. There are back-to-back fireplaces; the fireplace in the main house has a wood mantel and rectangular opening.

T–442
107 South Washington Street, Easton
Circa 1800; Private

107 South Washington Street, restored in the late 1960s, has the typical Federal townhouse form: it is two-and-one-half stories tall with a side-hall plan. This is one of the best maintained and most elegant of East-

on's early buildings and, along with its neighbors (T–9 and T–10), gives South Washington Street an appearance similar to that the town must have had 175 years ago. The main facade is laid in Flemish-bond brick and has a three-brick beltcourse (which, curiously, is recessed into the wall) between the first and second stories. The paneled door and transom are set within a frame of pilasters carrying an architrave and dentiled cornice. The windows have lintels with double stone keystones finely chiseled with reedings and flutings. Beneath the cornice, in a position usually occupied by a bed molding, is an intricately carved chain motif. A tall chimney rises above the south gable end. Although the beltcourse, window openings, and roof are continuous with 109 South Washington Street (T–10), this house was probably built after its neighbor. The first story's interior has been greatly altered, but there still are two Federal mantels. The upper floors, on the other hand, have survived almost intact, with their original pine flooring and window and door trim.

T–443
111 South Washington Street, Easton
Mid-nineteenth century; Private

This is a small frame house, two stories tall and three bays wide, covered with weather-

board. Its street facade has a side entrance with transom and sidelights in the south bay and a one-story porch with chamfered posts and ornate brackets. The gable roof has a box cornice with bold crown-and-bed moldings; the cornice has returns on the gable ends, probably a bow to the Greek revival. There is a gable-roofed meat house with wide vertical siding in the rear garden.

T–444
HARDCASTLE HOUSE AND CARRIAGE HOUSE
18 North Aurora Street, Easton
Circa 1900; Private

Built by Edward B. Hardcastle on what was known as Silk Stocking Row, Hardcastle House is a large frame structure that resists stylistic classification. Its symmetry, hip roof, and pedimented entrance pavilion and dormers are characteristic of Georgian architecture. On the other hand, the oriel windows on the second story of the facade are more suggestive of the Gothic revival of the mid-nineteenth century. The central double doors are emphasized by a pedimented pavilion that extends from the house's one-story porch. The tympanum of the pediment is filled with a geometric pattern of small cobblestones embedded in plaster or stucco, a most unusual detail. The interior possesses some fine features, including an open-well

T-443

T-444

247

T-446

T-447

stair with slender balusters, mantels with applied wood ornament, and tile surrounds and hearths. To the rear of the house is an elaborate, two-story carriage house that is sheathed with vertical siding and covered by a gable roof topped by a cupola with louvered openings.

T–446
400 Block of Goldsborough Street, Easton
Various dates; Private

As Easton grew during the mid- and late nineteenth century, its buildings and streets followed the pattern common to most towns and cities: the main houses faced the street; then came gardens, both kitchen and formal, then, placed behind them, were outbuildings on the alleys. The alley behind Goldsborough Street near the railroad tracks is probably the least disturbed in the town. Along it are garages, servants quarters, and even a jerkinhead-roofed pigeon cote.

T–447
BATEMAN-TILGHMAN-HOWARD
HOUSE
216 South Street, Easton
Circa 1875; Private

In 1881 Henry Bateman sold this property, with a two-and-one-half-story house, to Oswald Tilghman for $2,400. Colonel Tilghman was a prominent lawyer and had served

as an officer in the Confederate army. His wife, Patty Belle, was a daughter of Dr. Samuel A. Harrison, whose research formed the basis for *A History of Talbot County, Maryland,* which Colonel Tilghman published in 1915. The Tilghmans' house, now divided into apartments, has a facade resembling Easton's Federal-period townhouses, but it is taller, partly because it is raised on a high foundation. This height led Cynthia Ludlow, in her book *Historic Easton,* to make a comparison between 216 South Street in Plimhimmon (T–162), Tilghman's grandmother's home. The main facade has an entrance with a transom and sidelights in the west bay and a one-story porch with ornate brackets.

T–448
SAINTS PETER AND PAUL ROMAN
CATHOLIC CHURCH AND RECTORY
213 and 215 Goldsborough Street, Easton
1866; 1870; Private

It was only after the Civil War that Catholics regularly held services in Easton. Until then Redemptorist Fathers from St. Mary's Church in Annapolis came by ferry whenever possible. Many Protestants were active in founding the parish, including Mr. and Mrs. Howes Goldsborough, whose correspondence concerning these affairs is extant. It has been suggested that the Catholic par-

ish was established because the county's landowners and farmers wanted to attract new workers—Irish and German immigrants, many of whom were Catholic—to fill the void left by the emancipation of the slaves. From this church's south gable end extend a central vestibule and corner bell tower. The vestibule is gable-roofed with wide eaves, ornate barge boards, and exposed, shaped rafters. Directly above the vestibule is a conspicuously Gothic feature, a rose window. The church has recently undergone renovation and remodeling to restore its original appearance and to adapt it to liturgical changes instituted by Vatican II.

The 1870 rectory is a simple two-and-one-half-story, three-bay brick house with a side-hall plan. The main (south) facade has a door in its west bay and a one-bay gable-roofed porch with a cornice and returns, a treatment echoed by the gable above.

T–449
HORSEY-WOODWARD HOUSE
212 Brookletts Avenue, Easton
Circa 1890; Private

This large, rambling house is impossible to class stylistically. It is a two-and-one-half-story, T-plan structure with a three-and-one-half-story entrance tower. The T-plan section is covered by steep intersecting gables

T-448

T-449

T-451

T-452

with pinnacles and sawn wooden decorations at the roofs' gable ends. The tower is surmounted by a bracketed mansard roof with very narrow, gable-roofed dormers with wide eaves, carved barge boards, and lancet-arched windows.

T-451
LARRIMORE-FLECKENSTEIN HOUSE
17 North Aurora Street, Easton
Circa 1885; Private

Victorian in its irregularity and picturesqueness, the Larrimore-Fleckenstein House for some reason lacks the fantastic intricacies of the volumetric expression that characterize structures of this period. It is a two-story, L-plan house with intersecting gables and a two-story, hip-roofed pavilion at the juncture of the two sections. This pavilion, surmounted by a balustrade, accommodates the main entrance and encloses the stair. A Doric-columned porch shades the first story of the east gable end and the north elevation to the gable-roofed rear section. Behind the house is a formal garden laid out in the 1920s.

T–452
LEONARD-PRICE HOUSE
312 Goldsborough Street, Easton
Circa 1900; Private

The Leonard-Price House is one of the few buildings in Easton designed in the nationally popular shingle style that emerged in the 1880s in New England, where centennial celebrations sparked interest in colonial architecture. Builders were particularly fascinated by the shingle-covered cottages of the New England shores, and the major characteristic of this style—as the name suggests—is a covering of wood shingle from roof to foundation. This two-story, four-bay, gambrel-roofed house is a self-contained structure without projections or additions, in direct contrast to the volumetric expression of Victorian buildings in the same period: even the porches have been cut out of the building mass so as not to compromise its regular lines. The first story is recessed behind an arcaded porch supported by square shingle-covered columns with moldings. The second story has four windows with upper sashes of twenty-five panes. On the interior, the house displays the spaciousness and informality common to shingle-style dwellings. There is a deep entrance hall with an enclosed stair against the east wall and a broad arched doorway leading to the rear. The fireplaces with tile surrounds and slender engaged columns are noteworthy.

T–453
SHANNAHAN HOUSE
402 Goldsborough Street, Easton
Mid-nineteenth century; 1878; Private

This large frame house reflects the architecture of two periods. The two-story, three-bay section with a gable-end facade dates from the mid-nineteenth century. Regular in form and restrained in detail, it is covered with German shiplap and has a side-hall plan typical of houses of that period. The main entrance is in the east bay and is shaded by a one-bay, gable-roofed porch, which replaces the original three-bay porch. The roof ends in cornices and returns, and the implied tympanum has double round-arched windows. In 1878 William E. Shannahan, one of the founders of Shannahan-Wrightson Hardware Company (T–404), added the two-story, gable-roofed wing on the east. From its north elevation extends a two-story, polygonal bay window with vertical boarding and fish-scale shingles. An identical bulge was added to the west elevation of the earlier structure. A porch with an outstanding balustrade of sawn-wood ornament and turned balusters shades the east and south elevations of the wing; the south porch was enclosed in this century. There is a two-story wing on the rear of the older section; this may date from the original construction. Behind the house is a large, one-

T-453

T-454

T-455

and-one-half-story, two-bay carriage house covered in German siding; it now serves as a medical office.

T–454
ADKINS HOUSE
13 North Aurora Street, Easton
Circa 1880; Private

This is one of the earliest houses to be built on the part of Aurora Street known as Silk Stocking Row. The two-and-one-half-story, three-bay frame structure has a gable-end principal facade and a side-hall plan. Originally covered with German siding, the walls have been obscured by vinyl siding since 1970. The main entrance is located in the north bay and is reached from the street via an uncovered porch made of material from an earlier one-story porch. Openings are regularly spaced, and the gable has a small window. The interior has had very little alteration and presents many original details, including the mantels and stair with step brackets. The grounds follow the principles discussed in T–446: there is a late-nineteenth-century garden behind the house with two outbuildings beyond.

T–455
LELAH PERRY HOUSE
11 South Street, Easton
Mid-nineteenth century (?); Private

This is a frame house composed of a two-story, two-bay main part with a one-and-one-half-story, three-bay wing on the east. The main entrance has a transom and side-lights and is located in the east bay of the south gable end of the main block. A balustered, Doric-columned, one-story porch covers the first story. The wing on the east has a steeply pitched gable roof perpendicular to that of the main house; its shed dormer is a late addition. Although many exterior and interior details have been removed during remodelings, those remaining in the wing (a fragment of a simply molded, Federal-style chair rail) suggest an early construction date. The house bears the name of one of its former owners, Lelah Perry, a skilled and widely respected seamstress.

T–457
OAK HILL
317 North Washington Street, Easton
Early nineteenth century; with alterations; Private

Taking its name from the tall trees surrounding it, Oak Hill is today a duplex composed of two, two-and-one-half-story,

three-bay sections covered with wood shingles. The building of this house probably began under the Reverend John Bowie, who purchased the property in 1796. What Mr. Bowie's house looked like is impossible to say, but early interior details (including a fragment of a chair rail, pine flooring, and three six-panel doors with H and L hinges) suggest that the section on the east probably formed a part of the original construction. The section on the west may have been built at this time, but, if so, most of its early woodwork has been removed. During the nineteenth century the house was enlarged to its present two large sections with two, one-and-one-half-story wings. These wings were removed sometime before 1919, and they are now used as separate residences. In this century the house's two sections were completely covered with shingles, and the colonial revival, two-story porch was added; in 1940, the sections were remodeled to form a double house.

T–458
36 and 38 Dover Street, Easton
Circa 1885; Private

This double building is among the most enthusiastically decorated, late-nineteenth-century commercial structures in Easton. (See also Hill's Drug Store, T–13.) Similar to 16 and 18 North Washington Street

T-457

T-458

T-459

T-460

(T–405, T–406), it is a two-story, four-bay building divided in two by three pilasters. These pilasters run the full two stories and have recessed panels, molded-brick rosettes, and corbeling at the bottom, center, and top. The double corbeling at the top rises to form a base on which rest miniature pediments. The first story is obscured by modern storefronts, but the second story's four windows, with their rubbed-brick segmental arches, remain undisturbed. The entire composition is surmounted by an elaborate cornice of pressed tin with a row of dentils and a pierced-fan design.

T–459
506 Goldsborough Street, Easton
Circa 1871; Private

Except for the enclosed porch on the west, this small, Victorian cottage is identical to the Blake House (T–414). It is the only brick building in a neighborhood of small frame dwellings.

T–460
115 South Street, Easton
Circa 1870; Private

Small and compact, this two-story, three-bay house is distinguished by its elaborate porch ornament. The brackets, unusually large and ornate for such a modest dwelling, are offset by the simple posts and plain bal-

ustrade. The main entrance is located in the east bay and is fitted with a transom and sidelights.

T–461
WRIGHTSON HOUSE
202 Dover Street, Easton
Late nineteenth century; Private

Square in proportion, this two-and-one-half-story, three-bay frame house has a hip roof and deep porch (now enclosed). Moreover, this is one of the few houses in Easton influenced by beaux-arts classicism (see T–408), a style usually reserved for public structures. Although domestic use seems to have limited the application of the more formal elements, the style is clearly present in the monumental treatment of the door: placed in the center of the house, the entrance is defined by a two-and-one-half-story pavilion and is approached by a broad flight of stairs flanked at the top by pairs of columns supporting a large entablature. The entrance proper has a three-centered arch filled by a large fanlight of leaded glass with interlocking muntins; the sidelights are treated similarly. Above the entrance is a three-part window emphasized by a frame of broad pilasters and an entablature. Completing the monumental assemblage is the large, ogee-roofed, tripartite dormer. Its central window has a Gothic upper sash and is

surmounted by a round arch. A secondary entrance on Hanson Street is less ambitiously treated. The interior has an elaborate stair with slender balusters. There are wood cornices carved with classical details in the major rooms and mantels with carved details including festoons and engaged columns. The house has been divided into offices and apartments.

T–462
NORTH HOUSE
122 Goldsborough Street, Easton
Circa 1880; Private

This two-and-one-half-story, two-bay Victorian frame house's most prominent feature is a two-story, twelve-sided tower on its northeast corner. The tower's nine exposed sides are sheathed in imbricated shingles, and it is surmounted by a twelve-sided conical roof. The house's interior retains many original details, including first-floor mantels decorated with neoclassical motifs such as festoons, urns, and fluted columns. The exquisite latticework in two first-floor double doorways is especially notable. Dr. Charles L. Davidson, a prominent physician and an organizer of the area's first hospital (T–2), owned the house in the early part of this century.

T–461

T–462

T-463

T-464

T–463
SEXTON'S HOUSE
Third Haven Meeting House Grounds,
Easton
1867; Private

In 1823 the minutes of the Third Haven
Meeting noted that a sexton's house was
needed because the meeting house had "at
different times suffered considerable injury
for want of a person living convenient to
take care of it." Accordingly, a small sexton's house was constructed on the grounds.
Completed by 1828, this early structure later
burned; it was replaced in 1867 with this
one-and-one-half-story frame dwelling. The
three-bay house has a one-room plan with a
brick chimney and fireplace on one gable
end. A steep window stair rises against the
chimney to the plainly finished loft.

T–464
BARN, SAINT AUBINS FARM
510 Diamond Street, Easton
Circa 1803; Private

Nicholas Hammond, a leading citizen of
Easton in the early nineteenth century and
first president of the Eastern Shore branch
of the Farmers Bank of Maryland, erected
this barn as the major outbuilding of his
farm, Saint Aubins (T–67). The barn is
noteworthy for its fine brick work, especially
its unusual molded cornice. Well pro-

portioned and detailed, this structure is one
of the finest early barns in the area and
clearly shows the pride and care with which
country estates were planned. The building
has been carefully converted into a
residence.

T–465
HAMMOND HOUSE
208 Goldsborough Street, Easton
Circa 1850; Private

Built in a style common in the mid-nineteenth century, the Hammond House is a
two-and-one-half-story, three-bay frame
structure with a side-hall plan. Its gable end
main facade, proportion, and detail reveal
the influence of the Greek revival style.
The interior retains many original features,
including a marbleized slate mantel and the
stair with turned balusters, heavy round
newel, and decorated step brackets. These
details are catalogue items, possibly ordered
from the Keystone Slate Mantel and Slate
Works in Philadelphia or the George O.
Stevens Company in Baltimore. The house
was once the residence of Dr. and Mrs. William T. Hammond. Dr. Hammond was active in the founding of the Memorial Hospital in Easton, and he gave his name to the
trophy of the Chesapeake Bay Yacht Club
which is the prize of that organization's annual regatta.

T–466
WRIGHTSON-JONES HOUSE
209 Goldsborough Street, Easton
Circa 1880; Private

The two-and-one-half-story, three-bay
Wrightson-Jones House is an example of the
continuing popularity of the central-hall-
plan dwelling. Shaded by a modern porch
supported by fluted Doric columns carrying a
pedimented entablature, the house's entrance has a three-centered arched fanlight
and sidelights with molded panels beneath.
There is a two-story, board-and-batten, gable-roofed carriage house behind the house.

T–467
STANLEY HOUSE
128 South West Street, Easton
Circa 1850; Private

Two stories tall and two bays wide, this
modest brick house illustrates how proportion and detail help achieve a dignified
composition. Openings are regularly spaced
on all elevations and are surmounted by flat
lintels. The bright orange brick is laid in
common bond with narrow mortar joints
and contrasts strongly with the white lintels
and window trim. The entrance has a transom and sidelights, and the paneled door is
trimmed with deep bolection moldings. The
gable roof is edged with a wide cornice and
returns, which are treated with a bold cyma-

T-465

T-466

T-467

T-468

T-471

recta molding. There is a one-bay wing with a steep gable roof appended to the rear gable wall.

T–468
CAST-IRON FENCE
15 South Hanson Street, Easton
Mid- to late nineteenth century; Private

This is one of the finest nineteenth-century cast-iron fences remaining in Easton. Compact, regular, and fanciful, the fence makes full use of the nature of cast iron as a medium for ornament. Unfortunately there is no evidence of a maker's plate, so the artisan is unknown.

T–471
MORRIS-SARGENT HOUSE
6 South Street, Easton
Circa 1864; Private

This house was built by Jeremiah Morris, whose wife was the granddaughter of Captain Clement Vickers, a prosperous steamboat operator; the house has remained in Morris's family. It is a two-story, L-plan frame dwelling covered by shallow gable roofs. The main entrance, located in the gable-end facade, has a segmental-arched transom and sidelights. A porch with Doric columns and a simple balustrade stretches across the first story and around the corner to the rear gable end. The roof terminates

in a cornice with returns that are enriched by a row of consolelike brackets. The house has undergone very little alteration and presents an almost pristine mid-nineteenth-century appearance.

T–472
108 South Harrison Street, Easton
Early nineteenth century; with additions; Private

This house, a part of which may have served as the residence of Dr. Tristram Thomas, the father of Philip Thomas, twenty-eighth governor of Maryland, once stood on Dover Street where the post office stands today. In the 1920s, John Williams acquired property on Harrison Street and moved the house, which had grown into a three-part telescopic dwelling, to this site. Because it has undergone so much alteration, it is difficult to assign specific dates of construction, but interior details provide some evidence. The two-story, three-bay section on the north, although largely rebuilt, has wide yellow-pine flooring and a fragment of a chair rail of a simple Federal-period type. The window and door frames in the two-story, three-bay central section appear to be from later in the nineteenth century, and the two-and-one-half-story, two-bay wing on the south has window and door trim that reveals Greek revival influence. Today the house is divided into apartments.

T–473
VICTORIAN FARM BUILDINGS
near St. Michaels
Mid-nineteenth century; Private; National Register

These structures were saved from destruction when they were moved in June 1975 from their original site on the north side of U.S. Route 13 in Somerset County to Talbot County. The matching outbuildings are covered with vertical boards in the walls and with horizontal boards on the gables. Interesting features include the elaborate tracery in the eaves, the turned pendants at the corners, and the finials above the gable ends.

T–474
Streetscape, August and Locust streets, Easton
Circa 1900; Private

Housing for Easton's working people developed its own simple architectural forms, and these dwellings, constructed along Locust Street, illustrate two types commonly used in the late nineteenth and early twentieth centuries. Built of frame, they are two stories tall and two bays wide with a two-bay front porch and gable roofs either facing or parallel to the street. Variety on the porch posts and brackets helps the houses escape starkness.

T-472

T-473

T-474

T-476

T-477

T-478

T-475
DONCASTER HISTORIC TOWN
Near Shaw Bay and Wye River
Archaeological Site; Private; National
Register

The Doncaster Historic Town site was one of the first land grants on the Eastern Shore, and the town, begun in 1684, was one of the first planned towns in Maryland, indeed on the entire continent. The site was an early seat of commerce and may have been the second-largest port on the Eastern Shore during the final decades of the seventeenth century. At its peak Doncaster contained inns, a chapel, warehouses, a ferry, stores, stocks and a whipping post, and a public square. It was a contender for the location of the Talbot County seat, and the town's failure to acquire that honor led eventually to its demise. Based on the surface debris observed in the cultivated sections of the site, many foundations remain *in situ* below the plow zone. No photograph is available.

T-476
CHESAPEAKE BAY SKIPJACK
RELIANCE
Knapps Narrows, Tilghman
1904; Private; National Register

The skipjack *Reliance* is one of twenty ships that make up the last fleet of working sail-

ing vessels in North America. Watermen used bugeyes during the nineteenth century, but by the 1890s rising costs and dwindling oyster harvests made that ship obsolete. The watermen then adapted the lines of their flat-bottomed crab skiffs to create a new boat, the skipjack. Built at Fishing Creek, *Reliance* is a sloop-rigged sailing vessel with an overall length of 60 feet, a beam of 14 feet, and a draft 2½ feet. Now used for oyster-dredging, her gear includes four pairs of dredges, dredge cables, and front and starboard dredge rollers. All running rigging is manila, and all deck hardware is iron. Her deck layout includes a small cabin aft with three berths. The vessel is built of Eastern Shore pine, and all repairs have been made to original specifications.

T-477
SHARPS ISLAND LIGHT
Sharps Island
1882; Public; National Register

The Sharps Island Lighthouse, sited to guide mariners away from the shoals off Poplar Island and Black Walnut Point, was built on an island that has since completely submerged. It is the third lighthouse to direct sailors through these waters. The first, a small wooden house with a lamp on top, was built in 1837 on the northwest tip of the island. Because of severe erosion, a new

screwpile structure, similar to the Hooper Straits Lighthouse (T–275) now in St. Michaels, was erected about one mile to the east of the first site, but it was washed away by the ice floes during the severe winter of 1881. The present lighthouse is a four-story, steel-covered brick structure resting on a steel caisson 30 feet in diameter. Before it was automated, its interior resembled some of the other caisson towers built on the Bay, with a kitchen, watch room, and quarters for the two assigned watchmen.

T-478
ST. MICHAELS MILL
St. Michaels
1890s; Private; National Register

St. Michaels, easily accessible by water and convenient to other towns, was an ideal center for milling, and there are records of windmills located in this area as early as 1664. These were eventually replaced by water-driven gristmills, such as Wye Mill (T–51) near Wye Creek. Mills like Wye Mill stood all along the Eastern Shore, and by the 1860s as many as thirty mills were in operation. These, in turn, were replaced by more modern structures, and today there are a few gristmills that remain untouched by modernization.

St. Michaels Mill stands on Chew Avenue near the waterfront. Built in the 1890s,

T-479

T-480

the structure has a main part of brick construction, laid in common bond with seven courses of stretchers to one course of headers. On the northeast and southwest sides of the structure there is a three-brick corbeled cornice. The mill was in operation until very recently, and the interior and machinery are intact.

T-479
ST. LUKE'S METHODIST CHURCH
Bellevue
1886; Private

St. Luke's is a simple frame building overlooking the Tred Avon River in Bellevue. Although the church was built in 1886, the congregation that it serves was formed many years before that and is primarily made up of black watermen and their families. Notable features include the pointed-arched windows, the round-arched window in the gable, and the bell tower with its belfry and finial.

T-480
TRINITY A.M.E. ZION CHURCH
St. Michaels
1901; Private

This small, simple frame church served the only A.M.E. Zion congregation on the Eastern Shore. A.M.E. Zion churches, common in Maryland's urban centers, were rare on

the Eastern Shore because the Methodist Episcopal Church was firmly entrenched here. In fact, the congregation disbanded in the 1950s, and the church is now occupied by a Holiness congregation. The austerity of the structure is offset by the pointed arches of the openings and the corner brackets under the eaves of the gable-end facade.

T-481
WATERS METHODIST EPISCOPAL
CHURCH
Oxford
1886; with additions; Private

The social hub of Oxford's black community, this church is the oldest black Methodist church in Oxford. It was built in 1886 on the site of the original church, which was built in 1873 and burned in 1884. It has undergone many alterations, including the addition of aluminum siding and the replacement of all windows. The church rests on a concrete-block foundation, and a tower with a belfry and short spire rises on the southwest. During the height of racial tensions in the late 1880s, this church, like so many black churches on the Eastern Shore, was vandalized by the Ku Klux Klan.

T-482
ST. JOHN'S UNITED METHODIST
CHURCH
Wittman
1876; Private

Many of the churches that are now used by black congregations were originally built for whites. This church, built by whites in 1876, was given to a black congregation in 1886 and continues to serve this small fishing village on Cummings Creek. It is raised on a brick foundation, and the original siding is covered with aluminum siding. Decorative features include shingles, a round window, and the tower with a bracketed cornice below the belfry. The bell, replaced by electronic chimes, has been placed on the church lawn.

T-483
JOHN WESLEY CHURCH
Oxford
1873; Private

Wesley Church is the oldest church built by blacks for a black congregation still in use in Talbot County. Only Bethel A.M.E. Church (T-412) in Easton is of a comparable age, having been built for a black congregation in 1877. This church is a simple, one-story, gable-roofed structure now covered with asbestos shingles. A cornerstone in the northeast corner is

T-481

T-482

T-483

inscribed: John Wesley M.E. Church 1873. The church is used today primarily as a mortuary chapel.

T–484
EASTON ARMORY
40 South Harrison Street, Easton
1927; Public

Sir Walter Scott would have approved of the Easton Armory, a crenelated brick and stone structure inspired by medieval fortifications. The main block is laid in Flemish bond with dark headers; the remaining brickwork is finished in common bond. The monumentally treated main entrance is topped by a segmental arch and flanked by towers projecting from the plane of the facade. From the rear of the main block extends a twelve-bay gymnasium; it has six buttresses on each long elevation and is topped by a corbeled cornice with brick dentils. The building served as an armory until it was acquired by the Department of Natural Resources in 1976 as the eastern regional headquarters for the Natural Resources police.

T–486
TILGHMAN ISLAND BRIDGE
Tilghman Island
1934; Public

Built in 1934, this bridge, which carries Maryland's Route 33 over Knapp's Narrows to Tilghman Island, is a heel trunnion, rolling lift bridge with a counterweight suspended over the roadway. It is one of two historic movable bridges (see T–487) in Talbot County and one of fifteen historic movable bridges in the state road system. There is a small, square, frame, one-room bridge-tender's house on the west side of the road at the north end of the bridge. Unlike keepers' quarters at other movable bridges, this house is not connected to the bridge.

T–487
DOVER BRIDGE
Near Tanyard
Twentieth century; Public

This bridge carries Maryland Route 331 across the Choptank River between Talbot and Caroline counties. It consists of one swing-span, steel, six-panel, Pratt through truss 219 feet long, flanked by two steel, six-panel, Pratt through trusses each 215 feet long. As a combination of a swing movable bridge and metal through-truss bridge, this structure has few peers. (See the Harrington Bridge, D–583, in Dorchester

County.) Along with the Tilghman Island Bridge (T–486), it is one of fifteen historic movable bridges in Maryland.

T–488
SCOTT'S METHODIST EPISCOPAL CHURCH
Trappe
1880; Private

Scott's Church has long been a religious and political center for Trappe's black community. During the late nineteenth century, for example, the church was a meeting place for black members of the Republican party. The imposing structure has a central entrance tower surmounted by a belfry with louvered openings and a spire topped by a cross. The absence of windows in the towered, gable end gives the church a somewhat severe appearance. The north and south elevations have pointed-arched windows filled with colored glass.

T–492
OUTTEN LOG HOUSE
Grounds of Chesapeake Bay Maritime Museum
Early nineteenth century; Private

Relocated from its original location near the town of Trappe to its new location on the grounds of the Chesapeake Bay Maritime Museum, the Outten House is a small one-

T-487

T-488

room-plan log dwelling that measures just
15½ feet deep and 16 feet long. The small
building is a rare survival of a house type
that was extremely common in the eighteenth and early nineteenth century.
Though many of these small houses were
later adapted as kitchen wings or outbuildings, many others were abandoned or
destroyed, and few have survived with so
few alterations. The most significant features
of this house are the dovetailed hewn-log
walls, the tilted false-plate roof construction, and a variety of hand-wrought
iron hinges on the doors.

T-492

Index

CHRISTOPHER WEEKS is a writer and editor with the Maryland Historical Trust. He is the author of *The Building of Westminster in Maryland*, coauthor of *The Work of William Lawrence Bottomley in Richmond*, and editor of *Bel Air: The Town through Its Buildings*, *Historic Sites in Caroline County*, *Three Centuries of Maryland Architecture*, and *Between the Nanticoke and the Choptank: An Architectural History of Dorchester County, Maryland*.

THE JOHNS HOPKINS UNIVERSITY PRESS

WHERE LAND AND WATER INTERTWINE

This book was composed in Goudy Old Style text and display type by Brushwood
Graphics Studio, from a design by Gerard A. Valerio.